Medical Law in Albania

Medical Law in Albania

Denard Veshi

This book was originally published as a monograph in the International Encyclopaedia of Laws/Medical Law.

Founding Editor: Roger Blanpain
General Editor: Frank Hendrickx
Volume Editor: Herman Nys; Associate Editor: Tom Goffin

Wolters Kluwer

Published by:
Kluwer Law International B.V.
PO Box 316
2400 AH Alphen aan den Rijn
The Netherlands
E-mail: lrs-sales@wolterskluwer.com
Website: www.wolterskluwer.com/en/solutions/kluwerlawinternational

Sold and distributed by:
Wolters Kluwer Legal & Regulatory U.S.
920 Links Avenue
Landisville, PA 17538
United States of America
E-mail: customer.service@wolterskluwer.com

ISBN 978-94-035-4709-1

e-Book: ISBN 978-94-035-4719-0
web-PDF: ISBN 978-94-035-4729-9

This title is available on www.kluwerlawonline.com

The Author

Associate Professor Denard Veshi is a legal scholar whose primary area of expertise lies in medical law, with a particular focus on the regulation of healthcare services, patients' rights, medical liability and bioethics. His research is situated at the intersection of civil and public law, human rights, and European Union law and is characterized by a comparative and interdisciplinary methodology. Denard holds two doctoral degrees: a PhD in Law, Science and Technology (LAST-JD), which was a joint PhD program, and a second PhD in European Doctorate in Law and Economics (EDLE), which was a multiple PhD program. His academic training has enabled him to approach complex legal problems through a multidisciplinary lens, integrating legal doctrine with economic analysis and empirical perspectives.

His contributions to the field of medical law are particularly notable within the context of informed consent and end-of-life decisions. He has published extensively in peer-reviewed international journals, including those indexed in Scopus and Web of Science, and his work has appeared in leading Italian legal journals classified as Class A by ANVUR (Area 12). His scholarship addresses both theoretical and practical dimensions of medical law, encompassing civil, criminal, administrative, and deontological aspects, with attention to the legal regulation of emerging medical technologies and the rights of vulnerable groups in healthcare settings. Currently, Associate Professor Denard Veshi has published more than thirty papers indexed in Scopus, and his Hindex is 6, which is quite high for a legal scholar.

In addition to his research activities, Associate Professor Veshi has been the recipient of several Jean Monnet Modules funded by the European Commission, recognizing his contributions to EU legal studies. He coordinated a Jean Monnet Module on EU Health Issues from 2019 to 2021 and has contributed to the establishment of two EU Centres of Excellence.

This contribution is classified as a scientific monograph, as determined by the decision of the Department of Law at University College Bedër, Tirana, Albania, no. 1 of 11 April 2025, meeting no. 2025/007. This classification has been confirmed by two independent reviewers with expertise in the relevant research field, in accordance with Decision No. 112, dated 23.02.2018, *On the Determination of Criteria for the Award of the Scientific Degree "Doctor" and the State Standards for the Award of Academic Titles "Associate Professor" and "Professor."*

The Author

Table of Contents

Table of Contents

List of Abbreviations

ACPD	Albanian Center for Population and Development
ANC	Antenatal Care
ARTs	Assisted Reproductive Techniques
CCr	Criminal Code
CCrP	Code of Criminal Procedure
CCv	Civil Code
CCvP	Code of Civil Procedure
CRPD	Convention on the Rights of Persons with Disabilities
ECHR	European Convention on Human Rights
ECT	Electroconvulsive Therapy
ECtHR	European Court of Human Rights
ENOC	European Network of Ombudsman for Children
EU	European Union
FM	Family Medicine
FP	Family Planning
HBSC	Healthy Behaviors of School-Age Children
HCV	Hepatitis C
IDUs	Injecting Drug Users
ILO	International Labor Organization
KMCAP	Medical Commission for the Determination of Ability to Work
NMR	Neonatal Mortality Rate
OTC	Over the Counter
PAS	Physician-Assisted Suicide
PHC	Primary Healthcare Service
PHDs	Public Health Directorates
PNC	Postnatal Care

List of Abbreviations

RHA	Regional Health Authority
RHDs	Regional Health Directorates
SAA	Stabilization and Association Agreement
STI	Sexually Transmitted Infections
WHO	World Trade Organization

General Introduction

1. Each nation is shaped by its unique legal traditions and constitutional evolution. Albania, having declared independence in 1912, underwent profound and frequent transformations in its legal and political systems throughout the twentieth century. Under various foundational laws—referred to alternately as *Statutes* and, from 1950 onward, as *Constitutions*—Albania has successively adopted the forms of a constitutional principate (1914), parliamentary republic (1925; reinstated in 1991 and reaffirmed in 1998), democratic monarchy (1928), constitutional monarchy (1939), people's republic (1950), and socialist republic (1976). No other European state has experienced such frequent and radical shifts in its constitutional identity within such a condensed historical period. These recurrent changes have inevitably influenced the development and consolidation of legal doctrines, including those in specialized areas such as medical law.

2. In this context, creating an encyclopedia on medical law in Albania emerges as both timely and necessary, addressing critical gaps in the legal, healthcare, and academic landscapes. Most notably, Albania lacks a comprehensive and systematic body of scholarly literature or legal commentary dedicated to medical law, an area that is undergoing rapid evolution globally. The proposed encyclopedia would address this deficiency by providing a structured, detailed, and authoritative overview of fundamental topics, including but not limited to patient rights, medical liability, bioethics, health data protection, and the regulation of healthcare services.

3. Furthermore, there is an urgent need for an interdisciplinary legal approach to medical law in Albania. Such an approach must encompass civil and criminal liability and procedural, labor, administrative, and deontological dimensions of healthcare practice. By integrating these diverse fields, the encyclopedia would serve as a foundational resource for scholars, enabling a comprehensive understanding of Albanian medical law and its intersection with international standards. Simultaneously, it would provide healthcare professionals with practical legal guidelines relevant to a variety of clinical and institutional contexts, thereby enhancing both legal compliance and patient care.

4. Additionally, Albania's rapidly expanding tourism sector adds another dimension to the need for such a reference work. According to official statistics, Albania welcomed 11,696,111 foreign visitors in 2024,[1] a figure that surpasses four times the country's resident population, which stood at 2,402,113 as of September 18, 2023.[2] While specific data on medical tourism remain unavailable, it is evident that a portion of these visitors seek healthcare services, particularly in the private sector. Concerns regarding the quality and safety of medical care in such settings have been publicly raised, including official warnings from the Italian Embassy in Tirana.[3] The Embassy has urged Italian nationals to obtain comprehensive medical insurance, inclusive of accident coverage and provisions for medical repatriation, prior to engaging in medical procedures in Albania.

5. Given this background, an encyclopedia on medical law would also serve a regulatory and educational function in cross-border healthcare services. It would support efforts to align domestic practices with international legal standards and EU health policy frameworks, particularly relevant as Albania advances in its EU accession process.

6. In conclusion, the development of a medical law encyclopedia in Albania represents an essential scholarly and practical endeavor, addressing not only domestic legal needs but also the broader challenges posed by internationalization, medical tourism, and the complexities of contemporary healthcare governance.

7. This encyclopedia focuses on the case of Albania. Albania has been chosen as one of the EU candidate countries. This work also applies case law study. Although Albania is a civil law country, the role of the jurisprudence is fundamental since the Consultative Council of European Judges has already observed that in civil law countries, judges are guided by case law, especially that of the highest courts, whose task includes ensuring the uniformity of case law.[4] In addition, compared to other countries, the Albanian academic scientific output is low,[5] ranking last in Europe.[6] Thus, the application of a judicial approach might be useful for developing the national legal doctrine. This research is innovative because it is the first comprehensive medical law in Albania.

---

1. INSTAT (INSTITUTE OF STATISTICS, ALBANIA), *Citizens' movement in Albania, December 2024*, available online: https://www.instat.gov.al/media/14810/lëvizjet-e-shtetasve-në-shqipëri-dhjetor-2024.pdf, accessed on Jan. 27, 2025.
2. INSTAT (INSTITUTE OF STATISTICS, ALBANIA), *Population and Housing Census 2023*, 2023, available online: https://www.instat.gov.al/media/13615/cens-i-popullsise-2023.pdf, accessed on Jan. 27, 2025.
3. AMBASCIATA D'ITALIA A TIRANA, *Cure dentali in Albania: Attenzione!* 2023, available online: https://ambtirana.esteri.it/it/news/dall_ambasciata/2023/01/cure-dentali-in-albania-attenzione/, accessed on Jan. 27, 2025.
4. Council of Europe, *Opinion No 11 of the Consultative Council of European Judges. On the quality of judicial decisions,* Dec. 18, 2008, Available online: https://www.courtexcellence.com/__data/assets/pdf_file/0023/4919/ccje.pdf.
5. NHR, Albanian National H-index Ranking 2025, 2025, available online: https://www.courtexcellence.com/__data/assets/pdf_file/0023/4919/ccje.pdf, accessed on Jan. 27, 2025.
6. Euronews Albania, Albania ranks last in Europe for scientific research, according to study, 2023, available online: https://euronews.al/en/albania-ranks-last-in-europe-for-scientific-research-according-to-study/.

8. In addition, it shows the importance of case law as well as the impact of the ECHR, ECtHR, and EU law. This is fundamental since—at the moment of writing—there is no scientific contribution that underlines its importance. Furthermore, this is fundamental since the Albanian doctrine in medical law is not as developed as in other countries. Thus, by showing the similarities between Albanian law and foreign law as well as the impact of the ECHR, ECtHR, EU law, and EU Court of Justice on foreign law or jurisprudence, the same arguments can be taken also by the Albanian doctrine or judges.

§1. The General Background of the Country

I. Geography

9. Albania is located in Southeastern Europe, in the western part of the Balkans. It shares borders with Montenegro to the northwest, Kosovo to the north and northeast, North Macedonia to the east, and Greece to the south. To the west, Albania is bordered by the Adriatic and Ionian Seas, part of the Mediterranean. The Otranto Channel, just 72 km wide, is the shortest sea distance between Albania and Italy. The country covers an area of 28,748 km^2.[7] According to data from INSTAT in 2023, Albania's population is about 2,412,113:[8]

a. The geographical position of Albania has a profound influence on its diverse natural conditions, making it a favorable area for human settlement while also holding significant strategic, economic, and sociocultural importance. Albania occupies a highly strategic location at the intersection of key routes connecting Western Europe and the Mediterranean to Eastern Europe and beyond. Historically, this position between East and West has made Albanian territories the focus of various imperial conquests, including those by the Roman, Byzantine, and Ottoman Empires, and a site of conflict during both World Wars (Ziu, 2018, pp. 6–7).

A. *Climate*

10. Albania is situated within the subtropical belt, falling under the Mediterranean climate zone. This results in short, mild winters and hot, dry summers. However, Albania's climate exhibits significant regional variations, with notable contrasts in temperature, precipitation, sunlight, and air humidity across different

7. *See* the Albanian Encyclopedic Dictionary, Published by the Academy of Sciences of Albania, Tirana 1985, p. 1035.
8. According to Shqiptarja.com, the Institute of Statistics has published the 2023 Census data. Based on the population data, Albania has a total of 2,402,113 inhabitants. Compared to the 2011 Census, the country has 419,831 fewer residents, a decline of approximately 17%. Regarding religious affiliation, 1.1 million people identified as Muslim, 384,000 as Christian, 85,000 as atheists, and 332,000 as unspecified. Tirana, April 22, 2024.

provinces. These variations are influenced by the country's diverse topography, ranging from coastal areas to mountainous regions, creating distinct microclimates throughout the territory, etc.:[9]

a. The Mediterranean climate has both beneficial and adverse effects on health. The abundant sunlight supports the production of vitamin D (Karras et al., 2014, p. 864) which plays a key role in bone health and immune function while also improving mental health (da Silva Sabião et al., 2024; Corona et al., 2001) by boosting serotonin levels, which helps regulate mood. Furthermore, the traditional Mediterranean diet, rich in fruits, vegetables, whole grains, olive oil, and fish, is associated with a lower incidence of cardiovascular diseases due to its high antioxidants and healthy fats content (Dalamaga et al., 2021; Barrea et al., 2020).
b. However, the dry summer climate can present challenges, especially to respiratory health (Louie et al., 2018). While the dry air may reduce the prevalence of respiratory infections that thrive in humid environments, it can also worsen respiratory conditions like asthma and bronchitis, especially when combined with higher temperatures and air pollution, including smoke from wildfires.
c. Additionally, dry summers pose health risks to vulnerable populations, such as the elderly, children, and those with pre-existing conditions, increasing the likelihood of heat-related illnesses like heat stroke and dehydration (Bastos et al., 2021).
d. Historically, the Mediterranean's warm, wet winters have also created favorable conditions for the proliferation of mosquitoes and other vectors, which can spread diseases such as West Nile Virus and malaria, though the latter has largely been eradicated in modern times from most Mediterranean regions (Sainz-Elipe et al., 2010).
e. In summary, while the Mediterranean climate offers notable health benefits, it also necessitates public health measures to mitigate the risks associated with extreme weather conditions and seasonal disease vectors.

II. Cultural Composition

11. Nestled in the heart of the Balkans, Albania is a land rich in history, diversity, and cultural vibrancy. Its cultural identity is a tapestry woven over centuries, reflecting the influences of ancient civilizations, foreign rulers, and the resilience of its people. From its Illyrian roots to its modern-day cultural dynamism, Albania presents a fascinating narrative of continuity and transformation.

12. Albania's cultural roots trace back to the ancient Illyrians, who are considered the ancestors of today's Albanians. The Illyrians inhabited much of the western Balkan Peninsula, and their legacy is still evident in Albanian folklore, language, and traditions. Over time, Albania became a crossroads of empires and

9. FESH, Tiranë 1985, a.g.e, f.1035.

civilizations. The Greeks established colonies along its coastline, introducing classical influences, while the Romans integrated the region into their vast empire, leaving behind architectural marvels and governance systems. The Byzantine Empire's influence brought Orthodox Christianity and Byzantine art, while the Slavic migrations and Ottoman rule layered additional complexities onto Albania's cultural fabric. The Ottomans, who ruled Albania for nearly five centuries, left a lasting imprint on its architecture, cuisine, and religious practices. Yet, throughout these eras, the Albanian people maintained a distinct identity, often blending foreign elements with their indigenous traditions.

13. Albania is largely ethnically homogeneous, with Albanians making up 98% of the population. Minority groups like Greeks, Aromanians, Roma, and Slavs add cultural diversity through their languages and traditions (Albanian Identities, 2000). The Albanian language, with its Gheg and Tosk dialects, unites the nation, with Tosk forming the basis of the modern standard.

14. Moreover, culture in Albania thrives in everyday life through music, dance, and theater. Isopolyphony, a traditional style of Albanian folk music recognized by UNESCO, is a hallmark of the nation's intangible heritage. Its rich, layered harmonies tell stories of love, nature, and history, reflecting the soul of the Albanian people. Theater and performing arts also play a vital role in Albanian society. In 2023, over 1,100 performances were staged across the country, drawing an audience of more than 153,000 people.[10] Institutions like the National Theater and the Opera and Ballet Theater in Tirana are at the forefront of fostering artistic excellence, offering a platform for both classical works and contemporary Albanian creativity. Film, too, has seen a revival, with Albanian filmmakers gaining international recognition at events such as the Tirana International Film Festival.

15. Albania's dedication to preserving its cultural heritage is evident in its numerous UNESCO-listed sites. The ancient city of Butrint, the historic centers of Berat and Gjirokastër, and the evocative strains of isopolyphonic folk music are celebrated globally as treasures of humanity. These sites are not merely historical artifacts; they are living symbols of Albania's enduring identity.

16. Efforts to preserve and promote cultural heritage have also extended to the country's museums, castles, and archaeological parks. In 2023, these sites welcomed over a million visitors, a record number that highlights both the appeal of Albania's heritage and the increasing interest in cultural tourism. While foreign tourists are drawn to the archaeological parks and historic landmarks, domestic visitors frequently explore museums, reflecting a growing appreciation for cultural heritage within Albania itself.

---

10. INSTAT, Cultural Statistics of Albania, 2023, available online: https://www.instat.gov.al/al/temat/treguesit-demografik%C3%AB-dhe-social%C3%AB/kultura/publikimet/2024/statistikat-e-kultur%C3%ABs-2023/

17. Education plays a crucial role in sustaining and expanding Albania's cultural landscape. Approximately, 14% of university students in Albania pursue studies related to cultural fields such as architecture, arts, and literature. This academic focus nurtures the next generation of cultural custodians, equipping them with the skills and knowledge to preserve and innovate within Albania's cultural sectors.[11] Educational initiatives connect tradition with modernity, exposing young Albanians to global influences while preserving their heritage. Cultural exchange programs ensure Albania's culture evolves without losing its authenticity.

18. Albania's cultural landscape is not static; it is constantly adapting to the rhythms of modern life. Digital platforms have become essential in the dissemination and consumption of cultural content. Online streaming of Albanian music, virtual museum tours, and digital archives make culture more accessible, particularly for younger audiences and the diaspora. Urbanization and migration have shaped Albania's cultural identity, blending global influences with traditional practices. Tirana exemplifies this dynamic, hosting modern artistic events alongside enduring cultural traditions.

19. Albania's religious landscape is marked by the harmonious coexistence of Islam, Catholicism, and Orthodox Christianity, reflecting centuries of interfaith tolerance and unity through shared rituals and celebrations (Albanian Identities, 2000).

III. Political System

A. *The Administrative Organization of Albania from 1912 to the Present*

20. Since the declaration of independence in 1912, Albania's administrative organization has undergone significant transformations. These changes have been influenced by various historical events, leading to alterations in the nomenclature and functions of administrative units, including municipalities, districts, prefectures, and others:

a. On November 22, 1913, the country was divided into prefectures, subprefectures, and provinces as outlined in the "Immediate Canon of Administration Civil Code of Albania" (History of State and Law, 2018). Subsequently, the "Organic Law of the Municipality," enacted in 1921, along with the "Civil Code" ratified on February 24, 1928, established the village and municipality as the foundational administrative units.
b. In 1928, in addition to the existing divisions into prefectures and subprefectures, the commune was introduced as an administrative layer, with villages serving as the basic units of organization. By 1945, the administrative structure was simplified, focusing primarily on prefectures and subprefectures. A year

11. INSTAT, Cultural Composition, 2022, available online: https://www.instat.gov.al/al/temat/treguesit-demografik%C3%AB-dhe-social%C3%AB/kultura/publikimet/2023/statistikat-e-kultur%C3%ABs-2022/

later, the new administrative framework incorporated locality units in certain regions, replacing the municipality by 1947.

c. The administrative reorganization in September 1953 established twenty-six districts, substituting the prefecture with the county system. Each district encompassed several localities, with districts being comprised of three or more localities. However, in July 1958, the functions and powers of districts were curtailed, leading to a continued reliance on the twenty-six-district organization. Following 1967, specific rural units were called "united villages."
d. Albania's administrative division evolved again in 1990, categorizing the territory into districts, united villages, villages, and towns. On June 10, 1992, a more structured division was implemented, establishing districts, municipalities, and communes across twelve prefectures. Between 1992 and 2000, further modifications to the administrative-territorial structure were made, culminating in a configuration of thirty-six districts, sixty-three municipalities, and 309 communes by 2000.
e. The most recent administrative-territorial division, established in 2014, recognizes sixty-one municipalities within twelve districts (Shkodra, Kukës, Lezhë, Durrës, Tirana, Vlorë, Fier, Berat, Gjirokastër, Korçë, Dibër, and Tiranë). This reorganization reflects the country's socioeconomic development and the community's demand for enhanced public services aligned with European standards.

21. Since its shift to democracy in the early 1990s, Albania has worked to establish and strengthen its democratic systems. With a parliamentary structure, the nation focuses heavily on aligning governance and justice reforms with European standards, particularly in combating corruption and enhancing judicial transparency. Despite advancements, issues such as political distrust and systemic corruption continue to pose obstacles. Findings from the 2023 census underline key demographic changes, including urban migration and a declining population, which shape policy decisions and governance priorities. Addressing regional imbalances and fostering inclusion of minority groups are critical for fostering social cohesion and political harmony. While Albania faces challenges such as economic inequalities and workforce migration, its focus on institutional reforms and international cooperation provides opportunities to further its political and developmental goals.

IV. Population and Vital Statistics

22. In antiquity, the Illyrians inhabited the lands that now constitute Albania, one of the most prominent ethnic groups in the Balkan Peninsula. Historical accounts, alongside archaeological and linguistic evidence, confirm that the Illyrians occupied a vast territory stretching from the Adriatic and Ionian coasts in the west, to the Morava and Vardar River basins in the east, and from the Sava River in the north to the Gulf of Ambracia in the south:

a. Within this expansive region, the Illyrian ethnos developed over centuries through the amalgamation of Indo-European populations with indigenous communities. By the end of the Bronze Age, circa 1200 BC, a distinct ethno-cultural group had formed in the western Balkans, exhibiting shared characteristics that distinguished the Illyrians from neighboring non-Illyrian populations (History of the Albanian People, 2022, p. 42).
b. The Illyrians inherited key anthropological, linguistic, and cultural traits from their early ancestors, reaching a significant stage of development by creating state institutions between the 7th and 5th centuries BC, including forming tribal federations. Among the most prominent Illyrian tribes were the Taulants, Ardians, Dardanians, Dalmatians, Albanians, Penestians, Molossians, Kaons, and Thesprotes (Galaty, 2002). Illyrian groups, such as the Mesapians and Iapygians, even settled in Southern Italy. The history of the Illyrian states began in the 4th century BC and persisted for over two centuries until the Roman conquest of Illyria in 168–167 BC.
c. Illyria became part of the Roman Empire for nearly six centuries with the Roman conquest. According to Roman administrative divisions of the late 1st century AD, Illyria was incorporated into the Prefecture of Illyricum, which comprised four provinces: Prevalis (centered in Shkodra), New Epirus (centered in Durrës), Old Epirus (centered in Nicopolis), and Dalmatia (Kos, 2013). In AD 395, following the division of the Roman Empire by Emperor Theodosius I, the Illyrian-Albanian territories became part of the Eastern Roman Empire, later known as the Byzantine Empire (History of the State and Law, 2018, p. 53).
d. During late antiquity and the early Middle Ages, the descendants of the Illyrians, known as the Arbers, continued to inhabit the region (Sotirović, 2013). The Albanian territories were affected by successive invasions during the 5th and 6th centuries by Germanic tribes, including the Ostrogoths, Visigoths, Vandals, and Huns, and by Slavic invasions in the 6th and 7th centuries, which resulted in significant settlements and territorial destruction. The Byzantine Empire, which survived for a millennium after the fall of the Western Roman Empire, reorganized its territories into administrative units known as themes (History of the State and Law, 2018, pp. 55–56). By the 9th century, most Albanian territories were included in the Theme of Durrës, stretching from Tivari in the north to the Gulf of Vlora in the south and into the Drin Valley in the east. Other regions were incorporated into the Themes of Nicopolis, Thessaloniki, and Dalmatia.
e. Under Byzantine rule, a local feudal class gradually emerged in Albania. The weakening of central Byzantine authority in the 12th century allowed the Albanian feudal class to establish autonomous political entities, forming the Principality of Arbër (History of the State and Law, 2018, p. 76). From the 12th to the 15th centuries, the Albanian territories experienced the rise of independent feudal principalities, such as those of the Topias, Balshajs, Muzaks, Zenebishes, and Shpatajs. During this time, parts of the coastal regions came under the control of the Normans and later the Angevins before reverting to Byzantine rule.
f. By the late 14th century, Albania fell under Ottoman rule, and the Ottoman administrative and military system was established, incorporating the Albanian territories into the Sanjak of Albania. On March 2, 1444, the League of Lezhë,

led by Gjergj Kastrioti Skënderbeu, marked the formation of a unified Albanian resistance against the Ottomans. Skënderbeu's state extended from Dukagjini in the north to Devoll and Seman in the south and from the Adriatic coast in the west to the valley of the Black Drin in the east. The Ottomans once again subjugated. Following Skënderbeu's death, Albania and the region remained under Ottoman control for nearly five centuries as part of the Eyalet of Rumelia.

g. By the late 18th and early 19th centuries, Albanian efforts to break away from the Ottoman Empire intensified, culminating in the National Renaissance (Shadan, 2018). On November 28, 1912, Albania declared its independence, although neighboring states immediately threatened the country's territorial integrity. The London Conference of Ambassadors, held between December 1912 and August 1913, ultimately disregarded Albanian independence and treated the region as part of the Ottoman Empire's legacy, which had been defeated in the First Balkan War (Hall, 2002). Despite efforts by the Government of Vlora to preserve Albania's territorial integrity, the Conference of Ambassadors decided on July 29, 1913, to divide nearly half of Albania's lands among Serbia, Montenegro, and Greece. Following these events, the Albanian lands became a battleground during World War I.

23. In the interwar period, Albania was ruled by Ahmet Zogu, who declared himself King of the Albanians from 1928 to 1939. However, on April 7, 1939, fascist Italy invaded Albania, and the country became embroiled in World War II until its liberation on November 29, 1944, when the communist regime took power (Tase, 2012):

a. Albania remained under communist rule until 1991 when a multiparty system and free-market economy were introduced. After enduring a challenging transition to democracy, Albania became a NATO member in 2009 and has been a candidate for European Union membership since then. Albania continues to play a crucial role in maintaining regional stability, supporting Kosovo's independence, and contributing to resolving political disputes in the Balkans.
b. In October 2024, Albania officially began its negotiations for EU accession, marking a crucial step in its long journey toward EU membership.[12] On 15 October, during the EU-Albania Intergovernmental Conference in Luxembourg, Albania opened five key negotiation chapters. These include critical areas such as judiciary and fundamental rights, justice, freedom and security, public procurement, statistics, and financial control. These areas are pivotal to Albania's alignment with EU standards, especially in strengthening its rule of law and governance structures.
c. This step follows Albania's progress in implementing reforms required by the EU, particularly in the justice sector and public administration. The process has been complex and long, influenced by regional politics. Notably, Albania's accession track has now been decoupled from that of North Macedonia, leading to discontent in Skopje, which perceives the EU's decision as unfair.

12. European Council, Second Accession Conference with Albania, Oct. 15, 2024, available online: https://www.consilium.europa.eu/en/meetings/international-ministerial-meetings/2024/10/15/

A. Population Dynamics

24. The first comprehensive census of the Albanian population is documented in the cadastral register from 1431 to 1432; however, this data needs to be revised as it reflects only the population of the Sanjak of Albania, with Gjirokastra serving as its capital (History of the Albanian People, 2002, p. 326). A more extensive census was conducted in 1506, including data from Albanian territories, incorporating information from the self-governing mountainous provinces where the timar system had yet to be implemented. It is estimated that the population of Albania was approximately 1.5 million inhabitants before the fragmentation of its territories in 1913, which resulted in less than half of that number (around 740,000) remaining within the political borders of Albania (Ziu, 2018):

a. The general population census conducted in 1923, recognized as the first official census in Albania, reported a population of approximately 814,380 inhabitants.[13] Subsequent censuses were carried out from 1923 until 2011, during which several notable demographic trends emerged. Since the initial census from 1923 to 1989, Albania experienced a continuous population increase, primarily attributed to high natural growth rates.
b. However, the 2001 census marked a significant turning point in population dynamics, as it revealed a notable decline in the population by approximately 113,000 individuals compared to 1989 (Ziu, 2018). This trend was corroborated by the subsequent population and housing census conducted in April 2011, which reported a population of 2,821,977, indicating a further decrease of 7.7% relative to the 2001 census. According to data from the Institute of Statistics (INSTAT), as of January 1, 1921, the population was recorded at 2,829,741.

25. The observed decline in population can be attributed to several factors, including:

- high levels of emigration following the sociopolitical changes of 1990;
- a decrease in the birth rate, primarily due to the emigration of young people;
- an increase in the age of marriage and the implementation of family planning policies.

26. These dynamics highlight the complex interplay of socioeconomic factors influencing demographic trends in Albania over the past century.

Table 1 Population Numbers by District from the Last Two Censuses

The District	*Year 2001*	*–Year 2011*
Berat	193,020	140,964
Debër	189,854	136,630

13. FESH, a.g.e, f.1042.

The District	*Year 2001*	*–Year 2011*
Durrës	245,179	265,330
Elbasan	362,736	296,082
Fier	382,544	310,989
Gjirokastra	112,831	75,172
Korçë	265,182	220,438
Kukës	111,393	85,239
Lezha	159,182	135,609
Shkodër	256,473	217,375
Tirana	597,899	–763,634
Vlorë	192,982	184,279

27. It should be underlined that the last census, 2023, has only been partially published. For instance, the total Albanian population is 2,402,113 inhabitants, of whom 1,190,448 are males and 1,211,665 are females.[14]

B. *Religious Structure of the Population*

28. Albania is notable for its high level of religious tolerance. The population is characterized by the coexistence of various religious communities, including Muslim and Bektashi groups and Catholic and Orthodox Christian denominations. Most of the population identifies as Muslim, and these communities interact harmoniously, reflecting a broader culture of religious pluralism in the country.

29. According to the last census, census 2023, the following table includes their answers:[15]

Religion	Sex		
	Total	Male	Female
Total	2,402,113	1,190,448	1,211,665
Muslim	1,101,718	545,828	555,890
Muslim—Bektashism	115,644	58,854	56,790

14. According to Shqiptarja.com, the Institute of Statistics has published the 2023 Census data. Based on the population data, Albania has a total of 2,402,113 inhabitants. Compared to the 2011 Census, the country has 419,831 fewer residents, a decline of approximately 17%. Regarding religious affiliation, 1.1 million people identified as Muslim, 384,000 as Christian, 85,000 as atheists, and 332,000 as unspecified. Tirana, April 22, 2024.
15. Shqiptarja.com, "2023 Census, Religious Affiliation Data Published," available online: https://shqiptarja.com/lajm/censi-2023-publikohen-te-dhenat-e-besimit-fetar-mbi-200-mije-qytetare-te-pa-cilesuar

Religion	Sex		
	Total	Male	Female
Christian—Catholicism	201,530	98,349	103,181
Christian—Orthodoxy	173,645	84,157	89,488
Christian—Evangelists (Protestant)	9,658	4,302	5,356
Other religion or faith	3,670	1,535	2,135
Believers without denomination	332,155	162,380	169,775
Atheists	85,311	44,851	40,460
Prefer not to answer	244,331	123,221	121,110
Not available	134,451	66,971	67,480

V. Social and Cultural Values

30. Albania, a country characterized by its profound cultural heritage and historical transitions, represents a compelling case of the interplay between enduring traditions and modern societal transformations. Its social and cultural fabric is defined by deeply ingrained familial ties, evolving gender dynamics, and a growing emphasis on public health, reflecting the nation's broader developmental trajectory. Demographic changes, evolving gender roles, and a growing focus on health are reshaping the country, offering a window into how tradition and modernity can coexist. Recent statistics underscore these shifts, shedding light on the challenges and opportunities facing Albania today. Family remains a cornerstone of Albanian society, with extended networks deeply involved in daily life. Around 24% of households are now led by women, reflecting gradual shifts in family structures, though multigenerational homes remain common, preserving cultural traditions and fostering social cohesion. In rural areas, community ties, including the influence of neighbors and religious leaders, reinforce the social fabric, providing vital support in addressing economic and social challenges.

31. Albania has made notable progress in advancing gender equity, as evidenced by 55.7% of women aged 15 and older attaining higher education—a significant increase from 51% a decade earlier. Women's participation in higher education has risen significantly, with over 55% of women aged 15 and older attaining higher education—an encouraging indicator of progress.[16] This shift has challenged traditional gender norms, particularly in urban areas where women increasingly occupy professional roles and leadership positions. However, in rural regions, traditional expectations of women as primary caretakers and homemakers persist, reflecting a slower pace of change. The gender wage gap and limited access

16. INSTAT, The Population and Housing Census in Albania, 2023 https://www.instat.gov.al/media/13615/cens-i-popullsise-2023.pdf.

to economic opportunities remain pressing issues, highlighting the need for continued efforts to achieve gender equity. Policies aimed at addressing these disparities must be complemented by cultural shifts that challenge deep-seated stereotypes.

32. One of the most dynamic areas of change in Albania is the field of health, where traditional practices are being supplemented and, in many cases, replaced by modern healthcare systems. Historically, Albanian communities, particularly in rural areas, relied heavily on natural remedies and community-based care. These approaches were guided by generational knowledge and a sense of mutual support within families. Nevertheless, the rise of chronic diseases, which now account for nearly 89% of total deaths, has shifted the focus to modern healthcare and prevention.

33. Government programs like "Si Je?" represent a significant step forward in promoting preventive health. This initiative offers free annual check-ups for individuals aged 35 to 70, targeting early detection and management of conditions such as high blood pressure, diabetes, and obesity. Such efforts reflect a growing recognition of the importance of addressing health risks proactively, particularly in a country where the population is aging rapidly—nearly 20% of Albanians are now aged 65 or older (Sentell et al., 2018). These demographic changes have placed additional pressure on Albania's healthcare system, necessitating reforms that emphasize accessibility, education, and integrated care. By integrating modern healthcare approaches with Albania's traditional focus on community-based care, the country is striving to build a more resilient and inclusive health system for the future. Despite these advancements, disparities persist, particularly in rural areas where access to healthcare facilities and services remains limited (Tresa et al., 2024). Urban centers like Tirana benefit from better-equipped medical facilities and a higher concentration of healthcare professionals, while rural populations often rely on underfunded clinics. Addressing this gap is critical to ensuring equitable health outcomes across the country. Schools and community programs are increasingly focused on teaching young people about the importance of healthy lifestyles, including nutrition and physical activity (Sentell et al., 2018). This emphasis on education aims to instill long-term behavioral changes that can reduce the prevalence of preventable diseases. Moreover, involving families in health promotion activities helps create a culture where well-being is a shared responsibility. This approach not only enhances public health outcomes but also reinforces the social cohesion that is a hallmark of Albanian culture.

34. Furthermore, demographic changes are profoundly impacting Albania's social structure. Albania's population is currently estimated at approximately 2.4 million, reflecting a decline of 420,000 since the 2011 census, primarily attributed to emigration, particularly among young individuals seeking opportunities abroad (Lopasic, n.d., p. 90, paragraph 2). Simultaneously, the country is undergoing rapid urbanization, with nearly one-third of the population now concentrated in the Tirana region. Urbanization is profoundly reshaping Albania's sociocultural and economic dynamics. Urban areas are increasingly functioning as epicenters of innovation and economic integration, attracting younger populations who aspire to engage in the global marketplace. However, this internal migration has intensified regional disparities, particularly in terms of access to essential services and the preservation of intangible cultural heritage in rural areas. Mitigating these imbalances necessitates a multifaceted approach, encompassing strategic investments in infrastructure, the expansion of educational resources, and the implementation of cultural preservation initiatives aimed at sustaining rural communities. These measures are imperative for achieving balanced regional development while maintaining Albania's cultural distinctiveness amidst ongoing urbanization.

35. Albania's distinctiveness lies in its capacity to evolve while preserving its cultural heritage. The profound respect for family and community continues to provide a resilient foundation as the nation engages with new ideas and opportunities. Moving forward, progressive policies are key to preserving cultural heritage while addressing challenges like gender equity, healthcare, and youth emigration. By maintaining its cultural identity alongside embracing modernization, Albania exemplifies the harmonious coexistence of tradition and progress. This transformative journey, rooted in enduring values, will remain integral to shaping the nation's future trajectory.

§2. General Description of Healthcare System

I. The Historical Background

A. Development of Albanian Medicine over the Centuries

36. The history of the Albanian people and their territory is closely intertwined with that of neighboring countries, marked by periods of both peaceful coexistence and conflict characterized by wars and invasions aimed at territorial occupation and national assimilation. Throughout history, Albanians have primarily focused on defending their land and preserving their identity, resulting in a relatively modest influence on the cultures of their invaders:

a. In contrast, the invading forces sought not only to gain control but also to appropriate Albanian spiritual culture and identity, often attempting complete assimilation. Despite these challenges, historical documents and archaeological discoveries attest to the resilience of the Albanian people, demonstrating that they have made significant contributions to culture, development, and scientific progress, particularly in medicine and dentistry, over the centuries.
b. Notably, Dr. Flamur Tartari, in collaboration with archaeologist Fatos Tartari, has presented compelling evidence from documentary and archaeological sources regarding the advancement of medicine in ancient Albania. Excavations at key ancient sites have uncovered various artifacts including specialized dishes, medical instruments, artistic works, and symbols, all providing insight into the early development of medical practices in the region (Koçi, 2023).

B. Illyrian Medicine

37. The emergence and expansion of numerous Illyrian cities in the first millennium BC, particularly between the 4th and 2nd centuries BC, signified the establishment of a slaveholding society. This transition catalyzed advancements across various domains, including medicine. Initially, Illyrian medicine was steeped in magical and mythological beliefs, with early practitioners predominantly being pagan priests who attributed illnesses to "evil spirits" (Tartari, 2014). However, as economic and social structures evolved, a distinction between magic and medicine began to take shape, leading to the professionalization of medical practice. The accumulation of empirical knowledge, alongside the exchange of ideas with neighboring cultures, facilitated notable progress in medical understanding and treatment (Koçi, 2023):

a. Influential medical theories, particularly those of Hippocrates, permeated ancient societies, including Illyria, via Greek colonies such as Epidamnus, Apollonia, and Oricum. Historical and archaeological evidence points to King Gent of the Hadrians as the earliest known Illyrian physician (Koçi, 2023).
b. A wealth of archaeological materials related to medicine, first showcased by F. Tartari and H. Bllaca in the journal *Iliria* in 1989, dates to the 3rd and 2nd centuries BC. These findings include surgical instruments, ceramic vessels, pharmaceutical scales, and specialized spoons, indicating a sophisticated healthcare approach. Additionally, the presence of sewers, public baths, and monumental temples underscores Illyria's advanced hygiene practices and cultural sophistication (Tartari & Bllaca, 1989).
c. The Illyrians demonstrated extensive knowledge of medicinal plants, utilizing them for preventive and therapeutic purposes, particularly in urban centers like Dyrrah and Apollonia, which thrived during the Roman occupation. Prominent physicians from this era include Filonidh Dyrraheni, an author of a medical encyclopedia, as well as Kratus, a freed slave who practiced medicine, and Filolog, noted for his expertise in ophthalmology. While specific records for practitioners in Apollonia remain limited, it is suggested that the city also housed medical professionals, including Jatrokles, a student of Filonidh. Ancient texts, including those of Pliny, indicate that the number of physicians in Illyria may have reached as high as one thousand (Shehu, 2004, p. 48).
d. King Gent, who ruled from 181 BC to 168 BC, played a pivotal role in Illyrian history. The son of King Pleurat, Gent fiercely resisted Roman expansion within Illyrian territories, successfully strengthening the state both politically and militarily. He is recognized as the last sovereign of ancient Illyria and was notable for minting bronze coins inscribed with his name (Faniko & Karamuço, 2016).
e. Amid escalating tensions with Rome, Gent led a valiant resistance during the Third Roman-Illyrian War from his capital in Skodra (Shkodra). Despite his determined efforts, the superior Roman legions ultimately overwhelmed the Illyrian forces. In a strategic decision to protect his citizens, Gent confined himself within the city walls and ultimately capitulated to Roman consul Anicius to avert further violence against his people. This surrender, known as "La caduta di Skodra," occurred on June 15, 168 BC. While the Romans honored their

agreement, they exiled Gent and his family to Italy, where they were granted lands and titles befitting their royal status.

f. In Italy, Gent dedicated his remaining years to herbal medicine, engaging in the study of plants with medicinal properties until he died in November 146 BC. He was honored posthumously with a grand mausoleum, as the historian Titus Livius documented. King Gent is remembered not only as a significant political leader but also as a pioneering figure in medicine, particularly for his identification of the therapeutic properties of the plant Gentiana, which bears his name, thus securing his legacy within the annals of medical history (Koçi, 2023).

C. Medicine in Albania During the Ottoman Empire

38. The Ottoman Empire profoundly influenced the historical trajectory of Albania and the broader Balkan region. As a dominion of one of the most powerful empires of the time, Albania's political, military, economic, and cultural developments were closely aligned with the imperial framework. However, the benefits of this affiliation were unevenly distributed; the empire, while a formidable military power, afforded only modest developmental opportunities to its vassal states. Albania, positioned as a peripheral territory, attracted Ottoman attention primarily during military campaigns or when its educated elites were required for administrative roles, such as generals or provincial governors. Consequently, the cultural, economic, and social challenges faced by the Albanian populace were often relegated to the margins of imperial policy:

a. Within the Ottoman Empire, which spanned over six centuries, the evolution of medical practices reflected a complex amalgamation of Eastern and Western influences, resulting in a distinctive medical tradition. The contributions of Islamic culture to healthcare, particularly in areas such as hygiene and dentistry, have been well documented. Numerous historical texts, from both the Arab world and Western scholarship, highlight the significance of hygiene in Islamic teachings, including directives for dental care, which recommended brushing teeth multiple times daily (Çınaroğlu, n.d.; Benli, 2016).
b. Despite its rich cultural heritage, the medical sciences in the Ottoman Empire, including dentistry, fell behind the advancements taking place in Europe, particularly during the Renaissance. Unlike Europe, where dentistry evolved into a distinct profession because of the Industrial Revolution, medical practitioners in the Ottoman Empire were often generalists who also performed dental procedures. Notably, the works of 17th-century scholars, such as Evliya Çelebi, provide insight into the presence of dental practices within the Ottoman military (Imber, 2002; Shaw, 1976).
c. The Tanzimat Reforms of the 19th century represented a significant turning point in the modernization of medical education and practice within the empire. The influx of Western-trained doctors, dentists, and pharmacists into state institutions signified a shift toward contemporary medical practices. The establishment of the Medical School (Mekteb–I Tibyie) in 1838 and the creation of public hospitals facilitated the formal organization of health services (Çolaklar,

2014). By 1840, the Medical Assembly, tasked with overseeing civil health services, was founded, which aimed to regulate the licensing of health professionals, including pharmacists, midwives, and dentists, ensuring that practitioners were subjected to examinations to validate their qualifications.

d. Despite these advancements, significant challenges remained, particularly concerning the regulation of dental practice. Barbers, licensed to perform dental extractions, coexisted with numerous unlicensed practitioners, especially in urban areas, leading to complications and malpractice. In rural regions, dental procedures were frequently conducted by tradespeople without formal training. Itinerant "dentists" often performed extractions in public squares, operating with minimal knowledge of proper techniques or hygiene standards.
e. During the reign of Sultan Abdulhamit II, the establishment of the Royal House of Sciences in 1900 laid the foundation for modern Turkish universities, fostering the development of specialized institutions for medicine, dentistry, and other scientific fields. The relocation of the Medical School to a new facility in the European part of Istanbul in 1903, alongside the transformation of existing medical schools into faculties, marked a critical advancement in Ottoman medical education (Kurdak et al., 2008). Nevertheless, the empire's contributions to the progression of dentistry in Albania were relatively negligible.
f. Documentation indicates that a Turkish dentist, Javer Efendi, alongside other foreign medical practitioners, contributed to healthcare in Albania during this period, with notable involvement from Austrian physician Kaus Chirban. Prof. Kadri Kirçiku first highlighted these contributions in his work *The Zhvillimi i shëndetësisë në Shkodër në shek. XV–XX* (Development of Health in Shkodër from the 15th to the 20th Century). Ultimately, while the Ottoman Empire facilitated certain advancements in the medical field, its overall impact on the evolution of Albanian medical practice and education remained limited (Kërçiku, 1962).

D. Inheritance in the Health Service

39. The latter half of the 19th century represented a pivotal period for the healthcare sector in Albania, primarily attributed to the establishment of medical schools in Istanbul and Athens. These institutions produced a substantial number of Albanian medical graduates who contributed to health service development both domestically and abroad. Concurrently, hospitals were inaugurated in various Albanian cities, significantly enhancing access to medical care. Noteworthy figures such as Besim Omeri, who served as a professor at the Istanbul Military Academy and later as a rector at Istanbul University, played a crucial role in advancing medical practice in the region. Omeri was instrumental in founding the Turkish Red Cross and authored over fifty medical publications, thus profoundly influencing Turkish health policy:

a. Several Albanian physicians, including Mustafa Buda, Bilal Golemi, and Rifat Frashëri, continued their practice in Turkey, indicating the regional impact of Albanian medical professionals. In 1914, under the government of Wilhelm

Wied, the "General Directorate of Public Health" was established, directed by Dr. Mihal Turtulli, marking the inception of Albania's first public health institution (Luarasi, 1938, p. 13).

b. With the formation of the National Government of Lushnja in 1920, there was a renewed emphasis on health services, with Dr. Rifat Frashëri appointed as the head of this newly established health service. At that time, only fifty doctors were practicing in Albania, with merely one specialist among them (Organ of the Albanian Red Cross, 1926). Furthermore, Albanian medical personnel made significant contributions during the Vlora War in 1920. Furthermore, Dr. Petraq Popa returned from his medical practice in Turkey to establish a hospital in Vlora, providing critical care to wounded soldiers (Xhuvani et al., 1980).
c. Establishing a bacteriological laboratory in 1924 was a notable advancement in the country's medical infrastructure. This period saw the emergence of prominent medical figures, such as Anton Ashta, a malariologist, and surgeon Federik Shiroka, who contributed to the formation of specialized medical departments. To address the growing demand for specialists in hospitals and laboratories, the Albanian government, between 1927 and 1928, facilitated further training for physicians—including Jani Basho, Ismail Tartari, Bajram Iljazi, and Sabri Tefiku—by sending them to Rome, Vienna, and Paris to specialize in various medical fields.[17]
d. The years 1925 to 1928 were characterized by political stability and an enhanced state administration, attracting Albanian students and foreign medical practitioners to work in Albania. Following the law "On the Health Service in Albania," medical personnel, including dentists and pharmacists, were required to possess a high school diploma to practice. A statistical report issued by the General Directorate of Health, addressing the health and demographic conditions of the population between 1935 and 1940, indicates that the Albanian health service consisted of 164 general practitioners during this period. The health service was overseen by several general directors, including Mihal Turtulli, Refat Frashëri, Osman Jonuzi, Qemal Jusufati, Jani Basho, and Hamdi Sulçebe, from 1912 to 1944 (Gudha, 2002).
e. The exigencies of World War II intensified the demand for medical professionals, prompting many patriotic doctors and medical students abroad to return to Albania to contribute to the liberation struggle. Several medical practitioners, such as dermatologist Stefan Pano, displayed remarkable bravery, sacrificing their lives in the fight for national liberation.
f. Following the war, Albania transitioned to a socialist health service model. Young doctors began to receive training in socialist countries, particularly within the Soviet bloc, which contrasted with previous educational practices that favored Western Europe. In 1952, the Faculty of Medicine was established with assistance from the Soviet Union, alongside the opening of numerous hospitals across the country, thereby extending medical services to remote areas.

---

17. AQSh (Central State Archive), F.202, v.1927, D.65, fl.32. Notifications from the Ministry of Public Works regarding the sending of Jani Basho and I. Tartari for specialization in Vienna and Rome, Tirana, May 1927.

This era witnessed the introduction of new medical specialties, contributing to the advancement of healthcare despite the country's prevailing isolation.

40. Owing to their dedication and commitment, Albanian physicians successfully eradicated several diseases, including malaria and syphilis, owing to their dedication and commitment. Their research findings were presented at international scientific congresses and conferences, reflecting an increase in the scientific standing of Albanian medicine, even within a system that often discouraged such initiatives. Furthermore, preventive measures were implemented, leading to the production of vaccines for diseases such as typhus, Malta fever, tetanus, tuberculosis, measles, and cholera:

a. The establishment of the Institute of Hygiene and Epidemiology in 1969 marked a significant advance in the focus on preventive health measures and epidemiological research. Although the collapse of the dictatorial regime in the early 1990s presented numerous challenges for the healthcare sector, it simultaneously opened avenues for improved communication with Europe and opportunities for further development. The dedication of many doctors who served in underserved regions, often facing systemic neglect or political adversity, should not be overlooked, as their contributions were instrumental in the evolution of Albania's health service.
b. Following the fall of the communist regime, Albanian medical law underwent reform for two key reasons. First, it was necessary to incorporate democratic values, such as the right to self-determination. Second, international and supranational case law and legislation influenced the application, interpretation, and amendment of national laws.

II. Regulation of the Healthcare System

41. Albania's healthcare system has long been characterized by strong central government control. In 1992, Albania shifted to a pluralist system with a liberalized economy—at least in principle. By 1993, the first steps to reform the health services were launched. These reforms aimed to deliver high-quality primary healthcare, reducing reliance on secondary services, and funding it all through a national health insurance system to ensure direct support for healthcare services. From then on, special attention was given to the pharmaceutical sector as part of the healthcare reform.

42. In Albania, the state provides most healthcare services to the population, covering areas like health promotion, disease prevention, diagnosis, and treatment. Meanwhile, the private sector focuses primarily on pharmaceuticals, dental services, and a few specialized diagnostic services, which are mostly concentrated in Tirana.

43. The country's diagnostic and curative health services are structured into three levels: primary, secondary, and tertiary healthcare. Public health services and health promotion activities are managed within primary healthcare, supported and supervised by the Institute of Public Health, the 12 Regional Directorates of Health, and the 24 Directorates of Public Health.

44. Albania's health system is supported by several national institutions that operate under the Ministry of Health. The Ministry plays a central role in the public sector, taking charge of drafting and implementing health policies and strategies that regulate the system while also coordinating all actors within and outside the health-care system.

45. Public health and promotion services form the foundation of the Institute of Public Health's work. This is the only state institution under the Ministry of Health offering specialized expertise in these areas. Beyond this, various national institutions also play key roles, including the National Center for Blood Transfusion; the National Center for Child Upbringing, Development and Rehabilitation; the University Dental Clinic; the National Center for Biomedical Engineering; the National Center for Drug Control; and the National Center of Quality Safety and Accreditation of Health Institutions.

46. Outside of Tirana, the primary healthcare is organized and managed by the Regional Health Authority (RHA), relying on Public Health Directorates (PHDs) and Regional Health Directorates (RHDs) which operate in twelve regions. These Directorates coordinate all primary healthcare services in their areas. Each region has Hospital Service Directorates, while the twelve main towns host Regional Hospital Directorates. Health Centers function as independent units contracted to provide services under the mandatory health insurance scheme and the Basic Primary Healthcare Service Package.

47. The Health Center is the primary healthcare institution in Albania. It is publicly funded, non-profit, and operates with its own bank account. It includes a network of all service providers as its subordinates and carries out its activities in compliance with Article 100, point 2 of the Albanian Constitution, and the following legislative frameworks: Law No. 10107, dated 30.03.2009, "On the primary healthcare in the Republic of Albania"; Law No. 10138, dated 11.05.2009, "On public health"; Law No. 7870, dated 13.10.1994, "On the health insurances in the Republic of Albania," as amended; Law No. 10107, dated 30.03.2009, "On the healthcare in the Republic of Albania," as amended; and Article 10 of Law No. 10383, dated 24.02.2011, "On the mandatory healthcare in the Republic of Albania," as amended. The Health Center operates upon the proposal of the Minister of Health and approval by the Council of Ministers.

48. The Health Center implements all relevant Albanian laws and sublegal acts issued by the Minister of Health, the Local Health Authorities authorized by the Minister of Health, and the Mandatory Healthcare Insurance Fund. Regarding financing, Health Centers operate with an annual budget funded by the Mandatory Healthcare Insurance Fund. This budget is allocated across three main areas: staff salaries, utilities, and medicine. Additionally, Health Centers generate secondary income from healthcare services provided to patients who do not have a Health Booklet or for health services offered against invoices. These secondary funds are used for investments, pending approval by the management board. Proposals for such investments must first be submitted to the board. Interviewees report that this process is often lengthy or delayed due to subjective reasons. Such delays directly impact on the quality of services and often lead to patient complaints about the manager or staff of the Health Center, as patients are generally unaware of the significant role the board plays in the center's operations.

49. The Ministry of Health is the institution responsible for developing health policies and strategies in Albania. The Mandatory Health Insurance Fund is tasked with assigning funds to the Primary Healthcare Centers, as stipulated in Law No. 10383, dated 24.02.2011, "On mandatory healthcare insurance in the Republic of Albania," as amended. The Healthcare Insurance Scheme began implementation on 1 March 1995, serving as a vital mechanism for healthcare reform and an essential step toward improving the quality of services offered.

50. The highest technical institution in the area of public healthcare is the Public Health Institute, a national institution operating under the direct subordination of the Ministry of Health. Its main duties include studying and monitoring risk factors, conducting surveillance of contagious diseases, serving as a lab reference, and managing vaccination programs. Additionally, the implementation of many short-term research or promotional programs is part of its responsibilities. The Public Health Institute also plays an important role in providing training in public health.

51. However, the existence of Health Center Boards creates challenges in finding quick solutions to issues. Managers of Health Centers report that they must submit a request to the Board even for replacing missing or broken medical equipment. On the contrary, while a "repair fund" exists as part of the Mandatory Health Insurance Fund, requests are often delayed or denied. These complaints focus on unnecessary bureaucracy, which only slows down work processes and prevents the timely delivery of necessary healthcare services to patients. For instance, in cases of medicine shortages before the end of the year, there is no alternative but to wait for the new budget for the following year, regardless of the urgent need for such medicine. De jure, the directors of Health Centers are granted many competencies, but in practice, they exercise little to no actual power. According to the managers of Health Centers, even their appointments are made by the Management Board, a process that, in their view, does not make any sense.

52. Health Centers' staff (including ambulances) comprises managers, doctors, nurses, midwives and support staff. Thus, healthcare services are not provided in a single building but through a network of healthcare providers. Family Medicine (FM) is the fundamental professional discipline around which Primary Healthcare is developed. In exercising their specialty skills, the family doctors exercise their competencies in these three areas: clinical duties, communication with patients, and management of Health Center. The services benefited are detailed in the Primary Healthcare basic package and include: (i) care in natural disaster emergencies; (ii) care in cases of common emergencies; (iii) provision of uninterrupted (24/7) healthcare at the Health Centers; (iv) provision of care at the Health Centers with interrupted services (eight hours daily); (v) provision of care outside the Health Centers; (vi) healthcare for children; (vii) healthcare for women and reproductive health; (viii) healthcare for adults; (ix) healthcare for the elderly; (x) mental healthcare; (xi) health promotion and education.

A. *Social Insurance*

53. The Social Insurance system was established based on Law No. 7870, dated 13.10.1994, "On Health Insurances in the Republic of Albania." Since its establishment, it has covered a list of basic reimbursable medications and the payment of the family doctor in the public system. The system gradually developed with the widening of the scope of services covered, going from non-differentiated financing to the payment of healthcare packages. The Albanian Health Insurance model is a mixed one (Bismarck and Beveridge), based on mandatory and voluntary contributions and funding by the state budget. The economically active population pays health insurances, whereas the state budget funds (from general taxation) cover the non-active population and categories "in need," thus giving the system a solidarity-based approach.

54. The health insurance system is based on the single-payer model, meaning the Compulsory Health Care Insurance Fund manages the scheme in line with national healthcare policies. The Compulsory Health Care Insurance Fund uses health service payment methods to influence increased access, prevention, and improvement of population health indicators. Annual contracts with public and private providers of health services for the provision of healthcare packages serve as the mechanism for implementing the health insurance scheme.

55. The health insurance scheme covers primary care (except for mental health community centers, public dental care, and healthcare in schools), hospital services (except for psychiatric hospitals), and a list of reimbursable medications that the patient would receive reimbursement for. The mandatory health insurance scheme also includes healthcare packages covering medical visits, examinations, and treatment at public primary healthcare centers and public hospitals, approved healthcare packages at private hospitals, and drugs, medical products, and treatment offered by contracted healthcare providers.

B. *The Institute of Public Health*

56. The Institute of Public Health represents the higher technical institution in the field of public health and is a national institution under the direct dependence of the Ministry of Health. Its tasks include research and monitoring of risk factors, surveillance of infectious diseases, laboratory reference and the management of the vaccination program. The Institute of Public Health plays an important role regarding training in the field of public health.

C. The National Agency of Drugs and Medical Devices

57. The agency is responsible for the control of every activity in the pharmaceutical field. It exercises control over:

the activities of manufacture, its facilities and equipment;
wholesale and retail trade and storage conditions of medicines;
drug raw materials and auxiliary materials; and
the imported drugs from all licensed entities.

The pharmaceutical market in Albania is well regulated, with expanded service provision of pharmaceuticals by the private sector. In aligning with the EU legislation, the legal framework was progressively improved.

58. The healthcare quality has improved in the last twenty years as a result of professional exchanges with other countries and technological progresses. In 2006, a special institution was established, and the necessary legal regulatory framework was drafted for the accreditation of health institutions and the development of Medical Guidelines and Protocols. The development of guidelines and protocols was not followed by any implementation capacity assessment. Further efforts are needed to complete the capacity assessment, as well as to define and regulate the clinical audits, in cooperation with the Professionals‘ Orders and the State Health Inspectorate.

III. Financing of the Healthcare System

59. Healthcare in Albania is financed by: (a) the state budget; (b) mandatory and voluntary health insurance; (c) private health insurance; and (d) direct payments. Compulsory health insurance and private health insurance are regulated by special laws, as specified in Article 8 of Law No. 10 107, dated 30.3.2009. Hospital financing is also regulated by Law No. 9106, dated 17.7.2003, “For the Hospital Service in the Republic of Albania.” Article 24 specifies that public hospitals are financed by: (a) the Ministry of Health; (b) health insurance institutions; (c) local government; and (ç) local and foreign donors.

60. Healthcare services offered in healthcare institutions to foreign citizens residing in the Republic of Albania are based on relevant international agreements or the principle of reciprocity. In the absence of an international agreement or conditions for reciprocity, foreign citizens benefit from healthcare services according to the provisions of this law and the healthcare financing law.

61. Public hospitals are financed by: (a) the state budget; (b) health insurance institutions; (c) local government; (d) local and foreign donors; (e) income generated by services provided to third parties; and (f) other legal income. Income from contracts, fees, or payments made by patients for clinical and nonclinical services not covered by hospital financing institutions is transferred to the hospital's account as secondary income. Secondary income that has not been spent within a fiscal year can be carried over to the next hospital fiscal year (Article 16, Law No. 55/2022).

62. Furthermore, Article 5 of Law No. 7870, dated 13.10.1994, On Health Insurance in the Republic of Albania, regulates the state finances: (a) preventive health measures; (b) visit and examinations for diagnostic purposes by the specialist, healthcare hospital, as well as other cases defined by law; (c) emergency services; (ç) investments. Emergency services for extraordinary cases, such as mass accidents, epidemics and natural disasters, are organized by municipalities and communes with the support of the government for their financing. For such services, expenses are covered according to the criteria determined by the Council of Ministers.

63. Law No. 9355, dated 10.3.2005, regulates assistance and social services, specifically addressing the financing and provision of such services in Albania. The state provides social care services and other forms of support for people in need, according to the possibilities of the state budget. Financing of programs of economic assistance, payment for persons with disabilities and social services is covered by the State Budget and local government budgets. The sources of financing assistance and payment of disabled persons consist of: (a) funds of the central State Budget; (b) funds from local taxes and fees (Article 34, Law No. 9355, dated 10.3.2005 For Assistance and Social Services).

64. Hospital service costs include the cost of treatment, outpatient diagnostics, or hospitalization. The costs of public hospital services are calculated based on the institution's expenses for diagnosis, care, and treatment of patients, as well as other necessary costs for providing hospital services. General costs, such as depreciation, renovation, and modernization of hospital equipment, must not exceed 4% of total costs. The cost of hospital services is approved by the decision of the management board for tertiary hospitals, university hospitals, and regional centers. For day hospitals, on a municipal or regional basis, costs are approved by the healthcare services operator according to the methodology outlined in the minister's instruction. For inpatients or outpatients, public hospitals are authorized to offer services outside the preferential referral system against fees determined by the decision of the management board (Article 23, Law No. 55/2022).

65. The Ministry of Labor and Social Affairs programs the funds for block economic aid and payment of disabled persons in accordance with the assessment of requests received from local government units, and once every two months, it transfers them to the municipality or commune. The criteria and indicators used for block aid programming are proposed by the Minister of Labor and Social Affairs and approved by the decision of the Council of Ministers.

66. The Ministry of Labor and Social Affairs delegates once every four months the economic block aid fund to municipalities, which conditions the provision of economic aid with work and social care services in the community. The surplus of economic aid funds, created because of better block aid management, after approval by the Ministry of Labor and Social Affairs, remains with the local units. These funds serve to support programs that are implemented for work or community service within the year.

67. Funding sources for social care services, which are carried out by public and non-public institutions at the district, municipality or commune level, in residential institutions, in the center's day, family or mobile community services consist of: (a) funds delegated by the central State Budget; (b) funds allocated from local taxes and fees; (c) certain revenues from assets and other activities of the municipality; (ç) contributions of beneficiaries of social care services, defined in Article 23 of this law; (d) donations, sponsorships and other financing from organizations, natural or legal persons or other individuals, which are not included in letters "a," "b," "c" and "d" of this article (Article 37, Law No. 9355, dated 10.3.2005 For Assistance and Social Services).

68. Funds from the Central Budget for the financing of social care services are delegated by the Ministry of Labor and Social Affairs to municipalities, communes or districts at the beginning of the year in accordance with the assessment of needs and the possibilities of the State Budget. The methodology for calculating and distributing these funds is determined by the Ministry of Labor and Social Affairs in cooperation with the Ministry of Finance and is approved by a decision of the Council of Ministers.

69. To support new social care services and the development of social policies, the Ministry of Labor and Social Affairs establishes the Social Fund, which consists of: (a) a portion of funds programed for social care services; (b) extra-budgetary financing from organizations, natural or legal persons, or other individuals; (c) other revenues generated through the direct implementation of bilateral or multilateral agreements that the Republic of Albania establishes with other countries; and (d) income from its own resources and assets owned by the Ministry of Labor and Social Affairs. The rules governing the use of the Social Fund are determined by a decision of the Council of Ministers (Article 39, Law No. 9355, dated 10.3.2005, "For Assistance and Social Services").

70. Control over the use of assistance funds, payments for disabled persons, and social care services is conducted by specialized control bodies in accordance with Law No. 9009, dated 13.2.2003, "On Internal Audit in the Public Sector." Any violation of this law or its implementation of bylaws is classified as an administrative misdemeanor in accordance with Law No. 7697, dated 7.4.1993, "On Administrative Offenses."

71. Based on their financing structure, social care services are classified into public services and private services. Public social care services include services provided in residential institutions, in day care centers or at home for groups in need. These services are financed by the central budget and the independent budgets of local government bodies. Municipalities administer all social services for individuals residing in their respective cities or municipalities. Counties administer services when they are offered to individuals across multiple local units within the county. Private social care services, on the other hand, consist of privately funded social care services offered in residential centers, in day centers, or at home.

72. Both public and private legal entities providing social care services must be licensed by the Ministry of Labor and Social Affairs. The criteria and procedures for licensing are determined by a decision of the Council of Ministers. Public social care services funded by central or local budget funds are procured by local government bodies from private providers in accordance with the prevailing public procurement legislation. Local government bodies enter contracts with the winning private legal entities to deliver services within their jurisdiction. The Ministry of Labor and Social Affairs drafts the standards for social care services and monitors their implementation. These standards are approved by a decision of the Council of Ministers.

73. The Council of Ministers ensures the financing of extraordinary costs incurred in activities during health emergencies by utilizing the Council's reserve fund, in line with the provisions of the National Health Emergency Plan. All healthcare institutions, whether public or private, cooperate as stipulated in the National Health Emergencies Plan and act based on their respective health emergency plans, which are approved in cooperation with the Ministry of Health (Article 35, Law No. 10 107, dated 30.3.2009).

74. The National Center for Welfare, Development, and Rehabilitation was created by Decision No. 325, dated 23.6.2000, of the Council of Ministers, "On the Creation of the National Center for the Well-being, Development, and Rehabilitation of Children," as a separate budget unit. According to this decision, the center operates as a national and special budget unit under the Ministry of Health and Social Protection. Financing for the center is provided through funds from the state budget, allocated via the Ministry of Health and Social Protection. The center is a national institution that provides medical and social services through a multidisciplinary team to children aged 0–6 years with motor or mental health problems and serves the entire territory of Albania.

§3. Sources of Medical Law

I. International Sources

75. According to the Albanian Constitution (Article 5, Article 116(1)(b), and Article 122(2)), international treaties ratified by the Albanian Parliament are mandatory and hold a higher rank than internal legislation.

76. The Republic of Albania adheres to international law that is binding upon it, as stipulated in Article 5 of the Albanian Constitution. Albania follows a clear hierarchy of laws. According to Article 116 of the Albanian Constitution, normative acts that are effective throughout the entire territory of the Republic of Albania are: (a) the Constitution; (b) ratified international agreements; (c) the laws; and (ç) normative acts of the Council of Ministers. At the top of this legal hierarchy is the Albanian Constitution. In cases of conflict between laws, Article 122(2) of the Albanian Constitution grants superiority to a ratified international agreement over any national law that is incompatible with it. Specifically, in relation to the European Convention on Human Rights (ECHR), the Albanian Constitutional Court has ranked it at the same level as the Constitution.

77. Among various international treaties, this paper focuses solely on the application of the ECHR and the jurisprudence of the ECtHR. The ECHR has been signed by forty-seven states that are members of the Council of Europe, making it one of the most widely respected human rights instruments. Furthermore, the ECHR establishes the right to file an individual application (Article 34 ECHR), subject to the criteria outlined in Article 35 ECHR. Consequently, in cases involving the violation of human rights, an international judge may apply these provisions against the Albanian State.

78. In the first semester of 2024, the Constitutional Court of Albania demonstrated its deep engagement with the ECHR and the interpretative principles of the ECtHR.[18] Throughout this period, the court consistently addressed key provisions of the ECHR, including Article 6, which pertains to the right to a fair trial and appeared in a significant number of its decisions. Additional attention was given to Articles 5, 8, 13, and 14, which safeguard rights such as liberty, private and family life, and effective remedies, alongside protections against discrimination.[19] Protocols such as Protocol No. 1 on the protection of property, Protocol No. 4 on freedom of movement, Protocol No. 7 on procedural safeguards, and Protocol No. 12 on the prohibition of discrimination further enriched the court's deliberations, highlighting its comprehensive approach to human rights adjudication.

79. The Constitutional Court's reliance on these articles and protocols illustrates its dedication to ensuring fairness, equality, and accountability in legal proceedings.

---

18. Until now, in August 2024, the Albanian Constitutional Court has published fifty-five legal decisions.
19. In the first semester of 2024, the Albanian Constitutional Court cited the ECHR (Articles 5, 6, 8, 13 and 14) in the following cases: Decisions No. 1 of 25.01.2024, No. 2 of 29.01.2024, No. 3 of 30.01.2024, No. 4 of 31.01.2024, No. 5 of 13.02.2024, No. 6 of 15.02.2024, No. 7 of 20.02.2024, No. 8 of 20.02.2024, No. 10 of 28.02.2024, No. 11 of 28.02.2024, No. 12 of 28.02.2024, No. 13 of 07.03.2024, No. 14 of 07.03.2024, No. 16 of 12.03.2024, No. 17 of 13.03.2024, No. 18 of 19.03.2024, No. 19 of 21.03.2024, No. 20 of 03.04.2024, No. 22 of 04.04.2024, No. 23 of 04.04.2024, No. 24 of 09.04.2024, No. 27 of 11.04.2024, No. 28 of 11.04.2024, No. 29 of 16.04.2024, No. 32 of 23.04.2024, No. 34 of 24.04.2024, No. 35 of 25.04.2024, No. 38 of 07.05.2024, No. 39 of 14.05.2024, No. 40 of 14.05.2024, No. 42 of 29.05.2024, No. 43 of 04.06.2024, No. 44 of 04.06.2024, No. 45 of 11.06.2024, No. 47 of 11.06.2024, No. 49 of 20.06.2024, No. 51 of 20.06.2024.

By weaving in established principles from ECtHR jurisprudence, the court reinforced Albania's alignment with European human rights standards, emphasizing the universality of these norms. This integration of international principles into domestic practice not only strengthens the judicial system's credibility but also reaffirms Albania's commitment to upholding justice and safeguarding fundamental freedoms in accordance with the broader European framework. These decisions, rooted in consistency and meticulous application of human rights law, reflect the court's evolving role as a key guarantor of individual liberties and legal integrity.[20]

80. Thus, in the first semester of 2024, the Albanian Constitutional Court referenced the ECHR in 36 out of 53 legal decisions.[21] In one decision,[22] it considered the highest number of articles, examining 11 different provisions of the Convention. Additionally, the court cited the ECtHR's principles in 25 out of 53 decisions.[23] In another decision, the court referred to the highest number of different legal interpretations derived from ECtHR jurisprudence, demonstrating the breadth of its engagement with international standards.[24] As seen in several cases, the Constitutional Court often combined the consideration of both the ECHR and ECtHR principles in its rulings.[25] Overall, in the first semester of 2024, only 11 decisions did

20. Please notice that the dissenting opinions are also published in Albania. However, the list only considers the majority opinion.
21. In the first semester of 2024, the Albanian Constitutional Court cited the ECHR in the following cases: Decisions No. 1 of 25.01.2024, No. 2 of 29.01.2024, No. 3 of 30.01.2024, No. 4 of 31.01.2024, No. 5 of 13.02.2024, No. 6 of 15.02.2024, No. 7 of 20.02.2024, No. 8 of 20.02.2024, No. 10 of 28.02.2024, No. 11 of 28.02.2024, No. 12 of 28.02.2024, No. 13 of 07.03.2024, No. 14 of 07.03.2024, No. 16 of 12.03.2024, No. 17 of 13.03.2024, No. 18 of 19.03.2024, No. 19 of 21.03.2024, No. 20 of 03.04.2024, No. 22 of 04.04.2024, No. 23 of 04.04.2024, No. 24 of 09.04.2024, No. 27 of 11.04.2024, No. 28 of 11.04.2024, No. 29 of 16.04.2024, No. 32 of 23.04.2024, No. 34 of 24.04.2024, No. 35 of 25.04.2024, No. 38 of 07.05.2024, No. 39 of 14.05.2024, No. 40 of 14.05.2024, No. 42 of 29.05.2024, No. 43 of 04.06.2024, No. 44 of 04.06.2024, No. 45 of 11.06.2024, No. 47 of 11.06.2024, No. 49 of 20.06.2024, No. 51 of 20.06.2024.
22. The Albanian Constitutional Court, No. 2 of 29.01.2024.
23. In the first semester of 2024, the Albanian Constitutional Court cited the ECtHR's jurisprudence in the following cases: Decisions No. 1 of 25.01.2024, No. 2 of 29.01.2024, No. 3 of 30.01.2024, No. 4 of 31.01.2024, No. 5 of 13.02.2024, No. 11 of 28.02.2024, No. 13 of 07.03.2024, No. 14 of 07.03.2024, No. 16 of 12.03.2024, No. 17 of 13.03.2024, No. 18 of 19.03.2024, No. 19 of 21.03.2024, No. 20 of 03.04.2024, No. 22 of 04.04.2024, No. 29 of 16.04.2024, No. 30 of 18.04.2024, No. 33 of 23.04.2024, No. 34 of 24.04.2024, No. 37 of 07.05.2024, No. 38 of 07.05.2024, No. 39 of 14.05.2024, No. 40 of 14.05.2024, No. 42 of 29.05.2024, No. 47 of 11.06.2024, No. 49 of 20.06.2024.
24. The Albanian Constitutional Court, No. 19 of 21.03.2024.
25. In the first semester of 2024, the Albanian Constitutional Court cited the ECtHR's jurisprudence as well as the importance of the ECHR in the following cases: Decisions No. 1 of 25.01.2024, No. 2 of 29.01.2024, No. 3 of 30.01.2024, No. 4 of 31.01.2024, No. 5 of 13.02.2024, No. 11 of 28.02.2024, No. 13 of 07.03.2024, No. 14 of 07.03.2024, No. 16 of 12.03.2024, No. 17 of 13.03.2024, No. 18 of 19.03.2024, No. 19 of 21.03.2024, No. 20 of 03.04.2024, No. 22 of 04.04.2024, No. 29 of 16.04.2024, No. 34 of 24.04.2024, No. 38 of 07.05.2024, No. 39 of 14.05.2024, No. 40 of 14.05.2024, No. 42 of 29.05.2024, No. 47 of 11.06.2024, No. 49 of 20.06.2024.

not reference either the ECHR or the ECtHR, highlighting the pivotal role of these instruments in shaping judicial outcomes.[26]

81. In the first semester of 2024, the Supreme Court of Albania issued key decisions to unify judicial practice, emphasizing alignment with international human rights standards. These rulings, referencing the ECHR, particularly Article 13 on the right to an effective remedy, demonstrate the court's dedication to procedural and substantive justice.[27] While not explicitly mentioned in intermediate decisions, the importance of the ECHR and European Court of Human Rights (ECtHR) jurisprudence is evident in efforts to bridge domestic law with European norms. These actions strengthen fundamental rights, enhance legal consistency, and affirm Albania's commitment to the rule of law and integration into the European legal framework.

II. National Sources

82. The Albanian Constitution prevails over international treaties (Article 116 Albanian Constitution).[28] According to the Albanian Constitution (Article 5, Article 116(1)(b), and Article 122(2)), international treaties ratified by the Albanian Parliament are mandatory and hold a higher rank than internal legislation. As outlined in Article 116 of the Constitution, the normative acts that are effective across the entire territory of the Republic of Albania are: (a) the Constitution; (b) ratified international agreements; (c) the laws; and (d) normative acts of the Council of Ministers. At the top of this hierarchy is the Albanian Constitution. In cases of conflicting laws, Article 122(2) of the Constitution grants superiority to an international agreement that has been ratified by law, taking precedence over any national law that is incompatible with it. Specifically, regarding the European Convention on Human Rights (ECHR), the Albanian Constitutional Court has elevated it to the same level as the Constitution.

III. Importance of EU Law

83. Albania is a small Western Balkan country that has aspired to join the European Union since the early years of its democracy. EU-Albania relations were officially established in June 1991, and Albania's EU perspective was reaffirmed during the Thessaloniki Summit in June 2003 (Abazi, 2008).

26. In 2024, the Albanian Constitutional Court did not consider either the ECHR or the ECtHR in the following cases: Decisions No. 9 of 27.02.2024, No. 15 of 18.03.2024, No. 21 of 04.04.2024, No. 25 of 09.04.2024, No. 26 of 09.04.2024, No. 31 of 18.04.2024, No. 36 of 30.04.2024, No. 41 of 29.05.2024, No. 46 of 11.06.2024, No. 50 of 20.06.2024, No. 53 of 08.07.2024.
27. The High Court of Albania, No. 154 of 15.04.2024.
28. Albanian Constitutional Court, No. 55 of 27.07.2016; Albanian Constitutional Court, No. 16 of 10.04.2015; Albanian Constitutional Court, No. 5 of 05.02.2015; Albanian Constitutional Court, No. 5 of 05.02.2014.

84. The EU has a fundamental role in the Albanian legislation. Without going into details, a good example is the proposed constitutional reform of 2016, where the EU values and legislation had an essential role.[29] For instance, the Albanian constitution's premises included the importance of European values. In addition, Article 2(4) of the Constitution stated that, upon accession, the Republic of Albania delegates to the European Union institutions the necessary powers to fulfill the obligations arising from accession. Furthermore, the EU influence on Albanian legislation is reflected in several constitutional provisions, including the election of Albanian representatives to the EU Parliament (Article 64(4) of the Constitution), the obligation of the Albanian Government to inform the Albanian Parliament about EU bills (Article 80a of the Constitution), the direct application of EU law (Article 122(3) of the Constitution), and the potential transfer of currency powers if Albania decides to join the Eurozone (Article 161 of the Constitution).

85. Although the Albanian Parliament did not approve these norms in 2016, the same results might be achieved by reading the internal constitutional norms, the EU primary sources and by interpreting the EUCJ case law. Focusing on the interpretation of the EUCJ, the EUCJ has underlined the principles of direct effect (Case 26/62) and primacy (Case 6/64). Focusing now on the Albanian constitutional approach, lessons coming from comparative constitutional law should be considered (Ginsburg & Dixon, 2011). France, Italy, and Germany are EU founders. France is the typical example of a unitary State, while Germany is a typical example of a dualist State (Wollmann, 2008). Both of them—France (Title XV Constitution) and Germany (Article 23 Basic Law)—have established in their national constitutions the delegation of legislative power to the EU. However, Italian constitutional lawmakers have not established an explicit constitutional delegation to EU institutions. Nevertheless, by interpreting Article 11 of the Italian Constitution,[30] Italian Constitutional judges have delegated legislative powers to the EU.[31] Article 2(3) of the Albanian constitution[32] has a similar formulation to Article 11 of the Italian Constitution.

86. Until when Albania becomes part of the EU, it is important to highlight Article 70(1) of the Stabilization and Association Agreement (SAA) between Albania and the EU, which states that Albania agrees to ensure its existing laws, and future legislation will gradually align with the EU *acquis*. According to the Albanian legal hierarchy, national laws shall be aligned not only with the constitution

29. CDL-REF(2016)008-e Consolidated version of the Constitution of Albania integrating the draft constitutional Amendments, available online: https://www.venice.coe.int/webforms/documents/?pdf=CDL-REF(2016)008-e.
30. Italy agrees on conditions of equality with other States, to the limitations of sovereignty that may be necessary to a world order ensuring peace and justice among the Nations. Italy promotes and encourages international organizations furthering such ends.
31. The Italian Constitutional Court, by interpreting Art. 11, has recognized the direct effect and primacy of the EU law with three important decisions (No. 14 of Mar. 7, 1964; No. 183 of Dec. 23, 1973; and No. 170 of Jun. 8, 1984).
32. For the maintenance of peace and national interests, the Republic of Albania may take part in a system of collective security, based on a law approved by a majority of all the members of the Assembly.

but also with ratified international treaties (Article 116(1) of the Albanian Constitution), as is considered the SAA. Additionally, by considering the SAA an international agreement, Article 123(1) of the Albanian Constitution states that, based on international agreements, the Republic of Albania delegates to international organizations powers for specific issues.[33] This is also why the Albanian Constitutional Court has already applied the EU law as a source of authority upon which to base its own decisions (i.e., Albanian Constitutional Court V-56/16).[34] Similarly, the Supreme Court, in its unification and modification of judicial practices, also embraced the *acquis communautaire* as a guiding framework. For example, in one significant decision, the court applied the EU directive on the protection of employees in cases of employer insolvency.[35] This deliberate reliance on European Union legal standards not only enhanced the coherence of domestic law but also demonstrated Albania's commitment to harmonizing its legal framework with the broader EU *acquis*. Such efforts underscore the judiciary's pivotal role in fostering a legal system that upholds the principles of fairness, accountability, and integration within the European legal order.

IV. Importance of Case Law

87. In 2016, the Albanian constitutional legislator modified the Albanian constitution. The current version of Article 141(1) of the Constitution states that *the High Court shall decide cases relating to the meaning and application of the law in order to ensure the unification or evolution in judicial practice, in accordance with the law*. Based on this constitutional background, the role of jurisprudence is underlined in civil, administrative and criminal proceedings.[36]

88. Focusing on the civil proceeding, one of the cases of judicial review by the High Court is when the appealed decision is different from the judicial practice of the Civil Session or the recognized practice of the United Sessions of the High

33. The Albanian Constitutional Court, No. 3 of 30.01.2024.
34. In the first semester of 2024, the engagement of the Albanian judiciary with the European Union's legal framework underscored the growing influence of EU law in shaping domestic jurisprudence. The Constitutional Court, in its deliberations, demonstrated a particular focus on aligning national decisions with the *acquis communautaire*, as reflected in its rulings. One prominent instance involved the consideration of advisory opinions from respected organizations and bodies tied to the Energy Community Treaty. This highlights the Court's responsiveness to the integration of European legal principles in addressing complex legal issues, particularly those with cross-border or systemic implications.
35. The High Court of Albania, No. 154 of 15.04.2024.
36. Veshi, Denard, Enkelejda Koka, and Laert Sheme. "The Application of Human Rights by Judges In Civil Cases: the Case of Albania." *Ordine Internazionale e Diritti Umani* 1 (2025): 87–103; Koka, Enkelejda, Laert Sheme. The Enforcement of Human Rights by Albanian Constitutional Judges: A Focus on Individual Constitutional Complaints in Civil Matters Federalismi.it 2025 (2): 186–209; Veshi, Denard "Albania's Judicial Approach to Consumer Protection and the Influence of EU Law" Studi sull'Integrazione Europea 2025(1); Denard Veshi, Enida Bozheku, and Andrea Castaldo. "Reckless Medication (or Medical Negligence) in Albania: A Criminal Case Law Study" Federalismi.it 24 (2024): 279–297.

Court (Article 472(1)(b) of the Code of Criminal Procedure).[37] In addition, Article 481(8) of the CCrP ruling the cases of judgment on the unification or change of judicial practice, modified several times—by the Constitutional Court (Decision No. 46/1999 dated 28.6.1999) as well as by the legislator (Law No. 8812, dated 17.5.2001, amended by Law No. 44/2021, dated 23.3.2021)—states that the decision of the Civil Session and the United Sessions is binding on the courts in the trial of similar cases. Moreover, Article 482/a of the CCrP—added in 2021 (Law No. 44/2021, dated 23.3.2021) —underlines that the High Court will decide on a public hearing when the case represents importance for the unification or development of judicial practice (Article 482/a(1)(a) of the CCrP). Furthermore, in order to publicize the new judicial practice, the reforms of 2017 (Law No. 8812 of 17.5.2001 and Law No. 38/2017 of 30.3.2017) and 2021 (Law No. 44/2021 of 23.3.2021) have underlined that when the High Court—the United Session or the Criminal Session—modifies its practice, the decision shall be published in the Official Gazette (Article 485(2) of the CCrP). However, it should be underlined that these reforms have repeated the same goal of the legislator of 2000 since the same is stated also in Article 19(3) Law No. 8588 of 15.03.2000 "On the Organization and Functioning of the High Court of the Republic of Albania." Finally, a clear example of stare decisis is the case of Article 493(4) of the CCrP, which states that in the case of reexamination by lower courts, the guidelines given by the High Court are mandatory.

89. Focusing on the administrative proceeding, it shall be immediately underlined that Article 2(2) of Law No. 49/2012 of 3.5.2012 "For Administrative Courts and Judgment of Administrative Disputes" states *the provisions of this law are supplemented by the provisions of the Code of Civil Procedure, except in cases and insofar as this law does not provide otherwise*. It seems that Law No. 49/2012 operates as *lex specialis* to the proceeding that applies rules focusing on civil proceedings. Indeed, the rules of the CCvP are used for the rights and obligations of parties (Article 14 Law No. 49/2012), the requirements of the lawsuit (Article 21(1) Law No. 49/2012), notifications (Article 22(1) Law No. 49/2012), preparatory actions before the trial (Article 25(1)(ç) Law No. 49/2012), the trial (Article 34(1) Law No. 49/2012), the content of the decision (Article 41(1) Law No. 49/2012), appeal instruments and terms (Article 44(1) Law No. 49/2012), and the opposition to enforcement actions (Article 69 Law No. 49/2012). So, while the civil proceeding is based on a code, the administrative proceeding is based on a law. For clarity purposes, in Albania, while three-fifths approve Codes of all members of the Assembly (Article 81(2)(d) Constitution), laws are approved by a majority of votes of the Assembly (Article 78(1) Constitution). Nevertheless, it shall be underlined that

37. For instance, a recent concrete example of it is Decision No. 00-2023-4867 of 22.11.2023 that states *in the case under review, it is established that the decisions given by the Vlore Court of Appeal and the Lushnjë Judicial District Court do not contradict the practice of the Civil Session or the United Sessions of the High Court* (par. 17).

judges, in the case of conflict between a Code and a Law, have the rule *lex specialis derogat generali*[38] (*see* paragraphs 299, 300, 301 and 302).

90. Thus, as in the civil proceeding, one of the cases of judicial review by the High Court is when the appealed decision is different from the judicial practice of the Administrative Session or the recognized practice of the United Sessions of the High Court (Article 58(1)(b) Law No. 49/2012). In addition, Article 62(1)(b) Law No. 49/2012 underlines that the High Court will decide on a public hearing when the appeal case is different from either the practice of the administrative session or the practice of the United Session of the High Court. Furthermore, if the rule of administrative proceeding establishes that the court is composed of three judges, Law No. 49/2021 of 23.3.2021 added that in the case of the unification of judicial practice, the Administrative Session is composed of five judges (Article 62/a (3) Law No. 49/2012). Furthermore, to publicize the new judicial practice, the reforms of 2021 (Law No. 49/2021 of 23.3.2021) underlined that when the High Court—the United Session or the Administrative Session—modifies its practice, the decision shall be published not only on the website of the High Court (Article 62/a(6) Law No. 49/2012) but also in the Official Gazette (Article 63(2) Law No. 49/2012). In addition, Article 62/a (8) Law No. 49/2012 ruling the cases of judgment on the unification or change of judicial practice states that the decision of the Administrative Session and the United Sessions is binding on the courts in the trial of similar cases. Finally, a clear example of stare decisis, connecting with its role as nomophylactic, is the case of Article 63(1)(c) Law No. 49/2012 which states that the guidelines given by the High Court are mandatory in case of reexamination by lower courts. Thus, the rules regarding the importance of jurisprudence also confirmed the similarities between civil and administrative proceedings.

91. Focusing on criminal proceedings, in recent years, the role of criminal jurisprudence has been increasingly emphasized in Albania. For instance, the importance of uniform precedent jurisprudence has been established in Article 14/a of the CCrP, added in 2002 (Law No. 8813 of 13.6.2002) and modified in 2017 (Law No. 35/2017 of 30.3.2017) and 2021 (Law No. 41/2021 of 23.3.2021), which states that *the Supreme Court judges the unification and development of judicial practice …. and the change of judicial practice in united colleges*. The same reforms in 2002 and 2017 modified Article 432 of the CCrP by underlying that the judicial review of the Supreme Court against the decisions of the Court of Appeal can be made in the cases of *noncompliance or incorrect application of material or procedural law, necessary for the unification or development of judicial practice* (Article 432(1)(a) of the CCrP) or when the decision object of the appeal is contrary to the jurisprudence established by either the United Sessions or the Criminal Session (Article 432(1)(c) of the CCrP).

38. The High Court of Albania, Administrative Session, No. 151 of 07.07.2023, par. 47: The Labor Code is the *lex generalis*, which is applied to every aspect of the labor relationship, but there is no special regulation *lex specialis*. E.g.: if the particular law lacks provisions for ensuring and protecting health at work, then the rules of the Labor Code, or other applicable laws (as the case may be) will apply.

92. In addition, Article 437 of the CCrP—modified in 2002, 2017, and 2021—underlines that the Supreme Court will decide on a public hearing when the case represents importance for the unification or development of judicial practice (Article 437(1)(a) of the CCrP). Intending to decrease the appeal at the Supreme Court, the reforms of 2002, 2017, and 2021 have underlined that the decisions of the Supreme Court—not only of the United Sessions but also of the Criminal Sessions—are mandatory for all Courts for similar decisions (Article 438(8) of the CCrP), not only for the courts that reexamine the case, according to the guidelines established by the Supreme Court (Articles 440(1) and 447(2) of the CCrP). In simple words, Article 438(8) of the CCrP emphasizes the previous past decisions. Indeed, while Articles 440 and 447 of the CCrP have not been modified, Article 438(8) of the CCrP has been added recently. In addition, in order to publicize the new judicial practice, the reforms of 2002, 2017, and 2021 have underlined that when the Supreme Court—the United Session or the Criminal Session—modifies its practice, the decision shall be published in the *Official Gazette* (Article 441(2) of the CCrP and Article 19(3) Law No. 8588 of 15.03.2000 "On the Organization and Functioning of the Supreme Court of the Republic of Albania"). This policy further underlines the importance of the jurisprudence in Albania.

93. It shall be clarified that although it might seem that the Albanian legislator has underlined the importance of stare decisis in Albanian legislation, this is not the case. In other words, from the literal interpretation, the decision of the civil, criminal or administrative sessions is also mandatory for lower courts. However, these new reforms should be interpreted in the spirit of *civil law* tradition as well as Article 142(2) of the Albanian Constitution. So, the only case of a codification of stare decisis in Albanian legislation is in the case of reexamination by lower courts under the guidelines given by the High Court. So, the Albanian legislator has codified the importance of case law without recognizing the principle of stare decisis, which is typical of common-law countries.

94. To sum up, although Albania is not part of the common-law system, the recent reforms of civil, criminal, and administrative proceedings have underlined the importance of jurisprudence. This approach perfectly fits in consumer protection, where judges—due to various factors—have substituted themselves for national lawmakers.

V. Importance of Foreign Case Law

95. Foreign case law refers to judicial decisions issued by courts outside one's own jurisdiction. While such case law is not typically binding in other legal systems, it can serve as a valuable source of influence for several reasons: (1) foreign case law is often consulted when domestic courts are confronted with new or complex issues for which there is no established precedent. This might also be the case for bioethics and law; (2) courts and legal scholars frequently draw upon foreign case law as a source of fresh and innovative legal reasoning. This is particularly relevant when jurisdictions experiment with novel legal approaches or reforms that can inspire the evolution of domestic law. This might also be in the case of evolution of patient rights. For instance, in the decision of (partial) legalization of physician-assisted suicide by the Italian Constitutional Court, judges also considered the decision of other constitutional courts.[39]

96. In the first semester of 2024, the Albanian judiciary demonstrated its engagement with foreign jurisprudence as a means of enriching its legal reasoning and aligning domestic practices with broader international standards.[40] The Constitutional Court notably referenced a decision of the Italian Constitutional Court,[41] emphasizing the importance of comparative legal reasoning in addressing complex constitutional issues.[42] This reliance on foreign jurisprudence illustrates the court's commitment to integrating insights from well-established constitutional systems into its decision-making process, further strengthening the quality and depth of its rulings.

97. Similarly, the Supreme Court incorporated foreign jurisprudence in its efforts to unify and refine judicial practices. In one significant decision,[43] the court engaged with key German legal principles, including a landmark ruling by Germany's Federal Administrative Court.[44] This integration of foreign legal frameworks demonstrates a deliberate approach to fostering coherence and modernization within Albania's legal system. By drawing on international judicial practices, the Albanian courts underscored their dedication to ensuring that domestic rulings are informed by the best practices and experiences of other legal traditions.

39. Veshi, Denard, et al. "End-of-Life Situations in Some Western European Countries: Towards a Common European Approach?." *BioLaw Journal-Rivista di BioDiritto* 1 (2024): 267–278.
40. In the first semester of 2024, the Albanian Constitutional Court has published fifty-five legal decisions.
41. The Italian Constitutional Court, No. 22/2016.
42. The Albanian Constitutional Court, No. 34 of 24.04.2024.
43. The High Court of Albania, No. 154 of 15.04.2024.
44. Germany's Federal Administrative Court, Bergaderm and others v Commission (Case C-352/98 P); Bundesverëaltungsgericht; decision on "Kalkar" (BVerfGE 55, 250), 2016.

Part I. The Medical Profession

Chapter 1. Access to the Medical Profession

§1. Training of Physicians

I. Professional Practice for Health Professions

98. Professional practice is the practice of the profession by the intern for one certain period under the guidance and responsibility of a qualified professional and with experience, with the aim of obtaining the professional title and being able to exercise it independently. It is regulated by the "Regulation on the Organization of professional practice for health professionals in the Republic of Albania." This regulation is issued in accordance with Article 11 of Law No. 10171, dated 22.10.2009 "For Regulated Professions in the Republic of Albania" and the Order of the Minister of Health, No. 73, dated 01.03.2011. Approved by the Decision of the National Council of the Order of Doctors, No. 3, dated 22.04.2011, professional practice ensures the effective acquisition of practical/technical knowledge, along with professional ethics. It guarantees the intern the necessary skills and public responsibility required for the independent exercise of the profession. Professional practice is carried out in health institutions that meet the standards necessary for fulfilling the requirements and acquiring the practical, technical, and ethical knowledge of the intern. This practice is guided and developed under the direction and responsibility of a qualified and experienced professional who has been legally and independently exercising the profession for over three years. The Ministry of Health determines and approves the list of accredited institutions authorized to accept interns. This list is published by Professional Order. Professional Order also prepares, approves, and announces the list of professionals who are authorized to lead and supervise interns during the performance of their professional practice.

99. Based on Law No. 10171, dated 22.10.2009 "On Professions Regulated in Republic of Albania," the candidate who possesses an official document, which certifies completion of higher studies, to obtain his professional title and the right to exercise the profession as an independent is obliged to submit to professional practice, for a certain period. The professional who wishes to return to the profession after a break of more than five years is also required to undergo professional practice for a specified period. To begin the professional practice, every candidate is obligated to report to the central office of Professional Order to complete provisional registration and provide the necessary documentation. The rules and criteria for registration/membership, issuance of relevant documents as well as the fees for completing these processes are determined and managed by the Professional Order.

100. At the conclusion of the professional internship, each intern is required to take the state exam. The modalities and rules governing the state exam are defined in the regulation approved by the Ministry of Education and Science. The professional who passes the state exam and wants to practice the profession is forced to appear in the relevant Professional Order to make the definitive registration and membership.

101. The intern has the right to choose from the published list, the institution and the professional practice leader. The Ministry of Health orders the leading institutions and professionals' interns to create the conditions and take the necessary responsibilities for the development of normal practice in accordance with the program and standard contract signed between parties. The duration of the professional internship is not less than nine months for the intern doctor and dentist, six months (including the practice of the training program completed) for the pharmacist trainee, and three months for the nurse trainee and other professionals of this rank. For the professional who has more than five years of separation from practicing the profession, the period of internship (as the case may be) is not less than two months. Professional Order in cooperation with the academic staff of the Faculty of Medicine of the University State determines and designs the internship program.

102. Professional Order drafts the standard contract of professional practice, which reflects the rights and obligations of the parties to be respected during the performance of the practice and to be signed between the practice leader and the trainee. The candidate is exempted from the obligation to perform the professional practice if for a certain period in accordance with the specific criteria of the profession has been engaged in a professional activity, inside or outside the country, that has given him the opportunity to acquire a sufficient professional experience in the field of this profession. To evaluate and make sure if the candidate's experience is sufficient for them to be exempted from the obligation to perform professional practice, the Professional Order relies on an official document issued by the institution where he exercised his professional activity (Article 3 Regulation about "Organization of professional practice for health professionals in the Republic of Albania").

II. Documents with Which the Candidate Is Provided

103. After registration, the candidate is provided with the following documents for the purpose of use only during professional practice: (a) Individual Intern's Permit (Intern's Certificate)—which is given to the intern who fulfills the criteria of carrying out the internship for the period defined in Article 3 Regulation about "Organization of professional practice for health professionals in the Republic of Albania"; (b) trainee's card—it is a professional identification document; (c) professional practice program; (d) practice booklet and related to it; (e) the Appraisal

Form of the Intern—which is compiled and prepared by Professional Order in compliance with the internship program (Article 5 Regulation about "Organization of professional practice for health professionals in the Republic of Albania").

III. Practitioner's Rights

104. During the exercise of professional practice, the intern, among others, has the right to: (1) participate and become active in all activities of scientific, professional interest, theoretical and practical that are developed; (2) follow the programs of Continuing Professional Education with interest in his professional training. In addition, for actions that conflict with these rights or other actions that prevent them, create them difficulties or impossibility in the effective development of the professional practice, the intern can complain to the head of the institution, as well as to the closest Professional Order structures (Article 6 Regulation about "Organization of professional practice for health professionals in the Republic of Albania").

IV. Responsibilities of the Intern

105. The intern has the following responsibilities: (1) to regularly participate in practice and implement its program; (2) to create and maintain correct relationships based on courtesy and respect mutually with the professional who leads the practice, colleagues and other personnel as well as the head of the institution; (3) to know the Code of Ethics and Deontology, his activity and professional behavior based on the principles and provisions of this Code; (4) to treat with prudence, humanity, competence and high professional responsibility the patient and the public with whom he communicates; (5) to make efforts for the maximum acquisition of practical-technical knowledge that serves his professional development and training. Follow and participate in scientific activities, consultations, etc.; (6) to strictly implement and respect the rules and statutes of the institution where he performs practice; (7) at the beginning of the professional practice, sign the standard trainee contract; (8) to register at the National Center of Continuing Education (Article 7 Regulation about "Organization of professional practice for health professionals in the Republic of Albania").

V. Rights of the Professional Leading the Trainee

106. The professional leading the trainee has the right: (1) to cancel the contract in case of violation of its obligations by the intern and inform the nearest Professional Order structures; (2) for leading a complete cycle of a practitioner to benefit from five credits valid for the fulfillment of the continuing education program. Thus, for difficulties and obstacles that are created in the implementation of the approved program, the intern can inform the management structures on which the Professional Order depends (Article 8 Regulation about "Organization of professional practice for health professionals in the Republic of Albania").

VI. Responsibilities of the Professional Leading the Trainee

107. The professional leading the trainee must: (1) recognize the professional practice program and request its implementation on the part of the intern; (2) recognize the principles of the Code of Ethics and Deontology, as well as request the implementation and respect them in the development of practice; (3) ensure and be responsible for the progress of professional practice; (4) supervise the regular attendance of the intern and document it in the Booklet Practice; (5) be a contributor to the education and professional training of the intern and be friendly with him; (6) take care of the respect and implementation of the contract signed with the intern; (7) accurately and responsibly complete the Intern Evaluation Form (Article 9 Regulation about "Organization of professional practice for health professionals in the Republic of Albania").

VII. Rights and Responsibilities of Professional Order

108. The Professional Order: (1) through its structures, supervises and ensures the normal development of the practicing professional; and (2) collects and evaluates written complaint information sent by the leader of the intern, the intern, the head of the institution, Professional Order, the patient, the public, media, and other subject to professional disciplinary judgment (Article 10 Regulation about "Organization of professional practice for health professionals in the Republic of Albania").

A. Completion of Professional Practice

109. At the end of the professional internship, the intern submits a completed Form of Appraisal of the Intern near the central office of Professional Order. After the verification and evaluation of the Form by the committee set up for this purpose, the intern is provided with a Certificate of Internship signed by the President of Professional Order. This document is valid for registering in the state exam.

B. Apprentice Registration Fees

110. For all procedures carried out in the registration and documents issued, before and after completing the professional internship, the intern is obliged to pay the Professional Order the prescribed fee. The amount of this fee is calculated by the central finance office at Professional Order and approved by the Decision of the National Council (Article 12 Regulation about "*Organization of professional practice for health professionals in the Republic of Albania*").

C. Registration of the Trainee in the Professional Order

111. To carry out the professional practice, the trainee is obliged to register for provisional membership in the Professional Order. Registration for definitive membership is done after the candidate has passed the state exam. Registration and providing the intern with the necessary documents to carry out the professional internship are held near the central office of Professional Order. For this purpose, the practitioner must be presented with the following documents: (a) written request stating that he knows the Code of Ethics and Deontology, Oath and Statute of the Order and that he will respect and implement them meticulously. In this request, he must state the name of the professional and the institution he has chosen to carry out the practice; (b) Passport or Identity Card; (c) the original official document, Diploma, testimony or certificate proving the studies performed. For those who have completed their studies abroad, the original official document has to be unified by the Ministry of Education and Science or other authority responsible; (d) three pieces of 3x4 cm photographs. All the aforementioned documents must be provided as photocopies (Article 4 Regulation about "Organization of professional practice for health professionals in the Republic of Albania").

§2. Manpower Planning

I. Freedom of Establishment

A. Medicine as a Regulated Profession

112. The professions regulated in the Republic of Albania are the profession of: (a) doctor; (b) dentist; (c) pharmacist; (d) nurse; (dh) midwife; (e) physiotherapist; (g) the veterinarian; (h) the architect; (i) the engineer (Article 5 Law No. 10 171, dated 22.10.2009). Law No. 10 171, dated 22.10.2009 adopts general rules on the adoption of Professions in the Republic of Albania. The object of Law No. 10 171 is to set out definitions of the rules for the way of organization and functioning of regulated professions in the Republic of Albania. The purpose of this law is to: (a) define the criteria for practicing some important professions, which are related with the protection of public interest, public safety and health, respecting the principle of independent review and autonomy of professionals; (b) protecting and guaranteeing standards for some important professions so that their exercise should be done by qualified persons who meet the conditions and criteria provided by this law or other laws (Article 2 Law No. 10 171, dated 22.10.2009). This law applies to any person who seeks to exercise a profession regulated in the Republic of Albania. This law does not apply: (a) for the activities performed in the regulated profession related to the performance of functions in judicial authorities; (b) for professions, which, according to the legislation in force, have special requirements out of their nature (Article 3 Law No. 10 171, dated 22.10.2009).

113. A regulated profession is an activity or group of professional activities, the right of exercise of which or one of the forms of exercise is regulated by law or bylaws and is conditional on a certain level of education or the possession of qualifications on special professions (Article 4(a) Law No. 10 171, dated 22.10.2009). The profession is practiced as either a natural or legal person, in the capacity of a self-employed individual or as an employee, according to the requirements established by the relevant Professional Order. The Professional Order serves as a professional regulatory authority, functioning as an independent public entity. It represents the collective interests of professionals within a specific field and regulates the relationships between them in service of the public interest. The exercise of a regulated profession is done in accordance with the following principles: (a) freedom of competition of professionals; (b) the autonomy and independence of the intellectual and technical judgment of the professional; (c) correctness and quality of services for the protection of the beneficiary of the service and his public interests, guaranteeing the correct and legal exercise of the profession, regardless of the way or form of its exercise; (d) freedom of choice by the beneficiary of the service.

114. Law No. 10 171 requires training and professional qualification for the exercise of the regulated profession. A person seeking to practice a regulated profession must have completed the relevant accredited study program and/or professional qualifications in that profession, which are certified by official documents, issued domestically or abroad and recognized in the Republic of Albania in accordance with the legislation in force (Article 7 Law No. 10 171, dated 22.10.2009).

115. The criterion for exercising a regulated profession is for each candidate to: (a) carry out professional practice; (b) take the state exam; (c) be registered in the relevant Professional Order (Article 8 Law No. 10 171, dated 22.10.2009). In Article 9 of Law No. 10 171, dated 22.10.2009, the state exam conducts the knowledge testing of the candidate who aspires to exercise a profession regulated, ensuring uniformity in the evaluation of candidates at the national level, through verification of the necessary professional skills, according to the specifics of each profession. The content of the state exam is designed in accordance with the professional field of activity. After successful completion of the state exam, the candidate is awarded the relevant professional title. The following are exempted from the obligation to take the state exam: (a) the professional who, at the time of entry into force of this law, exercises or has exercised a regulated occupation; (b) the professional who acquires the right to exercise a regulated profession out of the Republic of Albania, in accordance with the determinations of the Council of Ministers.

116. Professional practice is designed to ensure the effective acquisition of technical knowledge and practical ethics related to the profession, with its methods determined by the competent authority upon the proposal of the relevant Professional Order. Professional practice is carried out under the guidance of a professional, either a natural or legal person. The respective Professional Order, through its own structures, ensures that the internship is carried out under the direction of a professional who has been practicing the profession for no less than three years and gives sufficient guarantees for the theoretical-practical preparation of the intern. During the development of the professional practice, the trainee is given a payment of no less than 50% of the basic salary. The payment or evaluation reward is provided by the professional who supervises the professional practice. Any individual who can demonstrate that, for a specified period and in accordance with the specific criteria of a regulated profession, they have been engaged in professional activity, either within or outside the country, and have thereby acquired sufficient professional experience in the field is recognized accordingly. The competent authority, in collaboration with the relevant Professional Order, establishes the criteria used to evaluate whether a candidate's professional experience is sufficient to exempt them from the obligation of completing professional practice, as determined through a final decision (Article 11 Law No. 10 171, dated 22.10.2009).

117. To obtain the right to practice a regulated profession, every professional must register with the relevant Professional Order (Article 12, Law No. 10 171, dated 22.10.2009). Upon satisfying the criteria of the profession, the professional has obligations to: (a) respect the laws and professional code of ethics; (b) make his professional title known to the public; (c) take care of updating their professional skills; (d) notify the relevant professional order of possible conflict of interest situations, related to the requested service; (e) inform the beneficiary of the service about his membership in the relevant professional order and provide information about his professional experience, as well as about potential conflict situations interest, related to the requested service (Article 16 Law No. 10 171, dated 22.10.2009).

B. Registration/Licensing Procedures

118. Procedures for registration or licensing are carried out by the Registration and Licensing Sector and Professional Practice at the National Council of Order of Doctors of Albania and from the Regional Councils Registration and licensing procedures. There are two categories of doctors:

1. Newly graduated doctors
2. Foreign doctors who seek to practice the profession in the Republic of Albania, as well as Albanian citizen who have graduated or specialized abroad and register for the first time as a member of the Order (Article 9 Law No. 10 171, dated 22.10.2009).

119. Procedures to be followed:

a. The doctor's individual file is opened, which is completed with all the documents that are required in the aforementioned regulations; (b) they are registered in the provisional register and provided with the trainee's booklet, as well as with other accompanying documents for professional practice.
b. With the completion of the professional practice and the successful passing of the state exam and in accordance with the requirements of the bylaws, the registration is done in the National Registry as a member of the Order of Doctors of Albania. The doctor is then provided with a license.

120. For newly graduated doctors, the procedures are carried out based on the Regulation "For Organization of Professional Practice" approved by the decision of the National Council No. 3 dated 22.04.2011 and of the Regulation "On Professional Practice for Health Professional in the Republic of Albania" of the Ministry of Education, according to which, the Registration, Licensing and Professional Practice Sector creates the provisional register. The Order of Doctors of Albania issues the provisional certificate of the practitioner for exercising the profession provided to newly graduated doctors. This certificate is issued by the Registration Department, Licensing and Professional Practice (Article 10 Law No. 10 171, dated 22.10.2009).

121. For doctors who are foreign citizens, as well as those Albanian citizens who have graduated or specialized abroad, who register for the first time as a member of the Order, the following procedure is followed: (a) the doctor's individual file is opened, which is completed with all the documents that this regulation provides; (b) the doctor is registered in the National Registry as a member of the Order of Doctors of Albania; (c) the file is presented to the licensing commission for review and signature; (d) the members of the licensing commission if convinced of the regularity of the documentation sign the license; (e) the Registration Sector, Licensing and Professional Practice equips the applicant with the license to practice in the profession of "Doctor."

C. *Competent Provincial Medical Association*

1. Registration/Licensing Procedures in the Regional Council

122. Registration and licensing procedures in the Regional Council are conducted in full compliance with all norms and requirements outlined in this regulation. In the Regional Council, doctors are registered, become members, are licensed, and are relicensed according to the following criteria: (a) all doctors currently practicing within the jurisdiction of this council; and (b) Albanian citizen doctors who have completed their qualifications or specializations either domestically or abroad, who were previously registered as members of the Order, and who practice the profession within the jurisdiction of that Council. The individual files of the newly graduated doctors who have passed the State Exam and/or Albanian doctors who have completed their studies or specializations abroad, as well as foreign doctors registered and licensed for the first time by the National Council, are sent to the Regional Council where they will practice the profession after registration. In any case, the files completed in the Regional Council by the secretary of this Council and the incoming files in its administration are submitted for verification to the President of the Regional Council, who orders registration of the doctor and equips him/her with the license for the individual practice of the profession. The license must be signed by the President and the secretary of the Council, and the seal of the Regional Council is affixed.

123. In case the doctor has not practiced the profession for a period of more than five years, he will be subjected to work voluntarily at a state health institution for a period of six months. In this case, the doctor will be equipped with the appropriate license after finishing the period of retraining of professional skills and submitting the relevant documentation at the Regional Council of the Order of Doctors. In the case of refusal to register as a member, a decision is issued expressing the reasons for this refusal.

124. The license for the individual practice of the medical profession is issued to the doctor/specialist who is registered as a member of the Basic Register of the Order of Doctors of Albania. This license is valid for five years, and at the end of the term, it is renewed based on the criteria defined by Law No. 10 171, dated 22.10.2009. The Regulatory Medical Authorities also issue a Certificate of Professional Conduct or other equivalent document as the most effective common mechanism for the exchange of information about doctors.

The Certificate of Professional Conduct includes, among others:

Certificate value:

Full name of the Order of Doctors (full address, phone number, e-mail and holder's signature);
Date of issue;
Certificate registration number;
Date of scanning of the Certificate;
Logo and seal of the institution.

Doctor's Identity:

Full name;
Paternity;
Date of birth;
Number of the register of the Order of Doctors;
The doctor's unique number.

Primary medical qualifications:

Name of the qualification, description, name of the body that awarded the diploma;
Number of degrees and graduation date;

Specialism:

Name of qualification and description of specialization.
Registration status:
Date of full registration of the doctor.

2. Union of Doctors

125. Any merger or grouping of doctors must be based on a written contract that respects the independence of everyone. This contract is communicated in advance to the Regional Council of the Doctors' Order, which verifies whether it complies with the laws and the Code of Medical Ethics and Deontology. In any association or grouping of doctors, regardless of its legal status, the exercise of the profession remains personal, with each doctor maintaining their independence and professional responsibility. Furthermore, in such cases, the patient's right to choose their doctor is an unchangeable ethical and deontological principle that must always be respected. Any grouping agreement or contract with a professional purpose between doctors from one side and other employees such as nurses and chemists is sent to the Regional Council of Doctors' Orders, which verifies compliance with applicable Laws and the Code of Medical Ethics and Deontology (Article 64 The Code of Medical Ethics and Deontology).

3. The Right to Strike

126. Doctors have the right to request that social and health bodies create the most suitable and optimal conditions for carrying out their professional activities. To achieve this, doctors utilize the resources and opportunities available to them that are most appropriate and least harmful to patients. Nevertheless, doctors also have the right to organize and participate in strikes, provided that the essential condition of guaranteeing emergency services and necessary care for patients is upheld (Article 65 The Code of Medical Ethics and Deontology).

§3. Licensing of General Practitioners and Medical Specialists

127. The registration, membership and licensing in physician's profession are regulated by Law No. 10 171, dated 22.10.2009; membership and licensing in physician's orders (Law No. 10 171, dated 22.10.2009) were approved by Decision No. 7, dated 08.07.2016 of the National Council; amended by Decision No. 4, dated 07.07.2017 of the National Council; amended by Decision No. 8, dated 21.12.2018 of the National Council; amended by Decision No. 4, dated 08.11.2019. This Regulation was drafted in support of Law No. 123/2014 "On the order of doctors in the Republic of Albania," Law 10107 "On Health Care in the Republic of Albania," Law 10171 "On Regulated Professions in the Republic of Albania," Statute of the Order of Doctors of Albania, as well as the Regulation "On Practice Professional for the Health Professional in the Republic of Albania." The purpose of this Regulation is to establish criteria and norms for registration, membership and equipment with the license for the individual exercise of the doctor's profession.

128. Licensing and relicensing are a mandatory process for natural or legal persons that provide health services in the Republic of Albania (Article 27 Law No. 10 107, dated 30.3.2009). The Licensing Commission is established by Order of the

President of the National Council. It consists of three members, two doctors/ one lawyer and performs the following functions and duties: (a) verifies the documentation of the doctors‘ files presented to him by Sector Registration, Licensing and Professional Practice and when it turns out that they are in accordance with the requirements and criteria provided for in this regulation, sign doctors' licenses. Licenses must be signed by all members of the commission; (b) examines and gives answers to complaints, which are submitted by the Registration Sector, Licensing and Professional Practice related to ambiguities and objections received for problems related to memberships, are equipped with a license, etc. Review of complaints is done with the presence of everyone to the members of the Commission; (c) in case of refusal of membership or equipment with a license, the commission comes out with a separate written decision arguing the reasons for this refusal. Membership registrations in the Order of Doctors of Albania are carried out by the Regional Councils of the Order of Physicians (Article 7 Law No. 10 171, dated 22.10.2009).

129. The Order of Doctors of Albania creates and administers the Basic Register of Membership. The process of creation and administration of the Basic Register of Doctors lies in the foundation of the Order's mission and activities. The National Council and the Regional Council are the structures that decide on membership within the Physician's order and the equipment with a license for the individual exercise of the profession. The Central Apparatus of the National Council is the authority responsible for creating, updating and ensuring the good administration of the Basic Register (Article 3 Law No. 10 171, dated 22.10.2009).

130. The Basic Register of Doctors‘ Order is the basic document, which reflects the situation and quantitative and qualitative changes of doctors working in health structures. The register reflects the progress of training and ethical-professional and scientific education doctors in years. A well-administered and regularly updated register of doctors plays an important role in the renewal of the License for the Individual Exercise of the Profession under the criteria provided in this Regulation. The Basic Register of Doctors‘ Orders is in electronic and written form (manual), according to the approved formats (Article 4 Law No. 10 171, dated 22.10.2009).

The basic register of the Order of Doctors must contain the following data:

A. IDENTIFICATION DATA:
   1. Name, Fatherhood, Surname and Previous Surname
   2. Doctor's Unique Code (File No.)
   3. Gender
   4. Date of birth
   5. Place of birth
   6. Nationality/Citizenship
   7. No. Personal Letter of Notification
   8. Place of residence (residential address)
   9. Contact address (Cel. Tel. Fax. e-mail)

B. PROFESSIONAL DATA:
   1. University/Faculty

2. Date of graduation
3. No. of the Diploma (Accounting by the competent authorities for doctors with a foreign diploma)
4. Specializations
5. University/Faculty where the specialization was carried out
6. The period during which the specialization was carried out
7. No. of the Diploma of Specialization (Accreditation by the competent authorities for doctors with a foreign diploma)
8. Professional qualifications
9. Scientific Degrees/Scientific Titles/ and other evaluations

The place where the doctor practices (Public/private hospital, etc.)

C. MEMBERSHIP DATA:
1. Date of membership to the Order of Doctors of Albania
2. Regional Council
3. Date of payment of membership fees
4. Date of issue of the first license
5. The date of issuance of the currently valid license
6. Disciplinary measures given to the doctor
7. The date of the fall/abolition of the disciplinary measure
8. Deregistration from the Order of Doctors of Albania (Causes/reasons and decision)
9. Reregistration

Other supplementary notes.

I. Provisional Register

131. The provisional register serves for the registration of all newly graduated doctors that undergo professional practice and after completion of the state exam. The provisional register is kept in electronic and written (manual) form. An individual file is opened for each doctor who is subject to provisional registration. The following documents are administered: written request for membership where he affirms that he knows the Code of Ethics and Medical Deontology, the Physician's Oath and the Statute of the Order and that he will respect and implement them accurately; self-declaration according to the format determined by the Order of Doctors; photocopy of passport or Letter of Notification; official document certifying university studies, list of grades; for those who have completed their studies abroad, the official document counted by the Ministry of Education; three photos of 3x4 cm; registration fee. The provisional register is kept by the Registration/Certification Sector (Article 5 Law No. 10 171, dated 22.10.2009).

II. Regional Registers of the Order of Doctors

132. Regional Registers are created near each Regional Council and serve to reflect not only the number of doctors and the mechanical movement of the region's doctors but also update with qualitative changes in ethical education, professional training, competence, performance, professional conduct, collection of membership fees, disciplinary measures, etc. The register is in electronic and written format (according to the model approved by these regulations). New registrations as well as other data resulting from the updating registry process are reported to the Registration/Certification Sector at the National Council to reflect it in the National Basic Register of the Order (Article 6 Law No. 10 171, dated 22.10.2009).

III. Criteria and Documentation Needed for Membership

133. Members of the Order of Doctors of Albania are Albanian and foreign citizens who have graduated with the title of doctor and appear in the Basic Register of the Order of Doctors. In order to register as a member of the Order of Doctors of Albania, they must present the following documents:

For Albanian citizens:

1. Valid Passport or Identity Card;
2. The request for membership, in which it is stated that he knows the Statute of Order of Doctors of Albania, the Oath of Doctor and the Code of Medical Ethics and Deontology and promises to observe them scrupulously;
3. Professional Curriculum Vitae;
4. The official document which certifies studies, qualifications, completed specializations and titles won;
5. If he has practiced the profession before, reference documented by the governing body the health or social-health institution where he served;
6. Proof of Criminality from the relevant body or certification from the court and the prosecutor, where it is proven that no sentence has been served;
7. three pieces of 3 x 4 cm photographs;
8. For young doctors, the official document which certifies that he has completed professional practice and passed the state exam.

   (Article 8 Law No. 10 171, dated 22.10.2009)

For foreign citizens

1. Residence permit in the Republic of Albania.
2. Passport or identity card
3. Good Standing Certificate from the Order/Chamber or Association of Doctors of his own country, where it is proven that he is registered and practices his profession and that he has been convicted or serving a sentence;
4. Diplomas and certificates of specializations completed by him/her issued from the competent Albanian authority, as well as copies of the diploma and specialty.
5. Recommendation from a local specialist in the same field, member of the Order of Doctors.
6. The foreign doctor resident in Albania must know the Albanian language.

For the non-resident doctor, he/she must work with a translator.

The documents brought by foreign citizens must be of translated into the Albanian language in accordance with the laws in force.

IV. License Renewal

134. The license is renewed at the Regional Councils where the doctor is registered and practices the profession. The renewal of the license for the individual exercise of the profession is completed within thirty days of submitting the required documents. The issuance of the license for the individual exercise of the profession is based on data collected and verified through periodic assessment and reassessment of the doctor's competence, performance, and professional behavior. For this purpose, to be equipped with the license, the application must be submitted by the applicant to the Order of Doctors with the following documents: (a) self-declaration according to the standard form issued by the Order of Doctors; (b) recertification by the National Development Education Center. As of January 2020, every doctor must obtain 150 credits to renew the individual license to practice the profession through the Order of Doctors of Albania. Additionally, an official evaluation reference, issued by the Directorate of the health institution where the doctor works, is required. This evaluation assesses the doctor's competence, performance, professional behavior, public opinion, and feedback from patients in accordance with the standard form issued by the Order of Doctors of Albania.

V. Removal from the List

135. In the event that the criteria for license renewal are not met, the Regional Council of the Order of Doctors has the authority to refuse the renewal of the doctor's license. A doctor whose license renewal has been denied has the right to file a complaint with the Registration, Licensing, and Professional Practice Sector at the National Council of the Order of Doctors of Albania. Upon receiving the complaint and retrieving the file from the relevant Regional Council, the case is forwarded to the Licensing Commission for review. The Licensing Commission then issues a decision on the matter, and the decision is binding for every Regional Council (Article 11, Law No. 10 171, dated 22.10.2009).

VI. License Suspension

136. The criteria for the suspension or temporary removal of the license are defined in the Statute of the Order of Doctors of Albania (Article 12 Law No. 10 171, dated 22.10.2009).

VII. Deregistration from Membership

137. Deregistration from the membership of the Order of Doctors of Albania takes place in cases where: (a) the doctor submits a written request for deregistration of membership from the Order and presents the reasons why he wants to deregister; (b) the doctor was sentenced by a final decision by judicial bodies regarding criminal offenses related to the practice of the doctor's profession; (c) in other cases provided by the laws in force. In the basic register of the Order of Doctors of Albania, an entry is made regarding the deregistration of the doctor and the reasons for this deregistration. In no case does the doctor hide from charter register. Doctors who have been deregistered as members of the Order of Doctors of Albania, in accordance with letter "a," have the right to submit a request for reregistration after completing all procedures for initial registration (Article 13, Law No. 10 171, dated 22.10.2009).

VIII. Appeal

138. Regarding any decision made by the Regional Council concerning the non-registration or non-renewal of a license, the doctor has the right to file a complaint within fifteen days with the Registration, Licensing, and Professional Practice Sector at the National Council. Similarly, for any decision made by the Licensing Commission regarding the non-registration of doctors, as well as decisions appealed to the Registration, Licensing, and Professional Practice Sector concerning the decisions of the Regional Council, the doctor has the right to file a complaint in accordance with the Code of Administrative Procedures, addressing the competent judicial body (Article 14, Law No. 10 171, dated 22.10.2009).

IX. Maintenance of Registration Subject to Restriction Structures Responsible for Membership Registration

139. The Registration/Certification Sector and the Commission operate under the National Council Licensing. The Registration, Licensing and Professional Practice Sector performs these functions and tasks: (a) creates the National Register in which all member doctors are registered; (b) updates this registry by adding new memberships, which are reported to it periodically by the Regional Councils, as well as those carried out by the sector itself resulting and reported from updating regional registers, other official sources, as well as from the sector itself; (c) cares for the good administration of the registry on the official website and reflecting in it correctly the data and new changes for each doctor; (d) creates the provisional register for newly graduated doctors for professional practice and the state exam; (e) open individual files for foreign doctors seeking to practice in the Republic of Albania, as well as for Albanian citizen doctors who have completed their studies and specializations abroad and join the Order for the first time Doctors and registers them in the National Register; (f) supervises and takes care of the good administration of the registers at the regional councils.

Chapter 2. Practice of Medicine

140. The practice of medicine, whether in private or public institutions, must be conducted under a formal written contract that explicitly defines the obligations and rights of the respective parties. Public hospital directorates are authorized to enter both full-time and part-time contracts with medical and non-medical personnel based on institutional needs. For personnel employed according to the approved organizational structure, the hospital directorate executes full-time employment contracts in compliance with the applicable legislation governing employer-employee contractual relations. Each draft contract is submitted in advance to the Regional Council of Doctors' Orders, which provides written feedback, including remarks and suggestions (Article 62 of the Code of Medical Ethics and Deontology). Additionally, for medical personnel required to meet hospital service needs, the hospital directorate may enter into part-time contracts in accordance with the legislation in force regulating such contractual relationships (Article 26, Law No. 55/2022).

141. Public hospitals give doctors the opportunity to offer outside the established work regime from the employer outpatient consultation services for patients outside the referral system, according to the determinations made by decision of the Council of Ministers. The hospital that enables dual practice approves the category by decision of the management board outpatient consultation services, the relevant fees, as well as the service contract model with the doctor practicing dual practice in the public hospital, without affecting the provision of public hospital service. The income provided by this activity will be transferred to the budget of the hospital (Article 27 Law No. 55/2022).

142. In the absence of a contract or prior agreement on royalties, doctors appoint fees which are usually paid by the patient or through an administration which regulates the fees of doctors, always in accordance with the legal or bylaws of this field. In determining fees, doctors must be careful and prudent, consider the economic situation of the sick, the possibilities of the service they offer and other circumstances. The doctor has the duty to explain and justify with arguments the cost of the service (Article 63 of the Code of Medical Ethics and Deontology).

143. The doctor is required to make an accurate assessment of the patient's condition and appropriately apply the resources of medical science, relying on the patient's anamnesis, clinical signs, and the examinations deemed necessary and essential (Article 14, The Code of Medical Ethics and Deontology).

144. The doctor, except in emergencies and extraordinary circumstances, must not take on the follow-up of a patient or prescribe treatments that exceed their professional abilities and competencies. They must limit their practice strictly to the specialty they are legally recognized for, as well as related disciplines. When required, the doctor has a duty to consult with colleagues within or outside their specialty and to implement the decisions of such consultations accurately and honestly (Article 15, The Code of Medical Ethics and Deontology).

145. Care for maintaining the well-being and health interests of the patient must be the doctor's primary concern. The relationship between the doctor and the patient should rely on mutual trust. Free choice of doctor and institution treatment by the patient is his right, which constitutes the basic principle of these relationships. The doctor is obliged to respect and create all the possibilities for the patient to exercise this right (Article 18 The Code of Medical Ethics and Deontology).

146. The doctor must ensure dedication, good behavior, and professional competence toward the patient. They have a duty to devote all the necessary time to the patient, providing information and making the most accurate diagnostic and treatment decisions. The doctor must carry out their mission with respect and adherence to professional and ethical standards, without abusing the patient physically, emotionally, or materially. He is not allowed to impose his personal, philosophical, moral or political will upon the patient (Article 19 The Code of Medical Ethics and Deontology).

147. The doctor must alleviate the suffering of the sick. In any case, the doctor must devote the necessary time to the patient, not only to diagnose and treat him appropriately but also to assist him morally and relieve suffering. The doctor must be careful and rational in interventions and diagnostic and treatment procedures, in order not to burden and annoy the sick with unnecessary and unjustified excesses (Article 24 The Code of Medical Ethics and Deontology).

148. Regardless of the profile or the institution in which a doctor works, public or private, his obligation to respect and implement the provisions of the Code of Medical Ethics and Deontology in the exercise of profession remains unchanged. The exercise of the profession of any profile and in any institution, whether public or private, is personal and independent. The doctor is responsible for the decisions and medical acts that are performed. In any public or private institution, the exercise of the profession must be the object of a written contract, which is in accordance with the provisions of this Code and the nature and specifics of the relevant institution. A doctor does not have to sign a contract and agree to work for an institution that deprives him of opportunities for him to fulfill his ethical and deontological obligations. Regardless of the institution in which a doctor works, public or private, he is obliged that beyond the principles and rules provided for in the provisions of the Code of Medical Ethics and Deontology, to recognize the laws, norms and administrative rules of the state and of the institution where he works, which belong to the field of practicing medicine, the duties and rights of the professional doctor (Article 66 The Code of Medical Ethics and Deontology).

149. The doctor is not allowed to use personal professional publicity or in his favor the public or private institution in which he works. He must be careful not to allow the use of his name by the institution where he works for publicity purposes. Regardless of the public or private institution in which he works, as well as his social hierarchical position to which he belongs, the doctor is obliged to respond to any request from Order Doctors, to appear for a professional disciplinary trial or any information or cooperation requested by this organization (Article 66 The Code of Medical Ethics and Deontology).

150. Throughout his active professional life, the doctor has the obligation of updating himself with the latest science to preserve and perfect his knowledge. In particular, the doctor should be systematically engaged in continuous programs organized to develop his medical competence and increase his professional skills. The doctor has the duty to participate in the evaluation of his practice and performance professionally (Article 13 The Code of Medical Ethics and Deontology).

151. The doctor has the duty to contribute to the education and training of other doctors. If he is charged with the task of teaching, he must work to be a competent teacher and ensure that new colleagues or students benefit and are supervised appropriately (Article 16 The Code of Medical Ethics and Deontology).

152. In the framework of his mission and professional obligations, the doctor has the duty to contribute to the activities and programs for the education and promotion of health and help the public to know and understand health issues (Article 17 The Code of Medical Ethics and Deontology).

153. The use of knowledge and the practice of medicine is based on the principle of freedom and independence of the profession. The doctor must use the knowledge and all the resources of medical science for an effective treatment based on professional independence, freedom of action and personal responsibility. He should consider the advantages, the harmful effects and the possible consequences of the research and the treatments it prescribes (Article 12 The Code of Medical Ethics and Deontology).

154. The doctor must be grateful and show respect and courtesy to his teachers for the knowledge, professional skills and craftsmanship he has acquired from them. Absence of gratitude and respect toward teachers is inexcusable and morally reprehensible (Article 43 The Code of Medical Ethics and Deontology).

155. The person involved in the study is informed of the possibility of interruption and removal from study of his own free will at any moment (Article 53 The Code of Medical Ethics and Deontology).

156. The doctor participating in the study has the duty to conduct the research honestly, meticulously followed and implemented in all aspects of the research protocol. He must record the research results truthfully and report and publish them honestly by not claiming authorship unjustifiably (Article 54 The Code of Medical Ethics and Deontology).

157. The application of new diagnostic, treatment and preventive methods is only allowed after clinical examination by a special independent and competent commission. The adoption, performance and promotion of scientifically unproven methods is prohibited, it is considered a violation of legal acts, a violation of the Code of Ethics and Deontology Medical and subject to follow-up and confrontation with these acts (Article 55 The Code of Medical Ethics and Deontology).

§1. The Right to Work and Labor Relations

158. Relations between employed individuals are regulated by the labor legislation consisting of the following primary legal sources:

- Constitution;
- Conventions of the International Labor Organization (ILO) in the field of employment, ratified by the Republic of Albania;
- The Labor Code and the legal and bylaws in its implementation;
- Rules applying private international law;
- Internal regulation of the company;
- Collective contract, if signed;
- Individual employment contract;
- Professional customs.

159. The rights and obligations of employees are written in laws, bylaws, internal regulations of companies or institutions, collective labor contracts, as well as in the individual labor contract. To be familiar with them, every employee must be provided with these documents, depending on the work he performs and the place of work.

160. The right to work originates from the Constitution of the Republic of Albania. In the second part of the Constitution, basic human rights and freedoms are foreseen (*see* Articles 18, 20, 22, 23, 24, 26, 35, 46, 47, 49, 51, 52, 54, 55). Article 49 of the Constitution guarantees the right to earn a living through legal work and the freedom to choose a profession, workplace or professional qualification system. Based on Article 49 of the Constitution, no one can be denied the right to seek work, to be employed in case of agreement with the employer or to freely choose the profession. This right cannot be interpreted as an obligation of the state or independent persons to guarantee everyone an effective workplace.

161. The Constitution explicitly prohibits any citizen to engage in forced labor against their will or consent. Specifically, it stipulates that no individual may be required to perform compulsory labor, except in circumstances such as the execution of a judicial decision, mandatory military service, services necessitated by a state of war, a state of emergency, or a natural disaster posing a threat to human life or health. In the context of labor relations and related matters, the Constitution enshrines key provisions that uphold fundamental economic, social, and cultural rights. It guarantees every citizen the right to secure a livelihood through lawful work that they have freely chosen or accepted. Furthermore, individuals are afforded the liberty to select their profession, workplace, and system of professional qualification.

162. The conventions of the International Labor Organization ratified by the Republic of Albania are the source and orientation of rights and obligations at work. The Labor Code supports and respects the Constitution of the Republic of Albania. A number of its articles, such as—Article 8 (prohibition of forced labor), Article 9 (prohibition of discrimination), Article 10 (freedom of trade union), Article 32 (protection of personality), Chapter VIII (assurance and protection of health), Article 115 (equality in remuneration between the sexes), Article 146 (termination of the contract without reasonable cause), Chapter XVI on professional organizations or articles on the right to strike, are based on constitutional principles. Various bylaws, issued in implementation of the Labor Code, are part of the obligation to implement rights and obligations at work.

163. The legislation provides the parties to regulate the labor relations between the employee and the employer, according to the way they agree to build their relations. Employment rules in the private sector are determined by the companies themselves and approved by their management bodies. Of course, companies must respect the basic principles of non-discrimination between sexes and genders, political beliefs, external appearance of persons, etc. The hiring procedure can be done in different ways, such as: by competition, by selection after testing, without selection and without testing. Each company has its own rules and procedures on how to hire employees.

164. The State Inspectorate of Labor and Social Services is a specialized body of executive power for the protection and strict implementation of labor legislation in the field of labor relations and social protection. The State Inspectorate of Labor and Social Services serves as the executive body under the Ministry of Health, Social Affairs, and Youth. It is a specialized institution tasked with ensuring the strict implementation of legal and sublegal acts governing labor relations and social issues. Established by a decision of the Council of Ministers, this institution operates as part of the ministry responsible for labor matters, with regional inspectors stationed at employment offices to oversee compliance and address concerns. In addition, employees have the right to notify the union regarding violations of their employment rights operating within their workplace (if one exists) or the relevant trade union in their field of activity at the district or municipal level.

§2. Elements Required by Labor Legislation in an Employment Contract

165. The employee enjoys all the rights that are provided in the Labor Code and other relevant legislation. This means that the minimum rights that the law gives to employees are guaranteed even if there is no written contract. The employee in the case of a possible dismissal must prove the existence of this employment relationship and the time when it started.

166. The documents that the employee can provide to prove this employment relationship are: the work book, the social and health insurance book, the bank account where the monthly salary goes, the pay list, which is submitted by the employer to the tax authorities, or the declarations to the employment offices by the employer. The absence of a written employment contract is punishable by law. In fact, the employer is punished, which can be severely Criminalized by labor legislation supervisors and labor inspectors.

167. Albanian Labor Code provides in Article 21 that the employment contract must contain especially:

a. the identity of the parties;
b. workplace;
c. general job description;
d. date of commencement of work;
e. the duration, when the parties enter into a fixed-term contract;
f. the duration of paid holidays;
g. the notice period for termination of the contract;
h. the constituent elements of the salary and the date of its award;
i. normal weekly working time;
j. reference to the collective agreement in force;
k. the trial period;
l. types and procedures of disciplinary measures, if there is no collective agreement.

168. If the contract has not been concluded according to the law, the employer is obliged to conclude it within seven days from the day of employment. The employee cannot be sanctioned in cases where he was not allowed to sign a written employment contract. The employer, during any inspection by the institution that oversees the implementation of labor legislation, may be Criminalized with administrative sanctions up to thirty times the minimum wage (Article 202 of the Labor Code).

169. Like any contract, the employment contract can provide for many other elements besides what the Labor Code provides. This depends on the specifics of the work, the type of activity that the employee performs, other legal and bylaws that may provide for specific provisions, etc. For this reason, the parties to an employment contract can provide for other details if they do not violate the obligations stipulated by the labor legislation and the Albanian legislation in general. The law cannot foresee every detail of an employment relationship; therefore, it gives the opportunity to the parties to construct an employment contract, to include the mandatory elements that they must agree to and what their rights and obligations are in respect to aspects of protection at work, salary, working conditions, annual holidays, bonuses, payment for working hours outside normal working hours, notice periods, etc.

§3. General Obligations of Employees at Work

170. The employee is obligated to be fully informed of the terms and obligations outlined in the employment contract they have entered into with the employer. Additionally, the employee must familiarize himself with the workplace regulations or rules established by the employer through its internal policies. Throughout the course of employment, the employee is accountable to the employer for any benefits obtained on behalf of the employer during the performance of his duties under the contract, particularly monetary amounts. The employee is required to promptly return to the employer all items or funds received in the course of their work, except for tips and gifts explicitly permitted by agreement with the employer. Furthermore, the employee must immediately return to the employer all products or outputs generated through their work, as stipulated by the employment contract.

171. The employee respects the general and special orders and instructions of the employer. The employee is not obliged to follow the general and special orders and instructions of the employer, which change the conditions of the employment contract. The change of the contract is made by written agreement between the parties. The employee is not obliged to follow the general and special orders and instructions of the employer, which endanger his life and health (Article 23 of the Labor Code).

172. The employee faithfully protects the legitimate interests of the employer. During the validity of the contract, the employee must not perform any work paid by third parties, which harms the employer or competes with him. During the validity of the contract and after its termination, the employee must respect the principle of confidentiality such as the secret of the fabrication and of the activity that he had knowledge of when he was in the service of the employer. The employee has the right to report for any criminal offenses, violations of labor legislation or of the contract of which he is aware to the competent bodies (Article 26 of the Labor Code).

173. The employee is liable to the employer for the damage he causes when he violates contractual obligations intentionally or through negligence. The degree of care that the employee must show at work depends on the technical knowledge necessary to perform the specific work, considering the skills and qualities of the employee, which the employer knew or should have known. The damage, which is inherently related to the performance of the work, is borne by the employer. Damages include actual damage and lost profit (Article 27 of the Labor Code).

174. The duty of loyalty defined in Article 26 of the Labor Code includes the duty to preserve and act, according to the interests of the employer, to assist the employer, the prohibition of competition, the preservation of secrecy or otherwise the obligation of confidentiality. In principle, the employee acts with loyalty to the employer. Violation of this obligation constitutes a justifying reason to terminate the contract in an immediately justified manner (Article 153 of the Labor Code). It is worth noting that loyalty to the employer should not affect the personality of the employee. The employee cannot be loyal to an employer who violates his obligations to the state and the society via committing criminal offenses or other violations (Article 26 of the Labor Code).

175. An employee over the age of 18 may enter into a written agreement with the employer stipulating that, upon termination of the employment relationship, he will not engage in competitive activities against the employer. Specifically, the employee agrees not to establish a competing enterprise, work for a competitor, or otherwise act in ways that could harm the employer's business interests. A noncompete agreement is valid only if the employment relationship has provided the employee access to the employer's trade or business secrets, and the misuse of these secrets could cause significant harm to the employer. The enforceability of the noncompete agreement is contingent upon the employer compensating the employee during the noncompete period (up to one year) with an amount not less than 75% of the salary they would have earned if they had continued their employment. In cases where the salary is variable, the compensation is calculated based on the employee's average salary from the previous year, adjusted for inflation (Article 28 of the Labor Code).

176. The prohibition of competition ends in the period specified in the agreement. Regardless of the term set in the agreement, the prohibition of competition ends if it is proven that the employer no longer has any interest in its continuation. The noncompetition agreement does not apply when the employer terminates the contract for unjustified reasons or when the employee terminates the contract for a justified reason related to the employer (Article 30 of the Labor Code).

177. The employee who violates the prohibition to compete must compensate the damage caused to the employer. If the agreement provides for a fine in case of violation of the prohibition of competition, the employee can continue the competitive activity, after paying the specified fine; however, he must also pay the employer the difference between the fine and the damage caused. If the agreement provides for a fine in the event of a violation of the prohibition of competition, the court may reduce the fine, if it is excessive, considering the circumstances that led to these violations. The employer may request, when he has expressly provided for this right in writing, in addition to the payment of the fine and other compensation provided, also the prohibition of the competitive activity, if this measure is justifiable, considering the interests violated or endangered of the employer, as well as the behavior of the employee (Article 31 of the Labor Code).

§4. Obligations of the Employer in an Employment Relationship

I. Respecting the Employee's Personality

178. The employer has the obligation to respect and protect the personality of the employees in work relations, as well as to take all the necessary measures to guarantee the safety and protection of their mental and physical health. He should prevent any attitude that violates the dignity of the employee. The employer must ensure the prohibition of moral harassment by him and other employees, as well as display the provisions on moral and sexual harassment and the corresponding sanctions. The employer is prohibited from performing any action that constitutes sexual harassment to employees and does not allow the performance of such actions by other employees. Sexual harassment is any unwanted form of behavior, expressed by words or physical and symbolic actions, of a sexual nature, which aims or results in the violation of personal dignity when it creates a threatening, hostile environment, humiliating, disparaging or insulting, committed by an employer against an employee, a job seeker or between employees (*see* paragraphs 305, 325, 326 and 396). The employer is forbidden to harass the employees with actions, which have the purpose or result in the degradation of the working conditions, to such a degree that it may lead to the violation of the rights and dignity of the person, to damage his mental and/or physical health or act to the detriment of his profession.

179. Any person who identifies or receives information from any employee, who may have had violations of his/her rights and in particular physical and mental health or personal freedom, which cannot be justified by the job description or the realization of certain objectives, must immediately signal the employer or the relevant structures, when the person to whom the infringement is addressed is the employee himself. The employee who complains that he has been harassed in one of the provided ways must present facts that prove his harassment and then it is up to the person to whom the complaint is addressed to prove that his/her actions were not aimed at harassment, as well as show the objective elements, which are not related to the harassment or disturbance. The employee who complains that he has been harassed in one of the provided ways or the whistleblower of harassment should not be criminalized for this reason, fired, discriminated against, or be a victim of sexual harassment or any kind of harassment.

II. Obligation to Instruct Employees

180. The employer must inform the employees about the risks of fire and various explosions, as well as about the protective means to prevent the occurrence of such risks. The employer teaches employees how to use extinguishers and other fire protection tools. The employer shows the employees the exit routes in case of fire and organizes at least once a year firefighting exercises and how to evacuate (Article 66 of the Labor Code).

III. Obligation to Register Employees in a Special Register

181. Employers are obliged to keep records of salaries and contribution payments updated every month for all employees who work for them and present this record whenever requested by labor inspectors and authorized inspectors of the tax administration. Employers must keep a register, according to the rules provided in this code such as: date of work commencement, the duration of the leave, the dates on which the holidays were taken and the salary given for the paid annual holidays are recorded (Article 95 of the Labor Code).

IV. Termination of Employment for Employees in the Health Sector

182. The termination of employment contracts in the Republic of Albania depends on whether the employee is employed in private or public hospitals. In the case of employment in private hospitals, the Albanian Labor Code will be applied, particularly Law No. 7961, dated 12.07.1995 (as changed) as well as the CCvP, Law No. 8116, dated 29.03.1996. In this case, the parties will address their disagreement before the Albanian courts with general functional jurisdiction.

183. In the case of employment in the public sector, in addition to the Labor Code, the Code of Administrative Proceedings will also be applied, namely Law No. 44/2015. In the circumstances when the Code of Administrative Proceedings does not cover in full or in part, it envisages the application of the relevant provisions of the CCvP to be applicable. In these cases, the parties will address their dispute to the court which has jurisdiction over administrative issues, i.e., the Administrative Court.

184. In this context, the law delineates two primary mechanisms for resolving an employment relationship: normal termination and extraordinary termination. Normal termination adheres to the obligations stipulated in Article 143 of the Labor Code, including compliance with notification deadlines and other contractual obligations. Extraordinary termination, as defined in Article 153 of the Labor Code, allows for the immediate cessation of the employment contract without adherence to notification deadlines (*ultimo ratio*). However, such termination must be based on reasonable grounds that render the continuation of the employment relationship impossible under normal circumstances.

185. Furthermore, Articles 141–149 of the Labor Code contain rules for the termination of employment contracts of indefinite and definite duration. This type of contract is, like any other private law contract, based on the general principles of the CCv but specifically regulated by the Labor Code. Termination of the employment contract is primarily based on the principle of contractual freedom of the parties (i.e., the parties are free to terminate the contract according to their free will). In principle, the parties can terminate the contract for any justified reason. The termination of the individual employment contract for any justified reason, which respects the procedure of Article 144 of the Labor Code, the legal and contractual notice period under Articles 143 and 149 of the Labor Code, provided it is not carried out during an inappropriate period as regulated under Articles 107 and 147 of the Labor Code is considered terminated in accordance with the law. Otherwise, the employer must compensate the claimant.

186. Judicial practice has ruled upon termination of employment contracts under a fixed term or unspecified term. Termination of these open-ended contracts can only be done by complying with the notification procedure. In the doctrine and judicial practice, you often find the term "normal termination of the employment contract," which means the termination of the employment relationship by respecting the notice period from the employer, after the implementation of the contract termination procedure according to Article 141 of the Labor Code, which stipulates: "The contract with an indefinite duration ends when it is terminated by one party and the notice period has expired." While the term "extraordinary termination of the employment contract" is considered in the case of noncompliance with the notification deadline by the employer, which considers the termination with immediate effect based on Article 143/4 of the Labor Code. The termination of an employment contract produces varying legal consequences, depending on whether the contract is fixed-term or open-ended, reflecting the distinct nature of the obligations and protections associated with each type.

V. Termination of Indefinite Term Employment Contract

187. Article 141 of the Labor Code defines that: "Unspecified term contracts end when one party unilaterally decides to terminate the contract, and provided the notice period has ended." The main elements for terminating the employment contract are the express will of one party to terminate the contract and, on the other hand, the obligation of this party to respect the notice period.

188. In an employment contract with an indefinite term, the employer may terminate the employment contract with the employee with justifiable reasons, but only by respecting the contract termination procedure and the notice period as provided under Articles 143 and 144 of the Labor Code. An employer must have a reasonable or justifiable cause to terminate an employee's employment. In the absence of justifiable cause, the employee is entitled to seek compensation by filing a claim in court in accordance with the applicable legislation. Even in cases where the employer lacks a valid reason for dismissal, termination may still proceed, provided the employer complies with the legally mandated notice periods, which are determined based on the employee's length of service. Provided the employer initiates termination proceedings, the employer is obligated to pay a seniority bonus to employees who have worked continuously for the employer for more than three years.

189. According to Article 143 of the Labor Code, if an employer wishes to terminate an employer's contract after the probationary period (three months after commending work), he must notify the employee in writing at least seventy-two hours before inviting the employee to a meeting to discuss the reasons for considering termination. The employer, during this conversation, presents to the employee the reasons for the anticipated decision to be taken and gives him the opportunity to express himself. During this period, the employer cannot take the decision to terminate the employment contract until forty-eight hours have passed since the meeting. Notification informing the termination of the contract must be submitted to the employee within a period of forty-eight hours to one week after the meeting. In the written notification, the employer expresses the reasons for terminating the contract, which are related to causes such as the ability, the behavior of the employee or the operational requirements of the enterprise (*see* Article 143 of the Labor Code). The employer who does not respect the procedure defined in this article is obliged to give the employee compensation equal to two months' salary, which is added to other possible compensations. The burden of proof rests upon the employer to prove compliance with the procedure defined in Article 143 of the Labor Code. By placing the burden on employers to substantiate dismissals with credible evidence, the Albanian Labor Code protects employees from unjust practices while promoting fair and predictable employment relations.[45] These procedural safeguards ensure a structured approach to employment disputes, enabling courts to enforce accountability without compromising on fairness or the rule of law.

190. According to Article 144 of the Labor Code, the employer must give the employee a notification period depending on the period of employment. The parties must respect a notice period of two weeks when the employment relationship has lasted up to six months, of one month for the duration of more than six months in two years, of two months for the duration over two years to five years, and of three months for the duration of more than five years (Article 144 of the Labor Code). The notice period for the termination of the contract is extended until the end of the week or until the end of the month. The same rule applies when the notice period is suspended during the period of incapacity for work, pregnancy or holidays granted by the employer. When one of the parties terminates the contract without respecting the notice period, the termination is treated as termination of the contract with immediate effect. During the notice period, when the employment contract is terminated by the employer, the employee benefit, at least, of twenty hours of paid leave per week to look for a new job. Duration of the permit and the procedures for obtaining and using it must be defined in the collective or individual labor contract. The employee has the right to receive the salary during the notice period.

VI. Termination of the Employment Contract at an Inappropriate Time

191. The employer cannot terminate the contract at the time when, according to the legislation in force, the employee performs, benefits from temporary work disability payment from the employer or social insurance, for a period of up to one year, as well as when the employee is on vacation from the employer (Article 147 of the Labor Code). When the termination of the contract is made before the employee is called up, is temporarily disabled at work or is on leave given by the employer and the notice period has not expired, this period is suspended for the period of military service, temporary disability at work or vacations granted by the employer and resumes after the end of this period. When the employee is not at work in the following circumstances: (1) When the employee is unable to work or otherwise with a medical report, or hospitalized, or on maternity leave; (2) When

45. Administrative Court of First Instance Shkoder, No. 205, dated 04.04.2014.

the employee is on vacation approved by the employer, annual leave, several days' leave, marriage leave, leave for various occasions.

VII. Termination Without Justified Causes

192. The employee has the right to the salary he would have earned if the employment relationship had ended at the end of the notice period provided for in the law or by contract or at the end of the fixed-term contract (Article 155 of the Labor Code). In cases of immediate, unjustified termination of the employment contract by the employer, the court, at the request of the employee and evaluating all the circumstances, decides the compensation, up to one year's salary, which is added to the salary that he should receive during the notice period. For employees in the *public administration*, when there is a final decision to return to the previous place of work, the employer is obliged to implement this decision.

193. Article 146(1) of the Labor Code provides a list of circumstances when the termination of the contract by the employer is considered without reasonable cause:

a. the employee has claims arising from the employment contract;
b. the employee has fulfilled a legal obligation;
c. the employee violates the prohibition of discrimination, according to the provisions in this code and in the special law on protection against discrimination;
d. for reasons related to the employee's exercise of a constitutional right, but which does not entail the violation of obligations arising from the employment contract;
e. it is done for the reasons of the employee's membership or non-membership in the trade union established based on the law or because of his participation in trade union activity on the basis of the law.

This is carried out in violation of the provisions outlined in point 3 of Article 144 of this Code, which pertains to the grounds for terminating the employment contract.

194. If the contract is terminated without justified reasons, the employee has the right to file a lawsuit against the employer, in the competent court, within 180 days from the day of termination of the employment relationship. In the case where the unjustified motive is discovered after the expiry of this period, the employee must file a lawsuit within thirty days from the day of discovery of this motive (Article 155(4) of the Labor Code).

VIII. Termination with Justified Reasons

195. Article 153 of the Labor Code provides for the case when labor relations have been resolved for justified reasons. From the interpretation of this provision, it follows that to have a justifiable reason in cases of unilateral termination of the employment contract must be analyzed: the responsibility of the employee in the non-fulfillment of a contractual obligation (Articles 22–31 of the Labor Code, other obligations arising from legislation, collective contracts, individual contracts); correctness (*see* Article 422 of the CCv) and care in the fulfillment of obligations, trust and loyalty to each other, as important principles of the relationship of obligation in general and specifically of labor relations, as well as their noncompliance in the sense of Articles 698, 704 of the CCv; failure to fulfill the contractual obligation of work; (the noncompliance must have been committed with serious or repeated fault and with written or oral warnings of the employer); the existence of a causal link between the non-fulfillment of the obligation by the employee and the dismissal immediately from work. This non-fulfillment must have created a serious situation that, according to the principle of good faith, does not allow the employer to be asked to continue the employment relationship. The court decides if there are justified reasons for the immediate termination of the contract. When there were no justified reasons in terms of Article 153 of the Labor Code, then the employer has the right to follow the procedures as provided in Articles 143 and 144 of the Labor Code.

196. In the conditions when the termination of the employment contract was carried out without justified reasons and, moreover, when it is proven that the claimant has not performed any action that would compromise the fulfillment of contractual obligations, the court based on the principle "*compesatio lucri cum damno*" and in view of Article 155 of the Labor Code, has the right to assess the amount of compensation requested by the employee, this amount coincides with the salary of twelve months of work, benefiting at the same time the rights granted by Article 145 of the Labor Code for seniority at work (at least three years of uninterrupted period of work).

197. In cases of fixed-term contracts, Article 149 of the Labor Code provides that: "The fixed-term contract ends at the end of the specified time, without prior resolution." In the case the employer unilaterally wishes to terminate the employment contract before the end of the term, then the employer must follow the procedure as set out in Article 143 of the Labor Code only, without following the notification procedure as provided in Article 144 of the Labor Code.

IX. The Resolution of Conflicts at Work

198. When the parties cannot resolve their disagreement arising out of the employment relationship, they may bring a claim to court. Although it is recommended that before accessing the court, the parties resolve their disagreement amicably in a mutual settlement.

199. The burden of proof lies with the employer to demonstrate that both procedures have been duly followed. Should the employer fail to provide such proof, the court is obligated to determine the amount of compensation for each procedure separately, provided that the employee has explicitly requested this in their submission to the court. In accordance with labor legislation, when an employment relationship or contract is contested, it is the employer—not the employee—who must substantiate compliance with the legally prescribed procedures.

200. The employee has the right to seek the court to provide for compensation. In cases of an indefinite contract, the employee has the right to request a two-month salary compensation for breach of the procedure under Article 143 of the Labor Code, salary payments for the months that the employee has worked (if not paid to date), unpaid annual leave, seniority leave (if applicable), the notice period depending on the period of work, and up to one-year salary payment if the contract is considered by the court to have been terminated with immediate effect. In cases of fixed-term contracts, the employee has the right to request payment for the remaining months as per the contract, unpaid annual leave, seniority payment (if applicable), monthly salary (if not paid by employer) and two-month salary for breach of Article 143 of the Labor Code.

201. If an employee has an employment relationship that has lasted more than three years, he benefits from a seniority payment. The remuneration is half a month salary for each full year of work. When the salary is variable, the bonus is calculated on the average salary of the previous year and indexed. The employee does not benefit from the above reward, when during the termination of the contract, if the reason for termination results as per the fault of the employee. The employee loses the right to remuneration for seniority if he has been dismissed with immediate effect, for reasonable reasons (Article 145 of the Labor Code).

202. The employee is advised to produce the following documents when submitting a claim to court:

- Individual original work contract.
- Workbook completed by the employer after contract termination.
- Social and health insurance booklet completed by the employer.
- A copy of the list of payments made in the bank where he receives his salary.
- Any other document relevant to supporting the claim.

203. In sensitive sectors like healthcare, the integration of ethical considerations further elevates the legal framework governing employment. The Code of Medical Ethics complements the Labor Code by highlighting the professional and moral obligations of healthcare practitioners, underscoring those ethical breaches, such as violations of patient trust or professional integrity, constitute valid grounds for termination.[46] These dual legal and ethical obligations are designed to uphold public trust and institutional credibility, particularly in public healthcare. Additionally, procedural fairness remains central even in such cases, ensuring that disciplinary actions are rooted in justifiable grounds and adhere to due process.[47] Together, the

46. Administrative Court of Appeal of Tirana, No. 4201 of 11.10.2017.
47. The High Court of Albania, No. 00-2022-2596 of 31.10.2022 and No. 00-2022-3237 of 23.11.2022.

Albanian Labor Code and ethical frameworks promote a balanced and principled approach to employment relations, fostering accountability, transparency, and the protection of both employees and institutional integrity. By aligning these practices with broader European norms, Albania reinforces its commitment to fairness, legal certainty, and governance grounded in the rule of law.[48]

X. Resolving Conflicts at Work: Public Sector

204. In Albania, the process of terminating labor contracts within public sector entities, including hospitals, involves adherence to both the Albanian Labor Code and the Code of Administrative Procedure, specifically Law No. 14/2015. The Code of Administrative Procedures is the basic law that deals with the administrative act. Since most labor relations in the public administration are created and extinguished by means of administrative acts, this law is often combined with the Law on the status of civil servants or with the Labor Code, depending on the status of the employee. The Code of Administrative Procedures defines some rules for the implementation of administrative jurisdiction in case of appeals for opposition or cancellation of an administrative act related to the beginning of the employment relationship in the public administration or its termination, with dismissal/removal from office, transfer in another job position, etc. Also, in the chapter on the investigative process, it is foreseen that the burden of the process of proof is both participating subjects and the administrative body, treating the parties equally from a gender point of view.

205. Article 118 of Law No. 14/2015 is particularly significant in these contexts, as it dictates the judicial requirements for handling disputes related to public administration. Article 118 is pivotal in ensuring that terminations within public hospitals are executed with due legal care. It mandates that all decisions made by public authorities be well documented and justified, thereby promoting transparency and accountability in administrative actions. This provision is crucial in settings where employment decisions directly impact public health services, ensuring that any terminations are conducted fairly and are subject to rigorous scrutiny.

206. The termination of labor contracts in the Albanian public sector, especially in public hospitals, is governed by a detailed legal framework that integrates labor and administrative laws. Article 118 of Law No. 14/2015 is central to ensuring these terminations are justified, well documented, and procedurally correct. In public hospitals, where decisions can significantly affect public service delivery, Article 118 of Law No. 14/2015 guarantees that terminations are reviewed under stringent administrative protocols. This legal safeguard ensures that employees are afforded a fair hearing and that their right to contest wrongful terminations is preserved. For judges, this article serves as a critical framework to verify if due procedures have been followed and if the reasons for termination are supported by sufficient evidence and are consistent with public service standards.

48. The High Court of Albania, No. 00-2022-234 (41) of 07.02.2022.

207. Enforcement of Article 118 of Law No. 14/2015 enhances judicial oversight over employee rights within the public sector. By stipulating precise documentation and justification of administrative decisions, this article helps prevent arbitrary dismissals and upholds a rule-of-law culture within public institutions. Judges are integral to this process, tasked with ensuring compliance with legal standards and maintaining fairness and justice in administrative proceedings.

208. The strict application of Article 118 of Law No. 14/2015 influences broader employment practices within the Albanian public sector. It compels public entities such as hospitals to uphold high standards of fairness and transparency, protecting individual employee rights and boosting the credibility and trust in public institutions. This accountability fosters a disciplined, legally compliant administrative environment, essential for effective public service.

209. Administrative courts were established under Law No. 49/2012 "On the organization and functioning of administrative courts and adjudication of administrative disputes." The law determines the organization and functioning of administrative courts, as well as the status of judges who serve in them, the jurisdiction and competence of administrative courts, the principles and procedure of the trial, the parties in the process and other persons in the administrative trial, the administrative court decisions and their execution. The competent courts for reviewing administrative disputes are the administrative courts of first instance, the Administrative Court of Appeal and the Administrative College of the Supreme Court.

210. The Law on Administrative Courts specifies the organization, jurisdiction, and procedural rules for the administrative courts, ensuring that these courts specialize in resolving conflicts stemming from administrative decisions. The law is pivotal in delineating the exact types of cases these courts handle, which typically include disputes related to public service contracts, administrative Criminalities, and rights to public benefits, as defined in Article 11 of Law No. 49/2012. Articles 14 and 15 of Law No. 49/2012 further outline the precise procedural requirements for appealing against administrative decisions, guaranteeing that the aggrieved parties have a clear and accessible avenue for seeking redress.

211. The structural independence of the administrative courts from the administrative bodies whose decisions they review is crucial and is addressed in Articles 17 and 18 of Law No. 49/2012. These articles ensure that the courts operate without external influences, maintaining impartiality and fairness in adjudicating administrative disputes. Moreover, Article 23 of Law No. 49/2012 details the ethical standards and duties of administrative court judges, emphasizing the integrity and impartiality required to uphold justice.

212. Furthermore, the law elaborates on the powers and procedural mechanisms available to these courts through Articles such as 7, 17/g, 18/5, 21, 35, and 41 of Law No. 49/2012. These sections are critical as they describe how the courts can challenge, annul, or enforce administrative acts. For instance, Article 35 of Law No.

49/2012 explicitly empowers the courts to make binding decisions regarding the legality of administrative actions, providing a necessary check on the administrative powers.

213. The procedural rights of individuals in administrative proceedings are meticulously laid out in Article 15/c and Article 3 point 3, as well as Article 7 point (a, 9) 41 of Law No. 49/2012. These articles ensure that individuals have the right to a fair hearing and are entitled to comprehensive and reasoned decisions from the courts, aligning the process with international standards of fairness and due process.

214. Currently, 6 (six) administrative courts of first instance operate in Albania: Durrës, Gjirokastër, Korçë, Shkodër, Tirana and Vlorë and the Tirana Administrative Court of Appeal. The Tirana Administrative Court of Appeal has seven judges, while the administrative courts of first instance have thirty-six judges.

XI. Discrimination in Employment

215. Law No. 10 221, dated 04.02.2010, "On protection against discrimination" provides as its subsection the treatment of the protection of discrimination in employment. According to this law, it is forbidden to discriminate against a person in relation to his right to employment. Discrimination includes any difference, limitation or exclusion based on the mentioned legal causes and related to: the announcement of job vacancies; the recruitment and selection of employees; the treatment of employees in the workplace, including their treatment when establishing or changing working conditions, remuneration, benefits and the working environment, treatment related to professional training or during the disciplinary process or related to dismissal or termination of the employment contract, or membership in trade unions and the opportunity to benefit from the facilities provided by this membership. Likewise, any kind of harassment, including sexual harassment, by the employer toward an employee or between employees is prohibited.

216. Discrimination which includes any difference, exception, limitation or preference based on any legal cause, which has the purpose or consequence of hindering or making it impossible to exercise in the same way as others, the rights and fundamental freedoms recognized by The Constitution of the Republic of Albania, with the international acts ratified by the Republic of Albania, as well as with the laws in force.

217. If discrimination comes as a policy dictated by higher hierarchical structures or links, then we encounter the term "instruction to discriminate," which is an instruction or request, based on hierarchical relationships, to discriminate against one or more people based on the mentioned legal causes.

218. Likewise, discrimination is also encountered in the form of "denial of reasonable adaptation," which constitutes that form of discrimination that occurs whenever there is a denial or objection to make necessary and appropriate changes or adjustments that are needed in a particular case and do not impose an excessive burden, in order to ensure the enjoyment and exercise on an equal basis of the basic rights and freedoms for persons with disabilities, or occurring in other legal conditions.

219. In Albania, the termination of an employment contract by an employer is a process that must strictly adhere to both labor and anti-discrimination laws to ensure fairness and equity in employment practices. Law No. 10221, dated February 4, 2010, "On Protection from Discrimination," provides a robust framework that is crucial in the context of employment termination. This law specifically addresses various bases of discrimination including, but not limited to, race, gender, age, disability, political beliefs, or any other condition that could lead to biased treatment.

220. The articles of the anti-discrimination law, such as Articles 3, 7, 12, 13, 34, 36, 37, and 38 of Law No. 10221, are particularly significant. They collectively ensure that all individuals receive equal treatment under the law and that any decisions related to employment, including terminations, are conducted without any form of discrimination. Article 3 of Law No. 10221 mandates equal treatment without bias, Article 12 of Law No. 10221 prohibits direct and indirect discrimination, and Articles 36 to 38 of Law No. 10221 provide the mechanisms for enforcing these rights and addressing grievances related to discriminatory practices.

221. The Labor Code is the basic law that regulates labor relations in Albania. It sanctions the principle of prohibition of discrimination. More specifically, the Labor Code provides that any type of discrimination in the field of employment and profession is prohibited. Non-discrimination and the right to employment are the main pillars provided by the Labor Code. Employment and profession mean professional orientation and training, employment in different professions, as well as employment conditions related to the distribution of work, its performance, remuneration, social assistance, discipline or termination of the employment contract.

222. The issue of wrongful termination in Albania underscores the importance of a legal framework that emphasizes objectivity, procedural fairness, and strict adherence to anti-discrimination principles in employment practices. Under the Albanian Labor Code, terminations must be based on clear and legally justifiable reasons, ensuring that employees are protected from arbitrary or unjust dismissals. The integration of anti-discrimination statutes into labor legislation strengthens this framework, mandating that employers substantiate termination decisions with concrete legal evidence. This requirement is particularly important in public institutions, where transparency and impartiality are fundamental to maintaining public trust. By embedding anti-discrimination principles into the procedural and substantive aspects of employment law, Albania demonstrates its commitment to fostering a fair and equitable labor market, aligned with international human rights standards.

This approach reflects the growing emphasis on ensuring that termination procedures are devoid of bias and grounded in objective, lawful criteria.

223. The interplay between anti-discrimination principles and employment termination procedures is critical in establishing an equitable work environment where decisions are based on merit and legality. Employers are required to meticulously document their termination processes, ensuring that they are transparent and withstand legal scrutiny. This dual emphasis on procedural integrity and substantive fairness ensures that employees are protected not only from explicit discrimination but also from decisions influenced by implicit biases, such as political affiliations, social status, or other irrelevant factors. Such legal safeguards are essential for both the public and private sectors, where adherence to non-discriminatory practices strengthens institutional integrity and workplace ethics. By promoting accountability, Albania's legal framework creates a culture of fairness in labor relations, fostering trust in judicial and administrative processes. These protections also set important legal precedents, reinforcing the necessity of compliance with both labor and anti-discrimination laws while contributing to the broader goal of sustainable, equitable, and inclusive employment practices. This comprehensive legal approach not only ensures justice in individual cases but also serves as a foundation for the continued development of Albania's labor market, balancing employee protections with employer obligations.

224. Every employer is obliged to implement, protect and promote the principle of equality and the prohibition of any kind of discrimination; to take the necessary measures, including disciplinary measures, for the protection of employees from discrimination and victimization, within one month of receiving knowledge; to respond effectively and in accordance with this law to complaints received due to discrimination committed by its employees, within one month of receiving them. The employer is obliged to raise awareness of this law by posting it in the public workplace, as well as to enable its full understanding with its own means or with the help of specialized entities.

225. Every employee has the right to complain to the employer, to the Commissioner for Protection from Discrimination, or to the court, if he believes that he has suffered discrimination. This provision does not limit the right to appeal to special institutions set up near different employment sectors. During the review period of the complaint, the employee has the right to continue working according to the terms of the contract. The employee has the right to receive information at any time regarding the handling of the complaint, as well as to receive explanations for the decisions taken by the employer, in response to his complaint, immediately after consideration. If the employer does not take steps to investigate and resolve the complaint of discrimination, the employee who made the complaint has the right to stop work, without losing the right to wages, for as long as is necessary to protect himself from discrimination. The employee returns the salary received if the alleged discrimination is not proved by a final decision. In particular, the costs associated with pregnancy and maternity cannot result in differences in individual rewards and benefits.

226. The law also provides for the procedures and ways of protecting everyone in case of discrimination. Thus, if a person alleges that he has been discriminated against, he may submit a complaint together with available evidence to the Commissioner, in writing or, in exceptional cases, orally, so that a record can be kept. Organizations with legal interests have the same right to initiate administrative procedures for protection against discrimination when they represent the interests of individuals by proxy. The Commissioner issues a decision, which is notified to the parties within ninety days from the day of receiving the complaint or, if a public hearing has been held, within ninety days from the day of the hearing. The decision contains the appropriate adjustments and measures, setting a deadline for their implementation.

227. If the Commissioner orders adjustments or measures, the person against whom the complaint is filed reports within thirty days to the Commissioner regarding the actions taken to implement the decision. In the event that the person against whom the complaint has been filed does not inform the Commissioner or does not implement the decision, the Commissioner shall impose a fine for the person against whom the complaint has been filed. The fine sanction is canceled if the person against whom the complaint was filed implements the decision within seven days after the sanction was imposed.

228. When deciding the measure, the Commissioner ensures that it is: effective and preventive and in proportion to the situation that caused the imposition of the measure. If a fine is imposed, the Commissioner determines the amount of the fine taking into account: the nature and scope of the violation and the impact on the victim; and the personal and financial circumstances of the offender, especially taking into account all sources of income and if the offense is committed by a private legal entity, balance sheet assets and profit, as well as total wages paid to employees, are taken into account.

229. The law also defines the measures of fines. As a last resort, especially when the physical or legal entity does not comply with the Commissioner's decision or does not pay the fine within three months after the deadline set by the Commissioner and the sanction has not been contested in court, the Commissioner may request the competent authorities to remove or suspend of the permission or authorization of the physical or legal entity to exercise its activity. In addition to administrative proceedings, the law also recognizes the path of judicial proceedings. Persons who claim that they have been discriminated against have the right to file a lawsuit in court. The object of the lawsuit is compensation according to the CCv or they can file a report before the competent bodies for criminal prosecution.

230. The administrative procedure before the Commissioner is not a condition for filing a claim and does not constitute an obstacle for the injured person to turn to the court or criminal prosecution bodies. Every person bears responsibility based on the provisions of this law when, with his actions or inactions, he has committed a discriminatory act within the meaning of this law. Individual responsibility does not exclude the responsibility of the state or private legal entity. The lawsuit is presented to the competent court no later than five years from the day the alleged discriminatory behavior occurred and no later than three years from the day the injured party becomes aware of this behavior. The injured party is not obliged to notify the Commissioner before filing a lawsuit for discrimination in court. The court notifies the Commissioner of the filing of any discrimination lawsuit. The court may ask the Commissioner, at any stage of the proceedings, to submit a written opinion, the results of his investigation, if the investigation has been done, or any other information that is relevant to the case.

231. The claimant has the obligation to bring evidence in support of the claim, using any type of legal evidence that can prove discriminatory behavior. After the plaintiff presents evidence on which he bases his claim and since which the court can presume discriminatory behavior, the defendant is obliged to prove that the facts do not constitute discrimination. The court's decision determines compensation if the court decides that there is a violation of this law, including a time limit for making compensation. The decision of the court is communicated to all interested parties, including the Commissioner. Compensation includes, among other things, the correction of legal violations and their consequences through restitution, appropriate compensation for pecuniary and non-pecuniary damages, or through other appropriate measures.

XII. Equality in Employment

232. The Constitution of the Republic of Albania, approved by Law No. 8417, dated 21.10.1998, amended by Law No. 9675, dated 13.1.2007 and by Law No. 9904, dated 21.4.2008, provides that all citizens are equal before the law and no one can be unfairly discriminated against for reasons such as gender, race, religion, ethnicity, language, political, religious or philosophical beliefs, economic, educational, social status or parental affiliation. No one can be discriminated against for the above reasons, unless there is a reasonable and objective justification.

233. Equality is a relative term, which is related to the creation of one connection between two or more categories. Based on logic, the differences between categories or objects that are compared potentially exist because no matter how similar all categories of things, people, events, judicial practices, judicial decisions, each of them carries its own specifics, which make it different from the same type of group. However, when we talk about establishing equality, we need a potential common characteristic that carries the essence of each of the categories we want to compare.

234. If we begin to analyze the category of "women" and the category of "men" in today's contemporary society, it is clear to all of us that each of them enjoys specific rights related to their different physical anatomy. On the other hand, both the category of women and the category of men together enjoy similar or identical and equivalent rights. Thus, as human beings, they equally enjoy constitutional rights related to work, family, creativity, professional organization or other types, and so on. Establishing equality, in this way, requires identifying the common criterion between the objects being compared and which may have compatibility. Only in this way will it be possible for us to evaluate the relationship of the elements we are comparing, to see if each of them actively participates and benefits from the common criterion in the same degree and in the same way, to reach the conclusion that only then, equality exists.

235. Within the field of discrimination in employment, equality is evidenced in three main directions:

- First, equality in employment begins from the moment of the creation or birth of the employment relationship, from the selection criteria, from the procedures that are followed for selection, from the exclusion of certain categories from participation in the competition, due to gender, but also within gender, there are cases of discrimination due to age. Thus, there are professions where the younger age of women is preferred in relation to the ages that pass twenty years of work, in positions such as secretaries, assistants, etc., women are preferred more than men in service positions, such as secretaries, sellers, etc., and men in leadership positions are preferred.
- Second, equality in employment continues with the way of fulfilling work relations, with the conditions that are created from: salary, the description of work, duties and competencies, the granting of permits, the treatment of pregnancy, etc. One of the elements of violation of women's rights in the work relationship is the violation of ethics by the employer, as well as cases of sexual harassment.
- Third, equality in employment is also observed in the way of graduation or the termination of the employment relationship, where it is observed that women are considered a category that is more fragile and often lose their job more easily, compared to men, for the same reasons, such as in case of job cuts, of employer restructurings, etc. For women, the rules of notification of the termination of the employment relationship are more easily violated, being satisfied only with the immediate notification of the termination of the work, without legitimate and reasonable reasons.

236. The anti-discrimination law provides a similar definition that naturally does not only relate to gender but also to other causes of discrimination. Harassment is that form of discrimination that occurs in the case of an unwanted behavior when it is related to any of the legal causes, which has the purpose or effect of violating the dignity of the person and creating an intimidating, hostile, contemptuous, humiliating or offensive environment for that person, as well as in the case of a less favorable treatment, carried out as a result of opposition or non-submission on the part of the person affected to such behavior. Wage discrimination. Initially, the principle of non-discrimination was applied due to discrimination based on gender in relation to unequal pay for women and men for the same work. The concept of "equal pay" was given a broader definition, not just for the net salary, which is received every month, but also for payments for services, rewards, bonuses, social security benefits, etc., and continuing until pensions. Even in the most developed European countries, the concept of equal pay for equal work between men and women came after working hard to educate the mentality that in order to promote equal pay, to prove both sexes are the same and no gender is more ladylike or more qualified simply because of gender.

XIII. Types of Discrimination

237. Any act or omission of the public authorities or of natural or legal persons who participate in life and public or private sectors, which create grounds for denying equality to a person or group of persons, or which exposes them to unfair and unequal treatment, when they are in the same or similar circumstances, compared to persons of others or other groups of people, constitutes discrimination. The elimination of all privileges and unfair discrimination is guaranteed for anyone, based on personal, political, economic, social and cultural rights provided by the Constitution of the Republic of Albania and international acts ratified by the Republic of Albania, as well as by laws in force.

238. Direct and indirect discrimination are two forms of discrimination that bring the same consequences in both cases. Direct discrimination is that form of discrimination that occurs when a person or group of persons is treated less favorably than another person or another group of persons in the same or similar situation, based on any legal cause. Indirect discrimination is that form of discrimination that occurs when a seemingly impartial provision, criterion or practice would put a person or group of persons in unfavorable conditions, in relation to another person or group of persons, as well as when that measure, criterion or practice, is not objectively justified by a legal goal, or when the means of achieving this purpose, or are not appropriate, or are not necessary and in fair proportion to the condition that caused it. They differ from each other simply by the way of achieving this discrimination or from proximity or distance cause-and-effect. Both these forms are equally illegal. Direct discrimination is more open, clear, direct and visible. While the concept of indirect discrimination goes beyond this and has become an important element of a legislative nature.

239. Association discrimination is that form of discrimination that occurs when there is a difference, restriction or preference due to association with persons belonging to groups defined by the law on protection from discrimination, as well as due to the assumption of such association. This allows the courts not only to deal with differences in treatment and direct discrimination but also to uphold policies that are as neutral as possible, which put a more vulnerable group at a particular disadvantage, for example, in cases where there is an indication that women are disproportionately more likely than men to be excluded from an employment contract. Such policies may be challenged on the grounds of their discriminatory effect and illegality in court, in case they are evidenced.

240. Sexual harassment is seen as one of the forms of gender discrimination. Usually, it is encountered in the form of harassment by employers or male superiors toward female employees or subordinates, although cases are not excluded when such harassment can also occur between fellow employees. It is not easy to identify cases of sexual harassment because they are often hidden due to mentality, fear, shame, etc. However, Albanian society has been shocked from time to time by cases of sexual harassment of public administration employees (even in high management positions) toward subordinates. The solution and sanction that has come in these cases has been the taking of administrative measures with dismissal, but there are still limited cases of criminal prosecution for abuse of office.

241. Gender harassment is any form of unwanted behavior related to a person's gender that is intended and/or has the effect of violating personal dignity or creating a threatening, hostile, humiliating, degrading or offensive environment.

Chapter 3. Illegal Practice of Medicine

242. As mentioned above, the legal practice of medicine is regulated by Law No. 10 171 of 22.10.2009 on Regulated Professions in the Republic of Albania. Article 5(1) Law No. 10 171 of 22.10.2009 includes the following regulated professions: (a) the doctor; (b) the dentist; (c) the pharmacist; (ç) nurses; (d) the midwife; (dh) physiotherapist; and (e) the veterinarian.

243. In the case of doctors, Law No. 8615 of 1.6.2000, For the Order of Doctors in the Republic of Albania, provides that doctors must enroll to receive the license to practice as doctors. In particular, according to Article 4(2)(a), Law No. 8615 of 1.6.2000 states that the Order of Doctors "completes the registration and keeps up-to-date the register of doctors for practicing their profession."

244. In relation to the illegal practice of medicine, the CCr should be referred to. The CCr does not have a general article dealing with the illegal practice of medicine. However, in general, the judge can establish the removal of the right to exercise a profession, or an activity. Article 39 of the CCr, as amended by Law No. 144, dated May 2, 2013, establishes that the revocation of this right restricts a convicted individual from performing any professional role or activity that requires a formal license, certification, authorization, or other approval from a competent regulating body.

245. The duration of this prohibition can range from one month to a maximum of five years, depending on the severity and circumstances of the offense. This measure is typically imposed following convictions for offenses wherein the individual has exploited or misused their professional authority, license, or role in committing the offense. Additionally, revocation is deemed appropriate when continued engagement in the professional role would contradict the protective aims of the legal framework designed to prevent such misconduct.

246. This legal provision acts as a safeguard for public trust, ensuring that individuals who have breached ethical or professional standards are temporarily or, in severe cases, indefinitely barred from holding positions that require a high degree of responsibility, integrity, and compliance with regulatory and ethical codes. Article 39 of the CCr, thus, serves as a critical regulatory measure to prevent further risk or harm, reinforcing the principle that professional privileges must be exercised within strict ethical and legal bounds.

247. In general, Article 246 of the CCr provides a useful legal framework for understanding how unauthorized professional practice is addressed within specific fields. Article 246/a of the CCr reflects a legal principle that could apply broadly to other essential professions where public safety and ethical practice are critical. In particular, the medical field, like accounting, demands high standards of professional conduct, rigorous qualifications, and accountability. Allowing unqualified individuals to practice medicine without formal licensure poses a significant risk to public health and safety, highlighting a potential gap in the current legal framework.

248. In this context, Article 246/a of the CCr could serve as a legislative precedent, underscoring the need for explicit prohibitions and sanctions in cases of unauthorized medical practice. By extending a similar model to the healthcare field, the legislature could establish a regulatory safeguard, ensuring that only qualified, licensed professionals are permitted to practice medicine. Such a measure would reinforce the integrity of the healthcare system and protect the public from potential harm caused by uncredentialed practitioners.

249. Article 94 of the CCr establishes as a criminal offense the practice of professions by an unauthorized person. In particular, Article 94 of the CCr establishes the termination of pregnancy carried out in places and by unauthorized persons. Specifically, it stipulates that any termination of pregnancy performed outside licensed public hospitals or specially permitted private clinics, or by a person who does not hold the qualifications of a licensed medical doctor, constitutes a criminal misdemeanor. This restriction also applies to terminations carried out beyond the legally allowed timeframe, except in cases where a legitimate health concern justifies the procedure.

250. According to Article 94 of the CCr, unauthorized termination of pregnancy is punishable by a fine or imprisonment for a period of up to two years. If the unauthorized procedure results in endangerment of life or leads to death, the punishment escalates, with potential imprisonment reaching up to five years. This legal provision underscores the requirement that such sensitive medical procedures are conducted by qualified professionals within approved settings, thereby protecting public health, ensuring accountability, and upholding medical and legal standards in critical healthcare services.

251. However, in other professions, the CCr provides specific provisions for certain professions, such as Article 143/a/7 of the CCr[49] (added by Law No. 23/2012 of 01.03.2012), 170/c of the CCr[50] and 170/ç of the CCr[51] (added by Law No.

---

49. Article 143/a/7 of Albanian CCr, *"Illegal trading of securities" (Added by Law No. 23/2012, dated 01.03.2012, Article 20): "A person who engages in unauthorized brokerage for the purchase or sale of securities shall be punished by a fine or imprisonment of up to one year. Where that offence has been committed in complicity, more than once, or has caused serious consequences, it shall be punished by imprisonment of two to five years."* [author' translation]
50. Article 170/c of Albanian CCr, *"Unlicensed banking activity" (Added by Law No. 23/2012, dated 01.03.2012, Article 25): "The conduct of banking activity by a person who has not been licensed for this purpose under the banking legislation in force shall be punished by a fine or imprisonment of up to three years. Where that offence has caused serious consequences to state interests or those of citizens, it shall be punished by a fine or imprisonment of up to seven years."* [author' translation]
51. Article 170/ç of Albanian CCr, *"Unlicensed financial activity" (Added by Law No. 23/2012, dated 01.03.2012, Article 25): "The conduct of one or several financial activities other than banking activity by persons who are not licensed for this purpose under the banking and/or financial legislation in force shall be punished by a fine or imprisonment of up to three years. Where that offence has*

23/2012 of 01.03.2012), 180/a of the CCr[52] (added by Law No. 135/2015 of 05.12.2015), and of the CCr 246/a[53] (added by Law No. 23/2012 of 01.03.2012). These provisions have been added with recent legislation. The sanctions start with lower offenses, such as fines or imprisonment for up to one year under Article 143/a/7 of the CCr, which addresses unauthorized mediation in securities trading. If this offense is committed in collaboration, occurs repeatedly, or leads to significant harm, the punishment may rise from two to five years of imprisonment. Moving up the scale, Article 246/a of the CCr deals with practicing as an expert accountant without registration or using accounting-related titles improperly, punishable by a fine or imprisonment of up to two years. This reflects the legal emphasis on accountability in professions that require official certification and public confidence. For more serious unlicensed activities, Article 170/ç of the CCr targets unauthorized financial practices, apart from banking, punishable by up to three years of imprisonment. If such offenses cause notable harm to public or private interests, the offense can increase to five years. Article 180/a of the CCr also criminalizes illegal or unregistered business practices, including tax-related noncompliance, with imprisonment of up to three years. The most severe offenses in this series are found in Article 170/c of the CCr, which concerns unlicensed banking activities, punishable by up to three years of imprisonment. If these activities lead to significant harm, the sentence may extend to seven years, the highest sanction in this set of articles.

252. This structured approach to offenses reflects the CCr's intent to ensure regulatory compliance and uphold professional standards across sectors. Based on the offense's severity, the code emphasizes the importance of lawful authorization, especially in roles where public trust and adherence to ethical standards are paramount.

---

caused serious consequences to state interests or those of citizens, it shall be punished by a fine or imprisonment of up to five years." [author' translation]

52. Article 180/a of Albanian CCr, *"Concealment of income" (Amended by Law No.144, dated 02.05.2013, Article 36): "Concealment or avoiding payment of taxes by not submitting documents or not declaring the necessary data envisaged by the effective legislation, by submitting forged documents, statements or false information in order to have personal material gains, for one's self or for others, by miscalculating the amount of taxes, fees or contribution, shall constitute a criminal offence and shall be punishable by a fine or up to three years of imprisonment. When this offence is committed with the intention of concealing or avoiding payment of a tax above five million ALL, it shall be punishable by two to five years of imprisonment. When this offence is done with the intention of concealing or avoiding payment of a tax above eight million ALL, it shall be punishable by four to eight years of imprisonment."* [author' translation]

53. Article 246/a of Albanian CCr, *"Practicing as an expert accountant and operating an auditing firm without registration" (Added by Law No. 23/2012, dated 01.03.2013, Article 31): "Acquisition of the professional title of certified public accountant, practicing the profession of certified public accountant, or using labels such as auditing company without being previously registered in a public registry of auditors, and using any kind of title which aims to create a similarity or confusion with these professional titles or designations, when an administrative measure has already been imposed, shall constitute a criminal offence and is punishable by a fine or imprisonment of up to two years."* [author' translation]

253. Finally, it is important to recognize that the illegal practice of medicine could be addressed within the broader scope of Article 143 of the CCr, which deals with the crime of fraud. This article defines fraud as the unlawful acquisition of private or public property through intentional deception, concealment of facts, or abuse of trust to gain an advantage for oneself or another party. The offense of fraud is punishable by up to five years of imprisonment (*see* paragraphs 341, 345, 346).

254. When fraudulent actions are carried out in collaboration with others, repeated, or result in significant consequences for the victims, the law increases the criminal offense to a prison term of two to six years. In instances where fraudulent conduct results in severe harm, the criminal offense may further escalate from five to ten years of imprisonment.

255. In cases of unauthorized medical practice, Article 143 of the CCr may be applicable if a person falsely claims to be a licensed medical professional, thereby deceiving patients and profiting from this misrepresentation. This form of deceitful behavior not only misleads individuals seeking care but also exposes them to potential harm, as unqualified practitioners may lack the necessary skills and knowledge to provide safe medical treatment. By categorizing such conduct as fraud, Article 143 of the CCr serves to uphold public trust in healthcare and ensures that those who misuse this trust for personal gain face appropriate legal consequences.

256. Overall, Article 143 of the CCr highlights the critical need for integrity and proper qualifications in professions that impact public welfare, including healthcare. By framing unauthorized medical practice within the context of fraud, this article reinforces the CCr's role in safeguarding individuals and society against the dangers of deceit, particularly in fields where professional competence and ethical standards are paramount.

257. Other crimes connected to the illegal practice of medicine are Article 88 of the CCr (Serious intentional injury),[54] Article 89 of the CCr (Non-serious intentional injury),[55] or eventually Article 87 of the CrC (Torture resulting into serious consequences),[56] Article 89/b of the CCr (Spread of infectious diseases),[57] Article

54. Article 88 of Albanian CCr, *"Intentional grievous bodily harm" (Second paragraph amended by Law No. 144, dated 02/05/2013, Article 18): "The intentional injury inflicting handicap, mutilation, or any other permanent detriment to health, termination of pregnancy, or which has been dangerous to life now of its inducement, shall be punished by three to ten years of imprisonment. The same offence, when committed against several persons, against the person who is the spouse, former spouse, cohabitant, or former cohabitant, close kin, or close in-law relationship with the offender, or when it results in death, shall be punished by five to fifteen years of imprisonment."* [author' translation]

55. Article 89 of Albanian CCr, *"Intentional minor bodily harm": "Intentional injury, inflicting temporary work incapacity of longer than nine days, constitutes criminal contravention and shall be punished to a fine or up to two years imprisonment."* [author' translation]

56. Article 87 of Albanian CCr, *"Torture with serious consequence": "Torture, like any other inhuman treatment, as long as it has inflicted handicap, mutilation or any permanent harm to the health of a person, or his death, shall be punished from ten to twenty years of imprisonment."* [author' translation]

110 of the CCr (Unlawful deprivation of liberty),[58] Article 121 of the CCr (Intruding into someone's privacy).[59] However, since the person is not qualified as a doctor, Article 96 of the CCr (Reckless Medication) cannot be applied.

258. During the unlawful practice of medicine, the potential offender may inflict severe or minor injuries, as any medical procedure inherently affects the victim's body. Depending on the severity of the harm caused, Articles 88 or 89 of the CCr may apply. Additionally, an unqualified practitioner might encounter infected individuals and, in some cases, intentionally spread infectious diseases. Moreover, in scenarios involving surgical procedures, patients may be prevented from leaving the hospital. Without proper qualifications, such actions could constitute unlawful deprivation of liberty or violations of privacy, as outlined in Articles 110 and 121 of the CCr.

---

57. Article 89/b of Albanian CCr, *"Spread of infectious disease": "Deliberate spread of infectious disease with high health risk, by actions or omissions committed by a person diagnosed as a carrier of the disease or by a person who intends to spread it, is punishable by imprisonment from two to five years. When this offense is committed through negligence, it is punishable by a fine or up to two years in prison. This same act, when it has caused serious consequences for the health or life of people, is punishable by three to eight years in prison."* [author' translation]
58. Article 110 of Albanian CCr, *"Unlawful deprivation of liberty": "(Paragraph II amended by Law No. 8733, dated 24.01.2001, Article 27): Unlawful detention of a person constitutes a criminal contravention and is punishable by a fine or imprisonment of up to one year. When this act is accompanied by severe physical suffering, committed in complicity, against several persons, or more than once, it is punishable by imprisonment of three to seven years."* [author' translation]
59. Article 121 of Albanian CCr, *"Stalking": "(Added by Law No. 23/2012, dated 01.03.2012, Article 15): Intimidation or harassment of a person through repetitive actions, with the intent to cause a state of constant and severe anxiety or fear for personal safety, of a relative or person with whom that person has a spiritual connection, or to force him or her to change his or her way of living, shall be punished by imprisonment of six months to four years. Where that offence is committed by an ex-spouse, former cohabitant, or person who had a spiritual connection with the injured party, the punishment shall increase by one-third (1/3) of the sentence imposed. Where that offence is committed against a minor, pregnant woman, or person unable to defend himself or herself, and where it has been committed by a person in disguise or accompanied by the carrying or use of weapons, the punishment shall increase by one-half of the sentence imposed."* [author' translation]

Chapter 4. Control over the Practice of Medicine

§1. Professional Liability

I. Civil Liability

259. In the medical profession, medical staff are expected to treat their patients with knowledge and skill appropriate to bring relief to the medical problem at hand. Apart from the Codes of Practice that the medical staff are to follow, they also must adhere to civil liability under civil and tort law. Public bodies shall also adhere to Law No. 8510, dated 15.07.1999 "On extra-contractual liability of state administration bodies."

260. Any liability for causing damage is regulated by Law No. 7850, dated 29.7.1994 on the CCv of the Republic of Albania. The person who, illegally and culpably, causes damage to another person or property is obliged to compensate for the damage caused. The person who caused the damage is not liable when he proves that he is not at fault. The damage becomes illegal when it is the result of the violation or violation of the interests and rights of others, which are protected by legal order or by good customs (Article 608 of Law No. 7850, dated 29.7.1994 on the CCv of the Republic of Albania) The damage must be a direct and immediate consequence of the person's act or omission. Failure to prevent an event by the person who has the legal obligation to avoid it charges him with responsibility for the damage caused (Article 609 of Law No. 7850, dated 29.7.1994 on the CCv of the Republic of Albania).

261. The person who suffers a non-pecuniary damage has the right to be compensated when: (a) has suffered an injury to his health, physical or mental integrity; (b) his honor, personality or reputation has been violated; (c) the right to the name has been violated; (ç) respect for private life has been violated; (d) the memory of a dead person has been violated. In this case, the spouse of the deceased person or his relatives up to the second degree may request compensation for non-pecuniary damage (Article 625 of Law No. 7850, dated 29.7.1994 on the CCv of the Republic of Albania). The pecuniary damage awarded consists of the loss suffered and the lost profit. The expenses incurred in a reasonable way to avoid or reduce the damage, those that were necessary to determine the responsibility and the extent of the damage, as well as the reasonable expenses incurred in order to secure compensation in extrajudicial ways, are also rewarded (Article 640 of Law No. 7850, dated 29.7.1994 on the CCv of the Republic of Albania).

A. *The Intersection of Medical Law and Civil Liability Through Case Law Analysis*

262. The intersection of medical law and civil liability in Albania represents a comprehensive legal framework designed to ensure accountability, patient rights, and institutional responsibility.[60] Rooted in key provisions of the CCv of Albania, such as Articles 608, 609, 659, and 704, the system addresses both contractual and noncontractual liability, holding healthcare providers accountable for negligence.[61] Laws like Law No. 7870 on health insurance and Law No. 9106 on hospital services further strengthen this framework by emphasizing institutional accountability and safeguarding patient protection. Notably, the recognition of non-economic damages, such as moral, existential, and biological harm, reflects a progressive approach that acknowledges the broader emotional and psychological consequences of medical negligence.[62] By adopting this victim-centered perspective, Albanian courts align with evolving European norms, emphasizing dignity and well-being alongside financial compensation, thereby reinforcing healthcare providers' obligations to prioritize patient safety and ethical care.

263. Additionally, the integration of ethical principles and European human rights standards underscores the sophistication of Albania's medical liability framework. Ethical standards, such as those enshrined in the Code of Medical Ethics, play a vital role in addressing breaches of patient trust, while provisions of the ECHR ensure alignment with broader justice standards.[63] Procedural safeguards, including reliance on expert testimony and structured claim processes under the CCvP, enhance fairness and transparency in resolving medical disputes. Institutional accountability is also a cornerstone, with healthcare systems held responsible not only for individual errors but also for systemic failures.[64] The dual avenue of civil and criminal liability further ensures that victims receive both justice and compensation, while the recognition of state responsibility in public healthcare underscores Albania's commitment to equity and trust in its healthcare institutions.[65] Through these mechanisms, the Albanian legal system promotes fairness, transparency, and the protection of human dignity in the healthcare sector.

B. Tort Liability of State Administration Bodies

264. Law No. 8510, dated 15.7.1999 regulates the External Contractual Liability of State Administration Bodies. State administration bodies are responsible for noncontractual property and non-property damage caused to natural or legal persons, private, domestic or foreign. The noncontractual liability of the state administration bodies is regulated by the provisions of this law and the CCv of the Republic of Albania.

60. The High Court of Albania, No. 00-2015-1152 of 13.01.2015, para. 5-7.1.
61. The High Court of Albania, No. 00-2022-2376 of 25.10.2022, para. 12, p. 8: "In reference to Article 50, of Law no.. 9106, dated 17.07.20013 'On the hospital service in the Republic of Albania' it is clear that the law charges the hospital, exclusively for non-compliance with the rules in the exercise of duties by employees and not for finding or not finding medications."
62. The High Court of Albania, No. 00-2022-2376 of 25.10.2022 and No. 00-2022-1671 of 18.07.2022.
63. The High Court of Albania, No. 00-2022-1671 of 18.07.2022.
64. Tribunal of First Instance of Tirana, No. 8130 of 12.10.2009.
65. The High Court of Albania, No. 00-2021-1107 of 23.12.2021.

265. Extracontractual liability of state administration bodies means the obligation of state administration bodies to compensate the damage that the latter have caused to the interests of private persons in the exercise of their public functions.

266. Article 3 of Law No. 8510 sets out the cases of responsibility of state bodies. State administration bodies are responsible for the damages they cause to private natural or legal persons in the following cases: (a) when they commit illegal actions or omissions; (b) when they perform legal actions or omissions, but which result in damage to the legal interests of private natural or legal persons; (c) when, although they perform legal actions or omissions, they cause disproportionate damage to the subjects to whom this action or omission is directed; (ç) when, due to the malfunctioning of the technical means with which the state administration bodies exercise their activity, private natural or legal persons are infringed on their legitimate interests; (d) when they cause a continuous risk to private natural or legal persons.

267. In the exercise of state functions, employees of state administration bodies are not liable for damages caused to private individuals or legal entities in the cases provided for in Article 3 of Law No. 8510. Employees of state administration bodies, exceptionally, are responsible for the damages they cause to private natural or legal persons when it is proven that they acted in bad faith. In the cases provided for in paragraph 2 of Article 3 of Law No. 8510, the state employing body, after indemnifying the injured party, has the right to demand from the guilty employee the return of the reward he paid (Article 4 of Law No. 8510, dated 15.7.1999 on the External Contractual Liability of State Administration Bodies).

268. State bodies are liable to return, concerning the physical transfer of an item or the restoration of a right, the enjoyment of which was suspended due to the actions or inactions of the state administration provided for in Article 3 of Law No. 8510. Also, the reward lies in paying an amount of money for it to balance a damage, which cannot be repaired directly.

269. If the damage is caused by a change in a legal or factual situation, which in turn originates in an act of the state administration, the competent body of this administration avoids the consequences, by restoring the previous state or, when such a thing is impossible, through the establishment of a similar condition. The elimination of the causes that bring about the damage does not apply when the restoration of the previous state or a similar state is impossible. This type of compensation does not apply, also, when the existing situation is caused by an administrative act, which has become irrefutable for the injured party (Article 7 of Law No. 8510).

270. In the case of causing property damage, the competent body of the state administration decides to accept the injured party's request for monetary compensation instead of elimination of the causes and restitution, only if this elimination of the causes and restitution is not possible. In the case of causing moral damage, the compensation is made in money. Moral damage competes with pecuniary damage and other non-pecuniary damages (Article 8 of Law No. 8510).

271. The state administration body is not responsible for the damage caused as a result of its action or inaction, if the damage could not have been avoided even if due care had been shown during the exercise of state functions, in accordance with the circumstances. The above exception does not apply in the case of malfunction of technical means (Article 9 of Law No. 8510). In any case, the compensation for damages includes lost profit, as well as non-pecuniary damage.

272. In the event that, in addition to the actions and inactions of the state administration body, the actions or inactions of the injured party also contributed to the damage, the amount of compensation that must be awarded depends on the extent to which the damage was also caused by the injured party. The role of the injured party in causing the damage and the amount of compensation to be paid in this case are determined through expert evaluations in accordance with the provisions of the Code of Administrative Procedures and the CCvP.

273. In cases where the damage is related to the violation of bodily integrity, health, freedom or personality, the compensation is made in money, always keeping in mind the role of the injured party in causing the damage. The claim for non-pecuniary damages falls when the disappearance of the causes in accordance with Article 6 is sufficient, as well as when the injured party is compensated in another way (Article 12.1 of Law No. 8510).

274. Article 13 of Law No. 8510 deals with indirectly injured claims. In cases of death, violation of bodily integrity or health, as well as in the case of unjust deprivation of liberty, as a result of the actions or inactions of the state administration bodies, the third party, to whom the injured party was obliged to do services at home or in his work, he is paid a monetary compensation for the damage caused to him by the services not performed. In case the death of a person is caused due to the actions or inactions of the state administration bodies, the latter are obliged to compensate the burial expenses of the one who has the legal obligation to pay them. When the deceased at the time of causing the damage was legally obliged to give alimony to a third party or such an obligation could be placed on him, and when the third party was left without this alimony obligation because of the obligee's death, then he is compensated for the damage through the assignment of a cash pension. The obligation for compensation of this nature remains even when the third party, at the time of causing the damage was not born. Even for the claims of third parties, the role of the injured party in causing the damage is verified.

275. Article 14 of Law No. 8510 covers areas of joint liability. When several state administration bodies are responsible for causing the damage, each of them bears responsibility for the entire damage. They respond to the injured party as debtors' solidarity.

276. If the entity causing the damage is not a state administrative body but operates under authorization from a public authority, the responsibility lies with the public authority holding the original competence. However, if the delegated entity causes the damage through its own fault, the delegating authority may seek compensation from the delegated entity (Article 16 of Law No. 8510).

277. Claiming compensation for damages caused by state administration bodies is prescribed within three years from the moment when the injured party becomes aware of the damage and the body that caused it. In the case where the damage is caused by a change in the situation, instead of being aware of the damage, the concept of being aware of the circumstances which made the situation illegal is introduced. The procedures for seeking and fulfilling compensation are done in accordance with the requirements of Law No. 8485, dated 12.5.1999 "Code of Administrative Procedures of the Republic of Albania." Article 19 of Law No. 8485 provides the decision of the state administrative body to recognize the responsibility for causing the damage to pay the relevant compensation and its amount, which constitutes an executive title.

C. Damages under Tort Liability

278. The United Colleges of the Supreme Court have unified the case law jurisprudence in matters concerning compensation in Tort Liability in cases concerning legal heirs and the death of minors in Decision No. 12 of 14.09.2007. The Claimants requested payment in favor of the legal heirs of the reward and compensation of funeral and other necessary and reasonable expenses caused by the car accident of 21.10.2002, in which the deceased heiress was found dead: Jetnor Yska, Rudolf Alimadhi and Ibrahim Baliqi. The Legal Basis were Article 31 of the CCv; Articles 2 and following of Decree No. 295, dated 15.9.1992 "For the mandatory insurance of the owners of motor vehicles for liability to third parties," approved with amendments in Law No. 7641, dated 01.12.1992, amended by Law No. 8729, dated 19.01.2001; Articles 4 and following of Regulation No. 622/1, dated 15.12.1992 to the Minister of Finance "For the implementation of mandatory insurance to the owners of motor vehicles for liability to third parties" and Articles 625 and 640 of the CCv.

279. Based on the comprehensive evaluation of the evidence presented and debated during the trial, including auto-technical and forensic expert reports, the courts of fact concluded that the deceased lost their lives as a result of a car accident on October 21, 2002, on the Fier-Seman national road. This incident was unlawfully caused by the negligence of Agron Vidhi, who was found guilty by a final court decision. He was convicted of violating road traffic regulations, resulting in the deaths of three individuals, and for fleeing the scene of the accident, receiving the corresponding criminal sentence.

280. The "Alfa Romeo" motor vehicle, with foreign license plates AN 457856, was not insured with a green card or with another insurance policy according to the legislation for compulsory insurance of motor vehicles. Therefore, in implementation of letter "b" of Article 17 of Decree No. 295, dated 15.9.1992 "For the compulsory insurance of motor vehicle owners for liability to third parties" (approved with amendments to the law), for the coverage of civil liability and compensation for the damage caused to third parties, is the responsibility of the Albanian Insurance Bureau, through the Compensation Fund administered for this purpose.

281. In such circumstances, based on Article 15 of the Constitution, Article 8 of the European Convention on Human Rights, Articles 17 and 24 of Decree No. 295, dated 15.09.1992, Articles 625, 640 et seq. of the CCv, Article 192 of the Family Code, etc., the claimants filed a lawsuit naming the Albanian Security Bureau as defendants. The claimants demanded the obligation of the defendant to compensate them, as the legal heirs of the victims, for the financial and non-financial damages caused by the accident resulting in the death of their sons, the late Jeton Yska, Rudolf Alimadhi and Ibrahim Baliqi.

282. The claimants claim that they have suffered severe violations of their health, personality, family relationships and interests, both in terms of pecuniary and non-pecuniary damages. Therefore, they demand the restoration of the situation before the accident, as if the death of the deceased had not happened, forcing the defendant to compensate them for the property losses due to the reduction of income in the family, as well as other non-pecuniary health damages for spiritual suffering, violation of values and the quality of their family and personal (private) life. The claimants request compensation for funeral expenses, those for care and healthcare of family members traumatized by the event, as well as legal defense expenses, calculating all damages, together with interests, at the time of the execution of the obligation.

283. Regarding the disagreement and the demands of the lawsuit, the court reasons that the general regulations of the CCv apply, as well as the special regulations of the legislation on noncontractual damages caused to third parties by motor vehicles. Article 608 of the CCv provides compensation for noncontractual damage caused by the injured party "to his person or property" and not those caused to the health or property of third parties. The court makes the same reasoning for the meaning of the provisions of Articles 17 and 18 of Decree No. 295, dated 15.09.1992 (*see* paragraphs 375, 382, 395, 506). Therefore, the court concludes that, exceptionally, only in the case of death, the survivors of the victim are compensated in the capacity of "heir," the property damages for food and living expenses and burial expenses, according to letter "a" and "b" of Article 643 of the CCv.

284. Guided by the fundamental principles governing civil dispute trials and the nature of the legal interests at stake in lawsuits seeking compensation for noncontractual damages, the United Colleges have reached a unifying conclusion: In cases involving obligations arising from harm caused, if the claimant seeks compensation "for all damages" or "for all pecuniary and non-pecuniary damages," such a request constitutes the claimant's disposition to seek compensation for each specific category of pecuniary and non-pecuniary harm. However, if the claim explicitly specifies compensation for particular categories of noncontractual damage, the court is obligated to confine its judgment and decision to those specific claims. Furthermore, the court has a duty to guide the parties by seeking clarifications regarding the nature of their disagreement. This ensures that the requests and objections are properly articulated, and the underlying legal rights and interests in dispute are clearly identified.

285. The principle of *alterum non laedere* (do not harm others) or *neminem laedere* (harm no one) stands as one of the foundational tenets of coexistence within a civilized society. This principle, rooted in the preservation of individual rights and societal harmony, is codified in the CCv and more specifically detailed within the provisions governing noncontractual civil liability, as outlined in Articles 608 the CCv et seq. This framework, often referred to as *Aquila's liability (lex Aquilia de damno)*, establishes that any individual who unlawfully infringes upon the rights or legal interests of another bears the obligation to provide compensation. The aim of such compensation is the principle of *restitutio in integrum*—restoring the injured party to their prior state *(status quo ante)* as if the unlawful act had never occurred. By adhering to this principle, the legal system ensures not only reparation but also the reinforcement of the societal commitment to accountability and justice.

286. Therefore, in application of Articles 608, 625, 643/a of the CCv, the United Panels of the High Court conclude to unify that: Any subject violated in personal and property rights and interests by the illegal fact, even if he is not the passive subject of that fact, he has the subjective right, the active legitimization, to demand (*ius proprius*) compensation for the property and non-property harm suffered. This active legitimation, in principle, is not conditioned by the enjoyment of the quality of the heir of a damaged person, but only by the claimants' own quality as damaged by the illegal fact.

287. In the case of causing death by an illegal act, as happened in the subject matter of this judgment, the members of the victim's family have active legitimacy to seek compensation for financial and non-financial damages. In the case of health damage, the person affected by his health and, depending on the circumstances, also the close members of his family, have active legitimacy. In both cases, the person who claims to have cohabited with the victim without marrying him (*more uxorio*) and, in exceptional circumstances, also other persons in the closest relationship of gender enjoy active legitimation.

288. Article 608 of the CCv stipulates: "The person who unlawfully and culpably causes damage to another person or their property is obliged to compensate for the damage caused." This provision addresses the foundational legal principle that an individual's wrongful and culpable conduct, which results in harm, creates an obligation for reparation. When an unlawful act is established, along with its causal link to the resulting harm, a legal obligation arises. This establishes the injured party's subjective right to seek compensation and imposes a corresponding duty on the responsible party to provide reparation. In interpreting this provision, the phrase "to the person or property" of the injured party encompasses both direct harm to the individual and the distinction between property and non-property infringements. These include not only material damage but also violations of intangible legal rights and interests, ensuring a comprehensive protection of personal and proprietary integrity under the law.

289. The United Colleges have reached a unifying conclusion affirming that the provisions of Article 608 of the CCv and Article 18 of Decree No. 295, dated 15.09.1992, are designed to safeguard third-party rights against unlawful acts. These provisions emphasize the protection of subjective rights, whether absolute or relative, including personal or property rights. Such rights encompass fundamental aspects of human existence, such as the right to life, health, personality, dignity, family, private life, and property. When these rights are violated through unlawful conduct, the injured party is entitled to seek noncontractual compensation as a relative subjective right. This framework underscores the legislator's intent to ensure accountability for harm and to uphold the legal and ethical standards necessary to protect individual and societal interests.

290. Under the provision of Article 18/b of Decree No. 295, dated 15.09.1992, "death" is regarded as the unlawful act itself that causes harm to the person of the victim, as referenced in Article 608 of the CCv. In the context of this judgment, the victim's fundamental right to life is violated, and this violation extends to the fundamental rights of others closely connected to the victim, including the claimants' as the victim's parents. These infringements manifest as violations of personal rights or property rights, resulting in various forms of non-pecuniary or pecuniary damage. A similar interpretation applies to "damage to health" as articulated in Article 18/b of Decree No. 295, dated 15.09.1992. Here, the injured individual's health may be compromised both in terms of property rights (as outlined in Article 641 of the CCv) and non-property rights (such as harm to health and personality, per Article 625/a of the CCv). Moreover, depending on the circumstances, such damage can also extend to the personal and property rights of those connected to the injured party, demonstrating the broader ripple effects of harm caused by unlawful acts.

291. Pursuant to Article 609 of the CCv for the acceptance of noncontractual civil liability, the material causal connection between the illegal and culpable behavior (action or inaction) and the damage caused must be verified. In the following, for the determination of concrete damages (violations) resulting from this illegal fact and the determination of the corresponding damages, the legal causal connection between them must also be verified.

292. The United Colleges have reached a unifying conclusion affirming that, under Articles 608 and 643/a of the CCv, surviving family members who shared a close and enduring relationship with a deceased minor whose life was lost due to an unlawful act are entitled to seek compensation. This compensation pertains to the loss of property in the form of lost earnings and the inability to benefit from the deceased's contributions over the course of a normal life. These contributions include not only general care and support but also the economic assistance the deceased would have provided to the family in the future. For purposes of active legitimization to seek compensation, it is immaterial whether the minor's parents or other family members had sufficient income for sustenance at the time of the minor's death. The right to claim arises from the legal and moral expectation of solidarity and mutual contribution within the family structure, ensuring that the financial and non-financial losses caused by the illegal act are justly remedied.

293. Non-pecuniary damage, provided in Article 625 of the CCv, as a broad and comprehensive category of noncontractual damages, includes any type of damage caused by the infringement of non-property rights and interests that are part of human values and that are not subject to evaluation directly economic in the market. In its essence, this provision recognizes the right to compensation for any non-pecuniary noncontractual property, which is "different from property." The listing of the "cases" of the non-pecuniary damage in its paragraphs "a" and "b" is not intended to limit, but to regulate in an express manner, for the effects of distinguishing the infringements, the right to compensation and the circle of entities that enjoy active legitimation.

294. Damage to health, or biological injury, fundamentally entails the violation of an individual's physical and psychological integrity, disrupting their overall well-being. This form of non-pecuniary damage, as specified under letter "a" of Article 625 of the CCv, constitutes a distinct category of harm. It is recognized as an independent basis for claims and compensation, separate from any other forms of non-pecuniary damages that the victim may have suffered because of the same unlawful act. This distinction ensures that the unique and intrinsic value of an individual's health and integrity is adequately safeguarded and addressed within the legal framework.

295. Since human life and health have no price, in compliance with the fundamental constitutional principle of equality before the law and the prohibition of discrimination according to Article 18 of the Constitution, the court must guarantee a uniform judgment and the same assessment of the percentage and amount of compensation for the biological victim, for any concrete form and degree of permanent or temporary violation of the physical or mental integrity of the victim, if the age is the same and the type of physical or mental health damage suffered is also the same.

296. Compensation for health damage according to Article 625/a of the CCv is requested independently of the request for financial compensation for the loss or reduction of the ability to work, provided for in Article 641 of the CCv. According to this provision, the pecuniary interest violated temporarily or permanently because of the health damage caused by the illegal fact is the human right, provided for in Article 49 of the Constitution, to acquire the means of living, thus, also to guarantee the right to property, through the legal work chosen with his free will. At the same time, the reduction of the injured party's property in the form of the expenses he incurs for care and for the treatment of the injured health as a continuous consequence of the same illegal fact also constitutes a legitimate interest.

297. Moral damage (*pretium doloris or pecunia doloris*) is an internal, temporary manifestation of the unjust perturbation (*non iure perturbatio*) of the spiritual state of a person, spiritual pain and suffering or a state of anxiety and spiritual torment that results because of the illegal fact. Anyone who suffers violations in the sphere of health and personality from illegal actions or inactions and through the fault of a third party has the right to request compensation for the moral damage suffered. This right, in the capacity of the injured person, belongs individually (*ius proprius*) to each of the close relatives of the person who lost his life, or his health was affected by the illegal fact, if their special family relationship is proven.

II. Criminal Liability

298. Article 59 of Law No. 7895 dated 27.1.1995 Criminal Code of the Republic of Albania includes elements of the convict's mental health when taking a decision on the suspension of the execution of the decision with imprisonment and probation (*see* paragraphs 390 and 525). Due to the low risk of the person, age, health or mental conditions, lifestyle and needs, especially those related to family, education or work, circumstances of the commission of the criminal offense, as well as of the behavior after the commission of the criminal offense, the court, when it imposes a prison sentence up to in five, years, may order that the convicted person keep in contact with the probation service and be put on probation, suspending the execution of the sentence, provided that he does not commit another criminal offense during the probationary period. The court orders the convict to fulfill one or more obligations, provided for in Article 60 of the CCr. For sentences of up to two years of imprisonment, suspended by the court, the probationary period is twice the time of the prison sentence given by the court. The probationary period, except for the rule provided in paragraph 3 of Article 60, is twenty-four months to five years. The trial period starts from the day after the announcement of the decision of the court that gave a decision on suspension of the prison sentence. The probation period can be shortened or extended depending on the method of the execution of probation and the personal conditions of the convicted, but without prejudice to the minimum and maximum term provided for in this paragraph. If the convict does not keep in contact with the probation service or does not fulfill the obligations as provided in Article 60 of the CCr, as ordered by the court, the court decides to replace the first sentence with another sentence, the extension of the term of supervision, within the probationary period, or the revocation of the suspension of execution of the decision (Law No. 7895, dated 27.1.1995 CCr of the Republic of Albania).

299. Law No. 7895, dated 27.1.1995 CCr of the Republic of Albania predicts criminal offenses committed intentionally against health (including mental health). Article 86 Law No. 7895, dated 27.1.1995 CCr of the Republic of Albania regulates torture and the deliberate committing of acts which a person is caused severe suffering, physical or *mental*, by a person exercising public functions, or with his instigation or approval, open or silent, on purpose: (a) to receive information or statements from him or someone else; (b) to punish him for an act committed or suspected to have been committed by/or another person; (c) to intimidate or pressure him or another person; (ç) for any other purpose based on any form of discrimination; (d) any other inhuman or humiliating act are sentenced to imprisonment from four to ten years.

300. Article 124/b of Law No. 7895 dated 27.1.1995 CCr of the Republic of Albania deals with Child abuse. Physical or psychological abuse of a minor by parents, sister, brother, grandfather, grandmother, legal guardian or any person who is obliged to take care of him, shall be sentenced to imprisonment from three months to two years. Forcing, exploiting, pushing or using a minor to work, to provide income, to beg or to perform actions that *harm his mental* and/or physical development, or his education, is punished with imprisonment from two to five years. When the offense causes serious health damage or the death of a minor, it is punishable by imprisonment from ten to twenty years (*see* paragraph 525).

301. The sale and purchase of transplants, as well as any activity related to the illegal removal and implantation of bodies, is punished with imprisonment from three to seven years. This offense committed by the person who abuses his position toward a child or another defenseless person shall be punished with imprisonment from seven to ten years. This offense, when committed more than once or in collaboration, is punishable by imprisonment from ten to fifteen years. When the above offense causes the death of the victim, or this offense is committed by a structured criminal group or criminal organization shall be punished with fifteen to twenty-five years of imprisonment (*see* Article 89/a, Law No. 7895, dated 27.1.1995 CCr of the Republic of Albania) (*see* paragraph 795).

302. The CCr of Albania punishes the use or *transplantation of organs* in its Article 110/a defined as a form of adult trafficking. Recruiting, transporting, transferring, harboring persons through threat or use of force or other forms of coercion, kidnapping, fraud, abuse of office or benefit from social, physical or mental condition or giving or receiving payments or benefits to receive the consent of the person who controls another person, for the purpose of exploiting the prostitution of others or other forms of sexual exploitation, forced labor or services, slavery or forms of similar to slavery, *the use or transplantation of organs*, as well as other forms of exploitation, both inside and outside the territory of the Republic of Albania, are punished with imprisonment from eight to fifteen years. When this offense is committed against an adult female person, it is punishable by imprisonment from ten to fifteen years. The organization, management and financing of human trafficking is punishable by imprisonment from seven to fifteen years (*see* Article 110/a, Law No. 7895, dated 27.1.1995 CCr of the Republic of Albania) (*see* paragraph 796).

303. When this offense is committed in cooperation, more than once, it is accompanied by ill-treatment and coercion with physical or mental violence against the victim, to perform various actions, brings serious consequences for health, or endangers his life, shall be punished by imprisonment for not less than fifteen years. When the offense resulted in the death of the victim, it is punished with imprisonment of not less than twenty years or more life imprisonment. When the criminal offense is committed using the state function or public service, the punishment with imprisonment is increased by ¼ of the sentence given (*see* Article 110/a, Law No. 7895, dated 27.1.1995 CCr of the Republic of Albania) (*see* paragraph 796).

304. Similarly, in its Article 128/b, the Albanian CCr punishes the use or transplantation of organs under the offense of Trafficking of Minors. Thus, the recruiting, selling, transporting, transferring, harboring minors for the purpose of exploiting prostitution or other forms of sexual exploitation, forced labor or services, slavery or forms similar to slavery, use or transplantation of organs, as well as forms other forms of exploitation, are punished with imprisonment from ten to twenty years. The organization, management and financing of the trafficking of minors is punishable by imprisonment from ten to twenty years. When this offense is committed in collaboration or more than once or is accompanied by mistreatment and the coercion by physical or mental violence of the injured party to perform various actions, or brings serious consequences for health, shall be punished with imprisonment of not less than fifteen years. When the offense resulted in the death of the victim, it is punished with imprisonment of not less than twenty years or more function or public service; the punishment with imprisonment is increased by 0.25 of the sentence given (see paragraphs 793, 796).

A. Forgery, Falsification and Fabrication of Documents

305. The legal framework in Albania addressing forgery, falsification, and professional misconduct demonstrates a nuanced balance between accountability and procedural efficiency, reflecting the country's commitment to upholding institutional integrity and public trust.[66] Article 186 of the CCr defines forgery as the intentional alteration or fabrication of documents with the purpose of defrauding or deceiving, emphasizing that fraudulent intent and deliberate action are prerequisites for criminal liability.[67] This safeguards individuals from unjust prosecution for inadvertent errors or procedural lapses. Similarly, Articles 608, 609, and 640 of the CCv provide a robust mechanism for addressing the moral and material harm caused by unlawful acts, even when criminal charges are not pursued, allowing victims to seek adequate compensation. Furthermore, the CCrP facilitates procedural efficiency by integrating civil claims into criminal proceedings, ensuring that punitive and restorative measures are addressed concurrently. This comprehensive approach underscores a cohesive justice system that aligns criminal accountability with equitable remedies for affected individuals.

306. In the context of professional misconduct, particularly within trust-based sectors like healthcare, the legal framework further underscores the importance of ethical responsibility and public accountability.[68] Articles 248 and 25 of the CCr address abuse of office by public officials, ensuring liability for actions that exploit

66. The High Court of Albania, No. 00-2010-155 (61) of 29.01.2010.
67. Court of Appeal of Gjirokastër, No. 136 of 02.10.2007.
68. Tribunal of First Instance of Berat, No. 445 of 29.09.2015.

authority or undermine public trust, while also holding participants in coordinated misconduct collectively accountable.[69] Additionally, Article 108/a of the CCr safeguards individuals from abuses of power, such as sexual harassment, by criminalizing behavior that exploits vulnerabilities or violates personal dignity.[70] These provisions reflect Albania's commitment to maintaining ethical standards and addressing systemic misconduct that threatens public welfare. Together, these legal principles not only ensure justice but also reinforce public confidence in institutional and professional frameworks, highlighting the judiciary's pivotal role in preserving the integrity of both the public and private sectors.

B. Case Law on Medical Negligence in Albania

307. This Section studies the Albanian judicial approach to reckless medication (or medical negligence) in Albania (Veshi et al., 2024).

308. First, medical criminal liability is not the most frequent option for evaluating medical errors or accidents. According to the Code of Medical Ethics, in the case of unethical behavior, physicians shall discuss it with their colleague and denounce him to the governing authorities of the institution and/or the Order of Doctors (Article 45 Code of Medical Ethics). Furthermore, in the case of errors by his colleagues or other support personnel, he shall discuss it with the governing authorities of the institution and/or the Order of Doctors (Article 46 Code of Medical Ethics). In addition, the Order of Doctors has its Disciplinary Commission (Article 16 Law No. 123/2014 "On the Order of Doctors of the Republic of Albania" of 25.09.2014), which is based on Article 17 Law No. 123/2014 and Article 11(1)(a) of the Statute of the Order of Doctors, can suspend or interrupt the membership in the Order of Doctors. It shall be underlined that only doctor's part of the Order of Doctors can exercise their profession in the Republic of Albania (Article 6(1)(a) Law No. 123/2014).

309. These mechanisms highlight the balance between professional accountability and judicial intervention, emphasizing the importance of maintaining professional standards within the medical community while reserving criminal prosecution for egregious acts of negligence.

310. Second, in Albania, there is a separation of powers between magistrates. While judges are nominated by the High Council of Judges (Article 136/a Constitution), prosecutors are nominated by the High Council of Prosecutors (Article 148/ç Constitution). In Albania, judges, in general, are bound by the charges done by prosecutors since only prosecutors, except in exceptional cases established in Article 284 of the CCrP, are entitled to make criminal charges and to start a criminal proceeding (Article 148(1) Constitution and Article 277 of the CCrP). However, with a final decision, the court can give a different qualification of the facts, under

69. The High Court of Albania, No. 00-2022-816 of 28.04.2022.
70. The High Court of Albania, No. 00-2022-1661 of 16.12.2022.

the condition that the "new" criminal offense stays within the same jurisdiction (Article 375(1) CCrP). In addition, in the case of a new qualification that puts the defendant in a worse position, the judge must notify the parties of this possibility and give them the necessary time to be protected by providing new evidence (Article 375(2) CCrP). Quite interestingly, it should be noted that Article 375 CCrP has been modified with the reforms of 2002 (Law No. 8813 of 13.6.2002) and of 2017 (Law No. 35/2017 of 30.3.2017), which are the same that codified in Albania the doctrine of *jurisprudence constante.* It is noteworthy that the reforms of 2002 and 2017 codified the principle of *jurisprudence constante*, which mandates consistency in judicial interpretations. This ensures greater predictability in medical criminal liability cases, reducing the likelihood of conflicting rulings.

311. Third, when deciding to prosecute, prosecutors shall determine whether the claim would be accepted by the court; otherwise, they shall choose to stop the proceeding not only for the cases established in Article 327(6)(a) of the CCrP, which refers to Article 328 of the CCrP (cases of dismissal of the charge or the case), but also to the cases where the court will decide to dismiss the case (Articles 387 of the CCrP) or when the court will find the defendant not guilty (Articles 388 of the CCrP). In addition to the general stigmatization of defendants in criminal courts (Walker, 1980), a study showed that defendant-physicians face symptoms of depression, as well as an increase in insomnia, headache, physical illness, and sometimes also excessive alcohol use and suicidal ideation (Charles et al., 1988). Obviously, this will affect their clinical competencies. Additionally, they show decreased administration duties (i.e., forgetting to ask for the insurance company's reimbursement) (Crane, 1998). The psychological toll on physicians involved in criminal proceedings is well documented, often leading to anxiety, depression, and professional burnout. Studies have highlighted how such proceedings may inadvertently impact clinical performance, undermining the broader healthcare system.

312. A significant challenge in prosecuting medical negligence lies in balancing the need for accountability with the recognition that medicine inherently involves risks and uncertainties. Medicine is not an exact science, and even under optimal conditions, adverse outcomes may occur despite adherence to standard protocols and best practices. Studies have shown that fear of criminal liability can lead to defensive medicine, where physicians prioritize avoiding litigation over providing patient-centered care. Defensive practices include over-prescription of diagnostic tests, unnecessary referrals, and avoidance of high-risk but potentially beneficial treatments, which can significantly increase healthcare costs while undermining efficiency and patient trust.

313. This research found fourteen different legal cases. All cases, except one,[71] dealt with the previous version of Article 96 of the CCr. Although the modification was made in 2001 and 2019, various decisions continued using the old criminal code version. This might contradict the application of Article 29 of the Constitution

71. Tribunal of First Instance of Elbasan, No. 2530 of 23.04.2021, Court of Appeal of Durres, No. 196 of 29.06.2021, The High Court of Albania, Criminal Session, No. 160 of 09.06.2022.

and Article 3(3) of the CCr that codifies the *pro reo* doctrine: if, during a criminal proceeding, the lawmaker changes the law, the most favorable law shall be applied (*see* paragraphs 413 and 501). Nevertheless, the sanctions given by the Albanian judges have been within the limits of the new version of Article 96 of the CCr. Thus, there is no constitutional violation, although the qualification should differ according to the latest criminal definition.

314. It should be clarified reckless exercise can be committed in the profession of the doctor, medical staff, and pharmacists.[72] In addition, this type of criminal offense can be committed by medical actions or omission since patients have entrusted their lives and health to the medical staff. The doctor must provide healthcare within his specialty to accurately determine the diagnosis, evaluate, treat, and care for their patients according to the degree of priority and importance of the patient's problem.[73] In addition, they shall implement patient protocols according to the current legislation,[74] also based on medical equipment that the hospital disposes of.[75] The application of patient protocols is particularly crucial in high-risk cases, such as those involving chronic conditions. Failure to implement specialized protocols can exacerbate patient outcomes, underscoring the need for precise procedural adherence. Moreover, advancements in the availability of medical equipment within Albanian hospitals have further raised the standard of care expected, creating a higher threshold for determining negligence.

315. Despite the changes to the CCr, in relation to the term "severe damages" established in Article 96 of the CCr before it was changed by the current law, jurisprudence[76] continues to agree with the interpretation that "severe damage" in medical malpractice means the exact definition given of the crime of severe injuries as established in Article 88(1) CCr.[77] Thus, judges will eventually interpret it in the same manner, considering also the doctrine of *jurisprudence constante,* codified in the recent reforms of the CCrP.

316. Criminal medical liability is personal (Article 29(1) Constitution and Articles 12–21 of the CCr). However, the research found a decision that considered the head of the medical department liable for the patient's death since, according to

72. The High Court of Albania, Criminal Session, No. 89 of 27.05.2015. Since the latest version of Art. 96 CCr does not include pharmacists, it would be interesting to know if the notion of "medical staff" would include also them.
73. The High Court of Albania, No. 1107 of 23.12.202—which is the appeal of the Court of Appeal of Vlore, No. 537 of 18.10.2018—as well as High Court, No. 142 of *22.11.*2017, which is the appeal of the Court of Appeal of Korçë No. 64 of 31.03.2016.
74. Court of Appeal of Vlorë No. 537 of 18.10.2018; The High Court of Albania, Criminal Session, No. 121 of 01.06.2016.
75. Court of Appeal of Vlorë No. 537 of 18.10.2018.
76. Tribunal of First Instance of Korçë No. 122 of 18.02.2015 (confirmed also by the Court of Appeal of Korçë No. 64 of 31.03.2016 as well as by the High Court, Criminal Session, No. 142 of 22.11.2017).
77. Intentionally inflicted injury that resulted in mutilation, disfigurement or any other permanent damage to health, termination of pregnancy, or was dangerous to life at the time of its infliction, is punishable by imprisonment from three to ten years.

the hospital's internal rules, there are no personal physicians per patient, but all doctors deal with all patients.[78] But, based on the constitutional principle that criminal liability is personal, the Court of Appeal quashed the decision and dismissed the case,[79] while the Supreme Court sent the case to the Court of Appeal in order to identify the criminal liability of the head of the medical department in the concrete case.[80]

317. Medical activity is a profession with high risks.[81] For this reason, judges must consider the result of the medical expertise, which is regarded as scientific evidence that, like all other types of evidence, will receive its evidential value and power only after the courts value it. However, although, as with other evidence, the act of medical expertise is not mandatory for the court, judges will not adopt the same conclusions of the acts of medical expertise but must argue in detail the differentiation in opinion through convincing arguments. The medical expert is not a body of criminal prosecution to conclude the mechanism of the (legal) events, but it helps magistrates with his scientific conclusions, which, taken and analyzed as a whole with other evidence, lead the prosecuting body or the judges to the relevant findings for the case under consideration.[82] In addition, these pieces of evidence shall not be reviewed subjectively[83] and shall be complete.[84] Moreover, the principle of beyond reasonable doubt will be applied; thus, the act of medical expertise shall clearly answer not only which medical act or omission the doctor should have done but also the correct medical drug that the doctor should have given.[85]

318. In case the judges are not convinced by the act of medical expertise since it might have irregularities, they can declare it invalid and ask to make another medical expertise by also establishing its composition as well as the questions that need to be answered by them.[86] Moreover, the team of medical experts is composed of experts in that particular medical field;[87] otherwise, the act of medical expertise is invalid.[88] However, if the legal questions are already answered, there is no need to remake the act of medical expertise.[89] Thus, the principles governing the validity of evidence, as outlined in Articles 178–179 of the CCrP, are equally applicable to the assessment and acceptance of acts of medical expertise. These provisions ensure

78. Tribunal of First Instance of Tirana No. 947 of 22.06.2009.
79. Court of Appeal of Tirana No. 355 of 28.04.2010.
80. The High Court of Albania, Criminal Session, No. 15 of 23.01.2013.
81. Tribunal of First Instance of Vlorë No. 296 of 11.06.2018.
82. The High Court of Albania, Criminal Session, No. 203 of 09.12.2015.
83. Court of Appeal of Vlorë No. 243 of 14.07.2010.
84. The High Court of Albania, Criminal Session, No. 104 of 20.03.2013.
85. The High Court of Albania, Criminal Session, No. 235 of 19.09.2012. If not complete, judges shall ask to review them wholly or partially.
86. Tribunal of First Instance (judge of the preliminary session) of Elbasan No. 2530 of 23.04.2021.
87. Court of Appeal of Durrës No. 196 of 29.06.2021 confirmed also by High Court, Criminal Session, No. 160 of 09.06.2022. In this case, the medical expertise was done by five experts. One of the experts was chosen for the second time in the same proceeding, which makes the act invalid. However, the invalidation is narrowed only to his part of the act of expertise.
88. *Ibid.*
89. Tribunal of First Instance (judge of the preliminary session) of Elbasan No. 2530 of 23.04.2021.

that the medical expertise presented in court meets established standards of reliability, impartiality, procedural integrity, and safeguarding the defendant's right to a fair trial. The rules require that the expertise is conducted by qualified professionals in the relevant medical field, free from conflicts of interest, and that its conclusions are supported by clear, scientific reasoning. In cases where these standards are not met, the expertise may be deemed inadmissible or subject to re-evaluation, ensuring that judicial decisions are based on credible and substantiated evidence.

319. Assessing medical liability in medical malpractice is challenging. The difference between medical criminal liability and "medical misfortune" is blurry. Indeed, the Tribunals of First Instance and the Courts of Appeal might make contradictory final decisions regarding the doctors' criminal liability, although it is the same situation.[90] As stated above, judges base their decisions on medical expertise. However, in one case, the expert better clarified his medical expertise during the proceeding.[91] In addition, in another case, two different acts of medical expertise might conclude contradictory results. For instance, in a patient's death, first, the act of medical expertise underlined the absence of medical liability, while after the family intervention of a second review, the prosecutor decided to prosecute the doctors.[92]

320. The assessment of criminal liability in medical malpractice is also challenging. For instance, in the first review of the death of a diabetic patient after surgery, the Court of First Instance of Vlora and the Court of Appeal of Vlora decided

90. Tribunal of First Instance of Tirana No. 2740 of 16.07.2015 (guilty) vr Court of Appeal of Tirana No. 1157 of 30.09.2016 (confirmed by the High Court, Criminal Session, No. 211 of 03.02.2022) (not guilty); Tribunal of First Instance of Vlorë No. 308 of 29.05.2014: guilty vr Court of Appeal of Vlorë No. 124 of 03.03.2016 (confirmed by the High Court, Criminal Session, No. 43 of 25.01.2022) (not guilty); Tribunal of First Instance of Vlorë No. 387 of 27.09.2013, uphold by the Court of Appeal of Vlorë No. 196 of 27.03.2014 (not guilty) vr. Tribunal of First Instance of Vlorë No. 296 of 11.06.2018, upheld by the Court of Appeal of Vlorë No. 537 of 18.10.2018 (confirmed by the High Court, Criminal Session, No. 1107 of 23.12.2021) (guilty); Tribunal of First Instance of Korçë No. 465 of 28.07.2015 (guilty) vr. Court of Appeal of Korçë No. 418 of 22.12.2015 (confirmed by the High Court, Criminal Session, No. 226 of 19.03.2021) (not guilty); Tribunal of First Instance of Berat No. 264 of 24.09.2013 (confirmed by the High Court, Criminal Session, No. 121 of 01.06.2016) (guilty) vr. Court of Appeal of Vlorë No. 174 of 12.03.2015 (not guilty); Tribunal of First Instance of Korçë No. 540 of 22.11.2011 (guilty) vr. Court of Appeal of Korçë No. 75 of 10.04.2012 (not guilty); Tribunal of First Instance of Lushnje No. 118 of 26.10.2009 (confirmed by the High Court, Criminal Session, No. 104 of 20.03.2013) (not guilty) vr. Court of Appeal of Vlorë No. 243 of 14.07.2010 (guilty); Tribunal of First Instance of Tirana No. 947 of 22.06.2009 (guilty) vr. Court of Appeal of Tirana No. 355 of 28.04.2010 (not guilty); Tribunal of First Instance of Sarandë No. 40 of 19.05.2010 (not guilty) vr. Court of Appeal of Vlorë No. 243 of 14.07.2010 (guilty).
91. Tribunal of First Instance of Lushnje No. 118 of 26.10.2009.
92. Tribunal of First Instance of Lushnje No. 118 of 26.10.2009, which declared the doctors not guilty, was also confirmed by the High Court, Criminal Session, No. 104 of 20.03.2013; Court of Appeal of Vlorë No. 243 of 14.07.2010 that declared the doctors guilty.

that there was no physician's medical liability,[93] while later, after the decision of the Supreme Court,[94] for the same facts, all courts[95] agreed that there was a physician's medical liability.

321. Thus, medical expertise is fundamental in the case of medical jurisprudence. Sometimes, judges might directly use the same medical expertise to both punish and dismiss the case within the same case.[96] Nevertheless, judges shall balance all the different medical proofs and consider the autopsy report and histopathology for the patient and the patient's diagnosis.[97] However, it shall be underlined that the assessment of medical liability shall be done by the judge of the proceeding and not by the judge of the preliminary session.[98]

322. Medical liability can be of various types, for instance, there is a criminal liability when: during the operation, there is an absence of an essential drug for the patient's life; the medical team had experience in that particular operation, even if this drug is not a drug used in Albania (but has been used by the same team of doctors in different previous operations) and even if the possibility that there would be a need for it was scarce.[99] In the case of reckless medication (as well as in the case of negligence in medical treatments), there is no possibility of cooperation;[100] thus, in the case of an operation done by a team of doctors, only the doctor who is liable for that particular step of the operation has criminal liability.[101] This does not mean

93. The same case decided in the same manner: Tribunal of First Instance of Vlorë No. 387 of 27.09.2013 and the Court of Appeal of Vlorë No. 196 of 27.03.2014.
94. The High Court of Albania, Criminal Session, No. 89 of 27.05.2015.
95. The same case decided in the same manner: Tribunal of First Instance of Vlorë No. 296 of 11.06.2018, confirmed then by the Court of Appeal of Vlorë No. 537 of 18.10.2018 and the High Court, Criminal Session, No. 1107 of 23.12.2021.
96. Tribunal of First Instance of Tirana No. 2740 of 16.07.2015 (guilty) vr Court of Appeal of Tirana No. 1157 of 30.09.2016 (confirmed by the High Court, Criminal Session, No. 211 of 03.02.2022) (not guilty); Tribunal of First Instance of Vlorë No. 308 of 29.05.2014: guilty vr Court of Appeal of Vlorë No. 124 of 03.03.2016 (confirmed by the High Court, Criminal Session, No. 43 of 25.01.2022) (not guilty); Tribunal of First Instance of Vlorë No. 387 of 27.09.2013, uphold by the Court of Appeal of Vlorë No. 196 of 27.03.2014 (not guilty) vr. Tribunal of First Instance of Vlorë No. 296 of 11.06.2018, upheld by the Court of Appeal of Vlorë No. 537 of 18.10.2018 (confirmed by the High Court, Criminal Session, No. 1107 of 23.12.2021) (guilty); Tribunal of First Instance of Korçë No. 465 of 28.07.2015 (guilty) vr. Court of Appeal of Korçë No. 418 of 22.12.2015 (confirmed by the High Court, Criminal Session, No. 226 of 19.03.2021) (not guilty); Tribunal of First Instance of Berat No. 264 of 24.09.2013 (confirmed by the High Court, Criminal Session, No. 121 of 01.06.2016) (guilty) vr. Court of Appeal of Vlorë No. 174 of 12.03.2015 (not guilty); Tribunal of First Instance of Korçë No. 540 of 22.11.2011 (guilty) vr. Court of Appeal of Korçë No. 75 of 10.04.2012 (not guilty); Tribunal of First Instance of Lushnje No. 118 of 26.10.2009 (confirmed by the High Court, Criminal Session, No. 104 of 20.03.2013) (not guilty) vr. Court of Appeal of Vlorë No. 243 of 14.07.2010 (guilty); Tribunal of First Instance of Tirana No. 947 of 22.06.2009 (guilty) vr. Court of Appeal of Tirana No. 355 of 28.04.2010 (not guilty); Tribunal of First Instance of Sarandë No. 40 of 19.05.2010 (not guilty) vr. Court of Appeal of Vlorë No. 243 of 14.07.2010 (guilty).
97. Court of Appeal of Korçë No. 418 of 22.12.2015.
98. The High Court of Albania, Criminal Session, No. 160 of 09.06.2022.
99. Court of Appeal of Tirana No. 191, No. 17.02.2016.
100. *Ibid.*
101. *Ibid.*

that more than one person would be liable for *culpa* in medical treatment for the same case.[102] However, this means that different doctors—without cooperating with one another—contributed, through their negligence, to the medical error.

323. In addition, medical negligence can also occur when the doctor forgets to advise the patient to do follow-up check-ups.[103] Nevertheless, he would not be liable if the doctor suggested them.[104] Moreover, there is a medical criminal liability when the doctor does not advise the patient to stay under observation. However, competent patients should decide for themselves.[105] Furthermore, Article 96 of the CCr will apply when doctors make a mistake in determining the diagnosis[106] or when the specialist has not been called at the correct time.[107]

324. Medical liability is not narrow. The doctors' criminal liability can also be for pre-operation and post-operation events. For instance, it is considered criminal liability when the clinical report has deficiencies.[108] In addition, there is a criminal liability when the post-operation infection is taken in the surgical aspirator tube.[109] Moreover, there is a medical liability when the doctor starts the medical operation without completing the necessary examinations that are necessary for the preparation of the operation.[110] Nevertheless, there is a need for a clear causal link between medical negligence and damage; otherwise, there is no medical liability for the doctors, although they might not have acted with high diligence.[111] Although doctors might have influenced the further deepening of the severe health condition of the victim, this does not make them liable for medical negligence.[112]

---

102. The same case decided in the same manner: Tribunal of First Instance of Tirana No. 1043 of 03.04.2015, confirmed then by the Court of Appeal of Tirana No. 191 No. 17.02.2016 and the High Court, Criminal Session, No. 222 of 19.03.2021.
103. Tribunal of First Instance of Tirana No. 2740 of 16.07.2015.
104. The same case decided in the same manner: Court of Appeal of Tirana No. 1157 of 30.09.2016, confirmed by the High Court, Criminal Session, No. 211 of 03.02.2022.
105. The same case decided in the same manner: Court of Appeal of Vlorë No. 124 of 03.03.2016, confirmed by the High Court, Criminal Session, No. 43 of 25.01.2022.
106. Tribunal of First Instance of Berat No. 264 of 24.09.2013, confirmed by the High Court, Criminal Session, No. 121 of 01.06.2016.
107. *Ibid.*
108. Tribunal of First Instance of Vlorë No. 308 of 29.05.2014.
109. The same case decided in the same manner: Tribunal of First Instance of Korçë No. 122 of 18.02.2015, confirmed by the Court of Appeal of Korçë No. 64 of 31.03.2016 and the High Court, Criminal Session, No. 142 of 22.11.2017.
110. The same case decided in the same manner: Tribunal of First Instance of Vlorë No. 296 of 11.06.2018, confirmed by the Court of Appeal of Vlorë No. 537 of 18.10.2018 and the High Court, Criminal Session, No. 1107 of 23.12.2021.
111. Tribunal of First Instance (judge of the preliminary session) of Elbasan No. 2530 of 23.04.2021.
112. Court of Appeal of Durrës No. 196 of 29.06.2021. In this case, after a car accident, the patient was sent to the hospital, and then he died. The medical expertise underlined that the link of causality is between car accidents and death and not between medical negligence and death, although the doctors' acts have further deepened the severe health condition of the victim.

325. In the case of patients with chronic diseases—diabetic[113] or HIV+[114] patients—specific (and not general) protocols shall be applied. Doctors will be liable even if the medical expertise does not give concrete answers to the legal questions asked by the judges if it is proven that specific, instead of general, protocols should have been applied, while in concrete, doctors applied the general medical protocols.[115] In addition, medical liability can also be asserted when an autopsy report is absent (since the patient's parents did not give consent).[116]

326. The general rules of criminal law or criminal proceedings will be applied also in the case of medical negligence. It is outside the Supreme Court's jurisdiction to evaluate (new) proofs.[117] In this case, the Supreme Court can decide to quash the decision of the Court of Appeal and send it to the same Court with a different composition,[118] to quash the decision of the Court of Appeal and uphold the decision of the Tribunal of First Instance,[119] uphold the decision of the Court of Appeal,[120] add a new sanction,[121] or simply reject the recourse.[122] In addition, special forms of criminal proceedings can also be applied.[123] Moreover, the prosecutor can include new investigations (if asked by the court)[124] and change the criminal charges.[125]

327. Thus, medical criminal liability is challenging. While general rules of criminal law or criminal proceedings will still be applied, medical criminal liability can be in various forms, not only when the doctor forgets to advise the patient to do follow-up check-ups[126] but also when doctors make a mistake in determining the

113. The same case decided in the same manner: Tribunal of First Instance of Vlorë No. 296 of 11.06.2018, confirmed by the Court of Appeal of Vlorë No. 537 of 18.10.2018 and the High Court, Criminal Session, No. 1107 of 23.12.2021.
114. Tribunal of First Instance of Vlorë No. 308 of 29.05.2014.
115. The same case decided in the same manner: Tribunal of First Instance of Vlorë No. 296 of 11.06.2018, confirmed by the Court of Appeal of Vlorë No. 537 of 18.10.2018 and the High Court, Criminal Session, No. 1107 of 23.12.2021.
116. The same case decided in the same manner: Tribunal of First Instance of Përmet No. 23 of 10.04.2014, confirmed by the Court of Appeal of Gjirokastër No. 163 of 17.07.2014 and the High Court, Criminal Session, No. 89 of 27.05.2015.
117. The High Court of Albania, Criminal Session, No. 226 of 19.03.2021; High Court, Criminal Session, No. 222 of 19.03.2021.
118. The High Court of Albania, Criminal Session, No. 52 of 25.02.2014; High Court, Criminal Session, No. 15 of 23.01.2013; and High Court, Criminal Session, No. 235 of 19.09.2012.
119. The High Court of Albania, Criminal Session, No. 121 of 01.06.2016; High Court, Criminal Session, No. 203 of 09.12.2015; and High Court, Criminal Session, No. 104 of 20.03.2013.
120. The High Court of Albania, Criminal Session, No. 142 of 22.11.2017; High Court, Criminal Session, No. 89 of 27.05.2015.
121. The High Court of Albania, Criminal Session, No. 121 of 01.06.2016.
122. The High Court of Albania, Criminal Session, No. 211 of 03.02.2022; High Court, Criminal Session, No. 43 of 25.01.2022; High Court, Criminal Session, No. 1107 of 23.12.2021; High Court, Criminal Session, No. 226 of 19.03.2021; and High Court, Criminal Session, No. 222 of 19.03.2021.
123. Tribunal of First Instance of Korçë No. 465 of 28.07.2015 or Tribunal of First Instance of Korçë No. 540 of 22.11.2011.
124. Tribunal of First Instance (judge of the preliminary session) of Elbasan No. 2530 of 23.04.2021. In this case, the judge asked the prosecutor three times to add investigation.
125. Tribunal of First Instance (judge of the preliminary session) of Elbasan No. 2530 of 23.04.2021.
126. Tribunal of First Instance of Tirana No. 2740 of 16.07.2015.

diagnosis[127] or even when the specialist has not been called at the correct time,[128] or when the patient starts the medical operation without completing the necessary examinations that are preparatory for the operation[129] or simply when doctors have not applied the specific medical protocols[130] or the clinical report has deficiencies.[131]

III. Vicarious Liability

328. The Albanian CCv also addresses situations involving vicarious liability, particularly in the context of employer responsibility. Under Article 618 of the CCv, an employer is held liable for damages caused to third parties by the fault of employees under their service, provided the harm occurs during the performance of duties entrusted to them. Similarly, legal entities are held accountable for damages caused by their governing bodies while performing their official functions. This framework ensures that accountability extends beyond the individual perpetrator, emphasizing the broader responsibility of employers and organizations in overseeing the actions of their employees.

329. An award for damages is also provided in case of damage to a person's health. The person who caused damage to another person's health is obliged to compensate the damage, considering the loss or reduction of the injured person's ability to work, the expenses incurred for his treatment, as well as other expenses related to the damage caused (Article 641 of the CCv). The amount of compensation for damages may change in the future, depending on the improvement or deterioration of the health or the increase or decrease of the capacity for work of the injured party, compared to the time of setting the compensation and the changes that the salary may have undergone of the injured party.

330. When the death of a person has been caused, the damage to be compensated consists of: (a) food and living expenses of his minor children, wife and parents unable to work who were dependent on the deceased, fully or partially, as well as persons who lived in the family of the deceased and who enjoyed the right to food from him; (b) appropriate expenses for the burial of the deceased, to the extent that they correspond to the personal and family circumstances of the deceased. The court, considering all the circumstances of the case, may decide that the reward be given in kind, in cash, all at once or in installments (Article 643 of the CCv).

---

127. The High Court of Albania, Criminal Session, No. 121 of 01.06.2016 which has confirmed the decision of the Tribunal of First Instance of Berat No. 264 Of 24.09.2013.
128. *Ibid.*
129. The same case decided in the same manner: Tribunal of First Instance of Vlorë No. 296 of 11.06.2018, confirmed by the Court of Appeal of Vlorë No. 537 of 18.10.2018 and the High Court, Criminal Session, No. 1107 of 23.12.2021.
130. *Ibid.*
131. Tribunal of First Instance of Vlorë No. 308 of 29.05.2014.

331. When the person who committed the illegal action or omission, in addition to the damage caused, also had an obvious benefit, the court, at the request of the injured party, considering the nature of the damage, the degree of guilt and other circumstances of the case, may calculate in compensation for damage, full or partial benefit (Article 644 of the CCv). When the death or health damage of a person who earns from social security is caused, the damage is compensated in the manner determined by law (Article 644 of the CCv).

332. Article 646 of the CCv provides guidance for determining compensation in cases where the injured party was neither formally employed nor insured. In such situations, the court calculates the amount of compensation for damages resulting from death or health-related harm by referencing the salary of an employee in a comparable category. This comparison considers the type of work that the injured party was performing or could have performed, ensuring equitable compensation aligned with the individual's potential earning capacity under similar circumstances.

333. In cases involving an injured minor, Article 647 of the CCv specifies the framework for compensation. When the minor reaches the age of 16 and does not have a salary from employment, they are entitled to seek compensation for the loss of their ability to work, calculated based on the average salary of an employee in a comparable category, as outlined in Article 646 of the CCv. Upon reaching the age of 18, the minor is further entitled to claim compensation equivalent to the average salary of a worker in the category they would have earned, or should have earned, had the health damage not occurred. These provisions ensure equitable redress for lost earning capacity, acknowledging the developmental stages of the injured party and their potential future contributions (Article 647 of the CCv).

334. Article 647/a of the CCv regulates the manner and criteria for determining civil liability and the amount of non-pecuniary damage. The award of non-pecuniary damage for the violation of a person's honor, personality or reputation aims to restore the violated right, proportionally to the damage suffered and is determined based on the circumstances of the case. For the determination of civil liability and the amount of non-pecuniary damage, the court also takes into account: (a) the manner, form and time of spreading statements or performing actions; (b) the degree of compliance with the rules of professional ethics by the author of the statements; (c) forms and degree of guilt; (ç) the fact whether the statements have correctly quoted or referred to the statements of a third person; (d) the fact if the statements are false, especially in the case of damage to reputation; (dh) the fact if the statements relate to issues of the private life of the injured person and their relationship with a public interest; (e) the fact whether the statements constitute opinions or statements that contain only factual inaccuracies unimportant; (ë) the fact if the statements are related to matters of public interest, or to persons in office state or candidates for elections; (f) performing actions to prevent or reduce the amount of damage, such as making a refutation for the false statement, as well as any other measure taken by the author of the statements to put the honor, personality or reputation of the injured person in place; (i) the fact whether the author of the false statements has benefited from their dissemination, as well as the amount of this benefit; (j) the fact whether the compensation can significantly burden the financial situation of the cause of the damage.

§2. QUALITY ASSURANCE

I. Accreditation and Licensing

335. Accreditation of health structures that carry out the activity of transplantation tissue cells is carried out by the National Center of Quality, Certification and Accreditation Health Institutions, according to the legislation in force. Licensing of health structures that will carry out the transplant process tissues, cells and organs in the Republic of Albania will be done according to the legislation in force (Article 28 of Law No. 10 454, dated 21.7.2011 For Tissue, Cell and Organ Transplantation in Republic of Albania) (*see* paragraphs 484–487).

336. Import and export of tissues, cells and organs, for transplantation purposes, are authorized by the Minister of Health. Relevant procedures and mandatory documentation, which the bank must complete for the tissues, cells and organs, which is the health structure that carries out the import and export of transplants, are determined by order of the Minister of Health. The list of requirements, which must meet the tissues, cells and organs imported from other countries, including tracking methods and conditions, recording of tracking data verifying the delivery of transplants, the system for declaring unwanted effects, as well as procedures for verifying equivalent quality and safety standards are defined with a special regulation, approved by order of the Minister of Health (Article 29 of Law No. 10 454, dated 21.7.2011 For Tissue, Cell and Organ Transplantation in the Republic of Albania).

II. Inspection

337. The Ministry of Health is the inspection authority of health structures transplantation, which organizes the inspection and takes the relevant measures to implement the requirements of the law. Inspection procedures are regulated by order of the Minister of Health. Representatives of the inspection authority have the right: (a) to periodically inspect the centers where activities related to transplantation are carried out of tissues, cells and organs. The interval between two inspections should not exceed two years; (b) to evaluate and verify the procedures and activities carried out in the centers transplants; (c) check any document or other data related to the object of the inspection (Article 30 of Law No. 10 454, dated 21.7.2011 For Tissue, Cell and Organ Transplantation in the Republic of Albania).

III. Tracing

338. By order of the Minister of Health, the regulation for the creation and operation of the tracking system for: (a) tracking from the donor to the recipient and vice versa of organs, tissues and cells selected, processed, stored or distributed in the territory of the country. Tracking also applies to all relevant data related to products and materials, which encounter the tissues, cells and organs in question; (b) the implementation of a donor identification system, to which a code is attached specific to each donation and product related to it; (c) recording and storing the necessary data to guarantee its traceability all stages. Data required for full tracking is stored for a minimum period of thirty years after clinical use. Data may also be stored electronically (Article 31 of Law No. 10 454, dated 21.7.2011 For Tissue, Cell and Organ Transplantation in the Republic of Albania).

IV. Adverse Effect Reporting

339. All centers that carry out the implantation of transplants of human origin report any adverse effects to tissue, cell and organ banks. The bank of tissues, cells and organs is notified of any case or effects unwanted and provided by the reporting structure with a report on the cause and the result. The procedure for the notification of unwanted effects, as well as the processing of data for the cases of unwanted effects in all links of the process are determined by regulation, approved by order of the Minister of Health. Tissue, cell and organ banks guarantee an accurate, fast procedure and verifiable, which enables the withdrawal from circulation of any product, which may relate to reported adverse effects (Article 32 of Law No. 10 454, dated 21.7.2011 For Tissue, Cell and Organ Transplantation in the Republic of Albania).

V. Quality Assurance of Continuing Education Activities: Accreditation

340. Accreditation is the process of approving continuing education activities and/or providers of continuing education activities, based on approved procedures, standards and criteria by decision of the Council of Ministers. Providers of continuing education activities are all public or private structures, academic or nonacademic, for-profit or not-for-profit, foreign and domestic, having expertise and experience in organizing continuing education activities in the field of health, according to the approved criteria. Providers of continuing education activities are obliged to ensure the quality of the activities they develop, through compliance with the quality criteria of accreditation, and the standards of continuing professional education. Criteria, standards and procedures for accreditation of continuing education activities, such as providers of continuing education activities, are approved by decision of the Council Ministers (Article 33/1 Law No. 10 107, dated 30.3.2009).

§3. Review Boards

I. Board of Continuing Education

341. The Continuing Education Board operates under the ministry responsible for health, which is chaired by the minister responsible for health, with the following composition: (a) representatives from the National Center of Continuing Education; (b) representatives from the Mandatory Health Care Insurance Fund; (c) representatives from the ministry responsible for education; (d) representatives from the National Center for Quality, Safety and Accreditation of Institutions Health; (e) representatives from the Order of Doctors; (f) representatives from the Nursing Order; (g) representatives from the Order of Pharmacists; (h) representative from the Order of Dentists. The Continuing Education Board is the highest decision-making body in the certification system and recertification of health professionals and accreditation of continuous education activities. The Board of Continuing Education meets no less than four times a year and, on special occasion, when necessary, the chairman can convene it even more often. Board meetings are valid when more than half of the members participate in them. Decision-making in the Board of Continuing Education is done by a simple majority (Article 33/2 Law No. 10 107, dated 30.3.2009).

342. The Continuing Education Board performs the following main functions: (a) designs criteria, standards and procedures for accreditation of continuing education activities and providers of continuing education activities, as well as the criteria and procedures of the process certification and/or recertification of health professionals; (b) approves the accreditation fees for continuing education activities; (c) approves the list of independent experts for each field of expertise, who will be included in the external evaluation of the activities, as part of the accreditation process, and the amount of their payment, according to the legislation in force; (d) examines the complaints made by health professionals about recognition procedures and registration of relevant credits; (e) reviews the complaints made by the providers of continuing education activities for the process of external assessment, which have not been resolved by the National Center for Continuing Education; (f) undertakes the necessary measures for the realization of the recertification exam for health professionals who do not meet the requirements of the certification program; (g) monitors the implementation of the certification program to ensure the fulfillment of its duties for responsible institutions. Members of the Board of Continuing Education are rewarded according to the legislation in force for remuneration of members of boards, councils or commissions (Article 33/2 Law No. 10 107, dated 30.3.2009).

§4. Disciplinary Organizations

I. Order of Physicians

343. Any medical act, or professional behavior in violation of the provisions of this Code, constitutes an object for prosecution and professional disciplinary judgment based on Law 8615, dated 01.06.2000 "On the Order of Doctors in the Republic of Albania" and in the Rules of Professional Disciplinary Court of the Order of Doctors (Article 68 The Code of Medical Ethics and Deontology). When according to the facts and evidence administered in the case file, it is proven that the member has performed behaviors or actions that are related to the exercise of the profession and constitute violation of the Code of Medical Ethics and Deontology, the law or the statute of the Order of Doctors in the Republic of Albania.

344. The professional who violates the obligations provided within the laws that regulate the field of his activity, or in the code of professional ethics will be administratively severely punished. The relevant professional order has the responsibility to define the types of administrative measures, the responsible authority, and procedures for issuing, appealing, the prescription or termination of these measures.

345. The Disciplinary Commission issues the following disciplinary measures: (a) written remarks; (b) remarks with a warning for the removal of the right to exercise the profession; (c) fine from ALL 15,000 to ALL 100,000; (d) proposal for dismissal from management functions in health and private institutions; (e) suspension from the right to vote in the governing bodies of the Order of Doctors for up to three years; (f) Exemption from the Doctors' Order for a period of up to three years (Article 17 (1) Law No. 123/2014, also *see* Article 15 Regulation about professional disciplinary judgment and Article 34 the Statute of the Order of Doctors of Albania).

346. In addition to the disciplinary measures, as complementary measures, the Commission has the right to appoint a retraining order or additional studies equal to twenty credits. The disciplinary measures can be canceled if the member has not received any other disciplinary measure as follows: (a) within one year from the date of their issuance; (b) within three years from the day of their issuance (Article 17 (1) Law No. 123/2014, also see Article 15 Regulation about professional disciplinary judgment and Article 34 the Statute of the Order of Doctors of Albania).

A. Appealing Disciplinary Decisions

347. Appeal against decisions made by Disciplinary Trial Commissions is done based on the terms and methods defined in the Regulation for Professional Disciplinary Judgment (Article 35 the Statute of the Order of Doctors of Albania). By decision of the National Council, near the National Council and Councils Regional, permanent commissions or working groups are created temporary, as needed. The activity of these commissions is based on the relevant regulations which are also approved, by decision of the National Council (Article 36 the Statute of the Order of Doctors of Albania).

B. Trial at First Instance

348. The Secretary of the Regional Council creates and responsibly administers the Register complaints/denunciations, their protocol, as well as the special file for each disciplinary issue. For every complaint/denunciation received at the Regional Council, the disciplinary process is initiated according to this time of action: The received complaint/denunciation is recorded in the special register, inventoried and numbered in the Case File.

349. The president and secretary of the Regional Council call the defendant doctor to the office of the council known as: (a) the complaint received against him and submitted a copy of it; (b) the procedures that are carried out for the professional disciplinary trial; (c) obligation to present a written defense within ten days from this moment and contradictory arguments and evidence for the submitted complaint; (d) the right to be represented and defended in the trial by a doctor, preferably the same specialty or a licensed lawyer, e.g., obligation to be present at the hearing or when the Trial committee deems his presence necessary.

350. The president or secretary meets the head of the public or private health institution to notify him of the complaint and to cooperate in carrying out the preliminary verification and other information. The president or the secretary meets the complaining/denouncing party to get information complementary regarding the claims, intentions and willingness to face the other party. To consider: (a) does the complaint stand or not; (b) whether or not there are witnesses and other materials that prove the appealed case.

351. The complaining party must be informed on: (a) the disciplinary procedure; (b) the right to be represented and protected by a doctor, preferably of the same specialty as the defendant's physician or licensed attorney; (c) the obligation to be present at the hearing or when the trial commission requests such a thing. The litigants are confronted, who are familiar with the contents of the file and if it is reasoned that the appealed case is not significant to necessarily pass it in the trial process, the possibility of reconciliation and closure of the case is offered and suggested. Whether the parties reach an understanding for reconciliation and the case is closed, a special document is drawn up with the conclusions, which is signed by the litigants, as well as the President and Secretary of the Council Regional.

352. In case of disagreement, the report of the case is decided for Disciplinary Judgment of the first degree where: (a) the verifying/reporting doctor (or doctors) is appointed, who is informed of the task that will perform and its importance by making this Regulation available for this purpose; (b) medical, forensic, and legal experts are appointed depending on the case in trial, to whom requests and questions related to the matter to be expert are presented. The composition of the Professional Disciplinary Judgment Committee and its chairman are determined (Article 16 Regulation about professional disciplinary judgment).

C. Preliminary Procedures for Trial at First Instance

353. Once the verifying/reporting doctor (or doctors) of the case is appointed, as well as appointed the Professional Disciplinary Judgment Committee and its chairman, the duties are given to the doctor (or doctors) verifier/relator, the deadlines for submitting the Report on Preliminary Verification of the Case. As soon as the Preliminary Case Verification Report has been made available, the file case is passed to the Professional Disciplinary Judgment Commission.

354. If the Professional Disciplinary Judgment Committee deems it necessary to appoint experts and after familiarizing themselves with the file materials, within the deadlines defined in this regulation, the Professional Disciplinary Judgment Commission announces the date for conducting the session, which the secretary of the relevant Regional Council communicates to the party's litigation. The Secretary of the Regional Council with the agreement of the Professional Disciplinary Judgment Commission sets the date of this trial, notifying the parties and other interested parties (Article 17 Regulation about professional disciplinary judgment).

D. Development of the First Instance Trial Session

355. The disciplinary process of the first instance judgment is organized and carried out under the auspices of the president and secretary of the Regional Council, who are responsible for the smooth running to its conclusion. Members of the Disciplinary Committee and the Support Team are notified of the date and time of the hearing and the case to be judged, no later than thirty days before the date set for the hearing. During these days in the office of the Regional Council they become familiar with the report on the Preliminary Verification of the Case and with the file materials as a whole. The preliminary verification, as well as the Disciplinary Trial of the first instance, are carried out no later than sixty days from the day of submission of the request for judgment (*see* paragraphs 440, 443, 483).

356. The first instance Professional Disciplinary Judgment takes place in two stages:

a. open phase;
b. closed phase and decision-making, I. The open phase, in which the Registrar officially opens the hearing. Warns the parties and the attendees to respect the rules for the normal development of the session. Otherwise, the session is interrupted, and the violating party is charged with the costs of the session. Then, the President continues by expressly communicating that:

> The complainant/petitioner_____________ sued the Regional Council of the District __________the doctor______________________for______________ ___________________.

357. Based on the implementation of Law No. 123/2014, dated 25.09.2014 "On the Order of Doctors in Republic of Albania" and the Regulation on Professional Disciplinary Judgment, he declares open the hearing session for Professional Disciplinary Judgment in the above-mentioned case."

358. In the session, the secretary of the relevant Regional Council keeps the minutes, where he notes the participation of the parties and other participants in the session, as well as presents file, reading the title of each document and making it visible to the parties. The session is chaired by the Chairman of the Professional Disciplinary Trial Commission, who gives the word to the verifying/reporting doctor (or doctors), who reads the Report on Preliminary Verification of the Case. The floor is given to the party that filed the complaint to present the complaint/request, as well as if he/she has to present or deliver other documents in connection with the case. Then the word is given to the defendant, to present his objections in relation to the complaint, as well as if there are other documents to present or deliver related to the case. The Chairman of the Professional Disciplinary Judgment Commission after listening to the parties, if he sees necessary, requires further details from the litigating parties, upon the case evaluation, may intervene for the amicable resolution of the submitted complaint. Then the floor is given to the experts, in case they have been called as such. Acting Chairman asks the members of the Commission if they have questions for the parties in the trial, for the narrator, as well as for the experts. If requests for additional verifications arise during the session, the Commission decides to suspend the session, reflecting this in the minutes, which are signed by the committee members and the secretary. The next session must take place within the time limit of sixty days from the date of filing a complaint/denunciation in writing to the relevant Regional Council. Before the closing of the session, the floor is given to the parties in the trial, first to the defendant, then the other party, if they have requests for clarifications and other explanations.

359. At the conclusion of the proceedings, the Chairman of the Commission inquires whether the complaining party wishes to proceed with the professional disciplinary judgment. If the complaining party consents to a settlement by mutual understanding or chooses to withdraw the complaint, this agreement is duly recorded in the session minutes, which are signed by both litigants, as well as by the Chairman and the secretary. Conversely, if the complaining party declines the proposed settlement or refuses to withdraw the complaint, this decision is similarly documented in the session minutes, signed by the Chairman and the secretary. In such instances, the Chairman formally announces the transition of the case to the second stage, involving a closed phase and decision-making.

360. The closed phase and decision-making is carried out without the presence of the participants in the process, and the secretary takes the participants in the process out of the room where the session takes place. The Professional Disciplinary Trial Commission of the first instance, in the presence of the secretary, continues the discussion without the presence of other people. The Chairman asks the members of the Professional Disciplinary Judgment Committee to express opinion and to argue it, for taking or not the punitive measure against the doctor. After considering the opinions of the members of the Disciplinary Trial Commission Professional of the first instance, the President presents his proposal, which is put to the vote open to other alternative proposals. The proposal, which has the majority, remains in force by simple voting. Then, it must be completed the decision sheet by the Professional Disciplinary Judgment Commission, according to form "B," which is administered in the case file. The Secretary, after inviting the attendees to return to the meeting room, keeping them calm and standing up. The Chairman of the Commission announces the decision. The Secretary of the relevant Regional Council together with the Commission's Lawyer, based on the minutes and the decision taken by the Professional Disciplinary Trial Commission, makes three copies of the decision, which are signed by the members of the Professional Disciplinary Commission, as well as the President of the relevant Regional Council and sealed with the seal of the relevant Regional Council. The decision is submitted to the litigants by the secretary of the Regional Council in the "C" format, where the parties are notified that this decision can be appealed within fifteen calendar days to the National Disciplinary Commission of the second level of Appeal. A copy of the decision is kept in the relevant Regional Council, as well as one copy is delivered to the litigants (Article 17 Regulation about professional disciplinary judgment).

E. Judgment at the Second Instance (Appeal)

361. The process of the Professional Disciplinary Judgment of the second instance (Appeal) is carried out under the auspices of The President, the Vice President and the lawyer of the National Council, who are responsible for the success of this process. Preliminary verification, if other additional data are required, as well as the Professional Disciplinary Judgment in the second instance (Appeal), are carried out no later than sixty days from the day of appeal against the decision. The National Commission of Professional Disciplinary Judgment of Appeal can make the following decisions: (a) upholds the decision of the first instance; (b) returns the case for retrial at first instance; (c) examines the case and makes a decision to change the decision; Except in cases where the case is returned for retrial in the first instance, all decisions of other judgments of the second instance (Appeal) are final and conclusive. Decisions that contain disciplinary measures against the doctor (doctors) are also communicated to the institutions where they practice their profession. The decision of the National Commission (Appeals) can be appealed to the Administrative Court, no later than fifteen days from the announcement of the decision or from its communication (Article 18 Regulation about professional disciplinary judgment).

F. Actions for Judgment in the Second Instance (Appeal)

362. The President of the National Council is notified of the case reached in Appeal, who carries out the procedures for the appointment of the Professional Disciplinary Judgment Commission of the second instance, as and of the relator/ verifier, who may be the previous relator. The defendant is also notified at the same time, who is given a copy of the appeal against the decision and is asked to bring his written arguments against it within ten days. The file of the Professional Disciplinary Judgment of the first instance, together with the appeal is submitted to the National Council, which makes it available to the Professional Disciplinary Judgment Commission of Appeal. The lawyer of the National Council after consulting with the Professional Disciplinary Trial Commission Appeal, sets the day and time of the session for which they have notified all participants (commission members, relator, litigants and experts, if any), not less than fifteen days before its development. The reporter, if necessary, undertakes supplementary verification actions for problems, which may be requested by the Professional Disciplinary Judgment Commission of Appeal or the experts (Article 19 Regulation about professional disciplinary judgment).

G. The Meeting of the Commission for the Development of the Trial

363. The Session of the Professional Disciplinary Judgment of Appeal is reflected in the minutes by respecting and applying the same rules as in the first instance trial and follows the following procedure: 1.a. The Chairman of the Professional Disciplinary Appeal Commission declares the opening of the session for the professional disciplinary trial, regarding the case against the doctor (doctors) "________________" presented by the complaining party Mr.________________, to Decision No.___, date. ________ of the Regional Council of the Order of Doctors ______________. 1.b. The speaker is given the floor, who reads the claims of the complaining party against Decision No. ___, date _______, of the Regional Council of the Order of Physicians ______________. 1.c. The floor is given to the other side to present its counterarguments. 1.d. Members of the Professional Disciplinary Judgment Commission are given the floor in turn to seek clarifications about the case and the claims of the parties in the trial.

364. The Professional Disciplinary Judgment Commission of Appeal decides to stop the session and reflects this in the minutes, taking signatures of all its members. The President of the National Council is notified of this action who orders the execution of further actions. After performing additional verifications or receiving an opinion of experts, the next session takes place no later than fifteen days. 1.f. In the case mentioned in the above paragraph (1.e), the floor is given to the experts and specialists of the support team and immediately after them the Chairman of the Judging Committee. The Professional Disciplinary of Appeal Commission declares the session closed to take the decision. 1.g. All participants in the process leave the premises where the trial is taking place. Only the members of the Professional Disciplinary Appeal Committee and the secretary are allowed to stay. The Chairman of the Professional Disciplinary Judgment Committee gives the floor in turn to the members of the commission, who present their reasoned opinions and proposals regarding the matter. The Chairman of the Commission, taking into consideration the opinions and members' arguments, makes its own comments and proposal regarding the judgment of the subject matter. 1.h. The proposal of the Chairman of the Commission is put to an open vote against other alternative proposals. The proposal, which receives a simple majority of votes, remains in force by completing the voting record according to the "B1" form, which they all sign. 1.i. The Secretary invites the litigants to return to the premises, where the process takes place, keeping them calm and standing up. The Chairman of the Professional Disciplinary Trial Commission of Appeals announces the decision. 1.j. The Secretary, who kept the record of the trial of the case together with the lawyer of the commission, relying on the minutes and the decision taken by the Professional Disciplinary Judgment Commission of Appeal, publishes the decision in four copies, according to form "D," which is signed by the Members of the Professional Disciplinary Judgment Committee of Appeal, the President of the National Council and sealed with the seal of the National Council. 1.k. A copy of the clarified decision is delivered to the litigating parties, one copy is administered in the archive of the National Council of the Order of Doctors of Albania, and one copy is administered in the file, which is submitted to the secretary of the relevant Regional Council. 1.l. The decision of the National Council is appealed to the competent court for the resolution of administrative disputes, within the deadlines set by the laws in force (Article 20 Regulation about professional disciplinary judgment).

H. Notification of the Institutions for the Decisions of the Professional Disciplinary Judgment

365. The decision of the Professional Disciplinary Judgment is made known to the institution in which the doctor practices the profession. The decision of the Professional Disciplinary Judgment, by which a disciplinary measure is taken against the doctor (or doctors), in cases of special interest, is made known to the Ministry of Health (Article 21 Regulation about professional disciplinary judgment).

I. Lack of Participation of the Parties in the Professional Disciplinary Trial

366. Litigation parties are contacted through the address stated by them in the complaint or in the database of the Order of Doctors of Albania. During the professional disciplinary trial, if one of the litigants is absent personally and/or not represented at the hearing by the authorized person, for justified reasons, the session is postponed by setting another date, which is communicated to all parties. During the first stage of the Professional Disciplinary Trial of the first instance, the unjustified absence of the litigating parties results in the postponement of the session and the appointment of another date, which is communicated to the litigants.

367. If the complaining party, whose absence has led to the postponement of the session, is absent again for unjustified reasons, the disciplinary trial commission may dismiss the complaint, considering the non-presentation of the party as withdrawal from the filed claim/denunciation. If one or both litigants are absent without justified reasons, the professional disciplinary trial is postponed to another date, which should not be more than fifteen days from the date of the undeveloped session. In case of repeated absence of the party or parties, the disciplinary trial continues in absence, and the committee of the Professional Disciplinary Appeal may charge the costs of this trial (Article 22 Regulation about professional disciplinary judgment).

J. Rewarding Participation in Disciplinary Processes

368. Members of Professional Disciplinary Judgment Commissions, secretaries, and teams' assistants in disciplinary proceedings are rewarded with fees from the Order of the Doctors in the Republic of Albania according to the manner and fees approved by the National Council of the Order of Doctors of Albania. When they are sent with services outside the district, they benefit from travel expenses and *per diem*, according to the fees defined in the Decision of the relevant Council of Ministers in force (Article 24 Regulation about professional disciplinary judgment).

II. Professional Codes

A. Professional Code of Ethics

369. The professional code of ethics, the content of which should be easily understandable by the professional, disciplines the exercise of the professional activity of every professional. The criteria and procedures for drafting the professional code of ethics are determined by the national bodies of professional orders. The professional code of ethics is guided by the following principles: (a) protection of public interests, through the correct exercise of the profession; (b) protection of trust and free choice by the beneficiary of the service; (c) ensuring the quality of professional services; (d) provision of appropriate data on the content and methods of exercising the professional services. The code of ethics is published and periodically updated by the relevant professional order (Article 17 Law No. 10 171, dated 22.10.2009).

370. The Doctor's Professional Order has created disciplinary commissions concerning ethics behavior (Article 18 Law No. 10 171, dated 22.10.2009). The manner of setting up and functioning of disciplinary commissions is defined in the statute and in the professional judgment regulating the Order (Article 16 Law No. 123/2014). Disciplinary commissions work next to the regional councils and the National Council as bodies of professional judgment. The regional disciplinary commission consists of 9 members elected by the Regional Council. The National Disciplinary Commission consists of 15 members elected by the National Council.

The Commission examines complaints made by any person or institution to the bodies of the Order, which are related to the exercise of the profession and constitute a violation of the Code of Ethics and Medical Deontology. The disciplinary commissions, next to the regional councils, exercise disciplinary powers at first instance trials. Their decisions are appealable to the disciplinary committee of the Council National, which exercises disciplinary powers of the second instance.

371. Disciplinary rules are also exercised through the Regulation about professional disciplinary judgment (approved by Decision No. 1, dated 08.04.2016, amended by Decision No. 8, dated 08.07.2016 of the National Council of Order of Doctors of Albania). The Professional Disciplinary Judgment and the Regulation of the Professional Disciplinary Judgment are based in Law No. 123/2014, dated 25.09.2014 "On the Order of Doctors in the Republic of Albania," in the Code of Medical Ethics and Deontology and in the Order of Doctors in the Republic of Albania Statute. Based on these normative acts, the Order of Doctors in the Republic of Albania undertakes actions and makes the professional disciplinary judgment of its member in cases where: (a) His professional competence or performance has serious deficiencies. (b) There is an allegation of medical negligence or professional misconduct. (c) He was convicted by the judicial bodies. (d) Because of his health condition he becomes incapacitated and irresponsible to exercise the profession. (e) His actions and behavior constitute a violation of the Code of Ethics and Deontology Medical and legislation in force.

372. The purpose of drafting and approving this regulation is: (a) to establish the basic principles and rules to ensure an objective disciplinary judgment on fairness and impartiality; (b) to protect the member of the Order from an arbitrary and undeserved punishment; (c) through the disciplinary trial, based on the complaints/ denunciations received in the Order of misdemeanors record (which constitute negligent medication) as well as medical errors to prevent their repetition in medical practices, in defense of patient and public health.

B. *Rules of Professional Conduct and Standards of Discretion, Probity and Dignity*

1. The Code of Medical Ethics and Deontology

373. Medical deontology is a set of principles and rules which the doctor is obliged to recognize and respect during the exercise of the profession. The behavior of the doctor outside the exercise of the profession must be exemplary in accordance with the dignity it requires in this profession. Doctors are obliged to know the principles and rules contained in this Code and adapt professional behavior.

374. Upon registration with the Order of Doctors, every physician is required to provide a written acknowledgment of this Code, alongside the doctor's oath, affirming their commitment to adhere to its principles with precision and full dedication.

This formal acknowledgment underscores the ethical and professional responsibilities inherent in the medical profession, reinforcing the obligation to uphold the highest standards of integrity and care.

375. The fundamental duty of every doctor, in their service to both individual and public health, is to safeguard human life, promote physical and mental well-being, and alleviate suffering. This core responsibility underscores the ethical commitment of the medical profession to prioritize the dignity, health, and welfare of patients above all else. His mission is humane, in respect of human life, of the individual and his dignity, for the protection of health, detection and treatment of diseases; the doctor is based only on science and his conscience, giving priority to the interests of the patient's health (Article 4 The Code of Medical Ethics and Deontology). The doctor is not allowed to use his knowledge contrary to these interests. The rules for the provision of mental healthcare are regulated by a separate law (Article 13 Law No. 10 107, dated 30.3.2009)

376. The doctor is obliged to provide healthcare, in times of peace and war, and medical assistance in accordance with the principles of effective treatment, the same for everyone, without difference in age, sex, race, nationality, religion, political views, economic status, social position, etc., respecting the rights and dignity of the patient (Article 5 The Code of Medical Ethics and Deontology).

377. In case of war or natural disasters, the doctor must be immediately engaged and made available to the competent authorities to offer his assistance (Article 6 The Code of Medical Ethics and Deontology). The doctor must respect and protect the best traditions of the medical profession, consistently practicing high professional standards and appropriate ethical behavior toward the patient, family members and any other person who asks for help (Article 7 The Code of Medical Ethics and Deontology).

378. Under no circumstances is a doctor permitted to exploit the privileges and advantages conferred by their professional status for personal or professional gain at the expense of the patient. Doctors holding administrative roles or serving in public office are further obligated to ensure the highest level of transparency in all matters that might present a conflict of interest. This principle upholds the integrity of the medical profession and fosters trust between doctors, patients, and the public. He is forbidden to use his function and position to increase the clientele or for other illegal personal benefits (Article 8 The Code of Medical Ethics and Deontology). The doctor, even outside the exercise of the profession, must keep his figure clean by avoiding any act that would invalidate his personality and human dignity and profession. Under no circumstances should he allow his name to be used for publicity and profitable purposes (Article 11 The Code of Medical Ethics and Deontology).

379. In the presence of a sick or injured person in danger of life, or when called for such a case, the doctor, regardless of his professional profile, has the duty to intervene in every place and circumstance to provide emergency assistance, assisting until the moment he makes sure he is getting qualified medical help (Article 9 The Code of Medical Ethics and Deontology).

380. Doctors have a duty to maintain good and honest relations with each other and with other members of the medical staff, respecting professional independence of each other, in the interest of the sick and maintaining the good name of the profession and the medical institution (Article 10 The Code of Medical Ethics and Deontology).

2. On Gifts and Financing

381. The doctor is prohibited from asking for or accepting gifts or illegal financing and compromising from companies, firms or individuals that sell medicines, equipment or other medical materials, apart from financing which is authorized only for accredited activities, which are organized for the purpose of education and professional doctor training (Article 59 The Code of Medical Ethics and Deontology).

III. Biomedical Ethics Committee

A. Disciplinary Commissions

382. Commissions operate next to the National Disciplinary Commission and the Regional Disciplinary Commission. The National and Regional Disciplinary Commissions consist of 15, respectively and 9 members, who are approved by decision of the relevant council. For any disciplinary trial case the trial bodies are established from the total number of these Commissions. Disciplinary Commissions are bodies of independent professional disciplinary judgment. They verify and examine complaints and requests that come from any person or institution in the Order of Doctors for violation of Medical Ethics and Deontology, for professional malpractice and medical errors. Criteria for selection and approval of members, organization of disciplinary processes are based on the regulation of the Professional Disciplinary Judgment, which is approved by decision of National Council (Article 33 the Statute of the Order of Doctors of Albania).

383. The disciplinary commission investigates and judges based on the facts and evidence administered and the hearing with the member of the Order, against whom disciplinary measures may be taken. Professional Disciplinary Judgment is independent, impartial, objective and fair. All complaints received in the Order of Doctors, without exception, are registered in the register of complaints and are subject to consideration in the relevant Regional Council only written complaints, according to the "A" format and signed by the appellant, who must note the contact number and his full address. The Order of Doctors accepts and undertakes disciplinary actions only for issues that belong to his legal attributes, which are related to the exercise of the profession by facing them with the normative acts in force (law, code, statute, decisions, etc.).

384. They are all subject to judgment in the hearing session and in the Disciplinary Commission appeal cases, except for those who agree to close the case. The parties in the trial have the right to be assisted in defense or to be represented in the trial by a person whom they appoint themselves. This can be a doctor, preferably with the same specialty to which the respondent doctor or licensed attorney belongs. When the Disciplinary Trial Commission of the first or second instance requires the presence of the parties, then they are obliged to be present, regardless of the presence of their doctor or lawyer.

385. The lawyer of the National Council of the Order of Doctors controls the implementation and compliance, gives instructions and takes measures to fix the identified defects. For problems that he considers necessary, he informs the President of the National Council of the Order of Doctors in the Republic of Albania. When the appealed case has been referred to the judicial bodies, the Order of Doctors carries out all actions in accordance with this regulation, creating a complete case file. From this one moment, the Disciplinary Action is suspended to be continued after the decision of final form by the judicial bodies if the case is related to the Order of Doctors from these bodies, and if there is reason to undertake a further disciplinary process.

B. *Disciplinary Action for Members of the Order of Doctors Who Are Foreign Citizens*

386. Foreign doctors practicing their profession within the territory of the Republic of Albania are subject to disciplinary proceedings in accordance with this Regulation like everyone else. In any case, they are obliged to appear with their translator. The disciplinary measure imposed on them is notified to the corresponding body of the respective country (To the Order, Chamber or Association) (Article 5 Regulation about professional disciplinary judgment).

C. *Disciplinary Judgment Committees*

387. Adjudication Commissions function next to the First and second instance Professional Disciplinary Regional Councils and the National Council. Professional Disciplinary Trial Commissions of the first instance are set up next to each Regional Council. These commissions consist of (nine members of which seven doctors and two lawyers. For each case under trial, only three of these two doctors and one lawyer are appointed as members of the Professional Disciplinary Trial Commission. The National Commission for Professional Disciplinary Judgment of the second instance is established by the National Council. This Commission consists of fifteen members, of which thirteen doctors and two lawyers. For each case in the second instance trial, only five of the members of this commission, four doctors and one lawyer are assigned to the composition of the Professional Disciplinary Trial Commission (Article 6 Regulation about professional disciplinary judgment).

D. Selection and Appointment of Commissioners

388. Candidates for members of Professional Disciplinary Judgment Commissions of first instance are selected by the Regional Council and approved by the decision of this Council. Candidates for members of the National Commission of Professional Disciplinary Judgment second instance (Appeal) are selected by the President of the National Council and approved by decision of the National Council. Legal candidates for members of Professional Disciplinary Judgment Commissions are preferable to be selected by lawyers (lawyers of health institutions or licensed lawyers), who have over ten years of work experience. Candidates for members of the Commissions of both levels are taken approval in advance, and only after they have agreed, they are proposed for decision in the relevant council (Article 7 Regulation about professional disciplinary judgment).

E. Selection Criteria

389. Candidates for members of Professional Disciplinary Judgment Commissions are selected guided by these criteria: (a) experience of not less than ten years in practicing the profession; (b) ethical-moral and professional prestige and reputation; (c) preferably experience in administrative activities; (d) it is categorically forbidden to elect persons who are appointed to leadership positions in the administration of state institutions or in party forums of any level (Article 8 Regulation about professional disciplinary judgment). The mandate of the member of the Commission, at both levels of judgment, is five years, with the right of reappointment (Article 9 Regulation about professional disciplinary judgment). The premature release from duty of the member of the Commission takes place when they: (a) submit a written request for resignation; (b) are convicted by a final decision for criminal offenses or misdemeanors administrative-disciplinary; (c) are absent three times, without justified reasons, in professional judgment sessions; (d) are disabled with mental health reasons (Article 10 Regulation about professional disciplinary judgment).

F. Establishment of Disciplinary Commissions

390. The composition of the Professional Disciplinary Commission, as well as the Chairman of the Commission is appointed: (a) for the first instance by decision of the President of the Regional Council, and in his absence, the deputy; (b) for the second instance (Appeal) by decision of the President of the National Council, and in his absence, the deputy. The chairman of the Commission (adjudicatory body) in both stages of the trial is a doctor (Article 11 Regulation about professional disciplinary judgment).

G. Prohibition for Participation in Disciplinary Commissions

391. It is forbidden to participate in Professional Disciplinary Trials, as well as in auxiliary teams' persons who are related by gender, kinship or any other social or friendly relationship with persons on trial. Their non-declaration leads to the suspension of the trial and the annulment of the decision when the trial has been completed. Measures are taken against the person, and the costs of the trial are charged (Article 12 Regulation about professional disciplinary judgment). For every case of complaint or denunciation in function of the disciplinary process, teams are established auxiliary composition: (a) a doctor with the duty of relator/reporter. Depending on the case, there may be more than one; (b) Secretary of the Disciplinary Trial Commission; (c) medical, forensic or legal expert, one or more depending on the case at trial (Article 13 Regulation about professional disciplinary judgment).

H. Tasks of the Relator/Reporter and Sequence of Actions in the Preliminary Verification

392. The relator has the duty to make an accurate and objective preliminary verification of the case and verify factors from several sources. To fulfill this task, the relator performs the following actions: (a) meets the defendant doctor to whom he asks for details or clarifications if they are deemed necessary; (b) if necessary, meet the director of the institution where the defendant doctor works; (c) obtain copies of clinical documents, as well as other documents related to the case; (d) obtain the necessary evidence from doctors and other medical personnel or other persons, where the defendant doctor works. Evidence is obtained in writing and signed by the person interviewed; (e) at the end of the preliminary verification, the relator/reporter drafts the final report of verifying the case, which he signs and delivers to the secretary of the Regional Council. The preliminary verification is completed no later than thirty days after the appointment of the relator (Article 14 Regulation about professional disciplinary judgment).

Part II. The Physician-Patient Relationship

Chapter 1. General Description

393. The Code of Medical Ethics and Deontology is the basic document of the medical profession, in which all the principles and professional standards are mandatory to be recognized and implemented by every member of the Order in the medical practice, as well as from any health institution. The National Council has the responsibility to draft and approve the Code of Medical Ethics and Deontology (Article 19 Law No. 123/2014) (*see* paragraph 487).

Obligation to comply with the Code

394. It is the duty of all doctors, medical students who assist or replace doctors on duty, as well as practicing doctors to recognize and apply the provisions of this Code throughout the professional career. Ignorance does not exclude anyone from responsibility and punitive measures for any offense committed (Article 67 The Code of Medical Ethics and Deontology) (*see* paragraph 933).

Notification of the Doctors' Order for violations

395. Each doctor has the duty to notify the relevant Regional Council of the Order of Doctors of all violations, which in his judgment and evaluation are in violation of the provisions of this Code (Article 69 The Code of Medical Ethics and Deontology) (*see* paragraph 488).

396. The Code of Medical Ethics and Deontology is the basic document of the medical profession, in which all the principles and professional standards are mandatory to be recognized and implemented by every member of the Order in the medical practice, as well as from any health institution (Article 19 Law No. 123/2014) (*see* paragraph 484).

Notification of the Doctors' Order for violations

397. Each doctor has the duty to notify the relevant Regional Council of the Order of Doctors of all violations, which in his judgment and evaluation are in violation of the provisions of this Code (Article 69 The Code of Medical Ethics and Deontology) (*see* paragraph 486).

§1. RIGHTS AND DUTIES OF PHYSICIANS AND PATIENTS

I. Diagnostic and Treatment Procedures

398. When processing the diagnosis and setting the treatment for his patient, the doctor must propose and describe those diagnostic and treatment procedures, which in his judgment are considered more suitable for the circumstances of the patient, scientifically proven contemporary and economically at a lower cost. The doctor is not allowed to take unjustified risks with his prescription for the health and life of the patient. He must formulate his descriptions in accordance with clinical guidelines and approved protocols, clearly and comprehensibly for the patient and for others (Article 27 The Code of Medical Ethics and Deontology).

II. Continuity of Treatment

399. Whatever the circumstances, the doctor has the duty to ensure the continuation of the treatment of his sickness. Even in case of a public danger, the doctor should not abandon his patients, except by Order from the responsible authorities in accordance with the Law. In cases where the doctor will leave the task for a while, or when he judges that the patient's problems or health condition are beyond his professional skills and knowledge, or out of other possibilities to treat him, then the doctor has a duty to take all measures for the patient to switch to continue treatment with another doctor relevant field able to undertake this treatment (Article 30 The Code of Medical Ethics and Deontology).

III. Changing the Treating Doctor

400. The doctor has the right to give up or refuse to continue the treatment of the patient and recommends his treatment at a doctor or other institution in the following cases: (a) for professional or personal reasons; (b) when the patient, capable and conscious of making independent decisions, loses trust in the doctor, and (c) when the patient, who is conscious, behaves inappropriately, becomes brutal and threatening to the doctor. Even in these cases, if the patient is in a medical emergency, the doctor has the duty to provide medical assistance until overcoming the situation or have ensured the continuation of treatment by another doctor (Article 31 The Code of Medical Ethics and Deontology).

IV. Medical Aid for Convicts

401. When the doctor who is called or works in an institution where convicts suffer the measure of punishment and notes that the person to whom he was called is a victim of ill-treatment, he should not only offer him medical help but also protect his rights and dignity. If, due to age, physical or mental condition, he is not good at defending himself, the doctor must notify the competent bodies recognized by law (Article 32 The Code of Medical Ethics and Deontology).

402. The doctor is categorically forbidden to participate or assist in violence or torture against the defendant. Forced treatment and feeding are allowed only in cases where the convict is not sick and mentally capable of making up his own mind. If an adult, mentally sound and conscious, refuses food of his own will, the doctor must respect the will of the sick (Article 33 The Code of Medical Ethics and Deontology).

V. Reports of a Doctor with the Treating Doctor and the Patient

403. The mutual relations of the doctor with the treating doctor and with the patient should be correct, sincere and honest, in respect of which doctors should apply these ethical rules and principles: (1) when the doctor is asked to provide medical care for a sick person, who has as a doctor curating another colleague: (a) if he is asked to receive medical treatment as a treating physician, he can accept it with the knowledge of the other treating doctor, when the patient himself wants to give up the latter; (b) if he is simply asked for a consultation, but not to change the treating doctor, he proposes one joint consultation with the attending physician. If he does not agree, he is given the required counseling and, if necessary, provided emergency medical treatment. In conclusion, with the patient's consent, the treating doctor is informed about everything; (c) if a sick person presents himself because his attending physician is absent, he is provided with care necessary medically until the return of his attending physician. To the latter, with consent of the patient, the necessary information is given. (2) If a sick person came without the recommendation and knowledge of his curative doctor, it is an ethical obligation and in the interest of the patient that the doctor, after receiving his consent, contact the attending physician in order to exchange their thoughts. (3) A consultant doctor who examined a patient together with a colleague or his colleagues is not allowed to reexamine on his own initiative the sick in continuation of the same disease, without the presence of the treating doctor or its approval, except in case of emergency (Article 47 The Code of Medical Ethics and Deontology).

VI. Complaints of the Sick

404. If the sick has complaints about healthcare or medication, then they must be given an immediate and appropriate response. The attending physician has the responsibility to deal with complaints constructively and honestly. In case during treatment, the patient has suffered serious injuries, regardless of the reason, it must be fully explained to him that what happened and possibly ask him for forgiveness, or, when he is 16 years old, his family members (Article 33 The Code of Medical Ethics and Deontology).

§2. Informed Consent

405. The patient has the right to be informed about the disease, examinations and treatments that their results are also proposed. The doctor has the duty to inform the patient in such a way honest and understandable, considering in each case his personality and psychic condition. If the patient is less than 16 years old or unable to understand the condition and the medication that is proposed, the information is given to the closest relative who has custody. If the doctor judges that informing the patient risks harming his mental and health condition, then he is not obliged to inform him or to get to know him of medical documentation. A severe diagnosis and fatal prognosis can be detected with a lot of discretion. However, family members should be informed and warned, except if the patient himself has previously determined the persons who can be informed about his condition (Article 25 The Code of Medical Ethics and Deontology).

406. A doctor is obligated to demonstrate understanding and mutual respect toward the patient's family members. They must keep the family informed about medical procedures, the care being provided, the patient's progress, and potential outcomes, as long as doing so does not conflict with the patient's expressed wishes. This responsibility underscores the importance of clear communication and compassion in fostering trust and support within the patient-caregiver-family dynamic (Article 26 The Code of Medical Ethics and Deontology).

I. Consent after Information (Informed Consent)

407. Law No. 44/2012 For Mental Health defines "Informed consent" as the consent obtained from a person for their inclusion or not in a procedure of assessing his needs, receiving or not receiving a service that meets his needs, only after the person has been fully informed about the procedure, service and alternatives others for assessing and meeting his needs.

408. It is an obligation for every doctor to obtain the consent of the patient before any intervention, examination or proposed treatments, after having informed him in detail and be convinced that the patient has understood. When the patient, able to express his will, refuses the proposed intervention, the doctor must accept the will of the patient, after having informed and convinced him of the expected consequences. If the patient is under 16 years of age, or unable to express his will for making decisions, the doctor cannot intervene without notifying the patient's relatives, except in cases of urgency or impossibility to contact these people. Informing the patient and obtaining consent or its refusal are expressed in writing in the clinical file of the patient and it is signed by him or the legitimate persons who have custody (Article 28 The Code of Medical Ethics and Deontology).

409. The doctor must try to enable his patient to benefit from all the rights, social or material benefits that are due to him by law due to his health condition.

Any abuse, fraud or falsification of medical documents for this consent is punishable by law (Article 29 The Code of Medical Ethics and Deontology).

410. Upon an investigation of the Albanian medical jurisprudence, the author could not find any relevant legal decision dealing with the right to choose medical treatment. Focusing on the primary legal sources, Article 6(1)(ç) Law No. 10.107 of 30.03.2009 codifies informed consent (IC) for medical treatments. Article 96 of the CCr punishes reckless medication, which might also include the case of medical treatment without the prior consent of the patient. While consent to medical treatment is established as a general rule (Article 6(2)(ç) Law No. 10.107 of 30.03.2009), IC has even been highlighted in the case of mental illness (Law No. 44/2012 of 19.4.2012 on the mental health), palliative patients (Law 138/2014 of 16.10.2014 on palliative care), and in cases of transplantation of tissues, cells, and organs (Law No. 10.454 of 21.7.2011 on transplantation of tissues, cells, and organs). In addition, Bylaw No. 101 of 04.02.2015 has established the right to free access to medical treatments. The Albanian Ministry of Health has also approved the Card of Patient Rights (Decree of the Albanian Ministry of Health No. 657 of 15.02. 2010). The Commissioner for Personal Data Protection has also established specific rules dealing with IC (Instruction No. 5 of 26.5.2010) since medical data are considered to be sensitive data (Article 3(2) Law No. 9887 of 10.03.2008 on the protection of personal data). The examination of the two main public bodies, the National Ethics Committee[132] and the National Committee of Health,[133] established as advisory bodies for medical issues, resulted in finding no relevant documents regarding IC. Furthermore, particular attention is given to Article 28 Code of Medical Ethics since this Code is mandatory for all physicians practicing in Albania.

II. Consent of the Patient or Waiver

411. Alleviating suffering and pain is one of the physician's essential duties to any sick person. This is especially important when treating a disease leading to death the doctor, in addition to the medication, which should be as light as possible and without hopeless excesses, must offer assistance and spiritual care, respecting the wishes and religious belief of the patient and preserving his dignity until the end. The doctor should inform the family members of the patient about his condition and try to find their cooperation in alleviating the suffering of the patient (Article 38 The Code of Medical Ethics and Deontology).

412. Speeding up the end of life or provoking death is against medical ethics. If the patient is unconscious, without hope of living, the doctor must act in his best judgment. The doctor must consult with other colleagues and the closest family

132. Decision of the Council of Ministers No. 595 of Sep. 21, 1998, which was abrogated on Jul. 15, 2015.
133. Article 6/1 Law No. 10 107 of Mar. 30, 2009, which was added with the law of 27/2019 of May 8, 2019. However, it should be mentioned that this Committee works more on the general policies rather than on the ethical policies.

members of the patient to decide on the therapeutic attitude to be maintained (Article 39 The Code of Medical Ethics and Deontology).

413. When a sick person dies, the attending physician must express his condolences to the family members and to explain the causes and circumstances of death. They must be informed with all the necessary details for the ambiguities and questions that may arise (Article 40 The Code of Medical Ethics and Deontology).

414. The doctor is not allowed to perform mutilating interventions without a very serious medical motive, without giving prior information to the patient and his consent. An exception is made only in urgent cases and when it is impossible to inform and obtain the patient's consent (Article 41 The Code of Medical Ethics and Deontology).

A. *Giver of Informed Consent: The Treating Party*

415.

a. In Albania, while the law only recognizes the right to informed consent (IC) (Article 6(2)(ç) Law No. 10.107 of 30.03.2009), the Code of Medical Ethics underlines that the physician shall give the information. According to the Code of Medical Ethics, in addition to the legal notion of a physician, there is also the notion of a curing physician who can give all the needed medical information. By interpreting this Code and considering the importance of IC, delegation to the medical staff, trainees, or assistants is impossible. Although the legal doctrine is absent for the division of pre-treatment information and therapeutic information, the interpretation of Article 28 Code of Medical Ethics and Articles 5 and 9 of the Decree of the Albanian Ministry of Health No. 657 of 15.02.2010 and of Article 2(6) and (7) Bylaw No. 101 of 04.02.2015, it seems that the Albanian legislature has considered a division between these two types of medical information. While Article 28 of the Code of Medical Ethics focuses only on pre-treatment information, the bylaw and the Ministerial order are divided into two different parts: pre-treatment information and therapeutic information.
b. It seems that the Albanian legislature has distinguished between these types of information for two main reasons, both of which aim to better protect patients. First, while in the case of contractual liability (violation of pre-treatment information), the plaintiff (the patient) shall prove only the contract and the absence of contractual fulfillment (Article 476(1) CCv), in the case of tort liability, the patient shall also prove the damage, the causality, as well as the physician's fault (Articles 608–612 CCv). Thus, contractual liability is easier to be proved by the defendant, whereas the physician, shall prove that s/he was not negligent. Second, it shall be underlined that the prescription for the contract liability is ten years (Article 114 CCv), while the prescription for the tort liability is only three years (Article 115(1)(dh) CCv).
c. In Albania, the importance of the timing of IC is established clearly in Articles 19 and 25 Code of Medical Ethics, as well as Articles 6 and 7 Card of Patient

Rights (Decree of the Albanian Ministry of Health No. 657 of 15.02. 2010). Indeed, the explanatory notes of these articles state that medical information shall be given at least twenty-four hours before the operation. Additionally, physicians shall spend the necessary time to explain all the medical information in a simple and comprehensive manner. However, Article 7 clearly states that information depends on the urgency of the medical treatment. Thus, in case of an emergency, the medical treatment cannot be delayed twenty-four hours from the time that the medical information was given.

d. In addition, the right to refuse medical information or medical treatment is established in Article 28 Code of Medical Ethics and Article 4 Card of Patient Rights. Patients can revoke IC even during treatment. This means that IC or medical treatment is not a duty but a right. This interpretation is consistent with the concrete application of the constitutional right of human dignity, the ethical principle of autonomy, and the right to self-determination. The law or bylaw do not establish cases where patients should not be informed. Furthermore, Article 25(3) of the Code of Medical Ethics considers the case of physician duty to not inform the patient if the information would damage the patient's psychological and physical health. These are rare cases for two main reasons. First, the next sentence of Article 25(3) of the Code of Medical Ethics states that severe diagnosis and fatal prognosis can also be communicated to patients with great caution. Second, the duty to not be informed is legitimate if the information brings psychological *and* physical health, which should be considered complementary.

e. Regarding the burden of proof, the general rules will be applied since neither the codes (CCv, CCr, CCvP, CCrP) nor the law nor bylaws establish ad hoc rules for the burden of proof. This makes the position of the victims more difficult since it is quite difficult to prove health damage. However, it should be mentioned that Article 260 of the CCvP establishes that those which are private documents, the books or documents of the medical staff that are written in conformity to the legal provisions are considered to be full evidence (Article 263 of the CCvP).

B. Receiver of Informed Consent and Its Object: The Patient and the Information

416.

a. Focusing on the Albanian legislation, in addition to the legal concepts of legal capacity (Article 1 CCr), and competency (Article 6 CCr), Article 7 recognizes minors older than 14 years old to conclude valid contracts through means that s/he disposes of his/her earnings from work. Nevertheless, it should be noted that the legal age for employment is 16 years old for the "easy jobs," which are jobs that do not impact child development and are yearly defined by the Council of Ministers (Article 99 Labor Code). Focusing on IC, Articles 25(2) and 28(3) Code of Medical Ethics establishes an age limit of 16. However, it should be mentioned that, as in Germany, in the case of an emergency, parents' consent is not needed.

b. In Albania, children less than 16 years old are not entitled to participate in the decision process. Indeed, this rule is also established in Article 20(2) Code of Medical Ethics. This rule is unconstitutional since it is not coherent with Article 6(2) of the Convention on Human Rights and Biomedicine (Oviedo Convention). Article 6(2) Oviedo Convention states that *the opinion of the minor shall be taken into consideration as an increasingly determining factor in proportion to his or her age and degree of maturity*. The Code of Medical Ethics should be aligned not only with the national legal system (constitution, law, and bylaws) but must also be in accordance with any international agreements ratified by the country (Article 116 Albanian Constitution). In July 2011, the Oviedo Convention came into effect in Albania. Consequently, Article 20(2) of the Code of Medical Ethics contradicts the Oviedo Convention, which also means that it is not in harmony with the constitutional principle established in Article 116 of the Albanian Constitution.

c. Focusing on the case of adults that are incapable to give IC, in Albania, from 2003, with the introduction of the Family Code, there is a similar institution as the *Betreuung*. While Article 10 CCv and Articles 382–387 CCvP considers only the case of incapacity to contract due to a state of pathological mental disturbance that prevents the free exercise of will, Articles 307–313 Family Code extends the power of the Guardianship (*kujdestari*) also to health issues (Article 310 Family Code). However, while in Germany there is a difference between the proxy of legal and economic issues and the legal institution of *Betreuung*, in Albania, the same person is nominated by the court for the legal and economic issues and health issues.

d. In Albania, it is interesting to notice the involvement of the patient's family. First, in the case that information cannot be given to the patient because this information can negatively impact his psychological and physical health, the information shall be shared with his family, except in cases where patients have clearly negated this approach. Second, and maybe more important, Article 26 (Informing Family Members) states that *the doctor has the duty to show understanding and concern to family members. She or he should keep them informed of the medical procedures and care provided to the patient, his progress and perspective, provided that such a thing does not go against the will of the patient.* [author' translation]

e. Upon reviewing the national policies dealing with sharing information with the family, the two different approaches were noticed: the information to the family can be given unless the patient has decided the contrary, *or* the information to the family is given only if there is the express consent of the patient (Pupe & Veshi, 2021). While the first approach is taken in France[134] as well as in Albania, the second one is applied in Italy,[135] Spain,[136] and Portugal.[137] Thus, while the German Code of

134. Article 35 (3) code of Medical Ethics in France states: *great care must be taken in revealing a terminal prognosis, but persons close to the patient should normally be informed, unless the patient has already indicated that he does not wish them to be informed or has designated third parties to whom the information should be given.* [author' translation]

135. Article 34(1) code of Medical Ethics in Italy states: *Information to third parties may be provided with the explicit consent expressed by the assisted person, without prejudice to the provisions of Articles 10* [the case of professional secrets given to other doctors] *and 12* [information about the patient given to him or his legal representative], *when the health or life of the person himself or of others is in grave danger* [author' translation]

Medical Ethics does not include at all a family right to be informed, in Albania, Article 26 of Code of Medical Ethics focuses on the right to family members to be informed.

f. While in Albania Law No. 10.107 of 30 March 2009 does not specify the object of IC, Article 25(1) Code of Medical Ethics underlines the importance of the subjective approach to IC; physicians shall consider the patient's personality and psychological health. This approach is similar to the current German approach established in 1962. In addition, Article 25(1) Code of Medical Ethics states that patients have the right to be informed regarding the disease and examinations as well as medical treatments and their results. Unfortunately, the Code of Medical Ethics includes neither the right to be informed of the nature or the purpose nor for any circumstances which are relevant to consent, including its risks. Nevertheless, the Code of Medical Ethics shall be interpreted in correlation with the Albanian legal framework. In other words, the Oviedo Convention and the Albanian Patient Card should be considered. Article 5 Oviedo Convention includes in the object of IC also the purpose and nature of the intervention as well as its risks. According to Article 116(1)(b) Albanian Constitution, since 2011, Oviedo Convention is part of the Albanian legal framework. Second, Articles 3 and 4 Patient Card include in the object of IC also any type of medical information related to him as well alternative medical treatments. According to Article 116(3) Albanian Constitution, *normative acts of ministers are effective within the sphere of their jurisdiction in the entire territory of the Republic of Albania.* Thus, although the Code of Medical Ethics has some gaps, these gaps are filled by the Oviedo Convention and the Albanian Patient Card.

g. In Albania, neither the legal framework nor the case law specify the modalities that information should be given. However, via the interpretation of the Patient Card as well as the Code of Medical Ethics, similar results are given. Both Article 25(1) Code of Medical Ethics and Article 4 Patient Card recognize the importance of comprehensive medical information. Despite medical information being better understood through oral communication, which provides the patient with the opportunity to ask various questions, for legal evidence, written forms are necessary. In addition, if patients do not speak Albanian, an interpreter is needed since the information shall be comprehensive for the patient.

136. This is the result of the international aspect of Arts. 9(2), 15(2), and 27(7) of the Spanish Code of Medical Ethics. In more concrete terms, Art. 9(2) states: *In the exercise of their profession, doctors will act correctly and delicately, respecting the privacy of the patient.* Art. 15(2) underlines that *the information is to be transmitted directly to the patient, persons designated by him or his/her legal representative. The physician shall respect the patient's right not to be informed, noting this in the medical record*; Art. 27(7) reads that *the doctor will preserve the confidentiality of patients in their social life, work and family.*

137. Article 50 (4) code of Medical Ethics in Portugal states: *the diagnosis and prognosis can only be made known to third parties, namely family members, with the express consent of the patient, unless the patient is minor or cognitively incompetent, without prejudice to the provisions of article 89 of this Code.* [author' translation]

§3. PRIVACY

417. In support of the Law on the Protection of Personal Data, the Order of Doctors maintains all personal data of its members. The National Register of Order of Doctors of Albania and the doctor's personal data are part of the privacy of the Order of Doctors. Personal data extraction or their processing in violation of the law on the protection of personal data constitutes an administrative offense (Article 15 Law No. 10 171, dated 22.10.2009).

418. The doctor is not allowed to interfere in personal or family problems of the patient nor try to influence his privacy, except when this is justified for professional reasons related to his illness or medical treatment (Article 21 The Code of Medical Ethics and Deontology).

I. Participation in the Session and Communication with the Media

419. For the participation of guests and the public in the professional disciplinary hearings, is decided for each case separately by the Relevant Professional Disciplinary Trial Commission, considering the preservation and non-infringement of privacy for both litigants. It is prohibited to provide information to the media before the final decision is announced by the Professional Disciplinary Appeal Commission (Article 23 Regulation about professional disciplinary judgment).

§4. DUTY OF MEDICAL SECRECY

420. The data that the doctor learns about his patient during the performance of his duties are considered medical secrets and constitute a professional secret. With the wish of the patient and in his interest, the doctor is obliged to keep and preserve the secret even from family members and other people of everything he was entrusted with and everything he saw and heard during his work with the sick. Even after the patient's death, except in cases where it poses a risk for the health and life of others, the doctor must not reveal the professional secret (Article 22 The Code of Medical Ethics and Deontology).

421. Regarding the disclosure of confidential information, a doctor is permitted to reveal a patient's medical secrets only under specific circumstances: when withholding such information poses a danger to the patient's life, or when disclosure is mandated by a legally recognized authority. This principle balances the ethical obligation of maintaining patient confidentiality with the need to protect life and comply with legal requirements. When the doctor uses the medical data of his patient to publish them, he is forced that the identity of the patient not revealed (Article 23 The Code of Medical Ethics and Deontology).

§5. COMPLAINTS

422. Complaints against decisions on giving disciplinary measures by the disciplinary commission of the regional council are presented to the disciplinary commission of the National Council of the Order of Doctors within fifteen days from the date of written communication of the decision. The disciplinary commission, within sixty days from the date of receiving the complaint, is obliged to give the decision on the submitted appeal. The decision of the disciplinary commission of the National Council appeals to the competent court for the resolution of administrative disputes (Article 18 Law No. 123/2014). The Order accepts and examines without exception the complaints and denunciations that come from: (a) patients, their families and other citizens; (b) Ministry of Health, as well as other public or private health institutions; (c) non-health institutions of public or private administration; (d) Members of the Order of Doctors, as well as other health professions; (e) mass media organs (Article 4 Regulation about professional disciplinary judgment).

423. In case of failure to meet the criteria for license renewal, the Regional Council of the Order of Doctors refuses to renew the doctor's license. The doctor, who was refused the renewal of the license, has the right to submit his complaint to the Registration, Licensing and Professional Practice Sector at the National Council of the Order of Doctors of Albania. After receiving the complaint of the doctor who was denied relicensing and after withdrawal of the file from the relevant Regional Council, the case is transferred to the Licensing Commission for treatment, who decides on this matter. The decision taken by the Licensing Commission is mandatory for each Regional Council (Article 11 Law No. 10 171, dated 22.10.2009).

424. Regarding any decision given by the Regional Council to the doctor regarding non-registration or non-renewal of the license, the doctor has the right to present within fifteen days complaint to the Registration, Licensing and Professional Practice Sector at the National Council. Regarding any decision given by the Licensing Commission regarding the non-registration of doctors, as well as related to the decisions appealed to the Registration and Licensing Sector and Professional Practice to the decisions of the Regional Council, the doctor has the right to file a complaint, in accordance with the Code of Administrative Procedures, addressing the competent court. Final decisions related to the complaint made by the doctor, referred to in the above paragraphs, are mandatory for the Regional Council (Article 14 Law No. 10 171, dated 22.10.2009).

§6. ACCESS TO MEDICAL RECORDS

I. Confidentiality

425. Professional confidentiality is the storage of data on the state of health of a patient to unauthorized persons. The persons who develop activities provided for in this law are obliged to maintain the confidentiality of all information received from the patient in health institutions, and his personal health data, according to the legislation in force. These persons are excluded from the obligation to preserve professional secrecy only when the information is given to the attending physician, the patient and/or residential institutions, as well as the bodies that have the right to request this information by law (Article 7, Law No. 44/2012 For Mental Health).

426. Regardless of the public or private health institution in which a doctor works, he has duty to respond to any official request to be made available and cooperated when investigations are carried out or various information related to it is requested his illness or any other matter. He should assist the authorities concerned, which must necessarily be officially legalized, adhering to the provisions of this Code for respecting and maintaining professional secrecy. It is a basic norm of medical ethics for every doctor, regardless of the institution where he works, to respect the patient's right to choose his doctor and when circumstances make it possible to have this doctor present in every medical treatment procedure to which this patient is subjected (Article 66 The Code of Medical Ethics and Deontology).

II. Issuance of Medical Documents

427. All diagnostic and treatment actions carried out in clinical practice in all types of outpatient service and profile, hospital, public or private, the doctor prescribes (records) special medical documents that are stored and maintained in accordance with the provisions that the health institution applies under conditions of respect and confidentiality of the profession. The doctor has the duty to create the patient's individual clinical file, which is completed and saved under the responsibility of the attending physician as an important clinical document, research-scientific and legal forensic. He has the duty to describe in the clinical record clearly understandable diagnoses, examinations and their interpretations, treatments and the arguments for every change he makes, as well as the medical consultations that are carried out for the patient (Article 34 The Code of Medical Ethics and Deontology).

428. In medical practice, the preparation of medical documents such as certificates, epicrises, and testimonies is essential, and their issuance should be carried out upon the request of the patient, family members, or legally recognized authorities. Every document completed and issued by a doctor must be accurate, fully reflective of medical findings, and legibly written. Additionally, the identity of the signatory and their signature must be clearly identifiable, ensuring the document's authenticity and reliability (Article 35 The Code of Medical Ethics and Deontology).

429. Any inaccuracy and inconsistency with medical findings and abuse in prescribing and the issuance of medical documents constitutes the object of follow-up and confrontation with the professional processes and legal disciplinary judgment for the responsible persons (Article 36 The Code of Medical Ethics and Deontology).

III. Personal Professional Indicators

430. The only indications that the doctor is allowed to present on the prescriptions, documents and the various announcements it publishes are: – name, surname, address, phone number and consultation hours (Article 61 The Code of Medical Ethics and Deontology).

431. The signs that the doctor is allowed to display at the entrance to his office are:

- his first and last name;
- consultation hours;
- legal (official) professional titles licensed and authorized by the Order of Physicians for exercise.

432. When the doctor holds a foreign diploma, then the country and the university that issued the diploma or certificate authorizing him to practice this profession must be specified (Article 61 The Code of Medical Ethics and Deontology).

Chapter 2. The Physician-Patient Relationship in Specific Terms

§1. The Minor Patient

433. In the exercise of the profession, the doctor must engage in the care of children, the elderly and the handicapped, especially when you notice that in the family or non-family environment where they live, they do not take enough care of their health. The doctor who is called to treat a minor, physically or mentally incompetent, must try to obtain the consent of his parents, relatives or legal representatives. An exception is made when the case is urgent, and the doctor is unable to communicate with these people. In case of suspicion of abuse or mistreatment of the child, or of a handicap, the doctor is obliged to notify the competent bodies recognized by law (Article 20 The Code of Medical Ethics and Deontology).

434. Article 124/b of Law No. 7895 dated 27.1.1995 CCr of the Republic of Albania deals with Child abuse. Physical or psychological abuse of a minor by parents, sister, brother, grandfather, grandmother, legal guardian or any person who is obliged to take care of him shall be sentenced to imprisonment from three months to two years. Forcing, exploiting, pushing or using a minor to work, to provide income, to beg or to perform actions that *harm his mental* and/or physical development or his education is punished with imprisonment from two to five years. When the offense causes serious health damage or the death of a minor, it is punishable by imprisonment from ten to twenty years (*see* paragraph 390).

435. The law on abortion requires authorization from the parents or a person who has parental responsibility in the case of a request for abortion by a minor. Regarding the deadlines within which abortion is allowed, the law provides that "Termination of pregnancy for medical reasons can be done up to the 22nd week of pregnancy, in the event that a committee consisting of 3 doctors, after examination and consultation, judges that the continuation of pregnancy and/or childbirth endangers life or women's health."

I. Child Health

436. The measures drawn up by the "Strategic Document and Action Plan for Sexual Health and Reproductive 2017–2021," aimed at improving reproductive health indicators in the country and reducing the still high levels of infant and child mortality.

437. The pediatric care service in our country is offered according to the levels of healthcare in:

- Primary Healthcare - health centers and ambulances in the village and child consultants in the city who follow care for the child's growth and development from 0 to 6 years old.

- Pediatric hospital care provided within the pediatric wards of regional hospitals Municipalities and Districts.
- The highest level of pediatric care is offered in the Pediatric Service of the State Medical University "Mother Tereza," in Tirana.

438. According to INSTAT 2021, the vaccination coverage is on average at levels over 97% fulfilling as well as the basic criterion where each vaccine antigen must be above 95% at the national level. Monitoring of children's growth and development is determined according to the Guidelines and Protocols of Clinical Practice, approved by Ministry of Public Health in 2014, which provide for frequent checks during the first three years. Thereafter, checks are required to be carried out once a year for the period between the four and six years of life. According to INSTAT 2021, during the year 2020, 256,146 children were registered with the children's consultant, and there are carried out 708,211 visits, an average of 2.8 visits per child per year. Of the total number of visits, 57.9% of them are carried out with the assistance of a specialist doctor and the rest were attended by midwives and nurses. The focus remains on increasing the number of medical staff in child consultancies in order to increase coverage and the quality of services, and to keep them intact even in case of difficulties created as a result of situations such as the COVID-19 pandemic.

II. Infant and Child Nutrition

439. Malnutrition indicators have declined between 2008–2009 and 2017–2018. Children report that they are too thin for their height and too short for their age has fallen respectively from 6% to less than 1%, and from 11% to 4%, respectively. The prevalence of stunting (short for age) is reduced with increasing mother's education level from 22% among mothers with no education or with only four years of education, to 8% among mothers with higher education. WHO and UNICEF recommend that babies be breastfeed within one hour of birth exclusively breastfeed during the first 6 months of life and continue to breastfeed until 2 years old and up. From the 6th month of life, breastfeeding should be combined with solid foods, semisolid and soft, safe and age appropriate.

440. The Baby Friendly Hospital Initiative (BFHI) initiative, which is of particular importance for ensuring the standards of best practices in the country's maternity hospitals and enables early initiation and long-term breastfeeding, needs a revitalization and operationalization, finding the necessary mechanisms that ensure its stability. Promotion and protection of breastfeeding, through the implementation of Law 8528, as amended, and bylaws in its implementation, takes on special importance, above all in pandemic situations or emergencies. Health personnel must know their responsibilities in accordance with the legislation and the body of the state health inspectorate must follow without interruption and with priority to law enforcement.

III. Adolescent Health

441. Adolescent health services in Albania are part of the package of primary care services, where some responsibilities of the family doctor and nursing staff are described in relation to adolescent health, as service providers for young people and adolescents. The health service in schools is a service financed by the Ministry of Health and Social Protection, with the aim of promoting health. Health service in schools includes oral healthcare.

442. There is little information about the mental health status of the population, especially among teenagers. However, an increasing trend is observed for mental health visits, in particular highlighted after the COVID-19 pandemic. However, it should be noted that the growth also comes because of citizens' awareness and the availability of mental health services. Having a focus on investment in prevention and early intervention programs, raising mechanisms of psychosocial support and counseling, as well as strengthening health education and mental health in schools and universities, increasing health knowledge, addressing stigma, and improving adolescents' help-seeking attitudes and behaviors, piloting began the establishment of Socio Health Centers, which are primary care Centers, enriched with trained staff who will provide psychosocial support to the entire covered population. Initially this project has been extended to 50 health centers, while it is expected to cover most of the Health Centers within 2023.

443. Access to services for young people with disabilities is a specific problem that needs further work. Strengthening health services for adolescents, by focusing in particular on mental health and sexual and reproductive health services, is essential not only for the protection of the individual right of children to health services but also to promote the coverage of adolescents with services, as well as to prevent the possible increase in the teenage birth rate, and the increase in prevalence of HIV among adolescents.

444. ADHS in Albania 2017/2018 reports progress regarding family planning and reproductive health, as 97% of all women and almost 96% of all men in the 15–49 age group knew at least one method of contraception, and 100% of unmarried men and women and sexually active knew at least one method of contraception. Albanian teenagers need to attend primary care centers for reproductive health advice; however, parental consent is required to take contraceptives.

445. The "Healthy Behaviors of School-Age Children" (HBSC) 2018 survey found that 73% of respondents reported a self-perceived "very good" state of health. In general, the prevalence of very frequent complaints was higher for tension, irritation and bad temper (about 11%), followed by headache and difficulty sleeping (both 6.6%), while the lowest was for dizziness (3.6%) and stomach pain (2.3%). The girls reported a higher prevalence of health complaints compared to boys. Meanwhile, boys reported a higher level of daily physical exercise than girls (respectively 29% against 20%). The overall prevalence of smoking among young people was 9.7%: 13.2% among boys and 6.5% in girls. About 78% of the children interviewed had never consumed alcoholic beverages, noting a large difference between boys (73%) and girls (83%). However, of the young 15 years old, 5.1% reported having used cannabis in their lifetime, and 2.7% stated that they had consumed it during the previous thirty days. Boys (5.5%) reported a higher frequency of consumption of cannabis than girls (1.1%).

446. A group of preventable risk factors such as: smoking, alcohol abuse, an unhealthy lifestyle diet and lack of physical activity have a great impact on the observed increase in the total noncommunicable diseases such as cancer, heart, liver and lung diseases. The prevention of dangerous behaviors and the promotion of physical activity among young Albanians remain the main challenges.

§2. The Mental Patient

447. Law No. 44/2012 For Mental Health aims to protect and promote mental health, prevent problems related to guarantee rights and improve the quality of life for people with mental health disorders. This law defines the procedure and conditions for the protection of mental health, through provision of healthcare, provision of a suitable social environment for persons with mental health disorders and through preventive mental health protection policies.

448. Law No. 44/2012 on Mental Health defines "mental health" as an individual's capacity to think, learn, and comprehend, as well as to live harmoniously with their own emotions and the reactions of others. The law further defines a "mental health disorder" as a fundamental impairment in thought, perception, orientation, or memory, which adversely affects behavior, judgment, the ability to recognize reality, or the capacity to meet life's demands. Such a disorder renders an individual mentally ill or indicates mental retardation, particularly when accompanied by pathological or severely aggressive and irresponsible behavior.

449. Law No. 44/2012 For Mental Health defines "Informed consent" as the consent obtained from a person for their inclusion or not in a procedure of assessing his needs, receiving or not receiving a service that meets his needs, only after the person has been fully informed about the procedure, service and others alternatives for assessing and meeting his needs.

450. Law No. 44/2012 on Mental Health defines "treatment" as the comprehensive set of activities involving assessment, diagnosis, therapy, and rehabilitation. This process encompasses the interaction between the patient and the multidisciplinary team within mental healthcare institutions, along with other actors involved in healthcare services. The law also defines "voluntary admission" as the admission of a person with mental health disorders to specialized mental health facilities with beds, aimed at providing necessary care and treatment based on the individual's informed consent. Conversely, "involuntary hospitalization" refers to the admission of a person suffering from a severe mental health disorder without their consent, subject to confirmation through a court decision.

I. Protection and Promotion of Mental Health

451. The protection and promotion of mental health are carried out through measures that contribute to ensuring or restoring the mental balance of the individual, empowering individual capacities, by promoting integrity, improving acceptance and combating discrimination and stigma in his social environment (Article 4, Law No. 44/2012 For Mental Health).

452. The general principles of care in mental health services are: (a) equal and non-discriminatory treatment of persons with mental health disorders in order to respect physical integrity and human dignity; (b) provision of healthcare for persons with mental health disorders in the least coercive environment, mainly at the community level, to avoid as much as possible displacements from the family environment to facilitate social integration and rehabilitation; (c) creating facilities for these people and their families in order to include them in social life; (d) provision of care for persons with mental health disorders by multidisciplinary teams that respond in a complex way to medical, psychological, social and rehabilitation; (e) exercising the rights of persons with mental health disorders, in accordance with international acts, ratified by the Republic of Albania (Article 5, Law No. 44/2012 For Mental Health).

II. Rights of Persons with Mental Health Disorders

453. People with mental health disorders enjoy: (a) constitutional rights, freedoms and legitimate interests; (b) the right to receive accessible and efficient health services under equal conditions as all other patients; (c) the right to treatment and protection, based on respect for individuality and dignity; (d) the right to accept or not the proposed diagnostic and therapeutic intervention, except other cases provided for in this law; (e) the right to receive appropriate information about their rights, as well as to be part of drawing up an individual treatment plan; (f) the right to request compensation for damage caused by the error in treatment or possible abuses; (g) the right to request a review of hospitalization or forced treatment; (h) the right to confidentiality on the data, due to their health condition; (i) the right not to be forced to be examined from a medical point of view, with the purpose of determining a possible mental health disorder, with the exception of cases and according to the procedure described in this law; (j) the right to be provided with adequate living, hygienic, and nutritional conditions; (k) the right to complain about the provision of mental health services. The exercise of the rights of persons with mental health disorders may be limited only in the cases provided for in this law. These restrictions are proportional to the dictated state health and cannot violate the essence of freedoms and rights (Article 6, Law No. 44/2012 For Mental Health).

III. Protection from Discrimination, Torture, Inhumane and Degrading Treatments

454. People with mental health disorders are provided with effective protection from discrimination and from any form of behavior that encourages discrimination, based on this law and legislation in force. No person with mental health disorders may be subjected to torture, cruel, inhuman or degrading punishment or treatment (Article 8, Law No. 44/2012 For Mental Health).

IV. Removal or Limitation of Capacity to Act

455. Removal or limitation of the ability to act of persons with mental health disorders is carried out according to the procedures provided in the CCvP. The Psychiatric-Legal Commission recommends to the subjects who have the right to make a request for removing or limiting the capacity to act, according to the CCvP, setting in motion legal procedures for removing or limiting the ability of the person to act with disorders of mental health. If the head of the mental health service finds that the legal guardian of the person with mental health disorders which is under the care of the mental health service does not fulfill his obligations, he may request the district court to replace the guardian (Article 9, Law No. 44/2012 For Mental Health).

V. Categories of Services

456. The health services which offer mental healthcare are: (a) primary healthcare services; (b) community mental health services; (c) specialized outpatient services; (d) specialized mental health services with beds; (e) special medical institutions; (f) services for children. Mental health services, provided in letters "a," "b" and "c," are offered also through private initiatives of patient groups, family members or third parties, according to the legislation in force. Rules for the organization and operation of these services are approved by the Minister of Health (Article 10, Law No. 44/2012 For Mental Health).

VI. Primary Healthcare Service

457. Primary healthcare service is the service provided by family doctors and nursing staff, who exercise their activity in primary healthcare institutions. The primary healthcare services are based on the basic care service package primary and in the referral system, which also includes the obligation of disclosure, referral and follow-up patients with mental health disorders (Article 11, Law No. 44/2012 For Mental Health).

VII. Specialized Outpatient Services

458. Specialized outpatient mental health services are services provided by doctors specializing in the medical discipline of psychiatry, nursing staff and support staff qualified who exercise their activity in public healthcare institutions and private (Article 12, Law No. 44/2012 For Mental Health).

VIII. Community Mental Health Service

459. Community mental health services provide preventive and curative activities and rehabilitation for people with mental health disorders. Community mental health services are provided by a multidisciplinary team and have as an objective: (a) preserving, developing and rehabilitating individual opportunities to overcome emergency or chronic needs; (b) social integration, psychosocial rehabilitation and social and professional rehabilitation (Article 13, Law No. 44/2012 For Mental Health).

IX. Specialist Mental Health Services with Beds

460. Specialist inpatient mental health services are specialist services within the general hospital or in specialized hospitals, which are organized and operate according to the legislation in force for the hospital service (Article 14, Law No. 44/2012 For Mental Health).

X. Mental Health Services for Children

461. Mental health services for children are provided by the National Therapeutic Center and Rehabilitation for Children. The National Therapeutic and Rehabilitation Center for Children is a public institution specialized center, which also offers specialized mental health services for children, in function of preserving and improving their mental health, with the aim of growth and development of the child, diagnosis and treatment, as well as disability rehabilitation. The organization and operation of the National Therapeutic and Rehabilitation Center for Children are regulated by the decision of the Council of Ministers (Article 14/1, Law No. 44/2012 For Mental Health).

XI. Children's Mental Health Services

A. Principles of Operation

462. Mental health services for children are provided to protect and improve the health of the population. The operation of mental health services for children is based on the principles of protection of children's rights and are a specific part of mental health services in all categories of mental health services (Article 15, Law No. 44/2012 For Mental Health).

463. The services offered in this center are as follows:

– Diagnosis.
– Evaluation and drafting of the individual plan.
– Outpatient and hospital treatment for all children with mental health problems.
– Education and rehabilitation service.

464. Children who receive services at this center are referred by primary healthcare services in accordance with the legislation. Primary healthcare service is the service provided by doctors of the family and nursing staff, who exercise their activity in primary healthcare institutions, including consultancies. The primary healthcare service is based on the basic service package of primary care and the referral system, which also includes the obligation of detection, referral and follow-up of patients with mental health disorders.

465. Under this package, mental health is an integral part of Primary Healthcare. This service assists individuals with mental health disorders and helps to improve the social condition (that is determinant of poor mental health) of patients and their families. Support provided in primary care is part of comprehensive mental healthcare, as well as an essential part of healthcare in general.

466. Children are referred by primary healthcare when: – they present signs of suicidal intentions; – assessment cannot be performed in primary care settings, e.g., psychotic symptoms, ADHD, etc.; – medication and treatment is needed, which is not carried out in the conditions of primary care (depressive disorder in the child, severe obsessive disorder compulsive); – the degree of disability is such that the person cannot go to school or meet friends; – signs of neglect or abuse appear.

467. For the children of the group aged 0–6 years, cases are also referred by the Children's Psychiatric Clinic and Adolescents in the Psychiatric Clinic of the University Hospital Center "Mother Teresa," Tirana.

468. Referred children are diagnosed by the medical services sector, which in the medical record also gives the relevant instructions for the actions that must be taken are undertaken continuously for the case evaluation process. Pursuant to the legislation in force, the case evaluation procedure includes assessment of the current problem of the individual or his needs—the evaluation, if the service can offer services that address the needs of the individual—as well as possible referrals.

469. For every patient (including children) who is referred to the services of mental health, an assessment is completed, based on the described procedures in the internal regulation, before providing services. This assessment should contain the elements of comprehensive assessment at the bio-psychosocial level, but not only such as: the patient's current problem; strengths and needs of the patient; the relevant diagnosis, which must be defined within thirty days from first contact; medical, family and social history; various psychiatric, psychological or social assessments.

470. The education and rehabilitation service is designed to provide direct support to children through various therapies tailored to their individual needs, as outlined in their personal records by multidisciplinary teams. Social workers play a critical role in this process by coordinating, advising, and referring cases in alignment with each child's individualized plan. Discussions with a social worker revealed that many of these children come from families with low educational and cultural levels, compounded by significant socioeconomic challenges. Consequently, these families often lack awareness of the rights of children with disabilities, underscoring the need for additional outreach and support to bridge this informational gap.

B. Educational-Therapeutic Kindergarten

471. The programs developed in this service are simple, based on the needs of children, where these programs can be easily developed by parents' home. The purpose of this service enables socialization among children, their interaction, where they learn to share toys and spaces. This service also includes the dissemination of good practices, which can be implemented even in the home environment by parents. Parents are constantly advised to develop these practices with children, where the therapists complete the observational protocols, which become part of their files.

472. Developmental therapy is performed daily for hospitalized children and several times per week for outpatient children. Development progress of the child during the provision of this service becomes part of the child's medical record the child. Speech therapy is performed daily for hospitalized children and several times a week for ambulatory children. Occupational therapy is performed daily for hospitalized children and several times a week for outpatient children. Diagnoses of children who received this service are children with autism, mental retardation, etc. Physiotherapy is performed daily for hospitalized children and several times a week for ambulatory children. Diagnoses of children who received this service are children with tetra paresis, hypotonia, hemiparesis, autism, etc. The progress of the child's development during the provision of this service is made part of the child's card.

473. For all the services offered above, counseling with parents is also offered, which these services should also be performed by them in the home environment. Every professional that provides these services, designs individual work plans for each child, where cooperation with parents enables the measurement of the child's development.

474. The Institution of the People's Advocate is part of the European Network of Ombudsman for Children (ENOC). The network's mission is to promote and protect children's rights in accordance with the Convention on the Rights of Children. The Institution of the People's Advocate has found that the challenges identified include a significant lack of information among parents regarding the responsible local structures tasked with protecting children, ensuring the continuity of therapies provided by specialized services, and facilitating the inclusion of children in educational institutions such as nurseries, kindergartens, and schools. Additionally, there is an evident shortage of specialized local-level services for children with health issues, particularly those aimed at empowering families and providing consistent guidance to create a nurturing family environment for children with mental health challenges. Furthermore, inadequate coordination and collaboration between central and local mechanisms, spanning medical, social, and educational structures, hinder the effective integration and protection of children and their families within society. The lack of promotional and awareness-raising activities targeting the central and local structures responsible for children with mental health problems further exacerbates these issues, highlighting the need for comprehensive systemic reforms and improved inter-agency cooperation.

475. The People's Advocate recommended taking measures for the drafting of the operating regulation and organization of the National Center for Prosperity, Development and Rehabilitation of Children, in accordance with the package of bylaws for implementation of Law No. 44/2012 "On health mental"; taking measures to increase the daily food quota for children, such as also the inclusion of mothers as beneficiaries of this service in this institution; taking measures to improve the children hospitalization rooms, creating warm and friendly environments for them; taking measures to install an elevator in the building, to avoid infrastructural barriers for children who receive the service of physiotherapy.

476. The sector of Mental Health and Addictology in the Ministry of Health and Social Protection should be strengthened in the exercise of its role as leader of the policy implementation process and mental health strategies in accordance with the legislation relevant in the field of health, social issues and protection of children, setting up an intersectoral working group for the design of work protocols between these areas; responsible state institutions, operating in this field, such as child protection units, community mental health services, day services for children at the local level, educational services, as well as primary health services, etc., must coordinate, cooperate and coordinate the work treatment, protection, integration and monitoring of the entire process in the interest child's highest, in accordance with Instruction No. 10, dated 25.2.2015 "On the ways, forms of cooperation and intervention procedures in aid of children at risk for institutions and structures principally responsible for the protection of the child." The Institute of Public Health must carry out studies, with a purpose of providing quantitative and qualitative data, which will help in the design of preventive and integrative policies.

C. *Family Care*

477. Family care for individuals with mental health disorders is coordinated by responsible state authorities, local government bodies, and non-profit organizations operating in this field. This cooperation involves the person with mental health disorders, their family, and a personal assistant as provided under the relevant legislation. Family care encompasses psychological and psycho-pedagogical support, personal and familial assistance services, as well as financial and service-based support in accordance with applicable laws. Families with members who have mental health disorders, in collaboration with state institutions and non-profit organizations specializing in care, treatment, and rehabilitation, work to support these individuals for their reintegration into the family, community, and broader society. Local government bodies, within their jurisdiction and in partnership with healthcare structures, undertake measures to provide comprehensive support to individuals with mental health disorders and their families, promoting their well-being and societal inclusion (Article 16, Law No. 44/2012 For Mental Health).

D. *Vocational Rehabilitation*

478. People with mental health disorders enjoy the right to benefit from policies of professional rehabilitation when their medical and educational conditions allow such a thing. The method of benefit and the inclusion of persons with mental health disorders in these policies are defined according to the legislation in force (Article 17, Law No. 44/2012 For Mental Health).

E. *Mental Health in Residential Social Care Institutions*

479. Persons who are in residential institutions of social care are offered counseling, treatment, rehabilitation and mental healthcare equally and according to health standards, approved by the Minister of Health (Article 18, Law No. 44/2012 For Mental Health).

480. Article 59 of Law No. 7895 dated 27.1.1995 CCr of the Republic of Albania includes elements of the convict's mental health when taking a decision on the suspension of the execution of the decision with imprisonment and probation. Due to the low risk of the person, age, health or mental conditions, lifestyle and needs, especially those related to family, education or work, circumstances of the commission of the criminal offense, as well as of the behavior after the commission of the criminal offense, the court, when it imposes a prison sentence up to in five¸ years, may order that the convicted person keep in contact with the probation service and be put on probation, suspending the execution of the sentence, provided that he does not commit another criminal offense during the probationary period. The court orders the convict to fulfill one or more obligations, provided for in Article 60 of this Code. For sentences of up to two years of imprisonment, suspended by the court, the probationary period is twice the time of the prison sentence given by the court. The probationary period, except for the rule provided in paragraph 3 of this article, is twenty-four months to five years. The trial period starts from the day after the announcement of the decision of the court that gave a decision on suspension of the prison sentence. The probation period can be shortened or extended depending on the method of the execution of probation and the personal conditions of the convicted, but without prejudice to the minimum and maximum term provided for in this paragraph. If the convict does not keep in contact with the probation service or does not fulfill the obligations provided in Article 60, as ordered by the court, the court decides to replace the first sentence with another sentence, the extension of the term of supervision, within the probationary period, or the revocation of the suspension of execution of the decision (Law No. 7895, dated 27.1.1995 CCr of the Republic of Albania).

481. Law No. 7895, dated 27.1.1995 CCr of the Republic of Albania predicts criminal offenses committed intentionally against health (including mental health). Article 86 Law No. 7895, dated 27.1.1995 CCr of the Republic of Albania regulates torture and the deliberate committing of acts which a person is caused severe suffering, physical or *mental*, by a person, exercising public functions, or with his instigation or approval, open or silent, on purpose: (a) to receive information or statements from him or someone else; (b) to punish him for an act committed or suspected to have been committed by/or another person; (c) to intimidate or pressure him or another person; (ç) for any other purpose based on any form of discrimination; (d) any other inhuman or humiliating act; are sentenced to imprisonment from four to ten years.

F. Voluntary Placement and Admission for Observation

482. Law No. 44/2012 For Mental Health defines "Voluntary admission" as the admission to specialized mental health services with beds of a person with mental health disorders to provide appropriate healthcare and necessary treatment after giving informed consent.

483. "Voluntary treatment" is treatment at the request or consent of the person suffering from mental health disorders or at the request of the legal representative of a minor under the age of 14 years old.

484. Law No. 44/2012 For Mental Health regulates the Admission and Treatment in Mental Health Services Specialized in Beds. A person with mental health disorders, admitted voluntarily to specialized mental health service with beds, receives voluntary treatment after releasing written approval on his part, subject to prior information. Treatment given to minors is subject to approval from their guardian or legal representative. Informed consent is ensured through the provision of complete information and suitable to the patient for the nature, purpose and effects of the proposed therapeutic intervention, documented in the standard form of informed consent of voluntary treatment, approved by order of the minister responsible for health. The content on discussion and approval form are part of the patient's clinical record. The patient signs for giving approval on a card, as well as in the informed consent form. The person with mental health disorders, his guardian or legal representative have the right to request termination, refusal or to complain about treatment at any point in the process, which can only be objected to when the criteria for involuntary treatment are met (Article 19, Law No. 44/2012 For Mental Health).

G. Voluntary Layoff Admission

485. An individual with mental health disorders may voluntarily be admitted to a specialized mental health service with inpatient facilities after providing written consent, following a comprehensive discussion about the need for hospitalization. This process ensures that the patient is fully informed about the care and treatment required. The standard informed consent form, approved by the minister responsible for health, is used to document this consent. Both the discussion details and the completed consent form are included in the patient's clinical record. The patient formalizes their approval for hospitalization by signing both a hospitalization card and the informed consent form. Prior to admission, the individual undergoes a preliminary examination by a doctor in a community health service or a specialized outpatient service. It is explicitly stated that voluntary hospitalization of individuals with mental health disorders in specialized mental health facilities cannot be used to assess their ability to work under any circumstances (Article 19/1, Law No. 44/2012 For Mental Health).

H. Involuntary Placement in a Unit of Mental Health

1. Compulsory Admission for Observation

486. Law No. 44/2012 For Mental Health defines "Involuntary hospitalization" as the hospitalization of a person suffering from a serious mental health disorder which is carried out without his approval and confirmed through a court decision. "Involuntary treatment" is the treatment of a person suffering from a serious mental health disorder which is carried out without his approval and confirmed through a court decision.

2. Involuntary Treatment

487. The subject of involuntary treatment is the person who is treated in such a way in specialized mental health services with beds, according to the definition of specialist doctor. The person with mental health disorders is treated involuntarily in the case that these conditions are met simultaneously: (a) when there is a serious mental disorder; (b) does not have the appropriate capacity to give informed consent; it regained the ability to consent to treatment and/or to prevent deterioration or harming his health or that of others. The decision for involuntary treatment of a person is taken by the specialist doctor only after having personally conducted his assessment. The sick person, his immediate family or legal guardian enjoy the right to be informed about the reasons for taking this decision and about the rights that the patient enjoys based on this condition. Treatment and information procedures for the patient and other interested persons are reflected in the clinical card, which is approved by order of the minister responsible for health (Article 20, Law No. 44/2012 For Mental Health).

3. Rights of the Person Subject to Involuntary Treatment

488. The patient who is subjected to involuntary treatment is explained in writing within forty-eight hours, the reasons for involuntary treatment, as well as being informed about his rights and obligations. The patient, during the actions of involuntary hospitalization, is represented personally and, in case the health condition does not allow it, through the legal representative. The patient who is subjected to involuntary treatment is guaranteed protection of his interests for all procedural actions related to him. The decision on involuntary treatment can be appealed to the court, according to legislation in force (Article 21, Law No. 44/2012 For Mental Health).

489. The person found in the circumstances provided for in Article 24/1 of this law is sent to specialized mental health service with beds from the medical staff of the services emergency, a person close to him or by any official or other person who is informed about his health condition. The State Police, at the request of the medical staff, help him during the performance of medical visits and transfer of the person to the specialized mental health service with beds, as well as guarantee the temporary protection of his property. In cases where help is missing from immediate medical personnel, the State Police are obliged to accompany the person, in the presence of family members or other relatives, to the nearest medical emergency service. The doctor in the specialized mental health service with beds, who decides for involuntary hospitalization of the person, immediately informs the medical or police personnel who have it accompanied by family members and other accompanying persons, as well as the legal representative, if it is present. The person enjoys the right to communicate with the persons close to him or his legal representative. The doctor in the specialized mental health service with beds, who decides for involuntary hospitalization, describes in detail in the medical record all the procedures followed and ensures the notification of the head of service for involuntary hospitalization, within twenty-four hours (Article 22, Law No. 44/2012 For Mental Health).

4. Re-evaluation of Involuntary Treatment

490. The head of the mental health service is required to order a written reassessment of a patient's condition and treatment plan within twenty-four hours of their placement in involuntary treatment. This reassessment must be conducted by medical personnel who were not involved in the initial involuntary treatment decision. The medical team performing the reassessment documents all necessary notes in the patient's medical record and reports their findings to the head of the service, including their opinion on the appropriateness of the treatment plan. If the head of the service determines, based on the reassessment, that the criteria for involuntary treatment are no longer met, they must order the immediate cessation of the treatment. This decision, along with detailed reasons, is recorded in the medical record. Conversely, if the reassessment confirms the necessity of continuing the involuntary treatment, the treatment proceeds according to the agreed plan, supported by two independent assessments. Following this decision, within forty-eight hours, the director of the institution providing the specialized mental health service submits a request to the court in the relevant judicial district to review the procedure carried out. A copy of this request is provided to the patient, a close relative, and/or their legal representative to ensure transparency and legal oversight (Article 23, Law No. 44/2012 For Mental Health).

5. Involuntary Treatment by Court Order

491. The sole judge examines the request submitted by the owner of the institution where the service is provided of specialized mental health with beds, for the evaluation of involuntary treatment, while receiving the opinion of a specialist doctor of an institution independent from the institution where he is treated the person subject to this procedure, as well as hears the patient personally, no later than forty-eight hours from her appearance. The decision of the single judge is immediately implemented by the specialized mental health service with beds. The decision of the court is reviewed periodically every twenty-eight days, at the request of the holder of the institution where the specialized mental health service with beds is offered. At any time, when the criteria for involuntary treatment are not met, the institution's owner where the specialized mental health service is offered with beds, the person with mental disorders mental health, which has not been deprived of the ability to act, subject to the involuntary treatment, the family members or his legal representative submit the request to the competent court for revoking the court's decision (Article 24, Law No. 44/2012 For Mental Health).

6. Rights of the Person Subject to Involuntary Hospitalization

492. The patient who is subject to involuntary hospitalization is explained in writing within forty-eight hours the reasons for involuntary hospitalization, as well as being informed about his rights and obligations. The patient is represented personally during the actions of involuntary hospitalization and, in case the health condition does not allow it, through the legal representative. The patient, who is subjected to involuntary hospitalization, is guaranteed protection of his interests for all procedural actions related to him. The decision on involuntary hospitalization can be appealed to the court according to legislation in force (Article 24/2, Law No. 44/2012 For Mental Health).

7. Reassessing Involuntary Placement

493. The head of the service, no later than twenty-four hours after the involuntary hospitalization, orders in writing the reassessment of the health status of the person hospitalized to involuntary in the medical record. The reassessment is performed by medical personnel who did not participate in the initial procedure. After reassessing the health condition, the medical staff completes the medical record with all the necessary notes and refers to the head of service if the involuntary placement is justified or unjustified, or the reasons for the person to be kept under the specified conditions. If after the reassessment, the head of the service finds that the reasons for the person to be kept in involuntary confinement conditions, orders the immediate removal of the person from involuntary placement. The decision of the head of service and his reasons are recorded in the medical record. If after the re-evaluation, the head of the service finds that the reasons for the person have not been reduced to be held in involuntary hospitalization conditions, the person continues to be held in such a way involuntarily in this service. After this decision, within forty-eight hours, the head of the institution where it is offered the specialized mental health service with beds, referred by the head of the service, addresses the court of the judicial district to assess the procedure is carried out. A copy of the request is made available to the patient, a close relative and/or his legal representative (Article 24/4, Law No. 44/2012 For Mental Health).

8. Involuntary Placement by Court Decision

494. The sole judge examines the request submitted by the owner of the institution, where it is offered specialized mental health service with beds, for the assessment of involuntary hospitalization, taking the opinion of a specialist doctor of an institution independent from the institution where he is admitted, as well as listens to the patient personally, no later than forty-eight hours from her appearance. The decision of the single judge is immediately implemented by the specialized mental health service with beds. The decision of the court is reviewed periodically every twenty-eight days, at the request of the holder of the institution where the specialized mental health service with beds is offered. At any time, when the health causes that led to involuntary hospitalization have subsided, the owner of the institution where the specialized mental health service with beds is offered submit to the competent court the request for the revocation of the judge's decision (Article 24/5, Law No. 44/2012 For Mental Health).

9. Special Medical and Surgical Treatments

495. Any medical and surgical treatment, including electroconvulsive therapy in persons with mental health disorders, applies, in any case, in the interest of the health needs of the patient, informing and obtaining the approval of the patient or his legal representative. Electroconvulsive therapy is applied after the informed consent of the patient himself or his legal representatives, according to the protocols approved by order of the Minister of Health. Electroconvulsive therapy is not applicable to minors. Rules of professional ethics, based on which medical and surgical procedures are performed, are also applied to people with mental health disorders (Article 25, Law No. 44/2012 For Mental Health).

10. Scientific and Medical Research

496. Scientific and medical research into persons with mental health disorders undertaken only after informed consent has been obtained from these patients. Scientific and medical research does not apply to people with mental health disorders, who are receiving involuntary treatment in the mental health service specializes in beds and people who do not have the ability to act (Article 26, Law No. 44/2012 For Mental Health).

11. Physical Limitation

497. Physical restraint of persons with mental health disorders is applied in the institutions of specialized mental health with beds and includes, according to the relevant protocol, the following elements: (a) holding the person by force; (b) forced use of medications; (c) immobilization; (d) isolation. Physical restraint is applied for short periods of time with clear objectives, according to protocols approved by order of the Minister of Health. The patient must be informed of physical limitation. The procedures followed, along with the justification for applying restraint, are carefully documented in the patient's medical record when the restraint occurs within a specialized service. If the restraint is implemented in another facility, the details are included in the official documentation or epicrisis that accompanies the patient to the specialized service. Continuous and active contact between healthcare staff and the restrained individual is maintained throughout the process, exceeding routine monitoring, as mandated by the approved protocols. The use of physical restraint as a punitive measure or for the convenience of healthcare staff is strictly forbidden. This ensures that physical restraint is applied ethically and professionally, solely to address therapeutic or safety needs, while safeguarding the dignity and rights of the individuals in care (Article 27, Law No. 44/2012 For Mental Health).

498. Physical restraint is applied in the conditions when: (a) is authorized by the psychiatrist in writing; (b) is carried out in the least restrictive/coercive form, which provides security and behavior to control the aggressiveness of the patient; (c) the force used is proportionate to the perceived risk; (d) the specialized mental health service with beds has the necessary infrastructure to implement the physical restraint as safely as possible, according to the standards approved by the Minister of Health. In any mental health service specialist with beds, where the restriction applies physical data, for each case, are documented in a separate register, in addition to the detailed documentation in the patient's clinical record. Patients' relatives and/or their legal representatives should be informed as soon as possible first when the patient is or becomes subject to physical limitation (Article 27, Law No. 44/2012 For Mental Health).

XII. Mental Health in the Execution of Criminal Decisions Institutions

A. Special Medical Institutions

499. Special medical institutions are institutions that serve for the treatment of persons with mental health disorders, who have committed a criminal offense, for which the competent court authority decided on forced treatment in a medical institution for detainees or of convicts who exhibit mental health disorders while serving their sentence, as well as for the treatment of persons, for whom the court has decided the temporary placement in a special medical institution, according to Article 239 of the CCrP.

500. The treatment of people in special medical institutions is the same as the treatment of other patients with mental health disorders. Special medical institutions are part of the integrated health system. The rules for the establishment and operation of these special medical institutions and security measures for their preservation are determined by the decision of the Council of Ministers (Article 28, Law No. 44/2012 For Mental Health).

B. Mental Health in the Institutions of Criminal Decisions Execution

501. Convicts and detainees who are in institutions for the execution of criminal decisions and suffering from mental health disorders enjoy the right to special health treatment near these institutions or in the Prison Hospital Center. Treatment and care for mental health are offered in a non-discriminatory manner and according to the health standards that apply to other categories as well as of persons with mental health disorders. The Ministry of Health, through mental health services, provides, according to needs, all the necessary assistance for diagnosis, treatment and rehabilitation of persons with mental health disorders (Article 29, Law No. 44/2012 For Mental Health).

XIII. Mental Health Monitoring

A. National Committee on Mental Health

502. The National Committee for Mental Health is an advisory body of the Minister of Health. The composition and mode of operation of this committee are approved by decision of the Council of Ministers, with the proposal of the Minister of Health. The National Committee for Mental Health advises the Minister of Health on the implementation of the obligations arising from this law and for important legal and technical organizational revisions in the field of mental health (Article 30, Law No. 44/2012 For Mental Health).

B. External Monitoring of the Mental Health Service

503. The People's Advocate, through the National Mechanism for the Prevention of Torture, Inhuman and Degrading Treatment, acting as a separate body under its authority, monitors regularly, through periodic inspections, the respect of rights and standards that are offered to people with mental health disorders in mental health service settings specialized with beds. It presents recommendations to the relevant bodies, with the aim of improving the treatment and conditions of patients and ensuring full respect of rights in mental healthcare institutions. The Ombudsman, through the National Mechanism for the Prevention of Torture, Inhuman and Degrading Treatment, during inspections in the mental health services of specialized with beds, is guaranteed free access to all places and environments of the institutions the mental health service, as well as the receipt of any information is guaranteed, according to the legislation in power. Monitoring procedures, duties and rights of employees of the National Mechanism for Prevention of Torture, Inhuman and Degrading Treatment is carried out according to the legislation in force (Article 31, Law No. 44/2012 For Mental Health).

C. Inspection

504. The inspection of mental health facilities is carried out by the inspectorate that covers the field of health in accordance with this law and Law No. 10 433, dated 16.6.2011 "For inspection in the Republic of Albania" (Article 31/1, Law No. 44/2012 For Mental Health) (*see* 675, 869, 899, 1153, 1175, 1177).

D. Participation of Non-profit Organizations

505. The Ministry of Health supports the initiatives of non-profit organizations that aim to assist in the realization of the strategic objectives of the Ministry of Health in the development and improvement of mental healthcare institutions, as well as those organizations that aim external and independent monitoring of respect for human rights in this sector. The activity of non-profit organizations in the premises of mental healthcare institutions with beds is regulated based on agreements of understanding and cooperation with the Ministry of Health. In any case, during this activity, these organizations respect the legislation in force and provide the necessary assurance of its ethical and legal use of personal and confidential data (Article 32, Law No. 44/2012 For Mental Health).

E. Sanctions

506. Violations of Articles 30–32 Law No. 44/2012 For Mental Health, when they do not constitute a criminal offense, constitute an administrative misdemeanor and are punished as follows: (a) Violation of disclosure of professional secrets, except in cases provided for in this law, is punished with the removal of the right to exercise the profession for up to three years. (b) Violation of point 1 of Article 19 and Article 19/1 of this law, carrying out voluntary treatment, without receiving the informed consent, shall be punished with the removal of the right to exercise the profession up to three years. (c) Violation of point 3 of Article 20 and point 4 of Article 24/1 of this law, failure to inform rights and reasons for the treatment, is punished with a fine of ALL 50,000. (d) Violation of point 4 of Article 22 and point 2 of Article 24/3 of this law, failure to notify within the deadline of the head of the service, is punished with a fine of ALL 50,000. (e) Violation of point 4 of Article 23 and point 4 of Article 24/4 of this law, noncompliance with deadlines imposed, shall be punished with a fine of ALL 50,000. (f) Violation of Article 25 of this law, performing special medical and surgical treatments, in violation of this article, is punished with the removal of the right to exercise the profession for up to three years. (g) Violation of Article 26 of this law, conducting scientific research without the patient's consent and patients who receive involuntary treatment, shall be punished with the removal of the right to practice the profession, up to three years and a fine of ALL 50,000.

507. The responsible authority for imposing and executing the fine is the inspectorate of the field of health. The main punishment is by a fine, when it is provided as a separate and complementary punishment and when it is given simultaneously with the measure of removing the right to exercise the profession. The appeal against the decision of the Inspectorate is made in accordance with the law on inspection. The execution of the decisions is done according to the legislation in force for administrative offenses (Article 34, Law No. 44/2012 For Mental Health).

§3. The Dying Patient

I. Advance Directives

508. Advances in medical discoveries have raised several issues related to end-of-life decisions (Grant & Sun, 2010). Within different types of end-of-life decisions, the main ones are withholding or withdrawing medical treatment from a conscious patient, withholding or withdrawing medical treatment from an unconscious patient, physician-assisted suicide (PAS), and euthanasia:

a. End-of-life decisions remain a national competence (Veshi & Neitzke, 2015). However, at a European level, the European Court of Human Rights (ECtHR) has clearly stated that withholding or withdrawing treatment from a conscious patient is considered legal.[138] In addition, the ECtHR, in several decisions,[139] has underlined the importance of advance directives (ADs), as the main instrument to communicate in the case of withholding or withdrawing medical treatments. Moreover, in recent years, the ECtHR also declared that death by euthanasia, also for nonterminal illnesses, is not a violation of (the positive obligation of) Article 2 of the European Convention of Human Rights (ECHR). Again, the absence of family involvement in the euthanasia process of a patient is not a violation of Article 8 ECHR.[140]
b. Focusing on the national level of Western European countries, while there are no doubts about the legalization of withholding or withdrawing treatment from a conscious patient, all of them have ruled ADs. (Andorno, 2008) It should be noted that ADs are used not only for non-treatment but also in the case of euthanasia[141] or also to give advance consent to compulsory hospital admission or treatment during a future mental health crisis.[142] Reviewing the case of PAS and euthanasia (Veshi et al., 2024), legalized versions of PAS or euthanasia exist in Low countries (the Netherlands, Belgium, and Luxemburg), Iberic Peninsula (Spain and Portugal), in German-speaking countries (Switzerland, which is the only country in Europe allowing assisted suicide by non-physicians, Germany, through a decision of the Constitutional Court,[143] and Austria, first through the Constitutional Court[144] and then by law), as well as Italy, through the intervention of its Constitutional Court.[145]

509. In Albania, while euthanasia and PAS are deemed criminal offenses (Articles 76, 79, and 99 CCr) and in violation of rules established in the Code of Medical Ethics (Article 39) (Boçari et al., 2010), Albanian law has acknowledged that withholding or withdrawing treatment from a conscious patient is considered legal since the patient can and does, in fact, consent to withholding or withdrawing medical treatment. This has also been codified in Article 6(2)(ç) Law No. 10.107 of

138. European Court of Human Rights (ECtHR): *Pretty v. the UK*, application No. 2346/02, para. 63.
139. Among others, ECtHR, *Lambert and Others v. France* [GC], application No. 46043/14.
140. European Court of Human Rights (ECtHR): *Mortier v. Belgium*, application No. 78017/17.
141. Chapter III of the Belgian Act on Euthanasia of May 28, 2002.
142. Dutch Law *Wet bijzondere opnemingen in psychiatrische ziekenhuizen*, which entered into force on Jan. 1, 2020.
143. German Constitutional Court, 2 BvR 2347/15.
144. Austrian Constitutional Court, VFGH, 2020: G139.2019.
145. Italian Constitutional Court, Ordinance 207/2018 of October 2018; Decision 242/2019 of September 2019; and Decision 135/2024 of Jul. 18, 2024.

March 2009. The legal and bioethical discussion regarding withholding or withdrawing treatment from an unconscious patient is quite complicated and it is directly correlated with the absence of an ad hoc law ruling on advance directives (ADs):

a. The importance of ADs has been recognized by several national and international scholars (Dudley, 2019; Veshi & Neitzke, 2015; Veshi & Neitzke, 2015; Veshi, 2015; Veshi, 2017; Vyshka & Kruja, 2011; Koka & Veshi, 2019). With the recognition of the importance of ADs, a patient's position evolves from a passive role of personal, physical, and mental protection to an active role of freedom and quality of life (Veshi & Neitzke, 2015). However, Albania does not have a specific law governing ADs.
b. Patients can express their medical declaration through ADs. An AD should be considered a medical declaration, which, based on the principle of extended autonomy, gives directives for future medical care in case of future incapacity. Citizens can express their medical declarations in two different forms: the "instructional medical directives" or the "surrogate will," both explained below. From a medico-legal perspective, these types of ADs should be complementary.
c. In the case of instructional directives, commonly known as instructional medical directives (or "living will"), citizens express their preferences regarding specific medical treatments that they want to permit or to reject in case of future unconsciousness. The second form of ADs, the surrogate will, gives enduring power for healthcare affairs to another competent citizen: the "surrogate." Surrogates must understand patients' wishes and values.
d. This Section focuses only on the analysis of "instructional medical directives." The term "living will" is confusing for people because the will takes effect only after an agent's death and is directed to other people (Spoto, 2011). Instructional medical directives are intended for a physician's acts to conform to a living patient's wishes. To avoid this confusion, it would be better to use the term *instructional medical directives* or *treatment directives*.
e. Instructional medical directives are written expressions of citizens' preferences regarding specific medical treatments that they want (to consent to or) to reject in case of future incapacity, which should be assessed by an impartial expert. It is thought that the origin of instructional medical directives could be the "Do Not Resuscitate" orders that physicians used to write in patients' case histories after discussing it with them and their families (Rabkin, 1976). Therefore, the instructional medical directive should be considered as the document in which the citizen expresses his or her preferences regarding specific medical treatments that he or she wants to consent to or to reject in the case of absence of future capacity.
f. It should be noted that in case of clear instructional directives that correspond perfectly in concrete medical situations, they should always have more weight in the decision-making process. These could be cases of chronic illnesses or neurodegenerative diseases affecting cognitive faculties. In these cases, the patient has received all medical and legal information regarding his future (probable) incapacity. But unfortunately, these are rare cases.

g. Although instructional medical directives are recognized as an important instrument to enshrine patient autonomy, some authors have underlined the risks of their implementations: life has an intrinsic value (or there is a principle of sanctity of life); they distort the patient–physician relationship; and they misunderstand the social role of physicians.
h. First, some bioethicists claim that life has an intrinsic value. Catholic bioethicists would state that instructional medical directives, which are directed at refusing life-sustaining intervention, infringe on the principle of the sanctity of life. The concept of the "sanctity of life" has a religious connotation that should not be used by a secular state (Brock, 2009). One objection derived from this principle is that if patients have the right to decide about their end of life, life will be less valued. Sick people could be considered less important than healthy citizens (Spoto, 2011). People with disabilities and old patients without families could ask for treatment to be withdrawn because they do not have families or relatives to take care of them.
i. The second main criticism focuses on the patient–physician dialog. A competent patient can decide and can reconsider it after taking into account physicians' advice. However, an incapacitated patient cannot revise his/her medical declarations. Furthermore, if instructional medical directives are general or vague or include only specific treatments that cannot be applied by analogy to a given medical situation, there will be difficulties in interpreting patients' wishes (Teno et al., 1997).
j. Physicians' social role could be considered as professionals who want to keep their patients alive, even through aggressive treatment. Physicians' perceptions of patients who could have written instructional medical directives, but did not, could be that these patients want to undergo aggressive treatment, or that these patients "did not want treatment withheld under any circumstances" (Kelly, 2006).
k. Although these problems exist, it should be suggested that the benefits of the instructional medical directives still outweigh the risks. Further, in case of incapacity, the instructional medical directives can create a bridge between patients and physicians. Moreover, instructional medical directives—especially if they were expressed through an intensive dialog with doctors—enhance patient's autonomy (Hunt & Ells, 2011). In addition, only the recognition of instructional medical directives leads to the equal treatment of competent and incompetent patients, which entails an application of the principle of equity, also protected in the Albanian constitution (Article 18). Instructional medical directives are based on the solid moral ground of the principle of autonomy. As Buchanan and Brock state, instructional medical directives are acts "of self-determination" which are based on the so-called extension view of autonomy. (Buchanan & Brock, 1989) They could be stated as follows: "just as we have a moral right of autonomy to affect our preferences over our interests in the present, so we have a moral right of precedent autonomy to effect (in advance) our preferences over our surviving interests."
l. From a strict Albanian legal point of view, instructional medical directives should be considered as unilateral legal transactions that produce legal effects in the non-pecuniary individual sphere: their aim is to (consent to or) reject

future medical treatment in case of an agent's incapacity. They should be viewed as an application of the right to self-determination recognized by Article 27 of the Albanian Constitution since there exists a right to life, but not a duty to live. The right to self-determination regarding health may be narrowed only in cases where a public intervention aims to protect the community (Article 6 Law 107/2009). However, the public intervention shall aim not only at the protection of others' health but also shall not damage, but (eventually) improve patient's health. This interpretation is similar to that of the European Court of Human Rights (ECtHR) which has stated that "therapeutic necessity cannot be regarded as inhuman or degrading...[when] ... the medical necessity has been convincingly shown to exist" (par. 82) and this medical treatment improves patient's health (ECtHR, *Herczegfalvy v. Austria*, Application No. 10533/83, par. 81). Although this legal decision deals with the interpretation of Article 3 ECHR (Prohibition of Torture), it is included here since this case underlines the patient's well-being even in situations where for public safety (e.g., a patient with COVID-19) physicians do not respect patient's right to self-determination.

m. By considering the general legal framework, in particular Articles 6–11 Albanian CCv instructional medical directives can be written only by people with full competency, reached at the age of 18 years old. Furthermore, simple opinions or declarations that do not aim to produce a legal effect on relationships with physicians must not be considered. Physicians must pay close attention to patients' medical declarations because on the one hand they should not take simple opinions into consideration, but on the other, they must be aware that patients' preferences change during a disease (Berger and Majerovitz, 1998). This could be achieved with a process of only four steps: understanding, appreciation, reasoning, and communicating a choice (Karel 2007). It is fundamental that the agents comprehend diagnostic and treatment-related information (understanding). After understanding the risks and benefits of a particular medical treatment, patients must have the ability to relate them to their own future eventual situation (appreciation) by comparing alternative treatments in a logically consistent manner (reasoning). In the end, they should convey a treatment choice (communicating a choice).

n. Although the Albanian legal framework does not establish specific rules regarding end-of-life decisions, the Albanian Code of Medical Ethics of November 2011 should be examined. The Code of Medical Ethics was published by the Albanian Order of Physicians[146] and is legally binding for all the physicians affiliated with it (Article 3). In other words, disciplinary sanctions may be applied in cases of its infringement (Article 68 Code of Medical Ethics and Article 1 Regulation of 08.04.2016 of the Albanian Federation of Physicians).

o. Clearly, Article 39 Code of Medical Ethics states that in the case of an unconscious patient with a terminal illness, the physician must act on his judgment by considering the patient's best interest. He, in consultation with other colleagues and with patient relatives, decides on the therapeutic treatment. Thus, instructional medical directives are not considered at all. In addition, physicians shall also consult other colleagues as well as patient relatives. All of them must seek

146. The Order of Physicians was formed for the first time in 1993.

to serve the patient's best interests rather than follow the patient's wishes. This rule does not protect patient autonomy and his right to self-determination. Physicians, the medical staff, and the patient's relatives should consider the patient's wishes and only act according to the patient's best interests when those wishes are unclear. This is the only policy that safeguards patient autonomy.

p. The current paternalistic formulation of Article 39 Code of Medical Ethics might be considered unconstitutional since it violates the fundamental principle of equity, established in Article 18 of the Albanian constitution. Accordingly, Article 39 makes a distinction between conscious and unconscious patients by allowing the right to refuse medical treatments only to the first group. This means that an unconscious person may not be considered a person, and all previous wishes may lose validity. Further, the instructional medical directive protects patient dignity, which is also the core principle of modern democratic constitutions. In 1998, for the first time in the Albanian legal history, dignity has become one of the main constitutional principles, also recognized in the preamble of the current constitution (Omar & Anastasi, 2008).

q. Moreover, Article 39 Code of Medical Ethics is also in contrast with international law, which Albania has ratified. In concrete, Article 9 of the Oviedo Convention states that "the previously expressed wishes relating to a medical intervention by a patient who is not, at the time of the intervention, in a state to express his or her wishes shall be taken into account." Although according to it, "previously expressed wishes" are not legally binding, Article 39 of the Albanian Code of Medical Ethics does not include at all the importance of them. As a result, Article 39 is also unconstitutional since the Albanian constitution recognizes that laws and other normative acts of the Council of Ministers shall be aligned not only with the constitution but also with ratified international agreements (Article 116 Albanian Constitution). Since July 2011, the Oviedo Convention entered into force also in Albania.

r. In addition, the formulation of Article 39 Albanian Code of Medical Ethics is also in contrast with *soft*-law documents published by the Council of Europe. Judges can also apply these *soft*-law documents since part of the doctrine has underlined that even nonbinding international documents may influence State behavior. The application of *soft*-law documents as a main source of law has also been done by the ECtHR (Veshi 2015). For instance, the ECtHR has applied the Convention on Human Rights and Biomedicine of 1997 toward the UK that has not ratified it yet (ECtHR, *Glass v. the UK*, Application No. 61827/00) or toward France that at that time had not ratified this convention (ECtHR, *Vo v. France*, Application No. 53924/00). In more concrete terms, Article 39 Code of Medical Ethics is in contrast with Principle 15 Recommendation REC(2009)11, which states that instructional medical directives that do not have a binding force should be treated as statements of wishes to be given due respect. The use of the term "due respect" is stronger than the phrase "shall be taken into consideration," used in Article 9 of the Convention of Oviedo.[147]

---

147. However, it must be mentioned that the French version of this recommendation uses the same expression that appears in the Convention of Oviedo.

s. Thus, instructional medical directives are an important instrument to highlight patient right to self-determination since according to the majority of the bioethicists, in case of a patient's incapacity, medical decisions at end-of-life must be made according to the so-called *three-step hierarchy* in the following order: (1) patient's wishes, (2) substitute judgments and only at the end (3) patient's best interest (Buchanan and Brock 1990), understood as objective medical criteria.

510. In addition, to increase the implementation of ethical principle of patient autonomy in end-of-life decisions, the paper suggested some policy recommendations. The need for ad hoc rules governing end-of-life decisions is fundamental to underline patient dignity since the medical community has applied a paternalistic approach to end-of-life decisions. By considering the international literature that has promoted patient autonomy, the authors asserted that the instructional medical directives in written forms should have legally binding force (or at least be highly considered by the medical staff) and should be without time or object limitations. Furthermore, rules should be established in the case of citizens who are incapable to write or in the cases of revocation when a situation of emergency and urgency exists.

511. In conclusion, ad hoc rules governing end-of-life decisions will enforce the ethical principle of patient autonomy. Until that moment, Albanian physicians as well as judges should apply the ethical principle of patient autonomy. The authors also suggest the application of the principle of human dignity in end-of-life decisions. Human dignity is one of the most important values crystallized in the Albanian constitution of 1998, which is mentioned not only in Articles 3 and 28 but also in the preamble. This value has already been applied by the Albanian Constitutional Court in case law (e.g., Albanian Constitutional Court No. 25 of 28 April 2014 and No. 33, of 10 April 2017). Furthermore, respect for human dignity has been codified in the European Charter of Medical Ethics, of which the Order of Physicians of Albania follows.

512. The previously expressed wishes relating to a medical intervention by a patient who is not, at the time of the intervention, in a state to express his or her wishes shall be considered (Article 9 Oviedo Convention). Moreover, by applying the medical jurisprudence of the ECtHR, the withdrawal of life-supporting medical equipment should be considered legal. Therefore, physicians should not be liable for intentional homicide (Article 76 PC), homicide committed in other specific circumstances (Article 79 PC), or for homicide by request of the victim (Article 99 PC) (*see* paragraph 607).

513. During COVID-19, the application of ethical principles has been challenged. Several countries have underlined the lack of intensive care beds and ventilators for patients. If the epidemic curve of infected individuals is flattened over a long period, the Albanian healthcare system will also suffer. The principle of justice is the main ethical principle that should guide the fair allocation of scarce medical resources during a pandemic. Although there should not be a distinction between patients with COVID-19 and others that need the same medical devices, priority should be given to younger patients (thus, maximizing benefits) as well as health-care workers and others who care for ill patients (thus, promoting instrumental value) (Rosenbaum, 2011; Emanuel et al., 2020).

514. While others might not have access to needed medical treatment, access to care should be guaranteed. This recommendation is also aligned with Principle 8 of the European Charter of Medical Ethics, which states that "while respecting personal autonomy, the physician will act in accordance with the principle of treatment efficacy, taking into consideration the equitable use of resources." Therefore, during this pandemic, physicians should protect human dignity and guarantee care to all patients (Principle 3 of the European Charter of Medical Ethics) while prioritizing some groups of patients without being liable for criminal charges.

515. Considering the scarce medical resources during a pandemic as well as the application of international law, in the cases of withdrawal or withholding of life-supporting medical equipment of unconscious patients who have previously expressed their autonomy via instructional medical directives even in the absence of specific rules governing ADs, physicians should not be liable for intentional homicide (Article 76 PC), homicide committed in other specific circumstances (Article 79 PC), or for homicide by request of the victim (Article 99 PC) (*see* paragraph 604).

II. Physician-Assisted Suicide

516. Article 99 Albanian CCr states causing suicide or a suicide attempt on a person because of systematic maltreatment or other systematic misbehaviors which seriously affect the dignity, committed by another person being the superior, or by the person having family or cohabitation relation shall be punished for three up to seven years imprisonment:

a. This Section studies causing suicide or suicide attempts in Albania by considering a case law approach from the Albanian judges. Through a judicial review, its goal is to understand if PAS is prohibited. In addition, this Section includes an analysis of the traditional literature against the legalization of PAS. In other words, the Section uses four arguments uncovered by the literature that have underlined the importance of criminalization of PAS. However, for each argument, the Section includes the contrary arguments to legalize PAS. Moreover, this Section examines the application of foreign jurisprudence, the ECHR norms, and the ECtHR's jurisprudence by the Albanian Constitutional Court. Its aim is to understand if the Albanian constitutional judges are aware of them. Thus, in other words, if a constitutionality request for PAS is asked in the future, this Section predicts what the Albanian Constitutional Court would answer since—as explained in section II—other national Constitutional Courts have used foreign jurisprudence, the ECHR norms, and the ECtHR's jurisprudence to legalize PAS.

b. The legalization of PAS is based on the protection of human dignity (Weber-Guskar, 2020). It shall be underlined that human dignity is fundamental in the Albanian post-communist constitution. Indeed, human dignity is not protected only in the preamble but also in Article 3 Constitution. As a result of it, the Albanian Constitution recognizes, in the case of violation of human rights, a constitutional complaint (Article 131(1)(f) or Article 134 (1)(g) Albanian Constitution). Thus, while in other countries (i.e., Italy: Article 134 Constitution, France: Articles 56–63 Constitution, or Portugal: Article 229 Constitution),[148] citizens do not have direct access to the national Constitutional Courts, Albania recognizes a constitutional complaint, which is also similar to what has been established in Germany (Article 93(1)(4a) German Basic Law), or Spain (Article 161(b) Constitution). The common historical background between these countries is that all these countries had a totalitarian regime, either communist, Nazism, or the Franco regime. Thus, constitutional complaints can be made about all the decisions of the Supreme Court that violate human rights.

517. Although human dignity is fundamental in the Albanian constitution, and the legalization of PAS is based on promoting human dignity, it seems that PAS in Albania violates Article 99 of the CCr. The review of the Albanian judicial approach to Article 99 of the CCr showed that Albanian jurisprudence has not dealt with PAS yet since all cases dealt with the systematic maltreatment given by victims' husbands.[149] Nevertheless, according to Albanian jurisprudence, the perpetrator can be a person with material dependence or any other dependence (official, professional, etc.),[150] and the object of a crime can also be deprivation of food or water.[151] Thus, it seems that Article 99 of the CCr criminalizes PAS since, also, in the case of PAS, there is a dependency between the patient and the physician. Furthermore, deprivation of food or water might be one of the cases of PAS:

a. The Albanian legislator has codified the traditional ethical doctrine that criminalized PAS. Focusing on the ethical analysis of PAS, there are some contrary arguments for allowing PAS. First, according to a part of the doctrine, there is

---

148. It should be mentioned that Art. 161(b) Spanish Constitution recognizes a constitutional complain to its citizens. It should be noted that from 1939 to 1975, Spain was ruled by the dictatorship of Francisco Franco Bahamonde, and the current constitution was published in 1978.
149. Court of First Instance of Tirana, No. 518 of 02.04.2010, confirmed by the Court of Appeal of Tirana, No. 941 of 24.11.2010, while the High Court, No. 89 of 13.03.2013 quashes the decision since one of the judges who participated in determining the security measures was also part of the trial of the merits; Court of First Instance of Kruja, No. 130 of 06.07.2015, confirmed by the Court of Appeal of Tirana, No. 827 of 24.06.2016 (that has canceled the suspensive execution of the punishment), which then was also confirmed by the High Court, No. 601 of 21.04.2022; Court of First Instance of Pogradec, No. 410-22 of 02.05.2017, confirmed by the Court of Appeal of Korçë, No. 81 of 19.09.2017, while the High Court, No. 221 of 13.09.2022 quashes the decision since the Court of Appeal used the same reasoning of the Court of First Instance without replying to the claims of the applicant.
150. The High Court of Albania, No. 221 of 13.09.2022, par. 21.
151. The High Court of Albania, No. 221 of 13.09.2022.

an alternative to PAS, which is voluntary self-starvation,[152] which is legally accepted (Lachman, 2015; White et al., 2014). This approach is also validated by previous national jurisprudence,[153] which bases its legal decisions on the right to body integrity: no one's body can be invaded or violated without consent. Self-starvation, from a medical perspective, does not bring pain (Sullivan, 1993; van Aarnhem, 2014). After a short period of starvation, the liver will produce ketone bodies; after a longer period, the brain will produce endorphins. At this time, the body will not feel the need to eat. In addition, the progressive inconvenience of renal functions will lead to loss of feeling of thirst. Although it is a voluntary self-starvation, palliative care and medical control are necessary.

b. Although this is an alternative between PAS and voluntary self-starvation, there are several differences. The two main differences consist of the outcome as well as the time phase. While in the case of PAS, death will occur in a few hours through the overdose of barbiturates, in the case of voluntary self-starvation, death will occur between one to three weeks through terminal dehydration. Additionally, starvation is considered inhumane and a criminal offense. As a result, it seems to be unethical to stimulate voluntary self-starvation.
c. Second, PAS might be considered as contrary to the ethos of the medical profession (Veshi, 2016). Based on this idea, Article 39 of the Code of Medical Ethics states hastening the end of life—thus, PAS—is contrary to medical ethics. The previous jurisprudence also underlined this approach.[154] This legal approach has been overruled since it did not make sense that the doctor was obliged to give the medical treatment only after the patient's informed consent while he was obliged to intervene by not letting the patient die when the patient is unconscious. Thus, currently, in Western countries, the doctor is not obliged to intervene if a patient does not want to be treated, even in the case of life-saving medical treatment.[155]
d. Third, PAS, sometimes, is not a free choice (Velleman, 1992; Reichlin, 2002). Palliative care is expensive. In addition, several people would like not to burden other family members. By considering that the law cannot discriminate between poor/rich families or people with children or not, personal elements and specific situations play an important role when valuing if PAS is the result of a free choice. It seems that this issue has also been highlighted by the Italian

152. Vicki D. Lachman, "Voluntary stopping of eating and drinking: An ethical alternative to physician-assisted suicide." *Medsurg nursing* 24.1 (2015): 56–60.
153. For instance, in the UK, Re E (Medical Treatment: Anorexia) [2012] EWHC 1639 at [7]: [p]eople with capacity are entitled to make decisions for themselves, including about what they will and will not eat, even if their decision brings about their death' or also in Australia: *H Ltd v. J* (2010) 107 SASR 352 at [64].
154. Germany: Bundesgerichtshof, NJW 1984, *2639*.
155. Bundesgerichtshof Jul. 3, 2019, 5 StR 132/18 and 5 StR *393/18*, revising decisions from courts in Hamburg and Berlin, both concerning assisted suicide services provided before 2015.

National Bioethics Committee, which gave guidelines for PAS,[156] as well as by the Italian Constitutional Court,[157] which did not allow the referendum regarding euthanasia.

e. Fourth, the slippery slope theory has been used as an argument against the legalization of PAS. According to it, from the recognition of withdrawing treatment from terminally ill persons to ADs for all citizens, then PAS by courts, and in some countries, PAS by legislators and also euthanasia (Lewis, 2007; Smith, 2005). However, from an ethical approach, since, under certain hopeless circumstances, it is ethical to refuse life-supporting medical treatments, it should also be considered legal, under certain hopeless circumstances, to request PAS (Beauchamp, 1999, p. 226). In addition, as stated in Sect. II, all the Constitutional Courts of Italy, Germany, and Austria underlined that there is no difference between refusing life-supporting treatments and PAS.

518. Another justification regarding PAS, if PAS is limited only to terminally ill patients, is the application of the double effect theory: physicians aim to alleviate patient suffering, while death is not their goal (Potter, 2015). Thus, the negative result, death, is the result of a positive action, end of suffering. In several cases, i.e., terminally ill patients, this is the only option for them to die with dignity:

a. Considering that other national Constitutional Courts have used foreign jurisprudence, the ECHR norms, and the ECtHR's jurisprudence to legalize PAS, it is important to understand the Albanian constitutional approach toward foreign jurisprudence, the ECHR norms, and the ECtHR's jurisprudence. Indeed, this Section reviews it by considering the decisions of the Constitutional Court over the last three years.
b. Albania has been part of the Council of Europe since 13 July 1995 and ratified the ECHR in 1996 (Law No. 8137 of 31.07.1996). Thus, Albanian judges shall also apply the ECHR norms and the ECtHR's jurisprudence since the Albanian Constitution (Article 5, Article 116(1)(b), and Article 122(2)) establishes that international treaties ratified by the Albanian Parliament are mandatory and have a higher rank than the internal legislation.

519. The Albanian legal framework addressing PAS reflects a nuanced intersection of criminal law and ethics, particularly as articulated through Article 99 of the CCr.[158] This provision criminalizes causing suicide or attempted suicide through systematic maltreatment or behavior that significantly undermines human dignity. Over time, the legislative focus has shifted to emphasize the family or dependent

---

156. National Bioethics Committee. Bioethical reflections on medically assisted suicide. 2019. http://bioetica.governo.it/media/3797/medically-assisted-suicide.pdf.
157. The Italian Constitutional Court, Decision 50/2022 of February 2022.
158. Law 144/2013 of 2.5.2013: "*Causing suicide or a suicide attempt on a person because of systematic maltreatment or other systematic misbehaviors that seriously affect the dignity, committed by another person who has material dependence, or any other dependence is punishable by a fine or imprisonment up to five years.*" [author' translation]

relationship between the perpetrator and the victim, underscoring the need to safeguard vulnerable individuals within intimate or dependent dynamics.[159] This change highlights the Albanian legal system's prioritization of protecting human dignity and ensuring accountability for actions that exploit positions of authority or dependency.[160] Importantly, the law requires a clear causal link between the systematic maltreatment and the suicide or attempted suicide of the victim. This evidentiary threshold ensures that not all cases of suicide are criminally prosecuted, but only those where a deliberate and systematic pattern of harm directly caused the tragic outcome.[161]

520. Additionally, the interpretation of Article 99 aligns with broader ethical and legal standards, emphasizing the principle of indirect intent or *"dolus eventualis,"* where the perpetrator is aware of the possible consequences of their actions but continues, nonetheless. The Albanian judiciary has emphasized that systematic maltreatment includes behaviors such as deprivation of food or water, severe psychological abuse, or continuous physical harm.[162] By this interpretation, the law indirectly criminalizes forms of PAS, particularly when there is a dependency relationship, such as between a patient and physician. The Code of Medical Ethics explicitly prohibits actions that hasten death, reinforcing the dual ethical and legal stance against both PAS and euthanasia.[163] These provisions underscore the Albanian legal system's commitment to balancing the sanctity of life with the principles of accountability and justice, while also upholding human dignity in cases involving vulnerable individuals. Through its integration of criminal law, judicial interpretation, and ethical obligations, the framework reflects a comprehensive approach to safeguarding life and ensuring that acts undermining dignity are met with appropriate legal consequences.[164]

159. The current version of Art. 99 CCr is: "*Causing suicide or a suicide attempt on a person because of systematic maltreatment or other systematic misbehaviors which seriously affect the dignity, committed by another person being the superior, or by the person having family or cohabitation relation shall be punished for three up to seven years imprisonment.*" [author' translation]
160. The High Court of Albania, No. 221 of 13.09.2022.
161. Court of Appeal of Tirana, No. 827 of 24.06.2016.
162. The High Court of Albania, No. 221 of 13.09.2022.
163. Court of First Instance of Pogradec, No. 410-22 of 02.05.2017, confirmed by the Court of Appeal of Korçë, No. 81 of 19.09.2017.
164. Court of First Instance of Kruja, No. 130 of 06.07.2015 confirmed by the Court of Appeal of Tirana, No. 827 of 24.06.2016.

Chapter 3. Specific Activities

§1. Abortion

521. Law No. 8045, dated 7.12.1995 For Termination of Pregnancy guarantees respect for every human being from the beginning of life. This principle shall not be violated, except when it is necessary and under the conditions defined in this law. Protection of this principle, information about the problems of life and national demography, education, social responsibilities, acceptance of the child in society and family policy are national obligations. Central and local government bodies fulfill these obligations and support any initiative that helps for their realization.

522. This law is based on the following principles: (1) The health service of all levels must use family planning services to avoid unwanted pregnancies. Termination of pregnancy is not considered in any case as a method of family planning. (2) The woman has the right to accurate information and counseling before termination of pregnancy. (3) In cases where termination of pregnancy is not contrary to the provisions of this law, it must be performed in safe conditions for the woman's health. (4) In all cases, women must be provided with health services for the treatment of possible complications after termination of pregnancy. (5) Counseling and family planning service must take place after termination of pregnancy, to avoid unwanted pregnancies. (6) Termination of pregnancy is allowed only when undesirable circumstances are proven by law and in any case with the consent of the woman (Article 2, Law No. 8045, dated 7.12.1995 For Termination of Pregnancy).

523. Voluntary termination of pregnancy is performed only by a specialist obstetrician gynecologist in state and private health institutions that meet the conditions defined in the relevant instruction of the Minister of Health and Environmental Protection (Article 3, Law No. 8045, dated 7.12.1995 For Termination of Pregnancy).

524. The doctor to whom the voluntary termination of pregnancy is requested must inform the woman in the first visit about: (1) The medical risks that termination of pregnancy brings for future pregnancies, as well as biological problems of medical intervention. (2) The rights, assistance and advantages guaranteed by law for the family, mother and child and the possibilities of adoption of the children expected to be born. (3) Institutions and organizations that can provide moral and financial support to women. (4) Clinics and hospitals that perform termination of pregnancy (Article 4, Law No. 8045, dated 7.12.1995 For Termination of Pregnancy).

525. The Minister of Health and Environmental Protection determines with a special instruction the content, the way of drafting and distribution of instructional materials with information as regulated by law (Article 5, Law No. 8045, dated 7.12.1995 For Termination of Pregnancy).

526. In case the woman, after receiving the information mentioned in Article 4, repeats her request for termination of pregnancy, the doctor requires written confirmation of the request. This confirmation is required after at least seven days have passed since the first request. When possible, in counseling and making the decision to terminate the pregnancy, the spouse or parent also participates. If the period of seven days leads to exceeding the deadlines defined in this law, the doctor may decide that this deadline should be at least two extra days (Article 6, Law No. 8045, dated 7.12.1995 For Termination of Pregnancy).

527. In case of confirmation, the doctor terminates the pregnancy under the conditions defined in Article 3 of Law No. 8045, dated 7.12.1995 For Termination of Pregnancy. When the doctor to whom the request is directed is not the one who will perform the intervention, then the request is returned to the woman together with a certificate on compliance with the procedures of Articles 4 and 6 of Law No. 8045, dated 7.12.1995 For Termination of Pregnancy to present to the doctor who will perform the termination of pregnancy. The state or private institution where the woman is accepted must include it in her card request and certification for compliance with procedures (Article 7, Law No. 8045, dated 7.12.1995 For Termination of Pregnancy).

528. In case of pregnancy out of wedlock in minor girls up to 16 years old, in addition to her request, Termination of pregnancy requires the approval of the person exercising parental authority or her legal guardian. The request of the girl herself must be made without the presence of the people mentioned in the above paragraph. Married minors are subject to the provisions of Article 7 of Law No. 8045, dated 7.12.1995 For Termination of Pregnancy (Article 8, Law No. 8045, dated 7.12.1995 For Termination of Pregnancy).

529. Termination of pregnancy for medical reasons can be done up to the twenty-second week of pregnancy, if a committee consisting of three doctors, after examination and consultation, judges that the continuation of the pregnancy and/or the birth of the child endangers the life or health of the woman. When the commission judges that the fetus has malformations incompatible with life, or disease invalid with uncertain treatment, decides to terminate the pregnancy at any time. The Minister of Health and Environmental Protection determines with a special instruction the cases mentioned in the first paragraph of this article, as well as the conditions that must be met by doctors and the commission (Article 9, Law No. 8045, dated 7.12.1995 For Termination of Pregnancy).

530. In cases where the woman assesses that the pregnancy creates psychosocial problems, the voluntary termination can be carried out within the twelfth week of pregnancy (Article 10, Law No. 8045, dated 7.12.1995 For Termination of Pregnancy). Termination of pregnancy for social reasons takes place within the twenty-second week, upon the composition of a commission of three specialists, doctors, social workers, lawyers, after examination and consultation, decide that the pregnancy is the result of rape or another sexual crime, as well as when other social reasons are proven. The instructions for handling these cases and the composition of the commission are approved by the Minister of Health and Environmental Protection (Article 11, Law No. 8045, dated 7.12.1995 For Termination of Pregnancy).

531. All terminations of pregnancy must be subject to a declaration confirmed by the doctor who performs the interruption, which is sent by the institution to the Institute of Statistics. The data for pregnancy terminations are sent from the state and private health institution to the Ministry of Health and Environmental Protection, according to the relevant instructions. The declaration and other information must not contain the identity of the woman (Article 12, Law No. 8045, dated 7.12.1995 For Termination of Pregnancy). All women's counseling is required to be given to women seeking pregnancy termination, the information and advice provided for in this law and in other bylaws for its implementation (Article 13, Law No. 8045, dated 7.12.1995 For Termination of Pregnancy).

532. In all cases of termination of pregnancy, the doctor who performs them is obliged to inform women about family planning services and advise them about contraceptive methods that are offered by the institution where he works and/or other state and private institutions (Article 14, Law No. 8045, dated 7.12.1995 For Termination of Pregnancy).

533. Any type of propaganda and advertising, directly or indirectly, by word or image, of institutions, methods, medications and products that cause termination of pregnancy is prohibited, except in scientific publications intended for doctors and pharmacists (Article 15, Law No. 8045, dated 7.12.1995 For Termination of Pregnancy).

534. No doctor can be forced to terminate a pregnancy against his will. Violation of the provisions provided in Articles 4, 6, 7, 12, 13, 14 and 16 of this law, when it does not constitute a criminal offense, is punished as an administrative misdemeanor with a fine from 50 thousand to 100 thousand Lek. Violation of the provisions provided for in Article 15 is punishable by a fine of up to ALL 100,000. Fines are issued by control bodies designated by the Minister of Health and Environmental Protection (Article 17, Law No. 8045, dated 7.12.1995 For Termination of Pregnancy).

I. Abortion and the Right to Life According to Article 2 of the ECHR

535. Abortion issues and the rights related to the fetus are provided under Article 2 ECHR. In relation to the issues of abortion, the claimant mainly at the time of drafting the requests addressed to the ECHR, in addition to using Article 2 ECHR, can also use as a legal basis the right to the protection of private and family life, the right to have access to court regarding access to information on abortion as well as the right to freedom of expression.

536. In the case of *Brüggemann and Scheuten v. Germany*, the applicant used as a legal basis Article 8 ECHR which guarantees the right to respect for "private life," arguing that only the woman had the right to decide whether to undergo an abortion. In another case, *X v. the United Kingdom*, the Commission argued that Article 2 ECHR does not provide protection for abortion. It does not include abortion in the list of permissible acts listed in the second paragraph which are not considered to be against this article. According to the Commission, this meant that there were only three possibilities: either that Article 2 ECHR does not cover the unborn fetus at all, or that it recognizes the right to life of the fetus with some implicit limitations; or that gives the fetus an absolute right to life. The commission excluded the interpretation of the idea of giving the fetus the quality of the bearer of the absolute right to life. It was not acceptable that the mother's life is considered of a lower value than that of the fetus.

537. Since 1950, since the drafting of the ECHR, debates had arisen as to whether "a trend toward further liberalization of abortion" could be tolerated. In an early case of the 1980s, there was an attempt to interpret Article 2 ECHR in favor of a positive answer to the first question, i.e., the recognition of the fetus as the bearer of the absolute right to life, equating it with the person born alive. When it was discussed about the limitations on the right in the content of the second sentence of the first paragraph of Article 2 ECHR, it was found that all the above limitations, by their nature, relate to persons who have already been born and do not apply to the fetus, it was concluded that both the general use of the term "toute personne" in the Convention and the context in which this term is used in Article 2 ECHR tend to support the view that it does not include the unborn child.

II. Abortion Issues in Albania

538. The Constitution of the Republic of Albania in its Article 21 states "that the life of the person is protected by law." The Republic of Albania has ratified the European Convention on Human Rights and the International Covenant on Civil and Political Rights, and Article 116 of the Constitution of the Republic of Albania states that international acts ratified by law have legal force throughout the territory of the Republic of Albania.

539. In Albania, the protection of the right to life has deep historical roots, supported by both domestic and international legal frameworks. From its earliest periods, life was regarded as sacred, with strong societal and legal prohibitions against acts such as abortion. Under customary law, governed by various traditional canons, any action endangering a woman's life was deemed a grave crime against life. The norms of the canons prescribed blood feud as the punitive measure for such violations, reflecting the seriousness with which the protection of life was upheld in Albanian tradition.

540. Over the years, a significant trend has emerged in the distribution of abortion types, with a marked increase in spontaneous abortions compared to terminations at the request of the woman. In 2009, spontaneous abortions accounted for 48.1% of the total number of abortions. This percentage grew steadily, reaching

67.2% in 2013. By 2018, spontaneous abortions constituted 79% of all cases, while terminations upon request dropped to 21%. This trend continued into 2020, with spontaneous abortions further increasing to 80.8%, leaving terminations at 19.2%. These statistics highlight a notable shift in the dynamics of abortion types over time. However, it should be considered that the overall trend of abortion has decreased, as have abortions on demand of the woman as well as spontaneous ones, with a higher decreasing trend in abortions on demand.

541. On December 7, 1995, the People's Assembly approved Law No. 8045, "For termination of pregnancy." Although its Article 1 stipulates that the Law guarantees the respect of every human being from the beginning of life, exceptions are also given that this principle can be violated when it is necessary and under the conditions defined in this law. Law "For termination of pregnancy" guarantees the respect of every human being from the beginning of their life, i.e., from the stage of their conception. Termination of pregnancy is allowed only for health reasons (mother and child) and for psychosocial reasons in the case of one out-of-wedlock pregnancy of minors up to 16 years old where termination of pregnancy is done with the approval of the parent or legal guardian.

542. In addition to cases of termination of pregnancy for health reasons, voluntary termination at the request of the mother is also allowed. The Albanian CCr, in its section V, deals with criminal offenses that endanger life and health from termination of pregnancy or failure to help. It provides for fines or imprisonment of up to five years in cases of termination of pregnancy without the consent of the woman excluding here the justified cases of protection of the woman's health. This offense is punishable by a fine or imprisonment of up to five years.

543. Pursuant to this section, Articles 94 and 95 also provide for sanctions for illegal abortion, considering it a criminal offense punishable by a fine or imprisonment of up to two years, and the measure is aggravated by a fine or imprisonment of up to five years when the cause of the abortion is threatened or caused the death of the mother. In Article 95, it is considered a criminal offense to provide means to terminate a pregnancy, being punished with a fine or imprisonment of up to one year.

544. From the interpretation of the above provisions of the Albanian CCr, it seems clear that abortion in Albania is not prohibited but limited. This is in connection with the constitutional provision of Article 21 of the Constitution of the Republic of Albania, which enshrines the right to life. The character of the absolute right in Albania, the right to life benefits from its importance and the ranking among other rights in the ECHR, in the Charter of Human Rights of the United Nations, etc., the sanctions provided for among them are mandatory for national law since Albania has joined these organizations, it benefits from its quality as the foundation of rights, the universal one, which guarantees and enables the exercise of all other personal and political rights, through which enable the very existence of the democratic system, which we have chosen as the most appropriate to regulate coexistence, at least in Western countries.

545. Law No. 8045, dated 7.12.1995 "On Termination of Pregnancy" for the first time legitimized the process of abortion but with the restriction that it should only be performed by a specialist obstetrician gynecologist in health institutions, which could be state or private but according to the instructions of the Minister of Health and Environmental Protection. Article 9 of this law defined the cases in which abortion was allowed with the authorization of a doctor. In the case where the doctor finds that the fetus has malformations incompatible with life, or a disabling disease with uncertain treatment, he must immediately inform the woman for her to make an appropriate decision regarding the abortion process, as well as the doctor who is obliged to provide detailed information about the negative consequences of abortion. Law No. 8045, dated 7.12.1995 "On Termination of Pregnancy" in Article 6 provides for a seven-day deadline regarding the submission of the request for abortions to the doctor who will perform the intervention and further in Article 8 of the law, the conditions for the realization of the request for abortion in the case of minor girls.

546. An analysis of the provisions of Law No. 8045, dated 7.12.1995, "On Termination of Pregnancy," alongside the relevant sections of the CCr, reveals a degree of ambiguity surrounding the regulation of abortion in Albania. The legal framework permits abortion as a legitimate process, allowing it to be performed without stringent procedural requirements up to the tenth week of pregnancy. Beyond this period, the procedure is restricted and requires the submission of a formal written request, thereby introducing limitations and procedural obligations.

§2. Sterilization

547. Sterilization means a medical surgical procedure, by means of which it is performed the permanent prohibition of an individual's ability to reproduce. Sterilization is a legal method for family planning and is performed only when: (a) the patient gives written consent; the individual meets the age criterion (Article 15, Law No. 8876, dated 4.4.2002 For Reproductive Health).

548. Every individual has the right, in accordance with his wishes, to undergo surgical sterilization methods (Article 16, Law No. 8876, dated 4.4.2002 For Reproductive Health).

I. Termination of Pregnancy and Sterilization

549. The doctor is prohibited from terminating pregnancy and performing sterilization procedures, except in the conditions provided by legal acts. The doctor is not allowed to terminate a pregnancy or perform a sterilization procedure without obtaining the consent of the interested parties after informing them about the indications, risks and possible consequences (Article 50 The Code of Medical Ethics and Deontology).

§3. In Vitro Fertilization

I. Reproductive Health

550. Sexual health is a state of physical, emotional, mental and social well-being in relation to sexuality and not simply the absence of disease, dysfunction or weakness. Sexual health requires a positive and respectful approach to sexuality and sexual relations, as well as the possibility of having satisfactory sexual experiences and safety, without coercion, discrimination and violence. For sexual health to be achieved and maintained, it is necessary to respect, protect and fulfill the rights of all persons.

551. Reproductive health encompasses the processes, functions, and systems related to reproduction across all stages of life. It ensures that individuals can experience a responsible, satisfying, and safe sexual life, possess the ability to reproduce, and exercise the freedom to decide if, when, and how to do so. As such, reproductive health is intrinsically linked to and forms a vital component of reproductive rights.

552. Reproductive rights refer to the fundamental rights of all couples and individuals to decide freely and responsibly the number of their children. They have the right to receive the information and methods to meet this and to achieve a higher standard of sexual and reproductive health. They also include the right to make decisions about reproduction without discrimination, force and violence, as provided in human rights legal frameworks.

553. Law No. 8876, dated 4.4.2002 regulates reproductive health in the Republic of Albania related to the organization, operation and supervision of all activities that are developed in the field of reproductive health, in private and public health institutions. It protects the individual's reproductive rights and that of the couple and ensures that the reproductive rights of everyone are protected in accordance with national laws and policies and other recognized international principles.

554. "Reproductive health" encompasses the overall physical, mental, and social well-being of individuals, free from diseases, disabilities, or other conditions that could impede the proper functioning of the reproductive system. It includes having the necessary conditions for reproductive functions and processes, as well as the ability to enjoy a safe and fulfilling sexual life. This definition emphasizes the right to reproductive autonomy, allowing individuals to decide freely on the timing and manner of reproduction while ensuring access to comprehensive information and services to support these choices (Article 2, Law No. 8876, dated 4.4.2002 For Reproductive Health).

555. Reproductive healthcare includes a range of methods, techniques and services that affect the reproductive health of people, preventing and solving their problems, as follows:

a. services and counseling, information, education, communication for family planning;
b. services and education for prenatal care, safe birth and postpartum care, especially breastfeeding.
c. services and education for children, adolescents and healthcare for women;
d. prevention and treatment for sexually transmitted diseases, HIV/AIDS, e infections and diseases of the reproductive tract;
e. safe abortion and management of complications related to abortion;
f. information, education and counseling on sexuality and reproductive health;
g. referral services for family planning, pregnancy complications, abortion, infertility, reproductive tract infections, breast cancers and cancers of the reproductive system, menopause, sexually transmitted diseases, including HIV/AIDS;
h. prevention and appropriate treatment of infertility (Article 3, Law No. 8876, dated 4.4.2002 For Reproductive Health).

556. Sexual health is part of reproductive health and means improving life and healthy sexual relations, information, counseling, reproductive care and sexually transmitted diseases. Sexual health includes: (a) normal development; (b) equal and responsible sexual relations accepted equally by every partner; (c) avoidance of diseases and any disability, coercion, violence and any practical behavior harmful related to sexuality; (d) the realization of an optimal sexual life (Article 4, Law No. 8876, dated 4.4.2002 For Reproductive Health).

557. Regarding information and care for sexual health, the doctor has the duty to work for the education and information of the population on issues of sexual health and prevention of sexually transmitted diseases. He should propagate and popularize the scientific methods of family planning and the use of scientifically proven and reliable contraceptives (Article 49 The Code of Medical Ethics and Deontology).

558. All individuals have the right to be informed, advised, educated and receive the necessary health and social service to have good sexual health, as well as exercise their reproductive and sexual rights and responsibilities (Article 5, Law No. 8876, dated 4.4.2002 For Reproductive Health).

559. Every woman, free and exempt from any form of discrimination, coercion and violence, has the right to be controlled and to decide freely on all matters related to her sexuality and sexual and reproductive health. Mutual respect of equal relations by women and men during sexual relations and reproduction means respect, non-violence of the integrity of each, understanding and sharing responsibilities for sexual behaviors and their consequences (Article 6, Law No. 8876, dated 4.4.2002 For Reproductive Health).

560. Safe Motherhood recognizes the right of every woman to receive the care she needs to have good health from pregnancy to childbirth. The main elements to ensure safe motherhood include access to high-quality care before, during and after birth, prevention of unwanted pregnancies, prevention of unsafe abortion and premature birth (Article 7, Law No. 8876, dated 4.4.2002 For Reproductive Health).

II. Reproduction Rights

561. All individuals and couples have the right to decide freely, but respecting the wish of each partner, for the time, number and interval of births, to be informed about the appropriate means of their realization, to seek the highest standards of reproductive and sexual health. This law guarantees every individual the decision-making for the exercise of reproductive rights according to their desire and interest, free from discrimination, coercion and violence (Article 8, Law No. 8876, dated 4.4.2002 For Reproductive Health).

562. Every individual has the right to choose his sexual relations and control his reproductive life. The choice must be made of his own free will, which means: (a) no woman should be forced to be pregnant; (b) any medical intervention related to reproductive and sexual health must be performed with the consent (acceptance) of the person on whom the intervention will be performed (Article 9, Law No. 8876, dated 4.4.2002 For Reproductive Health).

563. All individuals and couples have the right to benefit from the use of safe methods, affordable and acceptable family planning, according to their choice, as well as to other methods chosen for regulating fertility. All individuals and couples have the right to receive appropriate healthcare services to have a safe pregnancy and birth and a healthy baby. All individuals have the right to benefit from scientific progress and technological information about reproduction and sexuality, when they are safe and acceptable (Article 10, Law No. 8876, dated 4.4.2002 For Reproductive Health).

564. Women have the fundamental right to safe motherhood and the prevention of unwanted pregnancies that could endanger their lives. No woman's life should be jeopardized due to pregnancy, childbirth, or societal barriers stemming from gender inequality. The promotion and utilization of family planning services play a pivotal role in reducing the incidence of unintended pregnancies. Every woman is entitled to comprehensive health protection throughout her pregnancy, access to professional assistance during childbirth, and the benefit of modern medical practices and methods designed to minimize health risks to herself, the fetus, the newborn, and the child (Article 11, Law No. 8876, dated 4.4.2002 For Reproductive Health).

565. Every individual holds the fundamental right to health education, which encompasses access to accurate and comprehensive information necessary for informed decision-making in the realm of reproductive and sexual rights. This right ensures that individuals are equipped with the knowledge needed to make responsible and autonomous choices about their reproductive health. Moreover, the freedom to exercise reproductive and sexual health rights should remain unimpeded by external influences such as religion, philosophy, culture, or ideology, safeguarding the principles of autonomy and equality (Article 12, Law No. 8876, dated 4.4.2002 For Reproductive Health).

566. Every individual is entitled to medical care and essential health services necessary for safeguarding their health and overall well-being. This includes the right to access qualified care specifically addressing reproductive and sexual health needs. Motherhood and children hold a particular entitlement to healthcare and specialized support, ensuring their protection and well-being. Additionally, individuals of reproductive age have the right to seek medical examinations, appropriate treatments, and rehabilitation aimed at promoting healthy reproductive outcomes, reinforcing the importance of accessible and comprehensive healthcare services (Article 13, Law No. 8876, dated 4.4.2002 For Reproductive Health).

567. Reproductive healthcare and health services are provided by state medical services, from public and private legal entities, as well as from persons who have the right to exercise this activity in accordance with the legislation in force, that are licensed by the Ministry of Health for this type of activity. State medical services, public and private legal entities, as well as persons who have the right to exercise this activity in accordance with the legislation in force, are obliged to maintain the confidentiality and anonymity of the data, which are made known due to the activity that they exercise (Article 14, Law No. 8876, dated 4.4.2002 For Reproductive Health).

568. Every individual has the right to protect their reproductive abilities by complaining against actions, decisions, damages of third parties, when rights related to reproductive health are violated (Article 17, Law No. 8876, dated 4.4.2002 For Reproductive Health).

569. Every individual has the right to receive comprehensive information and access to health services, as well as medical and social assistance tailored to their chosen methods and techniques. These provisions must align with the individual's specific health condition, age, and personal characteristics, as recognized and regulated by law. Such measures aim to prevent unwanted pregnancies while ensuring that healthcare services are adapted to the unique needs and circumstances of each person (Article 18, Law No. 8876, dated 4.4.2002 For Reproductive Health).

570. Adolescents and young people are entitled to access information and services related to reproductive health. This includes comprehensive educational programs and resources aimed at preventing unwanted pregnancies, addressing abuse, and supporting their understanding of sexually active behavior. Such initiatives must be age appropriate and tailored to meet the specific developmental and information needs of this demographic (Article 19, Law No. 8876, dated 4.4.2002 For Reproductive Health).

571. All individuals have the right to: (a) treatment of infertility, including the application of modern methods and technologies for reproduction; (b) information on the content of supplementary reproductive technologies, efficiency, optimal periods for their implementation, medical consequences and possible consequences, as well as information on the validity of other methods for treating infertility. Couples and individuals will have the right to implement reproductive technologies only in the event of a mutual agreement (Article 20, Law No. 8876, dated 4.4.2002 For Reproductive Health).

III. Infertility

572. Infertility is the inability of a couple to conceive after twelve months of regular sexual intercourse, without the use of contraceptives in women under the age of 35 and after six months for women over the age of 35. Some doctors use the term sub-fertility to describe the inability of the couple to conceive, until proven sterile. Infertility is a unique medical condition, as it involves a couple and not a single individual. Infertility in married couples is not a rare condition, with significant psychological, economic, demographic and medical issues. In recent years, the demand for services dealing with infertility has increased substantially, although the prevalence of infertility remains roughly the same.

573. WHO reports 168 million couples in the reproductive period with primary infertility problems and/or secondary, mainly in developing countries. The WHO Task Force on the Diagnosis and Treatment of Infertility conducted a study with 8500 infertile couples and used standard diagnostic criteria to define medical conditions that contributed to infertility. In developed countries, the female factor of infertility was reported at 37% of infertile couples, the male factor of infertility in 8%, and together the male factor and female infertility in 35% of cases; 5% of couples had unexplained infertility and 15% of them, became pregnant during the study. This study illustrates that infertility should not be described as the result mainly of disorders of the female partner.

574. Infertility rates are significantly influenced by age, with notable variations in primary and secondary infertility. Primary infertility tends to be higher among women aged 20–24 and older women, whereas secondary infertility follows an opposite and more pronounced pattern. Regional variations in infertility rates have been observed, but the general trends for primary and secondary infertility often align across different areas, including Albania. A key factor contributing to infertility is the natural decline in female fertility, which becomes particularly evident after the age of 30. For this reason, it is recommended that women aged 35–40 begin infertility evaluations after six months of trying to conceive, and those over 40 undergo assessments in less than six months, reflecting the urgency to address age-related fertility declines.

575. Evaluation is also started earlier if the woman is at risk for early ovarian failure (major ovarian surgery, exposure to pelvic radiation or chemotherapy, autoimmune disease, smoking, family history of early menopause, advanced endometriosis, or pathology known tubes/uterus). The male factor can also be an indication for evaluation of early infertility such as: history of testicular trauma, adult parotitis, sexual dysfunction, chemotherapy/radiotherapy, or history of infertility with another partner.

576. Sexually transmitted infections (STIs) and infections of the reproductive tract are one of the other main causes of primary or secondary marital infertility; therefore, there is a need for prevention and treatment. Infertility is also related to lifestyle factors such as: body weight, smoking, stress. For this reason, lifestyle changes that can improve to achieve fertility are widely recommended such as: achieving an ideal body mass, quitting smoking and limiting alcohol and caffeine. Also, during the assessment of infertile couples, the doctor should not ignore the emotional state of the couple which may include depression, anger, anxiety and marital discord. It is currently estimated that more than 7 million babies have been born worldwide from IVF-ET and modifications, widely known as Assisted Reproductive Techniques (ARTs), since the reports of the birth of the first baby with in vitro fertilization in 1976 and 1978. With experience over the years, the percentage of success of these techniques has also increased. ARTs are calculated to contribute to 1%–3% of live births in the USA and Europe. Access to covered services for assisted reproduction has been associated with the increased use of ART techniques.

577. But the conservative therapy of the treatment of marital infertility is a prolonged costly therapy. WHO emphasizes that the psychosocial and socioeconomic impact of not having a child is greater in individuals, couples and communities, where diagnosis and treatment are more difficult for economic reasons. Knowledge of medication, use of protocols, types of medications and their dosage by medical personnel is a necessity and an urgent need, but often the cost is unaffordable for all couples. Thus, only a small portion of the world's population benefits from new reproductive technologies. Cost of infertility management is determined by the percentage of patients seeking treatment for infertility, its impact on the population and quality of treatment (total cost to society, multiple pregnancies, side effects and child health).

IV. Organization of Reproductive Health Service

578. The Minister of Health determines the structures and services of reproductive health, the criteria, the regulations of their operation, as well as the policy and development strategy for reproductive health (Article 21, Law No. 8876, dated 4.4.2002 For Reproductive Health).

579. The activity of reproductive healthcare services includes: (a) care before, during and after birth; (b) care for the growth and development of the child 0–6 years old; (c) care for the health of adolescents; (d) control and treatment of sexually transmitted diseases HIV/AIDS; (e) sexual information and education; (f) prevention of unwanted pregnancies through contraceptive methods for family planning; (g) voluntary termination of pregnancy; (h) sterility treatment and reproduction techniques; (i) treatment of diseases of the reproductive tract; (j) menopause treatment (Article 22, Law No. 8876, dated 4.4.2002 For Reproductive Health).

580. The reproductive health service is organized in public and private specialized clinics and licensed at all three levels of healthcare based on the instructions of the Minister of Health. Reproductive health services in primary healthcare carry out prevention, detection, treatment of reproductive health problems, health information and education, following pathologies in the reproductive system (Article 23, Law No. 8876, dated 4.4.2002 For Reproductive Health).

581. All pregnant women benefit from periodic medical follow-up of pregnancy for free birth and postpartum, especially mandatory prenatal and postpartum examinations that are determined by an act of the Minister of Health. The number and type of mandatory examinations and the period of their performance are determined with the instruction of the Minister of Health. All pregnant women have the right to perform mandatory examinations free of charge prescribed by the doctor and receive the personal notebook of pregnancy follow-up for free (Article 24, Law No. 8876, dated 4.4.2002 For Reproductive Health).

582. All children aged 0–6 years are entitled to benefit from preventive health measures, including free medical check-ups and follow-up care. The frequency and type of examinations, as well as the medical institutions responsible for conducting these checks, are established by regulations set forth by the Minister of Health. This framework ensures that early childhood health is prioritized and adequately monitored (Article 25, Law No. 8876, dated 4.4.2002 For Reproductive Health).

583. Contraceptive methods for family planning, acceptable for use in the country include condoms, vaginal barrier methods, oral contraceptives, implants, injectables, intrauterine devices, voluntary male and female sterilization and emergency contraception. Patients/clients should receive detailed information about the risks and advantages of each method (Article 26, Law No. 8876, dated 4.4.2002 For Reproductive Health).

584. Health information is divided into three main categories, as follows:

- Disease registers.
- Surveillance of diseases of special importance in public health.
- Data on the activity of health institutions.

585. The bylaws provide for the reporting method of the Abortion Registry; Register for people being tested for HIV; Family planning; Syndromic surveillance of STIs; Reporting domestic violence; Obstetric activity in health institutions or housing; The activity of the woman's consultant; Children's consultant activity.

586. National Agenda for Children's Rights 2021–2026 is a document which was drawn up on behalf of the Albanian Government by Ministry of Health and Social Protection and is a commitment to fulfill children's rights in Albania with a period of 2021–2026 (Decision of the Council of Ministers No. 659 dated 3.11.2020 "On the approval of the National Agenda for Children's Rights 2021–2026").

587. The year 2020 marked the conclusion of the implementation period for several key national frameworks, including the National Strategy for Development and Integration 2015–2020 and the National Agenda for Children's Rights 2017–2020. These initiatives, along with other significant national policies, were instrumental in advancing developments aimed at safeguarding children's rights and were designed to address the necessity of quality strategic planning in this critical area.

588. The National Agenda for Children's Rights consolidates and creates continuity of work carried out in the framework of the previous National Agenda for children's rights (2017–2020), addressing ongoing gaps and new challenges and reflecting innovative perspectives, and especially those related to the European Union Strategy for Children's Rights. This document with a cross-cutting approach forms the basis for enabling coordination of efforts between ministries and four different sectors; and to guide the national regulatory framework toward a harmonized and effective strategy for children.

589. AKDF presents a multidisciplinary and systematic framework, which should be integrated into all documents, plans and other national and local activities related to children, in the spirit of the United Nations Convention on the Rights of the Child (UN CCr), Convention on the Rights of Persons with Disabilities (CRPD), Council of Europe Strategy for Children's Rights (2016–2021) and the European Union (EU) Strategy for Children's Rights. AKDF is guided by the four general principles of the Convention on the Rights of the Child, namely: non-discrimination; the best interest of the child; life, survival, and development; and attendance.

V. The Situation of Maternal Health in Albania

A. *Antenatal and Postnatal Care*

590. Antenatal care (ANC) has been identified as one of the country priorities of health policies. Routine ANC in Albania includes periodic examination of the pregnant woman, a series of laboratory tests, such as: blood and urine tests, screening for STIs, Rh factor test, etc.

591. In Albania, ANC and postnatal care (PNC) are integrated into the primary healthcare system, and women have free access to these services. Births are mainly performed in the public sector in regional maternity hospitals, as well as in tertiary-level hospitals in Tirana. Although caesarean sections can reduce maternal and neonatal mortality, they should be performed when they have a medical indication.

592. The postnatal period is defined as the time from the exit of the placenta to forty-two days after birth. This is a critical period for both the mother and the newborn, as studies show that most maternal and neonatal deaths occur within two days after birth.

593. The number of deaths in Albania has decreased since the registered numbers since 1990. According to INSTAT statistics, there were 22.7 deaths/100,000 live births in 1990. In 2013, the number decreased to 11.8 deaths per 100,000 births alive. The numbers further decreased to 7 deaths/100,000 live births in 2019 and of 3.6 deaths/100,000 live births in 2020. This number increased to 7.2 deaths/100,000 live births.

594. Based on the data of the Ministry of Health and Social Protection, the main causes of maternal mortality are bleeding (hemorrhages), postpartum infections, pre-eclampsia and eclampsia during pregnancy, as well as unsafe abortion.

B. Birth Rate

595. According to INSTAT, in 2001, the synthetic fertility index was 2.3 children per woman. In the years then a decline is noted. In the developed world, a fertility rate of 2.1 is considered the replacement level of the population, or in other words, the average number of births per woman to keep the population level constant. The fertility rate in Albania, as in most developed countries, has reached one downward trend since 2013. In 2017 the average fertility rate was 1.48, and in 2020 it went to 1.34.

596. The Albanian government is following a pronatalist policy to increase the level of fertility in the country through financial incentives such as a bonus of the baby at birth that is offered since January 1, 2019; through the law that guarantees paid maternity leave for both mother and father and scheduled reduced work for the breastfeeding mother. Another aspect that affects the growth of the fertility level in the country is the opportunity offered to parents for long-term childcare day in institutions such as nurseries and kindergartens, with minimal accessible and easily affordable costs. In our country, all children attend free and quality education. Mothers' appropriate healthcare is provided free of charge, before and after birth. Children are guaranteed the right to free healthcare of the highest standard, as well as the benefit of treatment services for illness and for the rehabilitation of health. Periodic visits of the employees of the mother and child consultant to the apartment of the pregnant woman and the child up to the age of 1 (one) are mandatory.

597. They are performed according to the basic package of primary healthcare services and protocols standards for these services and are made to protect the health of the mother and the child. In the primary healthcare services, quality care is provided free of charge for the woman around birth including preconception care, pregnancy, birth and postpartum care. Also counseling and information related to issues of infertility, assisted reproduction methods, etc. An assessment of the most common problems is also provided. The Albanian government is working to promote healthy behaviors that can help in preserving and protecting the fertility of the population. The focus is on health-related promotion with the prevention, early detection and treatment of health conditions or problems that can threaten fertility. An important factor remains the reduction of exposures to environmental, occupational, infectious and iatrogenic agents (conditions resulting from medical activity) that may threaten the fertility of individuals.

C. *Family Planning*

598. Among the many issues concerning sexual and reproductive health, addressing the un-met need for family planning (FP) services remains a priority. Family planning plays a crucial role in fostering sustainable development within any society. Comprehensive family planning programs, which include access to modern contraceptive methods, empower couples and individuals to realize and exercise their fundamental right to freely and responsibly determine if, when, and how many children they wish to have. A wealth of international evidence underscores the transformative impact of effective family planning initiatives, demonstrating significant improvements in health outcomes, such as reductions in maternal, infant, and child mortality rates. Furthermore, these programs contribute to enhanced educational attainment, economic opportunities, and overall empowerment, particularly for women.

D. *The Situation of Family Planning in Albania*

599. Currently, the main modern contraceptive methods used in the Albanian context include pills, condoms and injections. Moreover, according to the National Security Strategy Contraceptives 2017–2021, in 2019 emergency contraceptives were also introduced in the basic family package planning services. Currently, contraceptives are available in Albania from the following three sources: free of charge (provided by the government); at subsidized prices (provided by social marketing programs); and at market prices (provided by the private sector). According to official information from the Ministry of Health and Social Protection, free contraceptives are available in 416 family planning clinics in the public sector in all districts of the country.

E. *Actors and Organizational Structure of Sexual and Reproductive Health Services in Albania*

600. In Albania, since 1997 all family planning services provided free of charge in the public sector are integrated into the health system at all three levels (primary, secondary and tertiary). In the public system, these services are offered in 416 family planning centers (of which 326 in Health Center and 90 in the consultant of women and maternity). In urban areas, family planning services, in addition to women's counseling centers, are available also in maternity hospitals, district and regional hospitals, university hospitals (tertiary level—only in Tirana). Meanwhile, in rural areas, family planning services are offered at the Health Center.

601. In these circumstances, the Ministry of Health and Social Protection, with the support of United Nations Population Fund, has started efforts to adopt the concept of "Total Market Approach" for contraceptive safety. The private non-profit sector is represented by social marketing and NGOs. The only social marketing institution operating in Albania is NESMARK. Albanian Center for Population and Development (ACPD) is the main NGO that provides reproductive health and family planning services, as well as the distribution of contraceptives.

F. Assisted Medical Reproduction

602. Assisted medical reproduction is designed to address the desire of individuals or couples to have children. Its primary goal is to treat medical conditions related to infertility that prevent a couple from achieving pregnancy through natural means (Article 30, Law No. 8876, dated 4.4.2002 For Reproductive Health).

603. Assisted medical reproduction includes clinical and biological practices, which enable in vitro conception, embryo transfer and artificial insemination, as well as all techniques of other equivalents that allow reproduction outside the natural process (Article 31, Law No. 8876, dated 4.4.2002 For Reproductive Health).

604. The application of reproduction techniques is carried out: when the individual has reached the age to marry; (b) when the spouses have failed in their efforts for a period of two years to have a child until the moment when embryo transfer and insemination are performed; (c) in the presence of a licensed specialist doctor; (d) only after obtaining written consent for each cycle from the individuals concerned (Article 32, Law No. 8876, dated 4.4.2002 For Reproductive Health).

605. Reproduction techniques are used only in cases where: (a) other methods of treatment against male or female infertility are not productive or suitable and do not guarantee the desired result; (b) prevent the transmission of genetic diseases, as well as other diseases, to the child which would result in his premature death, his mental retardation and his disability; (c) are considered an alternative to natural childbirth (Article 33, Law No. 8876, dated 4.4.2002 For Reproductive Health).

G. Artificial Insemination

606. By artificial insemination it is understood the benefit of semen from the donor and their injection to the wife. This is done when: her husband turns out to be infertile; the donor is not the wife's husband (Article 34, Law No. 8876, dated 4.4.2002 For Reproductive Health). Artificial insemination with the spouse is used only when the couple's inability to procreate does not result from the man's lack of reproductive capacity (Article 35, Law No. 8876, dated 4.4.2002 For Reproductive Health).

H. Application of Assisted Reproduction Methods

607. The doctor is not allowed to undertake a medical procedure of assisted reproduction, except in the conditions provided by law or other legal acts. In the treatment of marital impossibility to bear children, the doctor must necessarily possess the basic scientific and ethical knowledge and be familiar with the methods that are applied in accordance with universally accepted concepts recognized by law. The doctor has the task of informing partners in detail about the procedure, the possibilities of success and failure to obtain their informed consent (Article 51 The Code of Medical Ethics and Deontology).

608. When using assisted reproductive technologies, sex selection is not allowed for the future child, except in cases where there is a possibility of inheriting related diseases with sex (Article 37, Law No. 8876, dated 4.4.2002 For Reproductive Health). The human embryo is prohibited from being used for any other commercial, industrial, or experimental purpose (Article 38, Law No. 8876, dated 4.4.2002 For Reproductive Health).

609. Men and women have the right to preserve their sex cells. The conditions and requirements for the storage and placement of sexual cells will be determined by an act of the Minister of Health (Article 39, Law No. 8876, dated 4.4.2002 For Reproductive Health).

I. Artificial Fertilization In Vitro

610. Artificial fertilization means experimental fertilization of female eggs with the man's sperm of a couple outside the woman's organism. Participation is subject to consent written by the woman who donates the eggs and the man who donates the sperm (Article 40, Law No. 8876, dated 4.4.2002 For Reproductive Health).

611. Artificial fertilization is applied in one of the cases when: damage or defects in the tubes appear in the woman; (b) the man is infertile or a carrier of life-threatening genetic diseases; (c) the sperm of the male partner is unsuitable for carrying out a natural birth (Article 41, Law No. 8876, dated 4.4.2002 For Reproductive Health).

612. Violations of the rules provided for in the preceding articles of this law, when they do not constitute criminal offense, are called administrative misdemeanors and are punished by the Minister of Health or by persons authorized by him as follows: (a) for exercising a profession in the field of reproductive health by doctors of this specialty without license, with a fine from ALL 25,000 to ALL 100,000; (b) for the operation of private health institutions without a license in the field of health reproductive, with a fine from ALL 50,000 to ALL 1,000,000. In case of repetition of the violations provided for in letters a and b of point 1 of this article the following measures are taken: confiscation of the institution's equipment; removal of the right to exercise the profession; criminal report (Article 42, Law No. 8876, dated 4.4.2002 For Reproductive Health).

J. Action Plan of Sexual Health and Reproducers 2022–2030

613. The Sexual and Reproductive Health Action Plan 2022–2030 was prepared on behalf of the Government Albanian from the Ministry of Health and Social Protection and dependency institutions, in consultation with representatives of civil society organizations and national and international organizations that work and support the functioning of coordination mechanisms cross-sectoral for problems related to sexual and reproductive health in Albania. This new Sexual and Reproductive Health Action Plan aims to improve sexual and reproductive health status of the entire population by increasing equal access to services universal reproductive health, improve the quality, efficiency, effectiveness of services and improve their response to the needs of the population. Its successful implementation will require a comprehensive, cross-program and multi-sectoral response to address causes of preventable mortality, morbidity and disability in women, children and adolescents, as well as their underlying determinants, to promote positive development, health and well-being.

614. Decision of the Council of Ministers No. 405 dated 20.5.2020 "On the approval of the strategy of development of primary health care services in Albania 2020–2025" also treats adolescents as a group with specific health needs, including substance abuse, depression, sexual health and nutrition. The strategy proposes new models of integrated services for adolescents (e.g., HEADSS). A smaller number of doctors will be able to provide pediatric services, maternal and child consultation, prenatal care, mental health, cover emergency services, etc. Also, nurses and midwives will take on a greater role in medicine prevention, the well-being of the child or the follow-up of the pregnant woman.

615. The following bylaws have been adopted for the purpose of health service package: Decision of the Council of Ministers No. 101 dated 4.2.2015 "For the approval of the package of health services, in primary public health care, which is financed by the compulsory health care insurance fund": Order of the Minister of Health No. 62 dated 15.02 2014 "On the approval of the standards of quality and clinical practice guidelines for women's counseling and protocols child consultant in primary health care"; Order of the Minister of Health No. 157 dated 21.04.2014 for "Approval of Protocols of Clinical Practice for Women's Counselors and Child Counselors in Care Primary Health - Nutrition of pregnant women, infants and small children"; Order of the Minister of Health No. 470 dated 03.09.2013 "On the approval of indicators for monitoring the performance of Mother Consultants and Child Consultants in Primary Health Care"; Order No. 491, dated 17.11.2015

"Clinical practice guide for safe abortion" and information sheets, as well as obtaining the patient's consent in the hospital for the abortion surgical, curettage method and medical abortion; Order of the Minister No. 25 dated 22/01/2016 "On the approval of the Guidelines and Protocols of Family Planning."

K. Legislation Related to Reproductive Health

616. The Family Code which, among other things, provides in Article 261 that for surrogacy adoption, provided for in Law No. 8876, dated 4.4.2002 "On reproductive health," to be applied the same criteria and procedures for adoption, according to this code and relevant legislation.

617. The goal of Law No. 10 071 dated 9.2.2009 "On the ratification of the Council of Europe convention on protection of children from sexual exploitation and abuse" is to prevent and combat the sexual exploitation and abuse of children; to protect the rights of child victims of sexual exploitation and abuse; promote national and international cooperation against exploitation and sexual abuse of children.

618. Law No. 8045, dated 23.09.1999 "On Termination of Pregnancy" guarantees compliance with every human being from the beginning of life. This principle is not violated, except when it is necessary and under the conditions defined in this law. The protection of this principle, information about the problems of life and national demography, education of social responsibilities, acceptance of the child in society and family policy are national obligations.

619. This law is based on the following principles: (a) Health service at all levels should use family planning services, to avoid unwanted pregnancies. Interruption of pregnancy will not be considered in any case as a method of family planning. (b) The woman has the right to accurate information and counseling before pregnancy termination. (c) In cases where termination of pregnancy is not contrary to the provisions according to this law, it must be performed in safe conditions for the woman's health. In all cases, women must be provided with health services for the treatment of possible complications after pregnancy termination. (d) Counseling and family planning service after termination of pregnancy should be immediate, to avoid unwanted pregnancies. Termination of pregnancy is allowed, only when undesirable circumstances are proven in this law and in any case with the consent of the woman.

620. Law No. 8528, dated 23.9.1999 "On the promotion and protection of breastfeeding" as amended, aims to promote and protect breastfeeding, as well as regulate marketing of breast milk substitutes for healthy feeding of children.

621. The Decision of the Council of Ministers No. 116, dated 15.2.2017, titled *"On the way of presentation, the format and labeling content of breast milk substitute products,"* establishes specific obligations for producers and distributors of designated products. Before these products are placed on the market, compliance with labeling regulations stipulated in food legislation must be ensured. The labels for such products must be in the Albanian language and affixed to the product packaging either by the manufacturer or by the commercial entity, importer, or distributor prior to market placement.

622. Order No. 179, dated 13/04/2017 "On determining the main elements of the content of informative and educational materials for baby and child feeding," defines the main elements of the content of informative and educational materials for the feeding of babies and young children addressed to the public and health professionals, also defines the Promotion department as the responsible structure of the Ministry of Education and Culture for the approval of these materials and State Health Inspectorate as controller of these materials, when placed on the market.

623. Law 15/2016 "On the prevention and fight against infections and infectious diseases," aims to protect the population from infectious diseases, defining the rules and activities for timely detection, evidence, their prevention and control, for the elimination and eradication of morbidity and of mortality from these diseases. Also, this law, among other things, provides mandatory vaccination for children aged 0–18, according to the relevant vaccination calendar and instructions approved by the minister responsible for health, after the proposals of the above committees.

624. Law No. 10 454, dated 21.7.2011 "On the transplantation of tissues, cells and organs in the Republic of Albania" aims to guarantee compliance with the standards of quality and safety during the performance of the activity of tissue and cell transplantation and organs of human origin, realized in the Republic of Albania, for preservation of public health. Tissues, cells and their transplantation are an important part of the process of assisted reproduction techniques (*see* 869, 937 and 947).

625. Law No. 9952, dated 14.07.2008 "On the prevention and control of HIV and AIDS," amended, defines rules for prevention and control in taking measures for HIV and AIDS, care treatment and support for people living with HIV and AIDS. The law has a special article that refers to HIV prevention, control and AIDS in the family predicting that couples before marriage or pregnant women before birth, are encouraged to voluntarily perform the HIV test. It also provides for the release of regulations from the ministry responsible for health for counseling, prevention and HIV and AIDS control.

626. Law No. 9669, dated 18.12.2006 "On measures against violence in family relationships" has the purpose of preventing and reducing domestic violence in all its forms, through appropriate legal and other necessary measures. The guarantee of protection by legal measures and other necessary measures of family members who are victims of domestic violence, paying special attention to children, the elderly and persons with disabilities, as well as any individual who presents special needs protection. The law provides for the obligation of the ministry responsible for social affairs for the establishment of crisis management centers, for cases of sexual violence, to ensure the possibility of operation of emergency rooms near the hospitals where the victim is treated. It is also foreseen that the standards of establishment and operation of crisis management centers, for cases of sexual violence, are determined by instruction of the minister responsible for health.

627. Decision of the Council of Ministers No. 327 dated 2.6.2021 "On the coordination mechanism of work between the responsible authorities, for referring cases of violence to family relations, as well as its proceedings, for the support and rehabilitation of victims of violence," regulates the basic standard procedures for work coordination between the responsible authorities, for the prevention of domestic violence, for the protection, support and rehabilitation of victims of all forms of domestic violence, by guaranteeing human rights and promote gender equality, as well as eliminate them all forms of discrimination against women. The coordinated mechanism for the referral of cases of violence in the family is created near each municipality and aims to prevent and treat cases of domestic violence. The role of the Violence Management Center is also foreseen.

628. Instruction No. 816, dated 27.11.2018 "On the approval of service provision standards and the operation of crisis management centers, for cases of sexual violence" was prepared with the aim of the most efficient operation of these centers which have in the main focus emergency service, with one stop, in an integrated way, 24/7 and short-term (twenty-four hours to seventy-two hours), for victims/survivors of sexual violence, such as and for other members of their families. Also see Order No. 101, dated 21.2.2020 "On the approval of standard operating procedures (PSV) for handling cases of domestic violence and gender-based violence by employees/employees of health services, within the framework of cooperation as members of the mechanism coordinated referral."

629. Decision of the Council of Ministers No. 327 dated 28.5.2014 "On determining the format and the manner of data collection and reporting by care service providers health, public or private," provides for the obligation of the public and private healthcare provider, which exercise activity in the field of health in the Republic of Albania, in accordance with the type of activity and the license for the exercise of activity, with the aim of formulating health and support scientific research policies, and report data in the health information system.

VI. Health of Newborn and Children

A. Newborn Health

630. In the field of providing health services of a country, indicators such as infant mortality, maternal mortality and vaccination coverage are considered important in relation to quality of healthcare service, coordination and overall performance of the system of providing healthcare services. Neonatal mortality rate (NMR) of one country is widely used as an indicator of public health, the quality of health services, distribution of wealth and the general standard of living; however, the burden of neonatal disease remains the main cause of morbidity for both sexes, at all ages (Global Disease Burden, WHO 2019).

631. The neonatal period, the first 0–28 days of life, is the most fragile time for the survival of an infant and therefore the early childhood period is the most important stage of development throughout life and harmful childhood experiences are related with long-term disadvantages and ill health, at substantial cost to the individual and the economy. Therefore, investing in the early years and giving every child the best start in life is essential for reducing inequalities in health.

632. The neonatological service in our country is provided according to the levels of healthcare in:

- Primary Healthcare—health centers and ambulances in the village and child consultants in the city who attend to the care of the child's well-being and development from 0 to 6 years and this includes the follow-up of babies after leaving the maternity ward until the first twenty-eight days after birth.
- Neonatological hospital care provided within the maternity wards of hospitals Municipalities and Districts.
- The highest level of neonatal care is provided in Obstetrical Gynecological Hospitals: "Queen Geraldine" and "Koço Gliozheni" in Tirana.

633. The vast majority of newborns in Albania undergo medical check-ups shortly after birth, similar to mothers receiving postnatal care. The Strategic Document and Action Plan for Sexual and Reproductive Health 2017–2021 introduced a series of five-year measures aimed at improving reproductive health across the country. Notably, maternal mortality rates have declined over the years, reflecting progress in healthcare initiatives. However, concerning neonatal mortality, methodological changes in the evaluation process have led to an apparent artificial increase in reported numbers. Efforts are currently underway to review and reassess data from previous years to ensure accuracy and provide a clearer picture of progress in this critical health indicator.

634. More than 80% of all newborn deaths result from three preventable treatable conditions: complications from prematurity, birth-related deaths (including asphyxia in birth) and neonatal infections. Increased morbidity also plays an important role here and deaths from congenital anomalies.

635. Complications of prematurity are currently the second cause of death for children under 5 years. Regarding the neonatology service, the government has constructed new maternity hospitals with contemporary parameters of Neonatology departments in Korçë, Lezhë, Sarandë, and Berat. Neonatology services are near completion in "Queen Geraldine" and Kukes Maternity. In addition, the government has improved in structure other maternity hospitals in the country.

§4. Prenatal Diagnosis (Genetics in General)

636. Law No. 8876, dated April 4, 2002, represents a pivotal framework in Albania's legal and healthcare systems, establishing a comprehensive framework for reproductive health. Among its many provisions, the law places significant emphasis on prenatal diagnosis, a medical service aimed at detecting potential complications or congenital conditions during pregnancy. This legal framework not only recognizes the importance of prenatal diagnosis but also embeds it within a broader context of safeguarding individual rights, ensuring equality, and maintaining high medical standards.

637. Article 9(b) of Law No. 8876 explicitly states that every individual has the fundamental right to access comprehensive health services, including those related to reproductive health. This provision underscores the significance of prenatal diagnosis as an essential service, integral to ensuring the health of both the mother and the fetus.[165] The law establishes that such services are not discretionary but a necessary part of maternal healthcare, reflecting the state's commitment to protecting reproductive health as a fundamental right. Furthermore, the inclusion of Article 10(2) of Law No. 8876 reinforces this commitment by prohibiting any kind of discrimination. It ensures that all individuals, regardless of gender, socioeconomic status, ethnicity, or other factors, have equal access to prenatal diagnostic services. This legal safeguard guarantees that access to these services is universally available, upholding the principle of equity.[166]

638. Moreover, the law recognizes the importance of individual autonomy and informed decision-making through Article 11(3) of Law No. 8876, which protects the right of individuals to freely make choices about their reproductive health.[167] In the context of prenatal diagnosis, this article guarantees that pregnant women are afforded the autonomy to make informed decisions regarding the choice to undergo diagnostic procedures, free from coercion or undue influence. This emphasis on autonomy is further strengthened by the procedural and ethical safeguards enshrined in other provisions of the law.

639. In addition to ensuring access and equity, the law places significant emphasis on the quality of medical services. Article 13 of Law No. 8876 mandates that all reproductive health interventions, including prenatal diagnostics, meet established

165. Law No. 8876, dated April 4, 2002, Art. 9(b): "*Every individual has the right to choose their sexual relationships and to control their reproductive life. This choice must be made with their consent, which implies b) Any medical intervention related to reproductive and sexual health must be carried out with the consent (approval) of the person on whom the intervention will be performed.*" [author' translation]

166. Law No. 8876, dated April 4, 2002, Art. 10(2): "*All individuals and couples have the right to receive appropriate healthcare services for safe pregnancy, childbirth, and to have a healthy child.*" [author' translation]

167. Law No. 8876, dated April 4, 2002, Art. 11(3): "*Every woman has the right to healthcare protection during her pregnancy, to assistance during childbirth, and to benefit from the application of methods and practices that minimize the risk to her health, the health of the fetus, the newborn, and the child.*" [author' translation]

quality and safety standards. This provision ensures that the medical professionals conducting these procedures are adequately trained and that the diagnostic tools and techniques employed adhere to rigorous safety protocols[168] Furthermore, Article 14 of Law No. 8876 complements this by obligating healthcare providers to offer clear and comprehensive information to patients. Pregnant women must be fully informed about the nature, purpose, and potential outcomes of prenatal diagnosis, enabling them to make decisions based on accurate and complete information.[169]

640. The preventive role of prenatal diagnosis is particularly highlighted in Article 22 of Law No. 8876, which emphasizes the importance of early detection of potential medical conditions. Through this provision, the law frames prenatal diagnosis as a preventive measure that allows for timely medical or surgical interventions to address any detected complications.[170] By identifying risks early, prenatal diagnostics can significantly improve health outcomes, underscoring the laws on proactive healthcare measures.

641. Building upon these ethical principles, Article 24 of Law No. 8876 establishes the right of all pregnant women to receive free, periodic medical evaluations throughout pregnancy, childbirth, and the postpartum period. This includes essential prenatal and postnatal care as a mandatory part of maternal health services.[171] By implementing this provision into law, it ensures that prenatal diagnostic procedures are readily available to all expectant mothers, thereby reaffirming the state's dedication to safeguarding both maternal and fetal well-being.

---

168. Law No. 8876, dated April 4, 2002, Art. 13*: "Every individual has the right to medical care and essential basic medical services, which are fundamental to protecting their health and well-being as an individual, and enjoys the right to qualified care for reproductive and sexual health. Motherhood and the child have the right to healthcare and special support. Every individual of reproductive age has the right to request medical examinations, appropriate treatment, and rehabilitation for healthy reproduction."* [author' translation]
169. Law No. 8876, dated April 4, 2002, Art. 14*: "Reproductive Health Care and Services": "Reproductive health care and services are provided by state medical services, public and private legal entities, as well as individuals authorized to perform this activity in accordance with the applicable legislation, who are licensed by the Ministry of Health for this type of activity. State medical services, public and private legal entities, as well as individuals authorized to perform this activity in accordance with the applicable legislation, are required to maintain the confidentiality and anonymity of the information they are made aware of due to the activities they carry out."* [author' translation]
170. Law No. 8876, dated Apr. 4, 2002, Art. 22*: "a) Care before, during, and after childbirth; b) Care for the growth and development of children aged 0–6 years; c) Care for adolescent health; ç) Screening and treatment of sexually transmitted infections, including HIV/AIDS; d) Sexual education and information; dh) Prevention of unwanted pregnancies through contraceptive methods and family planning; e) Voluntary termination of pregnancy; ë) Treatment of infertility and reproductive technologies; f) Treatment of reproductive tract diseases; g) Treatment of menopause."* [author' translation]
171. Law No. 8876, dated April 4, 2002, Art. 24: *"All pregnant women are entitled to free periodic medical follow-up during pregnancy, childbirth, and the postnatal period, particularly mandatory prenatal and postnatal examinations, which are designated by a regulation of the Minister of Health. The number and type of mandatory examinations, as well as the timing of their performance, are determined by a directive from the Minister of Health."* [author' translation]

642. Specific provisions in the law directly address the implementation of prenatal diagnostic services. Article 27 of Law No. 8876 explicitly affirms the right to access these services, establishing it as a critical element of maternal healthcare.[172] Meanwhile, Article 28 of Law No. 8876 ensures that the methods, conditions, and procedural aspects of prenatal diagnostics are regulated through ministerial directives.[173] This provision allows for flexibility and the integration of advancements in medical technology while maintaining consistency with national health priorities and ethical standards. The importance of informed consent is central to Article 29 of Law No. 8876, which requires that pregnant women receive all relevant information in an accessible and comprehensible manner.[174] This provision is crucial in ensuring that women can make informed choices about their health and the health of their unborn child, free from external pressure.

643. In conclusion, Law No. 8876 establishes a robust legal framework that integrates prenatal diagnosis into the broader spectrum of reproductive health services. By embedding it within a rights-based approach, the law ensures that prenatal diagnostics are accessible, equitable, and delivered with the highest standards of care. The provisions of Articles 9(b), 10(2), and 11(3) Law No. 8876 safeguard equality and autonomy, while Articles 13, 14, and 22 Law No. 8876 operationalize these principles through quality assurance, transparency, and preventive care. Furthermore, Articles 27, 28, and 29 Law No. 8876 provide the specific legal scaffolding necessary to implement these services effectively and ethically. This comprehensive approach not only reflects Albania's dedication to advancing reproductive health but also empowers women to make informed decisions about their pregnancies, ensuring dignity, autonomy, and well-being for all.

644. Additionally, The Albanian Code of Medical Ethics provides guiding principles that, while not explicitly mentioning prenatal diagnosis, are directly applicable to its practice. Article 4 emphasizes the fundamental duties of physicians to protect life and health and to act in the best interest of their patients.[175] This provision is highly relevant to prenatal diagnosis, as the procedure aims to identify potential health risks to both the mother and fetus. By adhering to this article, physicians are obligated to utilize their expertise to safeguard maternal and fetal well-being through appropriate diagnostic measures.

---

172. Law No. 8876, dated April 4, 2002, Art. 27: *"In terms of reproductive health, prenatal diagnosis is permitted for all women."*
173. Law No. 8876, dated April 4, 2002, Art. 28*: "The rules, conditions, and specific methods for prenatal diagnosis will be determined by acts of the Minister of Health."* [author' translation]
174. Law No. 8876, dated April 4, 2002, Art. 29: *"For examinations related to prenatal diagnosis, information must be provided in such a way that the woman feels free to make her own choice."* [author' translation]
175. The Code of Medical Ethics of Albania, Art. 4, *"Duties and Mission of the Doctor": "The fundamental duty of every doctor, in service to the individual and public health, is to protect life, physical and mental health, and alleviate human suffering. In their humanitarian mission, with respect for human life, the individual, and their dignity, the doctor is committed to protecting health, discovering and treating diseases, relying solely on science and their conscience, and prioritizing the health interests of the patient. A doctor is not permitted to use their knowledge in opposition to these interests."* [author' translation]

645. Article 28, on the other hand, focuses on the necessity of informed consent. It requires that physicians provide clear and comprehensive information to patients about proposed medical procedures, enabling them to make autonomous decisions.[176] In the context of prenatal diagnosis, this means ensuring that expectant mothers fully understand the purpose, process, potential risks, and implications of diagnostic tests, empowering them to make informed and voluntary choices about their healthcare.

646. These articles collectively establish an ethical foundation for prenatal diagnostic practices, highlighting the importance of protecting health while respecting patient autonomy and informed decision-making.

§5. Psychosurgical Interventions

647. The Action Plan for Mental Health 2023–2026 highlights Albania's commitment to providing compassionate, ethical, and modern mental healthcare that aligns with international standards. As part of this vision, psychosurgical interventions, including electroconvulsive therapy (ECT), are recognized as essential tools for treating severe and complex mental health conditions, especially when other treatments have been ineffective. These procedures are carefully regulated to ensure they prioritize the health and rights of the patient. Article 25 of the Mental Health Law sets out strict rules for the use of psychosurgical treatments like ECT, making it clear that they can only be performed when medically necessary and in the best interest of the patient. Informed consent is central to the process, requiring the approval of either the patient or their legal representative, with all treatments conducted according to protocols authorized by the Ministry of Health. To protect vulnerable groups, the law prohibits the use of ECT on minors, reinforcing a strong ethical stance in mental healthcare.

648. While psychosurgical procedures represent only a small portion of mental health treatments, they play a critical role in helping individuals with severe conditions when other therapies have not worked. Including these advanced interventions in Albania's mental healthcare system demonstrates a commitment to ensuring that all patients, even those with the most challenging needs, have access to effective care. At the same time, the system remains grounded in respect for human

---

176. The Code of Medical Ethics of Albania, Art. 28, *"Informed Consent": "It is the duty of every doctor to obtain the patient's consent before any proposed intervention, examination, or treatment, after fully informing the patient and ensuring that they have understood the information provided. If the patient, in a condition to express their will, refuses the proposed intervention, the doctor must respect the patient's decision after informing them about the possible consequences. If the patient is under 16 years old or unable to express their will to make decisions, the doctor cannot proceed without informing the patient's relatives or the legitimate responsible person, except in emergency situations or when it is impossible to contact these individuals. The patient's information and their consent or refusal must be documented in writing in the patient's clinical file and signed by the patient or by the legitimate persons who have custody of them."* [author' translation]

rights, patient autonomy, and ethical practice. To support the safe use of these treatments, the Action Plan for Mental Health 2023–2026 focuses on improving facilities and training for healthcare professionals. It ensures that psychosurgical interventions are carried out ethically, using evidence-based methods and clear protocols. These efforts aim to strengthen the country's mental healthcare system so that it can respond to the growing and evolving needs of the population. By integrating advanced treatments into a broader mental health framework, Albania is taking a significant step toward a more inclusive and patient-focused care system. The plan reflects a commitment to modernizing mental health services while safeguarding the dignity, autonomy, and rights of every individual.

649. Patients with mental health problems are treated either through Voluntary Medical Treatment or Involuntary Medical Treatment. Both are ruled in Section V of Law No. 44/2012 For Mental Health, which was modified by Law No. 20/2021 of 15 February 2021. After hospitalization, there will be several treatments (Article 19 of Law No. 44/2012) for cases of voluntary medical treatment for patients with mental health problems (Article 19/1 added by Law No. 20/2021 of 15 February 2021).

650. Under Article 19 of Law No. 44/2012, individuals who voluntarily seek treatment for mental health issues within specialized facilities must provide informed written consent. This consent is given after receiving comprehensive information about the nature, purpose, and potential outcomes of the proposed interventions. The process ensures that patients are fully aware of the treatment plan and its implications. In the case of minors, the responsibility for granting consent lies with their legal guardians or representatives. The law requires that the consent be documented in a standardized format, approved by the Ministry of Health, and integrated into the patient's clinical record. Furthermore, patients or their legal representatives maintain the right to withdraw consent, refuse treatment, or raise objections at any stage of the process, unless specific legal criteria for involuntary intervention are met.

651. In addition, Article 19/1 of Law No. 44/2012, introduced by Law No. 20/2021 of 15 February 2021, governs voluntary hospitalization. It stipulates that admission to specialized mental health facilities requires written informed consent, which must follow a thorough discussion about the necessity of hospitalization to provide appropriate care. A critical requirement of this process is a prior medical examination conducted by a qualified physician within community-based or outpatient mental health services. This evaluation serves as a safeguard, ensuring that hospitalization is recommended only when necessary and that less restrictive forms of care have been considered. This step underscores the principle of proportionality, aligning with international mental healthcare standards that prioritize the least restrictive interventions suitable for a patient's condition. The process of obtaining and documenting consent is an essential part of the patient's clinical record, ensuring that everything is transparent and handled ethically. Additionally, the law explicitly prohibits the use of voluntary hospitalization for purposes such as assessing an individual's work capacity or other non-therapeutic objectives.

652. These legal provisions emphasize the importance of informed decision-making in mental healthcare, respecting the dignity and autonomy of individuals while ensuring their treatment is transparent, consensual, and ethically sound. The framework reflects a commitment to patient-centered care, ensuring that the rights and well-being of those with mental health conditions remain at the forefront of clinical and legal practices.

653. There is a specific procedure on the voluntary medical treatment for patients with mental health problems. Articles 20 and 24/5 of Law No. 44/2012 provide a comprehensive and regulated process to ensure such interventions are applied only when strictly required and in line with ethical and legal principles. In cases where involuntary medical treatment is necessary for individuals with mental health disorders, Article 20 of Law No. 44/2012 establishes that involuntary treatment may be administered to individuals diagnosed with a severe mental disorder who are unable to provide informed consent due to their condition. This treatment must also be essential for improving their mental health, restoring their ability to consent, or preventing harm to themselves or others. A specialist physician is the only authority permitted to authorize involuntary treatment following a thorough personal evaluation. Afterward, the patient, along with their family members or legal representatives, must be informed of the decision, its rationale, and the patient's rights in these circumstances. All steps and communications are documented in detail in the patient's clinical record, as mandated by the Ministry of Health.

654. When involuntary hospitalization is required, Article 24/5 of Law No. 44/2012 introduces judicial oversight to protect the individual's rights. This process begins when the head of the mental health institution submits an official request to the court for authorization. The request must include an independent evaluation from a physician who is unaffiliated with the facility where the individual is being treated. Within forty-eight hours, the judge must personally hear the patient's account, ensuring their voice is part of the deliberation. If the court approves the request, the decision is implemented immediately by the mental health facility. To prevent unnecessary or prolonged hospitalizations, the law mandates a periodic review of the court's decision every twenty-eight days to assess whether continued care is justified.

655. Additionally, the law permits the revocation of a court's decision for involuntary hospitalization at any time if the circumstances justifying such hospitalization no longer exist. This revocation can be requested by the individual undergoing treatment, their family, legal representatives, or the treating facility. By integrating medical expertise with judicial oversight, Articles 20 and 24/5 of Law No. 44/2012 create a framework that ensures a balance between the necessity of effective mental healthcare and the protection of individual rights. This system emphasizes the responsible and ethical application of involuntary measures, upholding the dignity and well-being of the individual.

656. After this short review, focusing on psychosurgical interventions, Article 25 No. 44/2012 states that medical and surgical treatments, including electroconvulsive therapy (ECT), for individuals with mental health disorders must always prioritize the patient's health and well-being. These interventions require informed consent, either directly from the patient or, if the patient is unable to provide it, from their legal representative. This requirement ensures that all procedures are conducted in a manner that respects the patient's autonomy and legal rights, aligning with ethical and professional standards of care.

657. Regarding ECT, Article 25 of Law No. 44/2012 introduces additional safeguards to regulate its use. The therapy may only be administered after obtaining informed consent, which ensures that patients or their representatives fully understand the nature, purpose, and potential effects of the procedure. Furthermore, all applications of ECT must strictly follow protocols established and approved by the Minister of Health. These protocols are designed to standardize the use of the therapy, ensuring it is applied consistently, ethically, and only when deemed medically necessary. To further protect vulnerable groups, the law explicitly prohibits the use of ECT on minors, reinforcing a commitment to safeguarding children and adolescents from intensive procedures that may not align with their developmental and emotional needs.

658. In addition, the article emphasizes that all medical and surgical procedures must comply with professional ethical standards. These rules ensure that treatments for individuals with mental health disorders are not only medically justified but also conducted in a way that respects the dignity, rights, and well-being of the patient. By integrating these requirements, Article 25 of Law No. 44/2012 reinforces the legal framework's focus on informed ethical and patient-centered care.

659. It shall be mentioned that Article 34(1) (dh) of Law No. 44/2012 states the violation of Article 25 of this law—thus, violations of psychosurgical interventions—is punishable by deprivation of the right to practice the profession for up to three years.

660. It is noteworthy that, although codes such as the CCr require a 3/5 majority vote in the Assembly under Article 81(2)(d) of the Constitution, this specific criminal sanction is incorporated into a law that can be passed by a simple majority of the members present, as stipulated in Article 78(1) of the Constitution. In practice, this means that a simple majority could theoretically consist of at least 36 members (the total membership of the Assembly is 140, the quorum requires at least 71 members).

661. Based on this background, it shall be mentioned that Article 4 Code of Medical Ethics states: The fundamental duty of every physician, in the service of the individual and public health, is to protect human life, physical and mental health, and alleviate their suffering. In addition, Article 20(2) Code of Medical Ethics states A doctor who is called to treat a mentally incompetent person must try to obtain the consent of his or her legal representatives. An exception is made when the case is urgent, and the doctor is unable to communicate with these people.

§6. Organ Transplants

I. Transplantation of Tissues and Organs

662. Taking organs, tissues or any other product from the body of a living or dead person is practiced only in the cases and conditions provided by law or other legal acts which belong to this field. The doctor is not allowed to take organs, tissues or any other product from the human body, nor their transplantation, if he is not qualified in this field nor have a trained collaborative team. He is also not allowed to do such an undertaking if he does not have available medical and technical equipment (Article 57 The Code of Medical Ethics and Deontology).

663. Law No. 10 454, dated 21.7.2011 regulates the Transplantation for Tissue, Cell and Organ Transplantation in Republic of Albania. This law aims to guarantee compliance with quality and safety standards during the performance of the activity of transplantation of tissues, cells and organs of human origin, carried out in the Republic of Albania, for the preservation of public health. This law defines: basic services involved in the activity of tissue and cell transplantation and organs; organization, operation, inspection, licensing and accreditation of health structures, involved in the activity of tissue, cell and organ transplantation; programming and coordination of work in this field; quality and safety standards for human tissues, cells and organs (Article 2 of Law No. 10 454, dated 21.7.2011 For Tissue, Cell and Organ Transplantation in Republic of Albania).

664. This law applies to all healthcare structures involved in the transplantation of organs, tissues, and cells in accordance with the applicable legislation in force. It ensures that all entities operating within this domain adhere to the regulatory standards and requirements established by the law, thereby promoting consistency, safety, and compliance across the transplantation field. It applies to all transplants that are performed: (a) within the same individual from one part of the body to another; (b) between individuals who are related by blood (grandfather, grandmother, parent, child, aunt, uncle, uncle, aunt, nephew, niece), with the exception of reproductive cells; (c) between individuals who are not related by blood (father-in-law, mother-in-law, spouse, wife), according to the conditions defined in this law; (d) for tissues and cells, including hematopoietic cells from peripheral blood, for umbilical cord (blood) and cells from bone marrow, for reproductive cells (eggs, sperm), tissues and fetal cells (Article 3 of Law No. 10 454, dated 21.7.2011 For Tissue, Cell and Organ Transplantation in Republic of Albania).

665. According to this legislation, the principles of tissue, cell and organ transplantation are as follows: (a) removal of tissues, cells and organs for transplantation purposes is performed only for therapeutic benefits to the beneficiary; (b) transplantation of tissues, cells and organs is performed only after the beneficiary and the donor has given free consent; (c) donation of tissues, cells and organs is based on voluntary donation, preserving the anonymity of both the donor and the beneficiary, the altruism of the donor and solidarity between donor and beneficiary, and in respect of life and health donors (Article 5 of Law No. 10 454, dated 21.7.2011 For Tissue, Cell and Organ Transplantation in Republic of Albania).

666. The law prohibits financial gain out of transplantation of tissues, cells and organs. Also, Brain and gonad transplantation is prohibited. In addition, genetic manipulation of the embryo is prohibited, even for transplantation purposes. It is also forbidden to donate organs from minor, living donors. The removal of the tissue, cells or organ cannot be performed on a person incapable of giving consent, except for the provisions of Article 20 of this law. Promotion and advertising for the purpose of soliciting or offering organs are prohibited (Article 6 of Law No. 10 454, dated 21.7.2011 For Tissue, Cell and Organ Transplantation in Republic of Albania).

667. The activities that are carried out during the process of transplanting tissues, cells and bodies are: (a) promotion of voluntary and unpaid donation; (b) the process of donating transplants; (c) selection of donors; (d) testing procedure; (e) transplant processing procedure; (f) procedure of conservation and storage of transplants; (g) transplant distribution procedure; (h) carrying out transplantation; (i) quality assurance procedure. These activities are allowed to be carried out only in specialized hospital health facilities for transplant services, licensed according to the legislation in force and approved by order of the Minister of Health (Article 7 of Law No. 10 454, dated 21.7.2011 For Tissue, Cell and Organ Transplantation in Republic of Albania).

668. Health structures of the transplant service are regulated by Article 8 of Law No. 10 454, dated 21.7.2011 For Tissue, Cell and Organ Transplantation in Republic of Albania. The health structures of the transplant service are (a) banks of tissues, cells and organs; (b) Center for Transplantation Coordination; (c) the transplant center.

669. Tissue, cell and organ banks are considered health facilities that perform the following processes: (a) selection, evaluation, testing of tissues, cells and organs; (b) their examination and processing; (c) preservation, storage, labeling and packaging of tissues, cells of organs and documenting data about them; (d) distribution of tissues, cells and organs intended for transplantation.

670. Banks of tissues, cells and organs are responsible for: (a) cooperation with the departments of pathology, forensic medicine, gynecological-obstetrical departments of healthcare institutions, with banks blood and with the healthcare centers that perform the removal and implantation; (b) keep records of their activity, including the type and quantity of transplants selected, tested, preserved, processed, stored and distributed institutions that carry out transplants, or discards, as well as for the origin and destination of theirs, intended for human applications, according to the requirements defined in the relevant regulations; (c) carry out the finding (research) of unrelated donors of hemopoietic cells, their examination and mediation of transplants of hematopoietic cells, donated from unrelated donors; (d) to keep data on the performed examinations of potential tissue donors, cells and organs; (e) keep the register of potential donors of hemopoietic cells; (f) provide, based on the request of the healthcare institution, data for potential donors of hematopoietic cells from the perspective of evaluation of their suitability for a particular beneficiary; (g) ensure and coordinate international cooperation in cell exchange hematopoiesis intended for transplant; (h) submit an annual report on their activity to the Ministry of Health (Article 9 of Law No. 10 454, dated 21.7.2011 For Tissue, Cell and Organ Transplantation in Republic of Albania).

II. Center for the Coordination of Transplants

671. The Center for the Coordination of Transplants is entasked to organize and mediate the process of transplantation between banks and transplant centers. It is managed under the Ministry of Health which approves by order the way it is organized and operated. The Transplantation Coordination Center performs the following tasks: (a) maintains the National Register of Persons awaiting tissue and cell transplantation and organs; (b) maintains the National Registry of Transplant Donors; (c) keeps the National Register of Transplants carried out; (d) coordinates the transplant removal and implantation teams; (e) designates the most suitable beneficiaries for the transplants removed, based on the results of Eastern typing analyses. Their selection is carried out only by the National Registry Persons waiting for tissue, cell and organ transplantation; (f) processes general data on removals, performed implantations and results for the previous year and drafts a report that is presented to the Ministry of Health by March 31 of the following calendar year; (g) methodologically coordinates the activities of banks to search for donors of hemopoietic cells; (h) ensures and coordinates international cooperation in tissue exchange, cells and organs intended for transplantation (Article 10 of Law No. 10 454, dated 21.7.2011 For Tissue, Cell and Organ Transplantation in Republic of Albania).

III. Transplant Center

672. Transplantation centers form an integral part of the hospital service system and can operate as either public or private entities. Public transplant centers are established by order of the Minister of Health, while private ones are licensed according to the legislation in force. Criteria for opening and closing transplant centers are determined by decision of the Council of Ministers. Transplantation centers carry out the removal and implantation of organs, tissues and cells based on this law and bylaws, in its implementation.

673. Transplantation centers perform the following tasks: (a) report on the persons registered for transplantation at the Center for the Coordination of Transplantation; (b) carry out the implantation only for the beneficiaries registered in the

National Registry of Persons waiting for tissue, cell and organ transplantation; (c) report on the transplants carried out at the Center for the Coordination of Transplantation; (d) cooperate with the Center for the Coordination of Transplants to designate the beneficiaries for more suitable tissues, cells and organs; (e) after receiving the data, according to Article 16 of Law No. 10 454, verify whether they have been completed all conditions related to the removal of transplants; (f) inform the Transplantation Coordination Center about the possible donor; (g) provide data required by the Center for the Coordination of Related Transplants with tissues, cells, organs. The provided data preserves anonymity in such a way that, as the donor, as well as the beneficiary, should not be identified; (h) document in writing the use of tissue, cells, organs removed in the protocol, which is attached to other accompanying documents for the removed transplant. This the protocol contains the date and place of removal, as well as the final purpose of removed grafts. In the event that a decision is made that the tissue, the cells and organs removed are inappropriate, the reason for the inappropriateness, as well as the means of further treatment are recorded in the protocol; (i) save data on the removals and implantations performed and record the data for bodies omitted in the protocol; (j) send the protocol to the Center for Transplantation Coordination within seven days from the date of making a decision on the final purpose of transplants. The centers cooperate with tissue banks and cells for the search of hematopoietic cell donors when selecting possible donors, more suitable not related by blood (Article 11 of Law No. 10 454, dated 21.7.2011 For Tissue, Cell and Organ Transplantation in Republic of Albania).

IV. Medical Ethics During the Transplant Process

674. The Medical Ethics Committee handles issues of tissue, cell and organ transplantation. The Medical Ethics Committee gives the health institution approval or rejection for regarding the realization of the removal of: (a) an organ for the benefit of the beneficiary, who is not related by blood (husband, wife, father-in-law, mother-in-law) with the donor; (b) regenerative tissue from a minor or a person incapable of expressing consent; (c) tissues, cells for the benefit of the beneficiary, who is not related by blood to the donor.

675. Members of the Medical Ethics Committee must not be in conflict of interest with their job position. They should not be part of the medical staff participating in the process of transplantation. The members of the Medical Ethics Committee maintain the confidentiality of all the data regarding the realization of their activities. In exceptional cases, the data is made known with the consent of the donor, beneficiary or a legal representative. Providing such a consent or refusal becomes part of the donor's medical records for the minor, or the person incapable of expressing his/her consent (Article 12 of Law No. 10 454, dated 21.7.2011 For Tissue, Cell and Organ Transplantation in Republic of Albania).

676. The National Transplantation Committee is an advisory body of the Minister of Health. The composition and mode of operation of this committee are approved by order of Minister of Health. The National Transplantation Committee advises the Minister of Health on the implementation of the obligations arising from this law and for important legal and technical organizational revisions in the field of transplants (Article 13 of Law No. 10 454, dated 21.7.2011 For Tissue, Cell and Organ Transplantation in Republic of Albania).

677. The doctor, who assesses the health capacity of the donor, informs him about the purpose, nature and consequences of transplant donation and the potential risks associated with them. When the donor is a minor or an incompetent person, the data in question is sent to his/her legal representatives. The information provided must be clear and understandable. The donor and the legal representative of a minor or an incompetent person enjoy the right to ask questions about the information received. The donor and the legal representative of a minor or an incompetent person may request that another witness be present when they are receiving the information. The doctor informs the people mentioned above for this opportunity in advance. All data, which the doctor uses to inform the donor, is described by him in an information sheet, which then becomes part of the documentation kept for the donor (Article 14 of Law No. 10 454, dated 21.7.2011 For Tissue, Cell and Organ Transplantation in Republic of Albania).

678. The donation of transplants can be carried out only after the donor has given his consent. Consent is given in writing and stored in the donor's medical records. For cases of removal of regenerative tissue from a minor or a person incapable of giving consent regarding the donation, the donation can only be carried out with the authorization of his/her legal representative. It must be noted that the opinion of the minor is taken into consideration as an increasingly determining factor, relative to his/her age and level of maturity. The donor or the legal representative of a minor or an incompetent person can withdraw their consent at any time. The doctor, who performs the removal, respects such a withdrawal, except when there are irreversible procedures, the interruption of which would endanger the health and life of the donor (Article 15 of Law No. 10 454, dated 21.7.2011 For Tissue, Cell and Organ Transplantation in Republic of Albania).

679. The transplant center which performs the removal, is responsible for assessing the health ability of the donor to determine the ability to donate transplants. Before removing a tissue, cell or organ from a donor, the relevant doctor evaluates: (a) his/her state of health through examinations or medical procedures; (b) the possible risks related to donating a transplant versus life or health of the donor; (c) appropriate procedures, in order to eliminate, in all possible ways, the health risks for the donor's life, related to the removal of the transplant.

680. The Minister of Health approves by regulation the Donor selection criteria, mandatory laboratory tests that must be performed before the donation of tissues, cells and organs, as well as the time limits that must be respected. Donor evaluation results and testing procedures are documented in the personal file of the donor and any anomaly is reported according to the requirements defined by regulation approved by order of the Minister of Health. The doctor, who evaluates the health status of the donor, decides whether the donor is able or not to donate tissues, cells or organs. Data related to the condition and health of the donor, are signed by the evaluating doctor and become part of the personal file with the donor's medical records. The transplant center, which performed the removal, also provides the necessary medical care to the donor for a long period after the removal of the tissue, cell or organ (Article 16 of Law No. 10 454, dated 21.7.2011 For Tissue, Cell and Organ Transplantation in Republic of Albania).

681. Every donor, before the tissue, cell and organ donation process, signs a form related to his health history, presented by the relevant structures, and bears personal responsibility. The form signed by the donor is signed also by the doctor who performs the evaluation of the donor. All data received from donors are confidential, including the laboratory results. The Minister of Health regulates by Order all types of documents for: verifying the suitability of donors, information received and given to donors and the way of donating tissues, cells, organs, as well as the treatment of donors after donation (Article 17 of Law No. 10 454, dated 21.7.2011 For Tissue, Cell and Organ Transplantation in Republic of Albania).

V. Treatment of Donors

682. Donors receive compensation, which includes reimbursement of expenses, and any experienced difficulties related to the donation process. Even if the donor is deemed unfit to donate, he has the right to receive compensation for his time. The value of the compensation for the cases mentioned above is made against the official certification of the corresponding structure. The amount and method of granting compensation are determined by decision of Council of Ministers (Article 18 of Law No. 10 454, dated 21.7.2011 For Tissue, Cell and Organ Transplantation in Republic of Albania).

683. The removal of tissues, cells and organs from a donor can only be carried out if: (a) performed only for medical benefits of the beneficiary; (b) there is, at the time of removal, no other comparable effective therapeutic method; (c) the donor or his/her legal representative have given consent, according to Article 15 of Law No. 10 454; (d) the tissues are regenerative or the organ belongs to one of the pair of functioning organs; (e) the removal of tissues, cells and organs from a donor can be carried out for medical benefits of the beneficiary, who is a blood relative (grandparent, parent, child, aunt, uncle, uncle, aunt, nephew, niece) with the donor, when the donor has given his/her consent to the beneficiary; (f) the removal of organs from a donor can be carried out for medical benefits to the beneficiary, who is a person unrelated by blood (father-in-law, mother-in-law, spouse, spouse) with the donor, only on the condition that: (g) the donor clearly declares in writing the desire to donate to the beneficiary; ii) the donation in question has been approved by the Medical Ethics Committee. The removal of tissues, cells or organs from a donor can only be carried out after the donor and beneficiary have declared their willingness to participate in the care program recommended by doctors in the post-removal phase (Article 19 of Law No. 10 454, dated 21.7.2011 For Tissue, Cell and Organ Transplantation in Republic of Albania).

684. For minors and incapacitated persons, regenerative tissue removal can only be performed when all the following conditions are met: (a) there is no possible, suitable donor able to give his clear and concrete consent; (b) the beneficiary is a parent, child, brother or sister of the donor; (c) the donation represents an opportunity to save the beneficiary's life; (d) the legal representative of the donor, a minor or an incompetent person, has expressed his/her consent for the donation according to Article 15 of Law No. 10 454; (e) The Medical Ethics Committee has approved the donation in question (Article 20 of Law No. 10 454, dated 21.7.2011 For Tissue, Cell and Organ Transplantation in Republic of Albania).

VI. Removal of Tissues or Organs from a Non-living Donor

685. Removal of tissue or organs from the body of a non-living person can be done only if the person in question during his/her lifetime or the legal representative of the minor or the disabled person have not openly expressed their disapproval. In these cases, consent to removal of the tissue or organ is taken from his/her relatives, in this order: wife, husband, older child, parent, sister, brother. The removal of the organ or tissue from a non-living person can only be done in the case when death is proven in accordance with the medical criteria, defined in regulation approved by order of the Minister of Health for death certification. The certification of the death of a potential donor is always carried out by three qualified doctors, who examine the donor independently of each other. Doctors, who certify death, do not participate in the transplant process (Article 21 of Law No. 10 454, dated 21.7.2011 For Tissue, Cell and Organ Transplantation in Republic of Albania).

686. The removal of tissue and organ from a non-living donor is prohibited when: (a) the non-living person or his/her legal representative has expressly objected to the removal of tissues and organs; (b) his relatives do not consent to the removal of the non-living person's tissue or organ; (c) based on the assessment of health capacity, it is not possible to exclude that the person, who is not living, suffered from a disease or condition, which may endanger health and the beneficiary's life; (d) it is impossible to identify the person who is not alive.

687. The procedures for assessing health capacity and conducting examinations on the deceased donors are established through regulations approved by the Minister of Health. The removal of tissues or organs from deceased foreign citizens is permitted only in accordance with applicable international agreements (Article 22 of Law No. 10 454, dated 21.7.2011 For Tissue, Cell and Organ Transplantation in Republic of Albania).

688. After removing the tissue or organ, the doctor records the list of tissues and removed organs, as well as the intended purpose of their use in the medical records of donors. Removed tissues and organs may be submitted for examination, processing, preparation, conservation, storage and further distribution only to a bank of tissues or organs (Article 23 of Law No. 10 454, dated 21.7.2011 For Tissue, Cell and Organ Transplantation in Republic of Albania).

689. The human body should be treated with respect during organ or tissue removal and during post-mortem examinations, and all procedures should be carried out in such a way that the body can be restored to its original appearance as much as possible (Article 24 of Law No. 10 454, dated 21.7.2011 For Tissue, Cell and Organ Transplantation in Republic of Albania).

690. Removal of the transplant from the donor is not possible if: (a) it is judged that the transplant may seriously endanger the health or life of the donor; (b) the donor is a person who is in custody or serving an imprisonment sentence. Exceptions include cases of donation between parents and their children, between siblings or between spouses; (c) during the evaluation of the health status of the donor, there is a suspicion that the donor suffers from a disease or condition, which may endanger the health or life of the beneficiary. it does not apply to cases where the risk to the beneficiary's health is small compared to the transplant that saves his/her life (Article 25 of Law No. 10 454, dated 21.7.2011 For Tissue, Cell and Organ Transplantation in Republic of Albania).

VII. Quality Management

691. The Ministry of Health undertakes all measures to guarantee the transplant health structures for their implementation based on principles of good practice. The transplant quality system includes standards and rules related to: (a) the documentation system; (b) environment and equipment; (c) staff; (d) the procedure of donor selection for tissues, cells and bodies; (e) procedures for accepting tissues, cells and organs in tissue banks and cells; (f) testing and processing procedure; (g) the labeling, documentation, packaging, storage and distribution procedure tissues, cells and organs; (h) the procedure for the treatment of tissues, cells and organs that will be disposed of, with the purpose for the prevention of contamination of tissues and other cells. These centers, responsible for the removal or implantation of transplants, operate as part of the hospital structure (Decision No. 206, dated 13.3.2013 For Determining the Criteria for Opening and Closing the Centers of Transplant).

692. Transplant health structures undertake all necessary measures: (a) to guarantee that the quality system includes at least the documentation of: (i) the standard operating procedure for each procedure that is performed; (ii) guides; (iii) training and reference manual; (iv) reporting form; (v) data of the donor; (vi) data on the final destination of tissues, cells and organs; (b) to ensure that this documentation is available for inspection by the competent authority/authorities. The health facilities of the transplant keep all the data necessary to guarantee its tracking. Rules for evaluating the quality and safety of tissues, cells and organs for transplantation purposes are determined by the regulation approved by order of the Minister of Health (Article 27 of Law No. 10 454, dated 21.7.2011 For Tissue, Cell and Organ Transplantation in Republic of Albania).

693. Health structures, which carry out activities in the field of transplant, must ensure the confidentiality of data for the non-identification of the donor and the beneficiary, according to the requirements of Law No. 9887, dated 10.3.2008 "For the protection of personal data in the Republic of Albania." In order to maintain confidentiality, the relevant institutions must take measures for the: (a) storage of the data system, as well as storage of any addition, removal or modification unauthorized data in the donor's file or by moving and transferring data; (b) designing procedures to resolve data inconsistencies and issuing to guarantee tracking of donations; (c) guaranteed that the identity of the beneficiary will not be known to the donor or his family in the case of donating reproductive cells; (d) guaranteeing donor data throughout the tracking process. Exceptions are made in cases where the data becomes known with the consent of the donor, beneficiaries or a legal representative, but always without violating the anonymity of the other party (Article 33 of Law No. 10 454, dated 21.7.2011 For Tissue, Cell and Organ Transplantation in Republic of Albania).

VIII. Criteria for Opening a Transplantation Center

694. Transplantation centers, apart from the requirements defined in Law No. 10 454, dated 21.7.2011 "For transplantation of tissues, cells and organs in the Republic of Albania," should also satisfy the following criteria:

A. Special construction criteria
   I. Operating room
      1. Hospitals that carry out the transplant should have a special room for carrying out the transplantation procedure.
      2. The transplant room should have only one operating bed.
      3. The transplanting room should be no less than 30 (thirty) m2, except spaces, which consist of corners and/or other spaces formed by split corners. In the performance hall space of transplantation, there can be no objects, which hinder the free movement of the operational hall team.
      4. In the space of the transplant hall, the floor-ceiling height should be no less than three meters. The parts of the corridor, which are in the operation block, should have a width of not less than two meters.
      5. The operating block consists of a sterile transplant room, a sterile dressing room of staff and an environment with complete sterilization.
      6. In those parts of the operating block, where sterilization is incomplete, there is a resting place for staff, separate dressing and undressing rooms, sanitary facilities, toilet room and shower.
      7. The doors and windows of the sterile rooms do not open to the non-sterile exterior and in these parts, there is no sanitary joint, toilet room.

8. The transplant room is ventilated and conditioned with a central air conditioning system with biological filters. The positive air pressure in the transplant room should be higher than in the rooms they have a connection with it.
9. Movement to the transplant room should be one-way.

   The lighting should be suitable for work.

   Floors should have smooth and nonabsorbent surfaces and easy for disinfection. The walls, the ceilings and floors of the rooms and corridors should be constructed in such a way that they can be maintainable and easily cleaned. Windows should be equipped with nets against insects and other poisonous animals.

II. Resuscitation unit
1. Reanimation units for transplanted patients are placed in suitable facilities, where medical personnel constantly monitor the patient. Resuscitation units are equipped with sinks.
2. In resuscitation units, the space for each resuscitation bed should be at least 12 (twelve) m2. Resuscitation room (box) for the recipient to be with one bed.
3. In each resuscitation box, at the head of the bed, there should be a central medical gas system, invasive monitor, mechanical ventilation apparatus. The bed should have built-in scales.
4. In resuscitation units, the space for each box should be suitable for operational personnel.
5. The resuscitation unit should not have a direct connection with the facilities of the visitors' patients, as well as with the hospital staff.

III. Rooms of transplant patients
1. Patient rooms with one bed should be no less than 12 (twelve) m2.
2. Rooms with two beds should be no less than 9 (nine) m2 for each bed.
3. For separate rooms for transplanted children, not less than 8 (eight) m2 for each bed.
4. The rooms for the recipient (the person who performed the transplant) should have one bed and for the donor two beds.
5. The nurse's room should be near the patients' rooms; be equipped with a sink, with a place where the medication is prepared, as well as with a call system to connect to each patient's room.

B. Criteria for medical staff at the transplant center
1. The team of health professionals working in transplant centers consists of:
   b) specialist doctor according to the type of transplantation to be performed.
   c) anesthesiologist/reanimator.
   d) nurse.
   ç) auxiliary staff.

2. The hospital ensures that the health professionals who perform the transplant process, have the necessary qualifications for carrying out transplant procedures according to the type of transplant being performed.
3. The hospital ensures that health professionals undergo continuous education and training in the field of transplants.

C. Criteria for maintaining documentation of the activity of the transplant center

1. The transplant center is obliged to have an archive for the storage of administrative and clinical documentation according to the "Records" legislation.
2. The transplant center is obliged to report to the Ministry of Health the activity of transplants, based on the National Statistical Program for Health, law no. 10 454, date 21.7.2011 "On the transplantation of tissues, cells and organs in the Republic of Albania," the law "On official statistics," the law "On prevention and fight against infectious diseases" and the law "On prevention and control of HIV/Aids."

Necessary equipment

A. The equipment for transplant rooms should be as follows:

1. Operating bed.
2. Anesthesia apparatus.
3. Monitor (with relevant files: etco2, nibp, ibp, ekg, o2 saturation, temperature, blood pressure, pap).
4. Cell-saver (for the recovery of blood lost in the operative field).
5. Hotline (for quick administration of fluids and blood).
6. Aspirator.
7. Hemogasanalysis apparatus (astrupogram).
8. Act meter.
9. Thromboelastograph (for heparin).
   Electric syringe.
   Perfusator.
   Extracorporeal circulation apparatus (for heparin).
   Contrapulsing balloon.
   Defibrillator.
   Medicine cabinet.
   Medication refrigerator.
   Table for back-table.

B. Resuscitation equipment to be as follows:

1. Reanimation bed with built-in scales.
2. Monitor (with relevant files: etco2, nibp, ibp, ekg, o2 saturation, temperature, blood pressure, pap).
3. Apparatus for mechanical ventilation.
4. Hemodialysis machine.
5. EKG device.
6. Ultrasound machine.
7. Echocardiograph.

8. X-ray machine.
9. Fibrobronchoscope.
   Hemogasanalysis apparatus (astrupogram).
   Electric syringe.
   Perfusator.
   Defibrillator.
   Portable aspirator.
   Medicine cabinet.
   Medication refrigerator.
   Medicine trolley.

C. Equipment for patient rooms should be as follows:
   1. The bed.
   2. Oxygen at the head of the bed.
   3. Call system for medical staff.
   4. Personal dresser.
   5. Closet.

A. *Closure Criteria of Transplant Centers*

695. The closure of transplant centers is done by order of the Minister of Health in case it is established the:

a. non-fulfillment of the necessary conditions for the exercise of their activity according to the criteria of defined in Decision No. 617, dated 12.9.2012 For Determining the Criteria for the Opening and Closing of Tissue Banks of Cells and Organs.
b. violation of laws and bylaws in force.
c. non-implementation, within the conditions and deadlines, of the tasks left by the Ministry of Health for correction of violations.

B. *Criteria for Opening a Bank of Tissues, Cells and Organs*

696. To open the tissue, cell and organ bank, the following criteria must be met:

1. Bank of tissues, cells and organs, apart from the requirements defined in Law No. 10 454, dated 21.7.2011 "For the transplantation of tissues, cells and organs in the Republic of Albania," must meet the criteria defined in annexes I and II, which are attached to Decision No. 617, dated 12.9.2012 For Determining the Criteria for the Opening and Closing of Tissue Banks of Cells and Organs.
2. The tissue, cell and organ bank must: a) have foreseen in its status the object of the activity, which it will perform in accordance with legislation in force; have a plan of services that will provide, which contains the type of tissues,

cells and bodies that will collect and process. The activity of the tissue, cell and organ bank is based on the regulations approved by the Ministry of Health.

3. The Minister of Health orders the closure of the bank of tissues, cells and organs in cases where one of the following situations is confirmed:
   a. does not meet the necessary conditions for exercising its activity according to the criteria defined in Decision No. 617, dated 12.9.2012 For Determining the Criteria for the Opening and Closing of Tissue Banks of Cells and Organs.
   b. violation of laws and bylaws in force.
   c. non-implementation, within the conditions and deadlines, of the tasks left by the Ministry of Health for correction of violations.

ANNEX 1

Construction criteria of tissue, cell banks

A. General infrastructure criteria
   Banks of tissues, cells and organs must respect urban and architectural norms in totality. Banks must:
   1. To ensure uninterrupted water supply sources, as well as sufficient water reserves in cases of resource interruption.
   2. To ensure sources of uninterrupted supply of electricity and to be equipped with independent electric power system (generator) to ensure the technical conditions of tissue preservation and cells.
   3. To meet the conditions for air conditioning and ventilation of the tissue and cell bank environments and organs, as well as ensure the physical and microbiological parameters for special work environments, according to criteria approved by order of the Minister of Health.
   4. To ensure fire protection measures.
   5. To provide measures for the prevention and protection of personnel from infections.
   6. To ensure the treatment and elimination of hospital waste according to the legislation in force.
   7. The tissue, cell and organ bank must have a central sterilization unit.
   8. Banks of tissues, cells and organs have renewable contracts for each year for maintenance of medical equipment and calibration of laboratory equipment.
B. Special construction criteria
   1. Banks of tissues, cells and organs must have a few rooms and surface area suitable in accordance with the activity of performance. The necessary premises for the performance of activities are as follows:
      – premises for administration and staff.
      – premises for dressing sterile and non-sterile staff with an area of not less than 9 m2.
      – premises for the cleaning and processing of tissues, cells and organs with a surface not smaller than 15 m2.
      – laboratory environment.

- facilities for deep freezing.
- premises to make the final control of tissues, cells and organs.
- premises for storage and distribution of tissues, cells and organs.
- warehouse for keeping sterile materials.
- premises for bank monitoring, alarm system.
- premises for the cold chain monitoring system.
- toilets for staff.

2. Administration premises must be separate from work premises. The connecting door of work premises with the administration part should not be opened directly to the outside environment. There should be no sanitary joints or toilet rooms in the work premises.
3. The premises of the bank must have:
   a) corridors not less than 2 meters wide.
   b) floors with smooth and nonabsorbent surfaces and easy to disinfect.
   c) the walls, ceilings and floors of the rooms and corridors are built in such a way that can be easily cleaned and maintained.
   d) all windows must be equipped with nets against insects and other poisonous animals.
4. Cleaning and processing facilities for tissues and cells must meet the criteria of the following:
   e) entry and exit to the processing environment must not be through the same door.
   f) suitable lighting for work.
   g) laminar flow cabinet and air filters, which meet the microbiological criteria according to the tissue to be processed.
   h) microbial load of the cleaning, processing, sterile clothing of the staff or introduction of sterile materials must be of class C, according to the criteria of the World Health Organization.
   i) the microbial load in non-sterile rooms and corridors must be of class D, according to the criteria of the World Health Organization.
   j) the positive air pressure in the cleaning room must be higher than in the connected rooms.
   k) the processing environment must have two doors that are not in the same direction. One door closes the room for the sterile clothing of the staff and the other door for the introduction of sterile materials. Both these rooms are of class C. The room for the sterile dressing of the staff is connected to the non-sterile room for the staff in charge of microbial class D. While the room for introducing sterile materials is connected to a non-sterile class D room.
   h) floor-ceiling height must be at least 3 meters.
   i) the processing room, as well as the connecting premises must be ventilated with a central air conditioning system with hygienic filters.

C. Criteria for equipment

1. The tissue and cell bank must provide the necessary laboratory equipment, medical devices instruments, measuring instruments and recorders certified and calibrated by the Directorate of General Calibration.
2. Necessary laboratory equipment for testing, control and validation of tissues, cells and bodies are as follows:
   - Refrigerated laboratory centrifuge.
   - Devices for the control of tissues, cells and organs for transmissible infectious agents' side of the transplant.
   - Equipment for controlling the microbial load of the premises and the transplant.
   - Laminar flow cabinet.
   - Equipment for carrying out microbiological control of the transplant
   - Equipment for complete control of clinical blood parameters.
   - Equipment for performing immunohematological analyses.
   - Multiparametric analyzer.
   - Equipment for carrying out chromosomal analyses.
   - Cytoflurometer.
   - Electrophoresis for hemoglobin.
   - Incubator 37°C.
   - Electronic scales up to 1000 mg.
3. Equipment for the cooling system, freezing and lyophilization procedures

   Tissue and cell banks must provide the necessary cooling, freezing and lyophilizers for the realization of procedures of processing and storage of products according to the desired tissue and cell be prepared as follows:
   - cooling refrigerators with a temperature of +4°C to +10°C.
   - vertical freezer with a temperature of -20°C, -40°C, -80°C or –100°C in accordance with the type of the graft to be stored.
   - equipment for deep freezing.
   - blood centrifuge.
   - automatic plasma extractor.
   - Adhesive.
   - temperature-controlled container for the transport of tissues and cells.

ANNEX 2

Criteria for medical personnel

1. Medical personnel working in tissue, cell and organ banks must have the education, the necessary experience and qualification in accordance with the tasks to be performed.
2. The regulation for the internal functioning of the bank of tissues, cells and organs is approved by ministerial order.

3. Criteria for documenting the activity of tissue, cell and organ banks
   a. The bank of tissues, cells and organs must document all their activity, including the type and quantity of tissues/cells selected, tested, processed, stored and distributed, discarded, as well as their origin and destination for human use, to make possible tracking all links of the activity according to the requirements defined in the relevant approved regulations from the Minister of Health.
   b. The bank of tissues, cells and organs is obliged to have an archive for the preservation of administrative and technical documentation according to Law no. 9154/2003 "On archives" and Law no. 10 454, date 21.7.2011 "For the transplantation of tissues, cells and organs in the Republic of Albania."
   c. The bank of tissues, cells and organs must report to the Ministry of Health on their activity based on law no. 7761, dated 19.10.1993 "On the prevention and fight against the disease stickers," amended, law no. 9952, dated 14.7.2008 "On the prevention and control of HIV/AIDS of Law no. 10 454, dated 21.7.2011 "On tissue, cell and organ transplantation in the Republic of Albania."

C. *Abuse of Human Embryos*

697. Abuse of human embryos for research purposes, or any other purpose is prohibited. It is considered a legal and ethical violation and is punished against these normative acts (Article 56 The Code of Medical Ethics and Deontology).

1. Criminal Offenses and Sanctions under Domestic and International Law

698. The Council of Europe Convention Against Trafficking in Human Organs is ratified by the Republic of Albania. It was signed in Sandiago de Compostela on March 25, 2015. The goal of this Convention is to: (a) preventing and combating the trafficking of human organs, enabling the criminalization of acts certain; (b) protection of the rights of victims of criminal offenses, determined in accordance with this Convention; (c) facilitation of cooperation at national and regional levels on anti-trafficking actions human organs. To guarantee the effective implementation of its provisions by the Parties, this Convention establishes a specific mechanism tracking (Article 1, Law No. 150/2015 On the Ratification of the Council of Europe Convention against Trafficking of Human Organs).

699. This Convention applies to the trafficking of human organs for the purpose of transplantation or other purposes and for other forms of illegal removal and implantation. For the purposes of this Convention, the terms: "trafficking in human organs" means any illegal activity related to human organs, as provided for in Article 4, paragraph 1 and Articles 5, 7, 8 and 9 of this Convention; "human organ" means a differentiated part of the human body, formed by tissue variety that preserves its structure, vascularization and capacity to develop physiological functions with a considerable level of autonomy. A part of an organ is also considered to be an organ if its function is to be used for the same purpose as the whole organ in the human body, maintaining the structure and vascularization requirements (Article 2, Law No. 150/2015 On the Ratification of the Council of Europe Convention against Trafficking of Human Organs).

700. Each party will take the necessary legislative and other measures to define the abuse of ***transplantation of organs*** as a criminal offense according to domestic law, when it is carried out with the aim of removing human organs from living or non-living donors: (a) when the removal was carried out without the free, conscious and specific consent of the living donor or in the case of the deceased donor, without authorized removal of his legal representatives as stipulated under the applicable domestic law; (b) when in exchange for the removal of the organs, the living donor or a third party has been offered or has received a financial gain or comparable advantage; (c) when in exchange for the removal of the organs, the deceased donor or a third party has been offered or has received a financial gain or comparable advantage (Article 4, Law No. 150/2015 On the Ratification of the Council of Europe Convention against Trafficking of Human Organs).

701. The following violations, when they do not constitute a criminal offense, constitute administrative misdemeanors and are punished as follows: (a) the performance of prohibited actions, defined in Article 6 of Law No. 10 454, is punishable by fine from ALL 500,000 to ALL 1,000,000 or with disqualification of practicing the profession for three years; (b) carrying out the tissue, cell or organ transplantation process without obtaining consent from the donor, in violation of Article 15 of Law No. 10 454, is punishable by removal of the right to practice the profession for three years; (c) carrying out the transplantation procedure, without respecting the procedures provided in Articles 19 and 20 of Law No. 10 454, is punishable by the removal of the right to exercise the profession, the person responsible for three years and suspension of the title of the relevant structure for a period of twelve months. In case of repetition, revocation of the title of the relevant structure, according to the legislation in force; (d) performing tissue or organ transplantation by a foreign citizen without an international agreement, in violation of point 3 of Article 22 of Law No. 10 454, shall be punished by deprivation of the right to exercising the profession of the responsible person for three years and suspension of the title of the relevant structure for a twelve-month period. In case of repetition, revocation of the title of the structure, according to legislation in force; (e) removal of the transplant from the donor when his life is in danger, when he is in custody or suffers a prison sentence, suffers from an illness that may endanger the beneficiary's life, in violation of Article 25 of Law No. 10 454 is punishable by disqualification for three years and suspension of the title of the relevant structure for a period of twelve months. In case of recurrence, revocation of the title of the relevant structure, according to the legislation in force; (f) non-notification of unwanted effects by the centers that carry out the transplant, in violation of point 1 of Article 32 of Law No. 10 454 is punishable by a fine of 500,000 (five hundred thousand) lek; (g) violation of confidentiality conditions, provided for in Article 33 of Law No. 10 454, on the part of the health structures is punished with the removal of the right to exercise the profession for three years. Carrying out the import and export of transplants without the authorization of the Minister of Health, in violation of Article 29 of Law No. 10 454, constitutes a criminal offense and is punished according to provisions of the CCr. The authority responsible for imposing and executing the fine is the Ministry of Health. The authorities responsible for removing the right to exercise the profession are professional orders. The procedures for imposing fines and appeals are regulated by Law No. 10 279, dated 20.5.2010 "On administrative offenses" (Article 34 of Law No. 10 454, dated 21.7.2011 For Tissue, Cell and Organ Transplantation in Republic of Albania).

702. The sale and purchase of transplants, as well as any activity related to the illegal removal and implantation of bodies, is punished with imprisonment from three to seven years. The offense committed by the person who abuses his position toward a child or another defenseless person shall be punished with imprisonment from seven to ten years. The offense, when committed more than once or in collaboration, is punishable by imprisonment from ten to fifteen years. When the above-mentioned offenses cause the death of the person or the offense is committed by a structured criminal group or criminal organization it shall be punished by fifteen to twenty-five years of imprisonment (*see* Article 89/a, Law No. 7895, dated 27.1.1995 CCr of the Republic of Albania).

703. The Albanian CCr punishes the use or *transplantation of organs* in its Article 110/a defined as a form of adult trafficking. Recruiting, transporting, transferring, harboring persons through threat or use of force or other forms of coercion, kidnapping, fraud, abuse of office or benefit from social, physical or mental condition or giving or receiving payments or benefits to receive the consent of the person who controls another person, for the purpose of exploiting the prostitution of others or other forms of sexual exploitation, forced labor or services, slavery or forms of similar to slavery, *the use or transplantation of organs*, as well as other forms of exploitation, both inside and outside the territory of the Republic of Albania, are punished with imprisonment from eight to fifteen years. When this offense is committed against an adult female person, it is punishable by imprisonment from ten to fifteen years. The organization, management and financing of human trafficking is punishable by imprisonment from seven to fifteen years (*see* Article 110/a, Law No. 7895, dated 27.1.1995 CCr of the Republic of Albania) (*see* paragraph 392).

704. When this offense is committed in cooperation, more than once, it is accompanied by ill-treatment and coercion with physical or mental violence against the victim, to perform various actions, brings serious consequences for health, or endangers his life, shall be punished by imprisonment for not less than fifteen years. When the offense causes the death of the victim, it is punished with imprisonment of not less than twenty years or life imprisonment. When the criminal offense is committed using the state function or public service, the punishment with imprisonment is increased by ¼ of the sentence given (*see* Article 110/a, Law No. 7895, dated 27.1.1995 CCr of the Republic of Albania) (*see* paragraph 393).

705. Similarly, in its Article 128/b, the Albanian CCr punishes the use or *transplantation of organs* under the offense of Trafficking of Minors. Thus, the recruiting, selling, transporting, transferring, harboring minors for the purpose of exploiting prostitution or other forms of sexual exploitation, forced labor or services, slavery or forms similar to slavery, *use or transplantation of organs,* as well as forms other forms of exploitation, are punished with imprisonment from ten to twenty years. The organization, management and financing of the trafficking of minors is punishable by imprisonment from ten to twenty years. When this offense is committed in collaboration or more than once or is accompanied by mistreatment and the coercion by physical or mental violence of the injured party, to perform various actions, or brings serious consequences for health, shall be punished with imprisonment of not less than fifteen years. When the criminal offense is committed using the state function or public service, the punishment with imprisonment is increased by ¼ of the sentence given (*see* paragraphs 394, 793).

706. According to the Council of Europe Convention against Trafficking in Human Organs, Albania shall endeavor to cooperate comprehensively, in accordance with this Convention, applicable international and regional instruments, reciprocal legislation, and domestic laws, to facilitate investigations and prosecutions of the criminal offenses defined under this Convention, including measures such as seizure and confiscation. Moreover, the Parties are committed to effective collaboration in implementing relevant international, regional, and bilateral treaties governing extradition and mutual legal assistance in criminal matters related to the offenses stipulated by this Convention. Where extradition or mutual legal assistance depends on the existence of a treaty, and a Party receives a request from another Party with which no such treaty exists, the requested Party, consistent with its international obligations and domestic legal framework, may treat this Convention as a sufficient legal basis for granting extradition or mutual legal assistance in matters involving the specified offenses (Article 17, Law No. 150/2015, On the Ratification of the Council of Europe Convention against Trafficking in Human Organs).

707. In addition, the Council of Europe Convention against Trafficking in Human Organs requires Albania to take the necessary legislative and other measures to protect the rights and the interests of victims in all phases of criminal investigations and proceedings, in particular: (a) informing them about their rights and the services available to them and, upon request, the follow-up given to their complaint, the charges, the stage of the criminal proceedings, except in special cases the proper handling of the case may be adversely affected by such notification, as well as their role in them and the results of their cases; (b) allowing them, in a manner compatible with the procedural rules of the domestic law, to be heard, to gather evidence and to present and consider their views, needs and concerns, directly or through an intermediary; (c) offering them the appropriate support services so that their rights and interests are properly presented and taken into account; (d) guaranteeing effective measures for their safety, as well as that of their families, from threats and revenge (Article 19, Law No. 150/2015 On the Ratification of the Council of Europe Convention against Trafficking of Human Organs).

708. The Convention also provides for each party to guarantee that victims have access from the first contact with the competent authorities, in the provision of information on the relevant judicial and administrative proceedings. Each party will guarantee that victims have access to free legal aid, in accordance with the domestic law when it is possible for them to have the status of parties in criminal proceedings. Each Party shall take the necessary legislative and other measures to ensure that victims of a criminal offense defined in accordance with this Convention committed in the territory of a different Party from where they reside, can submit a complaint to the competent authorities of their State of residence. Each Party shall ensure, by legislative or other means, in accordance with the terms provided by domestic law, the possibility for groups, foundations, associations or organizations governmental or non-governmental, to help and/or support victims with their consent during criminal proceedings related to the offenses defined in accordance with this Convention (Article 19, Law No. 150/2015 On the Ratification of the Council of Europe Convention against Trafficking of Human Organs).

2. Implications of Court Decisions Related to Blood Transfusions

709. The cases examined are situated within a robust legal framework that includes the Constitution of the Republic of Albania, Law No. 9739/2007 on Blood Transfusion Services, Law No. 10107/2009 on Public Health Care, and the Code of Administrative Procedures.[177] These laws define the scope of governmental responsibility in healthcare, the rights of patients, and the roles of public and private healthcare institutions.[178]

710. An administrative dispute regarding the validity of directives can arise when procedural and substantive issues, such as inadequate consultation with stakeholders, are identified, potentially leading to their invalidation.[179] Judicial oversight plays a critical role in ensuring that administrative actions adhere to principles of equity, transparency, and procedural fairness, particularly when such actions affect public health services and the private sector. This reinforces the necessity for compliance with statutory limits and constitutional guarantees of equality and access to healthcare, safeguarding against unjust financial burdens on patients.

711. Judicial scrutiny in cases involving medical negligence underscores the complexity of balancing accountability with the recognition of professional discretion. Courts often face the challenge of distinguishing between administrative errors, professional judgment, and criminal liability, particularly in cases where medical decisions align with established protocols and recognized standards of

177. Administrative Court of Appeal, No. 25 of 30.09.2015, para. 2; p. 6.
178. The High Court of Albania, No. 00-2017-1825 of 23.05.2017.
179. Administrative Court of Appeal, No. 25 of 30.09.2015, upheld by The High Court of Albania, No. 00-2017-1825.

care.[180] This cautious approach serves to protect medical professionals from unwarranted legal actions, ensuring that they are not penalized for decisions made in good faith within the scope of their expertise. It also highlights the judiciary's role in fostering an environment where medical practitioners can perform their duties without the fear of unjustified prosecution while still maintaining safeguards to uphold patient safety and professional accountability.[181] This balance demonstrates the cautious approach of the judiciary in distinguishing between administrative errors and criminal negligence, emphasizing the importance of shielding medical professionals from unwarranted legal actions when they adhere to recognized protocols.[182]

712. In Albania, the legal framework regulating the procurement and processing of blood products establishes clear responsibilities for both public institutions and private healthcare providers. Public institutions, such as the National Blood Transfusion Center, play a vital role in ensuring the availability, safety, and quality of blood products, which are essential for various medical treatments and emergencies. These institutions are tasked with managing and overseeing blood collection, testing, storage, and distribution to maintain public health standards and meet the needs of patients. Private healthcare providers, including hospitals and clinics, are equally accountable for compliance with established regulations. They are required to adhere to approved tariffs and follow stringent protocols for the proper handling, storage, and use of blood products. This dual responsibility underscores the importance of a harmonized approach to managing blood products, ensuring that safety and ethical considerations are upheld across the healthcare sector.[183] Cooperation between public entities and private healthcare providers is central to the effective functioning of this system. By working together, these actors can address challenges such as supply shortages, ensure equitable access to blood products, and maintain consistent service quality. This collaboration also serves to protect patient rights, prioritizing safety and reliability in medical procedures that rely on blood transfusions or related treatments.[184] The legal framework not only reinforces the obligations of all involved parties but also ensures that regulatory standards are consistently applied. This helps build trust in the healthcare system, promotes accountability, and safeguards public health. The emphasis on compliance and collaboration highlights the shared responsibility of public and private sectors in delivering essential health services and maintaining high standards of care for the population.

713. Albania's legal framework emphasizes the state's responsibility to ensure equitable access to essential healthcare, such as blood transfusions for conditions like thalassemia. Grounded in the Law on Public Health Care and the Constitution, it safeguards patient rights and ensures administrative actions support, rather than hinder, access to vital medical services, particularly for vulnerable populations.

180. The High Court of Albania, No. 00-2022-1277 of 25.10.2022.
181. The High Court of Albania, No. 00-2017-1825 of 23.05.2017.
182. Tribunal of First Instance of Vlore, No. 17 of 05.02.2016.
183. The High Court of Albania, No. 00-2016-2206 of 15.12.2016.
184. Albanian Constitutional Court, No. 9 of 26.02.2016.

714. The role of the courts in regulating administrative powers is particularly evident in these decisions. The judiciary provides a crucial balance between government regulation and the autonomy of private healthcare providers. By scrutinizing administrative decisions, such as those imposing tariffs, the courts ensure that executive actions comply with legal norms, respect procedural rights, and do not infringe upon private sector interests without just cause. These decisions are significant in setting precedents for the limits of administrative discretion, especially in sensitive areas like public health, where the potential for abuse of power could directly impact the well-being of citizens.

715. The criminal case involving allegations of medical negligence further highlights the judiciary's careful approach in holding medical professionals accountable. The court's insistence on a high standard for establishing criminal liability helps protect doctors from undue legal pressures while promoting adherence to professional standards and protocols. This balance is essential for maintaining a healthcare system where medical professionals can operate without fear of unfounded criminal charges, allowing them to focus on providing high-quality care.

716. In conclusion, the legal decisions analyzed in this report demonstrate the importance of a balanced approach to governance in Albania's healthcare sector. The judiciary plays a critical role in reviewing administrative actions and protecting both patient rights and professional autonomy, ensuring a more equitable healthcare system. These cases contribute significantly to the ongoing legal discourse in Albania regarding the role of state oversight in healthcare, the rights of private healthcare providers, and the protection of patients' interests. As Albania continues to develop its legal framework in alignment with European standards, the precedents set by these cases will serve as important reference points for future legislative and judicial actions.

D. Court Decisions Concerning Blood Transfusions

717. The Albanian judicial approach to administrative actions in healthcare reflects a crucial intersection between regulatory authority, legal compliance, and the protection of individual rights.[185] This is particularly evident in the governance of healthcare services, where administrative bodies like the Ministry of Health must operate within the boundaries set by law to ensure fairness and accountability. Judicial decisions in this context emphasize the importance of legislative intent as the guiding principle for administrative actions, ensuring that ministries and other public bodies respect their legally defined limits.[186] This adherence to legal and procedural standards fosters a system of checks and balances that safeguards the rule of

185. The High Court of Albania, No. 00-2017-1825 of 23.05.2017.
186. Administrative Court of Appeal, No. 25 of 30.09.2015, para. 2; pg. 6: Order No. 52, dated 28.01.2015 "On the approval of fees for the collection and processing of blood and its components" is based on Art. 14 of Law 9739/2007 "On Blood Transfusion in the Republic of Slovenia."

law, particularly in sectors like healthcare, which directly impact public welfare. Furthermore, the principle of collaboration between public authorities and private entities in healthcare regulation highlights the importance of balancing state responsibilities with the rights and interests of private stakeholders, creating a regulatory framework that is participatory and transparent.[187]

718. The broader implications of this approach for Albanian administrative law are significant. By reinforcing principles such as procedural fairness, proportionality, and accountability, the judiciary ensures that administrative actions align with constitutional mandates, such as equitable access to healthcare.[188] This legal framework underscores the importance of non-discrimination and the elimination of undue financial barriers to essential services, reflecting a commitment to upholding healthcare as a fundamental right. Moreover, the emphasis on harmonizing statutory provisions with international norms, such as fairness and participation, demonstrates Albania's evolving legal culture, one that prioritizes the rule of law and the fair distribution of resources.[189] Ultimately, this judicial interpretation strengthens the accountability of public institutions and creates a cohesive legal environment that supports the equitable and effective regulation of healthcare, contributing to the broader development of governance and public trust in Albania.

§7. Experiments on Human Beings

719. The doctor is not allowed to lead or participate in research or experiments, scientific, biomedical, except when such a thing is provided by law or other legal acts. The doctor who undertakes a research work with a preventive, diagnostic or doctors, including patients or volunteers, must submit the project to a special competent and independent bioethics commission to evaluate the scientific legality, ethical acceptability and to approve it. The doctor must carefully inform the person or

---

changed. Art. 14, point 2, of the above law provides that "The Ministry of Health annually proposes and controls the prices and fees used in the transfusion service in relation to its public or private partners. In Art. 14, point 2, of Law 9739/2007 "On Blood Transfusion in the Republic of Slovenia." as amended, foresees the competence of the Ministry of Health to propose and to check annually the prices-fees, which are used in the transfusion service, in relation to its public or private partners."

187. Administrative Court of Appeal, No. 25 of 30.09.2015; para. 2; pg. 5: Law No. 10107, dated 30.03.2009 "On health care in the Republic of Albania," defines the main principles and the legal framework for the regulation, organization and operation of the health care system in the Republic of Albania. *"This law applies to all natural or legal persons, Albanian or foreign, who operate in the health care system. According to this law, the health authorities are the Ministry of Health, as well as the regional structures depending on it. According to this law, health care by the health authorities is guided by several essential principles such as: the right to health care is a fundamental right of the individual, guaranteed to equal rights in health care, based on non-discrimination; the participation of different actors, patients, consumers and citizens, etc."* [author' translation]

188. The High Court of Albania, No. 00-2022-1277 of 25.10.2022.

189. Tribunal of First Instance of Vlore, No. 17 of 05.02.2016 (criminal session); upheld by Court of Appeal of Vlore, No. 88 of 18.05.2017.

persons involved in the project on the object of the research work, the expected benefits, the possible consequences and damages and take consent. If obtaining consent is impossible due to physical incapacity, mental or age of the patient, consent can be obtained from relatives (Article 52 The Code of Medical Ethics and Deontology).

720. The practice of conducting experiments on human beings is an essential aspect of biomedical research, requiring a careful balance between scientific advancement and the ethical obligation to protect participants. This complex area is regulated by rigorous ethical and legal frameworks designed to uphold human dignity and safeguard individual rights. These principles, articulated in several key legal articles, provide a comprehensive guide to ensure research practices adhere to the highest standards of integrity and respect for humanity.

721. Medical professionals are permitted to engage in research involving human subjects only under strict legal conditions, as outlined in Article 52 of the Code of Medical Ethics. Before any study is undertaken, it must be reviewed and approved by an independent bioethics committee, which assesses the scientific validity, ethical soundness, and overall justification of the project. Participants must be fully informed about the purpose of the research, the expected benefits, the potential risks, and any foreseeable consequences of their participation.[190] Informed consent is a fundamental requirement, ensuring that participation is voluntary and based on a clear understanding of the study. In situations where individuals are unable to provide consent due to factors such as age, mental incapacity, or physical limitations, consent must be obtained from a legal representative or a close family member. This process ensures that every participant, regardless of their capacity, is afforded equitable protection and respect.

722. A cornerstone of ethical research, as emphasized in Article 53 the Code of Medical Ethics, is the participant's right to withdraw from the study at any time and for any reason, without fear of negative consequences.[191] This principal safeguards personal autonomy and ensures that participation remains a matter of free will. Researchers bear the responsibility of clearly communicating this right to all participants as part of their ethical obligation to foster an environment of trust and respect.

190. The Code of Medical Ethics, Art. 52, *"Participation in Scientific Research": "Doctors are not allowed to lead or participate in scientific or biomedical research and experiments, except in cases where such activities are foreseen by law or other legal acts. A doctor undertaking a research project for preventive, diagnostic, or therapeutic purposes involving patients or volunteers must submit the project to a specialized, independent bioethics committee for scientific evaluation, ethical approval, and authorization. The doctor must carefully inform the individual or individuals involved in the project about the purpose of the research, expected benefits, potential risks, and possible harms, and obtain their consent. If obtaining consent is impossible due to the patient's physical or mental incapacity or age, consent may be obtained from the relatives."* [author' translation]

191. The Code of Medical Ethics, Art. 53, *"Right to Withdraw from Study": "The individual involved in the study must be informed of their right to withdraw from the study voluntarily at any time."* [author' translation]

723. Moreover, Article 54 of the Code of Medical Ethics underscores the vital importance of honesty and transparency throughout every stage of the research process.[192] Researchers must adhere strictly to approved protocols, record results accurately, and report findings truthfully. Any deviation from these principles—such as fabricating data, manipulating outcomes, or making unwarranted claims of authorship—is not only unethical but also undermines the credibility of scientific inquiry. This commitment to integrity is essential for maintaining public trust and ensuring that research findings contribute meaningfully to the advancement of knowledge.

724. The adoption of innovative diagnostic, therapeutic, or preventive methods is permitted only after thorough evaluation and approval by an independent clinical committee, as stipulated in Article 55 of the Code of Medical Ethics.[193] Such methods must be supported by a robust body of scientific evidence and must prioritize patient safety. The use of unproven or scientifically unsound methods is prohibited, reflecting a commitment to protecting participants from unnecessary harm. Placebo treatments, while ethically complex, may be employed in specific circumstances where evidence suggests potential benefits for patients and where harm can be definitively ruled out.

725. Additionally, Article 56 of the Code of Medical Ethics addresses the protection of human embryos, highlighting this as a particularly delicate and ethically significant area of biomedical research.[194] Such actions are deemed a grave violation of ethical and legal norms, reflecting a deep societal commitment to preserving the dignity of human life at all stages of development. This principle underscores the importance of treating all forms of human life with profound respect and care.

726. Similarly, the regulation of organ and tissue transplantation, as described in Article 57 of the Code of Medical Ethics, is governed by strict legal provisions.[195] These procedures may only be conducted by qualified professionals within adequately equipped facilities to ensure safety and compliance with established

---

192. The Code of Medical Ethics, Art. 54, *"Reporting Results": "A doctor participating in the study is obliged to conduct research with integrity, strictly following all aspects of the research protocol. They must record the research results accurately, report, and publish them honestly, without unjustly claiming authorship."* [author' translation]
193. The Code of Medical Ethics, Art. 55, *"Application of New Methods": "The application of new diagnostic, therapeutic, and preventive methods is only allowed after clinical review by a specialized, independent, and competent commission. The adoption, execution, and promotion of scientifically unproven methods is prohibited, as it constitutes a violation of legal acts, an infringement of the Code of Medical Ethics and Deontology, and subject to disciplinary action. Only treatment compared with a placebo may be allowed under conditions where, according to scientific data, the patient may benefit, but with a guaranteed exclusion of harmful effects."* [author' translation]
194. The Code of Medical Ethics, Art. 56, *"Abuse of Human Embryos": "Abuse of human embryos for research purposes or any other purpose is prohibited. It is considered both a legal and ethical violation and is punishable according to these normative acts."* [author' translation]
195. The Code of Medical Ethics, Art. 57, *"Organ and Tissue Transplantation": "The removal of organs, tissues, or any other products from a living or deceased human body is practiced only under the conditions and circumstances provided by law or other relevant legal acts related to this field. A doctor is not allowed to remove organs, tissues, or any other products from the human body,*

medical standards. Violations of these regulations, including unauthorized practices or procedures performed by unqualified individuals, constitute serious ethical and legal breaches.

727. The ethical and legal frameworks governing human experimentation, as articulated in Articles 52 through 57 of the Code of Medical Ethics, underscore the scientific community's obligation to uphold human dignity, protect individual rights, and adhere to principles of transparency and accountability. These provisions establish a foundation for fostering trust between researchers and participants, ensuring that scientific advancement is pursued responsibly and ethically. By rigorously following these standards, researchers not only advance the boundaries of knowledge but also safeguard the fundamental values that define and preserve our shared humanity.

728. The rights enshrined in the "Albanian Charter of Patient's Rights" serve as a vital cornerstone for promoting ethical practices in biomedical research involving human subjects. These rights prioritize patient empowerment, autonomy, and informed decision-making, principles that are fundamental to the ethical conduct of experimentation and the protection of human dignity.

729. Article 3 of the "Albanian Card of Patient's Rights" establishes the Right to Information, affirming that every patient has the right to access comprehensive information about their health condition, available healthcare services, and how to utilize them effectively.[196] This right extends to information about any scientific research or technological innovation that could be relevant to their care. In the context of biomedical research, this provision ensures that individuals are fully aware of any potential implications or benefits of research activities that may involve them.

730. Building upon this foundation, Article 4 underscores the Right to Consent, asserting that patients must be fully informed and equipped with all relevant information to actively engage in decisions concerning their health. This principle reinforces autonomy and ensures that medical practices and research align with ethical and legal standards.[197] This includes detailed explanations of proposed treatments, procedures, or participation in scientific research. Such information must be conveyed clearly, as it serves as a prerequisite for obtaining informed consent. Without

---

nor transplant them, unless they are qualified in this field and have a trained and qualified cooperative team. Additionally, such a procedure is prohibited if appropriate medical and technical equipment is not available." [author' translation]

196. Albanian Card of Patient's Rights, Art. 3, *"Right to Information": "Every patient has the right to access all information related to their health condition, healthcare services, and how to use them, as well as any scientific research or technological innovation that may be applicable."* [author' translation]

197. Albanian Card of Patient's Rights, Art. 4, *"Right to Consent": "Every patient has the right to access all information that enables them to actively participate in decisions regarding their health. This information is a prerequisite for any treatment and procedure, including participation in scientific research."* [author' translation]

this, no treatment, intervention, or research participation can proceed ethically. These rights collectively ensure that individuals are not passive subjects but active, informed participants in decisions affecting their health and well-being.

731. By embedding these principles into the framework for biomedical research, the ethical guidelines reinforce the importance of respecting patient autonomy and ensuring that all participation in scientific studies is voluntary, informed, and rooted in a clear understanding of the potential impacts. This approach protects individuals while fostering trust and transparency in the research process.

§8. Euthanasia

732. The term "euthanasia" derives from the union of the ancient Greek words euthanatos where the "eu" means good and "thanatos" means death. Thus, in the context of a translation, it simply means good death. These two words have caused philosophical clashes, but at the same time they have also served as the axis around which human thought has developed, trying to analyze them. The "eu" concept of good, in general as material and spiritual, has always been a point of reference for humanity, something ideal, which it has tried to understand and approach by closely relating it to the existence of its own kind. The concept of "thanatos" death, on the other hand, is also conceived as the embodiment of evil, of human suffering and pain, also as a reality that cannot be compromised in any way.

733. Literally euthanasia, in the most correct translation and approach to the philosophical thought of the ancient Greeks, is conveyed as the good, glorious, beautiful death, as the death that comes without pain and suffering, as the desirable death. This new concept has caused debates in the international arena and sparked intense discussions and controversies about ethics, law, deontology, etc.

734. Euthanasia is fundamentally rooted in the will of the individual performing the act. However, such an action must be solely driven by compassion, care for the patient, and a genuine desire to alleviate their suffering. If the action is influenced by other motives, such as economic gain or personal interests of the perpetrator or a third party, it no longer qualifies as euthanasia. Instead, it may constitute elements of the criminal offense of premeditated murder.

735. Another essential condition for considering an act as euthanasia is the patient's health status, which must unequivocally indicate a terminal condition that will inevitably lead to death, accompanied by unavoidable suffering and pain. In these cases, it is assumed that in the process of pain, although it remains to be discussed, since in many cases, it cannot be scientifically concluded that the patient feels pain (Giunta, F., 1997: 42). Finally, the process of ending the patient's life should be such, methodically studied, treating each case as unique, to ensure a quick death, eliminating pain as much as possible and the suffering and absolutely respecting and disrespecting the patient's dignity.

736. In 2022, the ECtHR declared that death by euthanasia, also for nonterminal illnesses, is not a violation of (the positive obligation of) Article 2 ECHR. The absence of family involvement in the euthanasia process of a patient is not a violation of Article 8 ECHR.[198]

737. However, while in other countries—i.e., Italy—different draft-bills have been presented in the Parliament to rule euthanasia.[199] While Albania has not initiated any draft-bills in parliament. It shall be noted that euthanasia is deemed a criminal offense in Albania (Articles 76, 79, and 99 of the CCr).[200]

§9. Others (Sexually Transmitted Infections)

I. Viral Hepatitis B and C

738. Albania has a prevalence of Hepatitis B (HBV) that is calculated to be 7%–9%, while the prevalence of Hepatitis C (HCV) is in the figures of 1%–1.5%. A case-based hepatitis B surveillance system has been established across the country in 2010. General hepatitis reporting system (undifferentiated) in the major system of reporting of infectious diseases shows the trend toward decreasing cases of viral hepatitis in general.

739. As for viral Hepatitis C, this number has not undergone a significant change. Most affected age group turns out to be 25–44 years old for both types of Hepatitis, which is also the most active age. It is worth noting that in the age group 0–18 years, the cases are close to 0. This fact is also due to high vaccination coverage in the country against HBV at 95% and additional vaccination programs for this age group.

740. Males are more affected than females for both types of viral hepatitis B and C. Thus, for the five-year period, 2016–2020, 484 cases of HBV were reported, of which 292 (60.3%) are men and 192 (39.7%) are women, and 107 cases were reported for HCV, of which 64 (59.8%) are male and 43 or 40.2% are female. The districts with the highest incidence are Berati, Durres, Shkodra, Tirana, Vlora; these districts have even the largest population. Most of the cases live in urban areas compared to rural areas. The most at-risk groups are people who have contact with people affected by these diseases, health personnel, people receiving multiple blood transfusions, drug users, men who have sex with men (MSM), pregnant women, Roma population.

---

198. ECtHR, *Mortier v. Belgium*, application No. 78017/17.
199. Draft-Bill No. S-124 presented on Oct. 13, 2022 "Provisions regarding medically assisted suicide and euthanasia treatment"; Draft-Bill No. C-313 presented on Nov. 23, 2022 "Provisions regarding medically assisted suicide and euthanasia treatment."
200. Hoxha, Dorina, et al. "Albania, the Right-to-Not Be Treated, and COVID-19." *BioLaw Journal-Rivista di BioDiritto* 4 (2021): 417–425.

741. The case-based surveillance system was initially deployed only in the Hospital Center "Mother Teresa" University in 2003 and then at Durrës Hospital and in 2010 has spread throughout the country based on the increase in laboratory diagnostic capacities. Given that the weight of the viral hepatitis disease is also measured through seroprevalence studies, below there are some important data. According to the seroprevalence studies in the group of pregnant women conducted in 2005, this group of which is also used to indicate the prevalence in the general population, the prevalence of these two diseases is respectively 6.4% for HBV and 1% for HCV. Research data show that the highest prevalence of HBV and HCV is maintained by risk groups.

II. Testing

742. In Albania, testing for hepatitis B and C is available in microbiology or immunology laboratories in the public sector, such as those affiliated with Local Units of Health Care, hospitals, counseling centers, voluntary testing facilities, as well as private clinics and laboratories. Individuals who test positive, even without clinical symptoms, are referred to specialist doctors for further evaluation and additional testing. The Ministry of Health and Social Protection has implemented a national prevention and screening guide for infectious diseases in pregnant women, ensuring that every pregnant woman is screened free of charge nationwide for HBV, HIV, syphilis, and rubella. This initiative has significantly reduced the transmission of these diseases from mother to child. The hepatitis B vaccination program was introduced in 1993 and expanded in 2000 to include newborns who are vaccinated within the first twenty-four hours of life and again during the first year. This program has achieved high coverage rates exceeding 95%, and subsequent adolescent vaccination efforts have nearly eradicated the disease among individuals aged 0–18.

743. In the same way, during the last years, vaccination programs have been offered to health workers, students of the Faculty of Medicine and other groups such as drug users, people who perform dialysis or transplants as well as repeated blood transfusions. Work is currently underway to finalize the strategic action plan for Viral Hepatitis B and C which includes aspects of prevention, control and early diagnosis and treatment.

III. Other Sexually Transmitted Infections

744. STIs are among the biggest causes of disease acute or chronic resulting in infertility, long-term disability and death in aged women reproductive. This surveillance includes the reporting of major syndromes associated with STIs transmissible and reported mainly in women. While in relation to men there are deficiencies and underreporting even though the source of information includes the structures of obstetrics and gynecology, urology, infection doctor and dermatologist.

745. Laboratory surveillance data indicate that the most common cause of STIs is *Gardnerella vaginalis*, accounting for 12.5% of cases, followed by *Ureaplasma urealyticum* at 7.1%. Other identified causes include *Trichomonas vaginalis* (5.5%), *Herpes simplex* (1.07%), and others. To ensure accurate identification of all STI causes, diagnostic capacities for *Chlamydia trachomatis* and *Neisseria gonorrhoeae* need to be strengthened.

IV. Syphilis

746. After a prolonged absence, syphilis reemerged in Albania in the early 1990s. Between 2014 and 2020, the number of reported syphilis cases saw a significant decline of 56%. Regarding gender distribution, 70% of the cases were male, and 30% were female. Analyzing the age distribution, children aged 0–14 years accounted for only 2% of cases, while the 15–24 age group comprised 9%. Most cases, 73%, were reported in the 25–49 age group, and individuals over 50 years of age represented 16% of the total cases.

V. HIV and AIDS

747. Based on statistical data, Albania continues to remain a country with a low prevalence of HIV infection. The prevalence of HIV infection in our country is about 0.05% (population according to INSTAT 2021). The first case of HIV was diagnosed in 1993 and until December 2021, 1,506 have been reported HIV cases.

748. Regarding the distribution of HIV positive cases by gender, 72% (1085 cases) of them are men and 28% (421 cases) are women. During the year 2021, 73 males and 31 females were reported diagnosed with HIV. The male/female ratio in positive cases expresses the risk of transmission to men who have sex with men. The sexual route of transmission of the HIV virus continues to be the most frequent route of transmission in our country, which is found in approximately 95% of cases; heterosexual underpass and homosexuals constitute 83% and 12%, respectively, according to cumulative data (1993–2021) in the moment of the person's HIV positive status being discovered for the first time. Vertical transmission or from infected mother to child accounts for 2.5% of the total.

749. HIV and AIDS remain urban phenomena in our country, as 72.6% of people are infected in residence in the city. The distribution by age group shows that the 35–44 age group predominates in our country (28.8%), followed by the 25–34 age group (26.8%) which is a sexually active age group. As part of the national response to the HIV/AIDS epidemic, several measures were designed and implemented measures, which include:

- Approval and implementation of the National HIV/AIDS Plan 2020–2025. The plan aims for Albania to remain a country with a low prevalence, with a health system capable of responding to it trends of increasing behaviors with risk for

HIV infection and providing care and treatment quality medical care for all people living with HIV/AIDS; provide an environment support for reducing stigma and discrimination and for social support.

750. Implementation of Law No. 9952, "For the Prevention and Control of HIV Infection in Albania," dated 14.07.2008. The law aims to strengthen preventive measures in the population general, vulnerable layers, support to infected persons through the protection of the rights of these persons, the promotion of counseling and testing services confidential as well as support with other health services for people living with HIV/AIDS. Preparation of relevant guidelines for HIV prevention in institutions of education, re-education, medical treatment institutions, residential institutions, social care, prisons and places of detention.

751. Strengthening of Voluntary Counseling and Testing Services in all Local Health Care Units where it is offered this service (2007 onward), enabling more access to testing and advice for HIV, Hepatitis and other STIs:

- Providing and monitoring free treatment with antiretroviral medications for Persons who Living with HIV/AIDS since 2004.
- Scaling up preventive interventions in vulnerable populations, including injecting drug users (IDUs), female sex workers, men who have sex with Men (MSM).

752. Conducting biological and behavioral studies in different risk groups such as IDU, MSM and female sex workers:

- Drafting and implementation of guidelines for testing pregnant women for several infectious agents: HIV, Syphilis, Hepatitis B and Rubella." Preparation of standards for the prevention program of HIV infection from mother to child.
- Expanding and strengthening healthcare provider-initiated testing.
- Cooperation with social service structures, civil society, educational structures and those of the local government for HIV prevention interventions, and in specific cases for children living with HIV.

Part III. The Physician in Relation to the Healthcare System

Chapter 1. Collegial Relationships

§1. Associations

I. The Doctor's Professional Order

753. In relation to the practice of professions related to medicine, in support of Articles 78 and 83, point 1, of the Constitution, upon with the proposal of the Council of Ministers, the Republic of Albania adopted Law No. 123/2014 for the Order of Doctors (Law No. 123/2014). The professional order aims to maintain high standards in the formation and exercise of the regulated profession related to medicine, as well as the protection of the public from the malpractice of the profession. The purpose of this law is to define the rules of organization and activity of the Order of Doctors and legal relations of medical professionals (Article 1 Law No. 123/2014). This law applies to all doctors who practice the profession in the Republic of Albania in the public or private system (Article 2 Law No. 123/2014). Article 3 of Law No. 123/2014 identifies the legal status of The Order of Doctors as a non-budgetary, professional, independent public entity, which represents and protects the common interests of the members of the Order and regulates the activities and relations between them.

754. As an independent professional self-regulatory authority, it is depoliticized and departmentalized, open and equal for all members, regardless of their social affiliations, racial, ethnic, religious or political beliefs. It is categorically forbidden that in the bodies and structures of all levels of the Order of phenomena or problems of a political, party, racial, ethnic character are discussed or religious reflections (Article 2 the Statute of the Order of Doctors of Albania). The order is run and managed in accordance with the Statute of the Order of Doctors of Albania (Order of Doctors in the Republic of Albania) is based on Law No. 123/2014, dated 25.09.2014 "On the Order of Doctors in the Republic of Albania," Law No. 10106, dated 30.03.2009 "On Health Care in the Republic of Albania" and Law 10171, dated 22.10.2009 "On professions regulated in the Republic of Albania." This Statute aims to regulate all the activities of the Order, its bodies and its structures, as an internal normative act for the implementation of the Law and the smooth running of activities.

755. The mission of the Order of Doctors is to maintain high standards in training and the exercise of professions in the field of medicine and the protection of patients and the public from malpractice of the medical profession (Article 4(1) Law No. 123/2014). To fulfill its mission, the Order of Doctors exercises the following powers: (a) grants and withdraws the individual license to practice the profession; (b) establishes ethical and deontological standards, mandatory for every doctor and monitors their implementation during the exercise of the profession; (c) periodically re-evaluates the competence and professional performance of the member Orders against established standards; (d) promotes the achievement of high standards in professional and ethical education and training members of the Order; (e) cooperates with the National Center of Continuing Education, other scientific and educational institutions to ensure high standards in Continuing Education (Article 4 the Statute of the Order of Doctors of Albania).

756. The Order of Doctors actively collaborates with the Ministry of Health and its subordinate institutions, as well as with other ministries, central bodies, higher education institutions, and various public or private organizations established under current legislation. Every six months, the Order provides the Ministry of Health with updates on memberships, disciplinary proceedings, and other matters of mutual interest. This information is also made publicly available on the Order's official website. Additionally, the State Health Inspectorate works closely with the Order of Doctors to support its functions. The Ministry of Health further collaborates with the Order in drafting legislation and developing key documents in the field of healthcare, ensuring alignment with professional and regulatory standards (Article 9 Law No. 123/2014, also *see* Article 5 the Statute of the Order of Doctors of Albania).

757. The Order of Doctors has its own budget, which is approved and administered by the National Council in accordance with the financial rules in force and with the internal regulation for the financial activity of the Order. The financial resources of the Order are: (a) members' quotas, the amount of which is determined by the National Council's decision and are mandatory for every member; (b) the fees imposed for acts and documents issued by the Order; (c) various donations and other legal income. The insured income is used to fulfill its goals and objectives in accordance with the statute and Law No. 123/2014 (*see* Article 10 Law No. 123/2014 and Article 37 the Statute of the Order of Doctors of Albania). The amount of quotation is determined by the decision of the National Council and is mandatory for every member. When for a period of more than one year the quotations are not repaid without justifiable reasons, his membership in Order of Doctors in the Republic of Albania and License are suspended for the individual exercise of the profession (Article 38 the Statute of the Order of Doctors of Albania).

758. The financial resources of the Order are used for: (a) salaries and fees for employees of the administration of the Central Executive Apparatus and regions, for the members of the National Council and those of the Regional Councils, for working groups, commissions, expertise, disciplinary processes; (b) rewards for work evaluation, assistance in case of disaster for members of the Order, as well as for employees of the Central Executive Apparatus and the Regional one, for commissions, working groups, etc.; (c) various cultural activities; (d) contribution to social and health insurance of employees; (e) obligations with the state and third parties, etc.; (f) operating expenses (office, transport, communications, energy, diet, photographic documentation, audiotapes and videotapes and others); (g) organization of scientific-professional and qualification activities (conferences, symposia, sessions, seminars, trainings, etc.); (h) scientific, informative and promotional publications for the Order; (i) investment and purchase of work tools and equipment; (j) participation in international activities, as well as hosting and escorting foreign delegations; (k) various commemorative, promotional ceremonies, and so on (Article 39 the Statute of the Order of Doctors of Albania).

759. All practicing doctors/specialists are members of the Order of Doctors the profession in the public and private health system in the Republic of Albania, who fulfill the conditions to be members according to Law 123/2014, dated 25.09.2014 “On the Order of Doctors in the Republic of Albania.” Membership in the Order is a prerequisite for practicing the profession. No individual can practice the profession in the healthcare system in the Republic of Albania without being a member of the Order of Doctors and without being licensed for the individual exercise of the profession issued by this Institution (Article 3 the Statute of the Order of Doctors of Albania). For the actions performed for membership registration, the equipment with the License for the exercise of the individual profession, membership card, as well as for acts and other documents that are issued by the Order, each individual pays the fees which are determined by the decision of the National Council Order (Article 8 the Statute of the Order of Doctors of Albania).

II. Membership

760. All Albanian or foreign doctors practicing the profession of doctor in the Republic of Albania must be members of the Order of Doctors and must meet the following criteria: For Albanian citizens (a) have a doctor’s diploma, specialist doctors and specialty diploma, issued by higher education institution inside or outside the country, recognized by the responsible ministry for education; (b) not to be convicted by a final decision for criminal offenses or for the commission of an intentional criminal offense at the time of membership application; (c) acknowledge and pledge in writing that they will comply with the requirements of the legislation in force, Statute, Doctor’s Oath and Code of Medical Ethics and Deontology.

761. For foreign citizens - Any doctor, foreign citizen, practicing the profession as a resident in Albania, or attached to a health institution when he comes periodically to exercise his profession, he must have also these documents: (a) residence and work permit in the Republic of Albania; (b) certificate of good professional behavior (Good Standing Certificate) from the Order/chamber or the association of doctors of his country, where it is proven that he is registered and practicing the profession and that no punitive measures have been taken; (c) the unification (validation) of the diploma and certificates of specializations completed by him/her; (d) recommendation from a local specialist in the same field, member of the Order of Doctors; (e) proof of knowledge of the Albanian language, certified by an authority licensed by the state. The non-resident doctor necessarily works with an interpreter. The Registration-Membership process, the administration of the Register, as well as the granting of the License for the individual exercise of the profession is carried out based on the Registration-Licensing Regulation, which is approved by the National Council (Article 6 the Statute of the Order of Doctors of Albania)

762. The membership of the member of the Order of Doctors is terminated in the following cases: (a) when he dies; (b) when the individual license to practice the profession is revoked by a disciplinary decision of the form decided by the bodies of the Order or the court; (c) when he is serving a criminal sentence with deprivation of liberty; (d) when the quotations are not settled in accordance with the deadlines set by the National Council of the Order and exceeds them for more than one year without justifiable reasons. The decision to terminate membership is officially communicated to the person and the institution where the convict served (Article 7 Law No. 123/2014).

763. The doctor/specialist doctor, who, for whatever reason, has not practiced the profession for a period over five years, in order to regain the right to practice the profession, must: (a) carry out the procedures of reregistration and re-membership in the Order of Doctors, in compliance with the requirements of this Statute and the Regulation on Registration and Membership and Licensing for the individual exercise of the profession; (b) undergo the exercise of supervised professional practice, in his own profile, for a period of six months. Be provided with the official document where to confirm the ability to exercise the profession independently; (c) to be provided with the license for the individual exercise of the profession (Article 7 the Statute of the Order of Doctors of Albania).

764. Regarding the decision that rejects the request for registration and membership, the applicant has the right to complain to the Central Executive Apparatus of the National Council no later than thirty days from the day of announcement and receipt of notification of the decision. The responsible commission or sector at the National Council examines it no later than thirty days from the submission of the complaint and takes the relevant decision, which it notifies the complainant. This decision is final. The applicant has the right to turn again to the relevant Regional Council with a request for membership only if he has met the conditions for acceptance of membership (Article 9 the Statute of the Order of Doctors of Albania).

765. Retired doctors and disabled doctors remain on the register as members of the Order of Doctors and have the right to maintain the membership without being obliged to pay the membership quota. If they are employed (in public or private institutions) or self-employed, they are subject to all the rights and obligations of the member of the Order. The member of the Order is temporarily deprived of the right to practice the profession or suspend it when: (a) there is a final decision of the National Disciplinary Commission of Order of Doctors in the Republic of Albania; (b) is serving a criminal sentence of deprivation of liberty by a final court decision; (c) has not paid the quotations within the terms provided for in the Statute of the Order of Doctors in the Republic of Albania; (d) has not fulfilled the obligations of the Code of Medical Ethics and Deontology; (e) has not passed the exams or tests assigned for a qualification or practical obligation provided by a final disciplinary decision. For the period of temporary removal (suspension) of the right to exercise the profession, the doctor maintains registration and membership in Order of Doctors in the Republic of Albania in accordance with the statutory provisions for members of the Order but does not enjoy the right to exercise the profession. Removal of the right to exercise the profession over three years is done only by a final court decision court. Procedural actions for the temporary removal of the right to exercise the profession (membership termination) are carried out in support of and in full compliance with legal provisions, the provisions of the Statute, the Code of Medical Ethics and Deontology and the Rules of Judgment Professional Disciplinary (Article 10 the Statute of the Order of Doctors of Albania).

766. The member of the Order of Doctors has the right: (1) to exercise the profession in his own profile; (2) to appeal to the bodies of the Order when their rights and opportunities for free exercise are violated and independent of any profession; (3) to choose and be elected in the bodies of the Order; (4) to participate in the examination by the bodies of the Order for problems related to his person; (5) to appeal to the forums of the Order the decisions of this body when he deems them unfair; (6) to request the creation of favorable conditions for the normal exercise of the profession, for his professional formation and development, as well as for the advancement of his career (Article 12 the Statute of the Order of Doctors of Albania, also *see* Article 6 Law No. 123/2014).

III. Duties of the Member of the Order of Doctors

767. The member of the Order of Doctors has the following duties: (1) to recognize and apply the Code of Medical Ethics and Deontology, the Law and the Statute of Order of Doctors in the Republic of Albania, as well as other laws and bylaws on health and care health in the Republic of Albania; (2) practice the profession and have good professional behavior in accordance with the requirements and the standards of the Code of Medical Ethics and Deontology, as well as in compliance with the laws and other administrative acts in the field of medicine; (3) work without interruption to increase the standards and quality of healthcare in the institution where he works, to participate regularly in the Continuous Medical Education programs, to be up-to-date and competent in the profession; (4) to disagree with the attitude and behavior of colleagues and other medical personnel, which do not conform to the standards and requirements of the Code of Ethics and Deontology Medical or endanger the health and life of the sick; (5) to pay the member's quota on time and any other obligation in relation to the Order in accordance with the requirements of this Statute and its other Regulations; (6) to be equipped with the License for the individual exercise of the profession (Article 8 Law No. 123/2014, also *see* Article 13 the Statute of the Order of Doctors of Albania).

IV. Control by Supervisory Committees

768. The main bodies of the Order are: (a) assemblies; (b) councils; (c) presidents of the order; (d) professional disciplinary trial commissions. Elections in the above-mentioned bodies must ensure representation to the extent of 30% from female gender, in accordance with Law No. 9970, dated 24.7.2008, "On gender equality in society" (Article 11 Law No. 123/2014, also *see* Article 14 of the Statute of the Order of Doctors of Albania). Special Instructions are drawn up and approved by the National Council to come to the aid of any election process for the governing bodies of the Order of Doctors, for the Presidents of the Regional Councils and the President of the National Council (Article 14 the Statute of the Order of Doctors of Albania).

769. The **National Assembly** is the highest governing body of the Order and consists of all members of regional councils. The Assembly holds regular meetings every five years. The meeting of the National Assembly is called by: (a) The President of the National Council; (b) when requested by one-third of all members of the assembly. During this timeframe, when it is necessary, it can be called to an extraordinary meeting. The regional assembly elects the regional council. The composition of the members of the regional assembly and their election procedures are defined in the Statute of the Order of Doctors (Article 12 Law No. 123/2014; also *see* Article 15 the Statute of the Order of Doctors of Albania).

770. The **Regional Assembly** is the highest governing and decision-making body of the Order of Doctors of the Region and consists of all its members. The Regional Assembly meets every five years. Between this period, in cases of necessity, the extraordinary meeting of the Regional Assembly is called, for which the written approval of the President of the National Council must be obtained. The meeting of the Regional Assembly is called by: (a) the President of the Regional Council; (b) at the request of one-third of the total number of members of the Assembly. The Regional Assembly elects the Regional Council.

771. The Regional Assembly elects the members of the respective Regional Council, following the principle of one member, one vote. The composition of the membership of the Regional Councils of the Order of Doctors is as follows: Regional Council of the Order of Doctors Shkodra District—5 members, 3 from Shkodra, 1 Malësia Madhe, 1 Puka; Regional Council of the Order of Doctors Lezha District—5 members, 3 Lezha, 1 Kurbini, 1 Rreshen; Regional Council of the Order of Doctors Kukës District—5 members, 3 Kukësi, 1 Tropoja, 1 Hasi; Regional Council of the Order of Doctors Dibër District—5 members, 3 Dibër, 1 Bulqiza, 1 Burreli; Regional Council of the Order of Doctors Durrës District—5 members, 4 Durrës, 1 Kruja; Regional Council of the Order of Doctors Elbasan District—5 members, 2 Elbasan, 1 Librazhd, 1 Gramsh, 1 Peqin; Regional Council of the Order of Doctors Berat District—5 members, 2 Berat, 1 Kuçovo, 1 Dimal, 1 Skrapar; Regional Council of the Order of Doctors Fier District—5 members, 3 Fieri, 1 Lushnja, 1 Ballshi; Regional Council of the Order of Doctors Tirana District—7 members, 6 Tirana, 1 Kavaja; Regional Council of the Order of Doctors Korça District—5 members, 2 Korça, 1 Erseka, 1 Bilishti, 1 Pogradeci; Regional Council of the Order of Doctors Vlora District—5 members, 5 Vlora; Regional Council of the Order of Doctors Gjirokastra District—5 members, 3 Gjirokastra, 1 Përmeti- Tepelena, 1 Saranda.

V. National Council

772. The National Council is the highest governing and decision-making body of the Order of Doctors in the Republic of Albania. The National Council consists of 25 members as follows: The newly elected Regional Presidents from the twelve Regional Councils; The other eight members are proposed by the members of the National Assembly themselves. The above members are elected by a simple majority of votes. Voting is open, except when the Assembly itself decides otherwise. The five members consist respectively of: the President of the Order, his Deputy, a representative from the Ministry responsible for health, a representative from the Compulsory Health Care Insurance Fund and a representative from senior educational institutions appointed by the President of the Order based on the criteria defined in the Statute.

773. If 1 (one) or more members of the National Council leave for any reason, his mandate passes to the next candidate on the final list of the Assembly elections of the national council with the most votes. Elections to the National Council are held every five years with the right to re-election to the members. The National Council meets no less than three times a year.

774. The national council is called by the (a) President of the Order of Doctors; (b) at the request of one-third of the total number of members of the National Council. The decisions of the National Council are mandatory to be implemented and respected by all structures and bodies of the Order at the central and regional level. Elections for the National Council and those for the Regional Councils are held at the same time. The organization and activity of the National Council is carried out based on the Regulation on the activity of the National Council, which is approved by the National Council (Article 17 the Statute of the Order of Doctors of Albania).

775. The National Council has the following responsibilities: (a) approves its own organizational structure and that of the regional councils; (b) determines the quotation and fees; (c) elects the President of the Order of Doctors and his deputy; (d) administers the movable and immovable assets of the Order at the national level, by determining funds in the administration of regional councils; (e) supervises all the activities of the bodies that depend on it; (f) approves the statute, the regulations of the Order as well as the Physician's Code of Ethics and Deontology; (g) set up ad hoc working groups for carrying out controls for the exercise of the doctor's profession. Elections for the National Council are held every five years. The elections for the National Council and those for the regional councils are held at the same time (Article 13 Law No. 123/2014).

VI. Functions and Responsibilities of the National Council

776. The National Council leads and supervises all the activities of the Order, the Regional Councils and Central Executive Apparatus. In fulfilling its functions and responsibilities the National Council: (a) drafts and approves the Code of Medical Ethics and Deontology and organizes its supervision and implementation; (b) drafts and approves the Statute and the internal Regulations of the functioning of the Councils and all sectors and other structures of the Order; (c) approves the organizational and administrative structures of the Order at the national and regional level; which approves the budget and its administration, as well as determines the funds under its Regional Councils administration; (d) represents and protects the common interests of the members of the Order in function of the free and autonomous exercise of the profession; (e) approves the Order's development strategies and organizes through its own structures and oversees their implementation; (f) sensitizes and informs public opinion about the mission and functions of the Order, such as declares his positions on special problems and situations as it pertains to the mission and its attributes; (g) cooperates with other factors and actors of the system for the improvement of standards of education and professional training of doctors and quality improvement of healthcare; (h) administers the movable and immovable assets of the Order at the central and regional level; (i) approves the membership fee and fees set for all acts and documents issued by the Order, elects the President and his Deputy; (j) set up ad hoc working groups to carry out checks on standards of professional practice and other activities of the Order; (k) approves the national activities of the Order; (l) maintains relations with homologous bodies and international forums and ratifies cooperation protocols; (m) elects the members of the National Commission of Professional Disciplinary Judgment (Appeal). For the realization of these tasks, the Council issues decisions which are signed by the President of Doctors' Orders (Article 18 the Statute of the Order of Doctors of Albania).

VII. Central Executive Apparatus of the National Council

777. The Central Executive Apparatus of the National Council coordinates and controls the activities of Regional Councils, technical-administrative and economic-financial activities of Orders. Ensures and controls the implementation and compliance with the Laws, as well as the Statute Regulations of the Order. Ensures and controls the implementation of Assembly Decisions and National Council, as well as; (a) provides and proposes membership fees, royalties, registration fees, membership, fees for the License for the individual exercise of the profession, as well as other fees which it approves in the National Council; (b) organizes and supervises the process of registration, membership and administration of the Registry of Doctors at the national and regional level; (c) Supervises the activities for equipping doctors with the License for the practice of the individual profession and determines the criteria for its issuance; appoints or approves according to the criteria specified in this Statute, commissions or specific work groups with a permanent character, which are approved by the Decision of the National Council; (d) systematically directs and supervises the activities of the Regional Councils; (e) organizes scientific activities, trainings and qualifying seminars for structure managers' of the Order, Disciplinary Commissions and others; (f) manages the publication and distribution of the Order Bulletin, ensuring its publications and printing; (g) it takes measures for the organization and administration of the electoral processes that take place near the Order of Doctors in implementation of orders, instructions and other administrative issued by the president (Article 19 the Statute of the Order of Doctors of Albania).

VIII. Regional Councils

778. The regional council consists of five to nine members, depending on the number of Doctors' Orders members. The regional council has the following functions: (a) the regional council elects its president and vice president; (b) administers the budget and all assets of the Order at the district level; (c) appoints the disciplinary commission at the district level; (d) set up ad hoc working groups to carry out checks on the exercise of the doctor's profession at the district level. Elections for the regional council are held every five years (Article 14 Law No. 123/2014).

IX. Presidents of the Order

779. The Presidents of the Order are elected by secret ballot by the National and Regional Councils and between no less than two alternative candidacies. The National Council elects the President of the Order of Doctors with the majority of votes of all its members. The mandate of the president is five years, with the right to re-election only one time. The regional councils elect the respective presidents of the regional councils. Their mandate is five years with the right to re-election only once. Candidates for presidents of the Order of Doctors must meet the following criteria: (a) be no more than retirement age at the time of election; (b) have at least fifteen years of professional experience; (c) have experience and reliable data on communication, organization and direction skills; (d) no punitive disciplinary measures have been taken against them in the last five years; (e) have prestige and ethical-moral and professional reputation; (f) have published scientific publications; (g) not to be convicted by a final decision for committing a crime or for committing a criminal offense intentionally. The function of presidents of the Order of Doctors is incompatible with any other administrative, public or political function. The presidents of the orders end their mandate early in the following cases: (a) when a decision is taken by the National or Regional Council, with the votes of not less than two-thirds of the members; (b) when they resign; (c) when convicted by a final court decision for committing a criminal offense; (d) when they lose the full ability to act; (e) when they become unable, for health reasons, to perform their duties, certified by competent medical commission. Election procedure, duties and powers of the presidents of the Order of Doctors are defined in the Statute of the Order (Article 15 Law No. 123/2014).

X. The President of the National Council

780. The President of the National Council is elected and dismissed by secret ballot from the National Council. For the election of the President, no less than two candidates are presented for voting in the National Council alternative candidacy. The President of the National Council has the following powers and duties: (a) directs and supervises all activities of the Order at the national level; (b) issues ordinances or instructions for the implementation of the decisions of the National Council; (c) calls the meetings of the Assembly, of the National Council which convenes extraordinary meetings of Assemblies and Regional Councils; (d) in the framework of relations with state administration institutions, as well as other organizations inside and outside the country, represents the National Council and expresses itself in its name; (e) in special cases, it authorizes the right to sign documents to the Vice President or the General Secretary; (f) himself appoints or dismisses the General Secretary, as well as the employees of the apparatus who are not chosen; (g) between two meetings of the National Council, it takes decisions on its behalf, which it ratifies at the next meeting of the Council; (h) calls heads of institutions, services or doctors when there is an incident in their services as the case may be, and advises them, refers them to the disciplinary process in the Order of Doctors or warns them; (i) approves the appointment or dismissal of non-elected employees at the Regional Councils. Undertake proposal initiatives in the legislative bodies for draft laws or documents important in the field of health; (j) proposes in the structures of the Order candidacies to be elected or dismissed in the bodies of the Order; (k) proposes to the National Council, members of the Order for various decorations and assessments; (l) organizes and maintains relations with international organizations and forums and ratifies in National Council agreements and cooperation protocols with them; (m) approves the salaries of all employees of the Central Executive Apparatus and its structures at Regional Councils, rewards, royalties, etc. Before any important decision-making, the President of the National Council is consulted with other leaders of the National Council (Article 20 the Statute of the Order of Doctors of Albania).

XI. Vice President of the National Council

781. The Vice President of the National Council is elected and dismissed by the National Council. The duties and functions of the Vice President are: (a) supervise and follow the implementation of the decisions of the National Council, as well as of the Ordinances and Instructions of the President of the National Council; (b) maintain contact with the Regional Councils and continuously monitor their activity; (c) monitor the administrative activity of the Central Executive Apparatus and sectors next to this Apparatus and is responsible for their progress in a special way regarding Continuing Medical Education, professional training, practice development professional and practice standards, etc.; monitor registration-licensing processes at the central and regional level and good administration of the National and Regional Basic Register; (d) inform and keep the President up-to-date on all the duties he covers; (e) in his absence and at his request, he assumes the powers of the President of the National Council for the period he is absent (Article 21 the Statute of the Order of Doctors of Albania).

XII. General Secretary

782. The General Secretary is primarily responsible for technical and organizational problems of the National Council and its Apparatus. He can be a doctor, lawyer, sociologist or economist. The General Secretary performs the following duties: (1) Directs and controls the progress of the work in the Central Apparatus of the National Council. (2) Maintains contacts with regional councils and coordinates their activities. (3) Cares for the creation and organization of commissions and working groups that rise to the councils of the Order and control their activity. (4) Organizes the meetings of the National Council. (5) Organizes public relations and contacts with state institutions and non-state organizations of the country, as well as with international organizations and forums. (6) Systematically reports and informs the President and in his absence the Vice President regarding the progress of the work and his specific duties. (7) Organizes and directs the work for the release of the Bulletin and takes care of other publications (Article 22 the Statute of the Order of Doctors of Albania).

XIII. Regional Council

783. The Regional Council is the highest governing and decision-making body of the Order of Doctors of the Region between the two meetings of the Regional Assembly. There are 12 Regional Councils, and they are created according to the territorial division. In special areas with decision of the National Council, sections or subregional councils can be established like mini structures. Regional Council elections are held every five years with the right to re-election of its members. The Regional Council consists of 5–9 members elected by the Regional Assembly according to criteria defined in this Statute and depending on the total number of members. In the event that one member of the Regional Council leaves for any reason, his mandate passes to the next candidate on the final list of the Regional Assembly elections with more votes (Article 23 the Statute of the Order of Doctors of Albania).

XIV. Criteria for the Selection of Members of the Councils of the Order

784. The candidacies for members of the National Council and Regional Councils are chosen among the most distinguished, dedicated doctors with professional skill and authority and should meet these criteria: (a) to be an Albanian citizen; (b) to be members registered with the Order for a period of ten years, non-stop; (c) to have ethical-moral and professional reputation; have experience and reliable data on communication skills, and have shown correctness in the application of norms and rules in social life, in communication with the public, patients, colleagues, as well as with managers; (d) not have been punished by a final decision for committing a crime or criminal offense, as well as not having taken disciplinary sanctions measures during the last five years; (e) not to have management functions in the state administration and not to take part in party leadership forums of any level, from which it must necessarily be resigned at the time of running; (f) to have contributions and to have been active in the structures and activities of the Order (Article 26 the Statute of the Order of Doctors of Albania).

XV. Premature Termination of the Council Member's Mandate

785. The mandate of the member of the Council (National and Regional) is prematurely terminated when: (a) requests his own resignation; (b) is punished by a final decision by the bodies of the Order or by the judiciary; (c) misuses the duty; (d) is absent more than 3 (three) times in the meetings of the Council without justifiable reasons; (e) is disabled for health reasons; (f) when they lose full capacity to act; (g) is appointed or elected to state or party leadership positions that conflict with the criteria provided in this Statute for the election of members of the National Council and Regional Councils (Article 27 the Statute of the Order of Doctors of Albania).

XVI. President of the Regional Council

786. The President of the Regional Council has the attributes of representing the Regional Council, as well as decision-making between two meetings of the Council. His decisions are ratified by the Council's meeting. He organizes, leads and supervises the activities of the Council and the Order of Doctors in the Region. For this purpose, the President of the Regional Council: (a) convenes and directs the meetings of the Council in accordance with the statutory norms; (b) draws up the action plan of the Council, detailed with objectives and deadlines implementation; (c) determines the tasks for the members of the Council and controls their implementation; which keeps the members of the council updated with the decisions of the National Council, Ordinances and the various Instructions coming from the Central Executive Apparatus of the National Council; (d) reports and systematically informs the Central Executive Apparatus about the activities of the Regional Council, the review of complaints, disciplinary processes, as well as for the implementation of instructions and orders received from the Apparatus; (e) keeps in control and takes care of the processes of registration, licensing, updating the register and its reflection on the website; (f) takes measures for the collection and payment of membership fees and other financial obligations (Article 28 the Statute of the Order of Doctors of Albania).

XVII. Council Meetings

787. The President of the Council (National or Regional), in his absence, his Deputy decides on the date, time and agenda of each meeting. The meeting of the Council (National or Regional) is notified in writing 7–14 days in advance, announcing the agenda. The above criteria may not apply only in special cases and circumstances. Each meeting must be attended by more than half of the members, who approve the agenda and the meeting's conduct in advance (Article 29 the Statute of the Order of Doctors of Albania).

788. The Council (National or Regional) makes decisions only on matters included in the meeting's agenda, unless a majority of the members present agree to consider and decide on issues not listed on the agenda. Decisions are made through open voting, except in cases where a majority of the members present decide otherwise. Decisions are approved by a simple majority of the votes of the members present at the meeting, except in situations requiring a qualified majority. In the event of a tie, a second vote is conducted. If the tie persists after the second vote, the President's vote is decisive (Article 30, Statute of the Order of Doctors of Albania).

789. A Council meeting, whether National or Regional, is considered valid when more than half of the members are present. If this quorum is not met at the start of the meeting, the President or the acting chairperson may decide to reschedule the meeting, issuing a new written notice (Article 31, Statute of the Order of Doctors of Albania). Minutes are recorded for every meeting, documenting the date, location, participants, topics discussed, decisions made, and the format and results of any votes. The President of the National or Regional Council designates a permanent individual responsible for maintaining these records. At the conclusion of the meeting, the minutes are signed by the secretary and the President or the deputy chairperson who presided over the session (Article 32, Statute of the Order of Doctors of Albania).

§2. HEALTHCARE CENTERS

I. The Public and Private Health Care Centres Which Operate in Albania

790. The following public and private healthcare centers operate in Albania:

University Hospital "Mother Theresa."
University Hospital "Shefqet Ndroqi."

American Hospital.
Hygeia Hospital.
Salus Hospital.
German Hospital.
Continental Hospital.
Villa Maria Hospital.

II. Health and Medical Care

791. The Albanian Government is the main provider of healthcare services in the country. The healthcare services are structured in three levels: primary healthcare; secondary healthcare; tertiary healthcare:

- Primary Healthcare Service (PHC) is provided in health centers/posts and polyclinics. PHC services at the community are the first level of access to healthcare.
- Secondary Healthcare is provided in regional and/or district hospitals.
- Tertiary Healthcare is provided at the University Hospital Centre "Mother Theresa" and "Tirana Military Hospital."

792. In each district functions a directory of Public Health, which coordinates all health services of the district. The exception is Tirana, where a pilot project is created referred as the Regional Health Authority. Ministry of Health aims to create in the future such regional authorities also in other Albanian regions, which will be coordinating the functioning of health services at regional level.

793. The Albanian Healthcare is organized autonomously on a regional basis and includes public and private clinics and specialists. Emergency services are available at all main hospitals. Hospitalization always requires a specific request from a specialized medical doctor or from a specialized medical structure. For emergency (ambulance) the number to call is 127.

794. The National Center of Drug Control is the responsible institution for the control of any activity in the pharmaceutical area. It exercises its control over: – Activity and production, premises and equipment. – Wholesale and retail and the conditions for storage of medicine Medical raw material and supporting package material. – Medicine imported by all the licensed subjects.

795. The National Center of Blood Transfusion aims at ensuring the gathering of blood and its products to optimally meet the needs for transfusions in treating individuals injured in accidents, severe and chronic anemia patients, cancer patients, patients to undergo surgical interventions, women who have severe case of bleeding during delivery, etc. The National Center of Blood Transfusion is composed of twenty-nine Blood Banks, of which three are found in Tirana and twenty-six in the other regions.

796. The National Center for Child Upbringing, Development and Rehabilitation in Tirana was established in 2000 as a national diagnosis, curing and training center. Its mission is to improve the quality of the lives of special needs children and to make them partners in the long road toward their rehabilitation, care and education.

797. The National Center for Biomedical Engineering aim is to offer maintenance of medical equipment with the goal of providing the best care to their patients by increasing the quality of their service as a combination of used medical equipment and the health institutions' staff (including medicine doctors, specialists, nurses, etc.).

798. National Center of Quality, Security and Accreditation of Health Institutions supports the Ministry of Health with the implementation of the long-term National Health Strategy in the following areas: Continuous improvement of the quality of the health system; Drafting, distribution and preliminary monitoring of Clinical Guidelines (Clinical Protocols) with the best clinical practices to assist the medical staff; Accreditation of Albanian public and private health institutions; Therapeutic education and empowering the role of patients as main and central stakeholders of the health system; Minimizing risks and mistakes in the health institutions: Increasing security for patients and the medical staff; Creating, gathering and using scientific evidence proved to be the best medical practices.

799. University Dentistry Clinic operates based on a regulation and respective guidelines by the Ministry of Health. It offers specialized services in maxillofacial surgery, therapy, orthopedics, pedodonthy and provides professional training for doctors during their specialization training.

800. The Helicopter Transport Unit's mission is to cover medical emergencies where the need presents itself for providing such a service. Their main activity includes the specialized medical transport by helicopter of patients in acute cases.

801. The Governmental Health Care Clinic's mission is to offer emergency and primary medical services for the senior state authorities. Its services consist of accompanying government delegations to enable provision of first medical aid in case of need.

802. The National Center of Continuous Education's mission is to encourage, deliver and improve the professional training for all categories of professional staff with the aim of enhancing the knowledge and developing the skills of the medical staff.

803. Tirana Health Centers have their own ambulatory points (satellites), to be as close to the public as possible. The satellites are part of the health centers and not regarded separately. Administratively speaking, they are subordinate to the

Regional Health Authority RHA, Tirana RHA and financially dependent on the Mandatory Health Insurance Fund and the Regional Healthcare Insurance Directorate.

§3. Professional Duties Toward Colleagues

804. The location where a doctor practices his profession must provide a suitable working environment, equipped with the appropriate medical and technical resources that correspond to and adapt to the nature of the preventive, diagnostic, and therapeutic medical acts they perform. A doctor must not practice his profession under conditions that compromise the safety of patients, or the quality of care provided to them and the public (Article 58, The Code of Medical Ethics and Deontology).

805. The relations between doctors should be based on the principles of a good society and mutual respect. The doctor must behave with correctness and honesty toward his colleagues. The doctor is not allowed to slander his colleagues, to lower the authority and their personality in front of patients and the public, harming them in the exercise of the profession. Doctors should not take their disagreements to public controversy. They should be resolved only in the way of reconciliation, in case of need also with the mediation of the institutional authorities or of the Order of Doctors (Article 42 The Code of Medical Ethics and Deontology).

806. Every doctor has the duty to preserve and respect solidarity with colleagues, for the benefit of maintaining professional integrity and respecting the norms of ethics and medical deontology. If a doctor is asked for professional advice or help by a colleague, he must be willing to give it honestly and to his best knowledge (Article 44 The Code of Medical Ethics and Deontology).

807. In case the doctor becomes aware of an inappropriate behavior of a colleague, in violation of the norms of medical ethics, he has the duty to: (1) identify the violation to his colleague, (2) inform the institution, and/or (3) the Order of Doctors. He is not allowed to discuss this with patients, family members or other colleagues (Article 45 The Code of Medical Ethics and Deontology).

808. Counseling and consultation among colleagues, when warranted by the patient's circumstances, is a critical practice that must be upheld. It serves not only to ensure the best possible treatment for the patient but also to enhance the professional integrity and development of physicians. Personal conflicts or disagreements between doctors that hinder consultation or participation are strictly impermissible and may be subject to disciplinary action. When a consultation is organized, the attending physician must inform the patient in advance, providing details about the purpose of the consultation and the doctors who will participate. The patient's consent is required for both the consultation itself and the participation of specific doctors, including those the patient may suggest, provided their choice does not compromise the patient's health. If the attending physician deems the patient's or relatives' choice of doctor inappropriate, they may decline the request. At the conclusion of a consultation involving two or more doctors, it is mandatory to document their conclusions in writing. This document must be signed by both the attending physician and the consulting doctors, ensuring clarity and accountability in the patient's care (Article 48 The Code of Medical Ethics and Deontology).

Chapter 2. Relationship with Other Healthcare Providers

§1. Pharmacists

809. The collaboration between physicians and pharmacists serves as a foundational pillar in ensuring the safe, effective, and regulated use of medicinal products. Comprehensive legal provisions underpin this partnership, specifically articulated in Articles 52 and 53 of Law No. 105/2014, which reflect efforts to harmonize national pharmaceutical practices with the standards set forth in European Union directives 2001/83/EC and 2001/20/EC. These legal frameworks underscore the critical importance of safeguarding public health through clear guidelines on the prescription and dispensation of medications.

810. Article 52 of Law No. 105/2014 outlines the regulatory mechanisms governing the issuance and management of medical prescriptions.[201] It mandates that medications may only be distributed through licensed pharmacies or pharmaceutical agencies upon presentation of a valid physician's prescription, except for over-the-counter (OTC) drugs, which are subject to approval by the Ministry of Health. For reimbursable drugs, prescriptions must specify the active ingredient, thereby promoting transparency and ensuring the availability of cost-effective therapeutic options. To ensure traceability and compliance, pharmacies are required to retain executed prescriptions for specified periods: standard prescriptions for two years, prescriptions for narcotics and psychotropics for three years, and prescriptions for highly toxic substances for five years. Notably, exemptions from these requirements are granted for certain categories of medications, such as biological drugs and vaccines, reflecting their unique characteristics and public health significance. In addition, pharmacies are authorized to supply medical devices in accordance with relevant legal provisions.

811. Article 53 of Law No. 105/2014 codifies the classification of medicinal products into those requiring a prescription and those that do not. Prescription-only medicines encompass pharmaceuticals that, due to their inherent risks, necessitate

---

201. Law No. 105/2014, Art. 52, "*Medical Prescription*": "*1. Medicines are sold in pharmacies or pharmaceutical agencies only with a doctor's prescription, except for OTC medicines, according to a list approved by the minister responsible for health. 2. Persons with medical qualifications, who are allowed to prescribe medicines, issue medical prescriptions based on the name of the active ingredient of the medicine, only for the list of reimbursable medicines. Executed prescriptions are kept in pharmacies for the following durations:*

a) 2 years for regular prescriptions;
b) 3 years for prescriptions for narcotic and psychotropic drugs;
c) 5 years for prescriptions for highly toxic poisons.

3. Exceptions to the rule stated in point 2 of this article are made only for:
a) biological medicines;
b) vaccines. [author' translation]

4. Medical devices are also sold in pharmacies according to the specifications set in the relevant law."

medical oversight.[202] These include drugs with potential for misuse, those associated with significant adverse effects, and substances subject to ongoing pharmacological investigation. Parenteral medications, by virtue of their administration route, also fall within this category. Conversely, OTC medications are classified as suitable for self-administration, provided they are utilized in accordance with the guidelines established by the regulatory authority. This bifurcated system ensures that pharmaceuticals with substantial health risks are subjected to rigorous professional supervision while facilitating access to safer products for public use.

812. The statutory provisions outlined in these articles underscore the critical interdependence between physicians and pharmacists, emphasizing their joint responsibility in promoting the safe and judicious use of medications. Physicians play a critical role in diagnosing and prescribing treatments, while pharmacists serve as the final checkpoint in dispensing and guiding the appropriate use of these treatments. This collaborative mechanism functions as a critical safeguard, minimizing the potential for errors, mitigating risks, and optimizing therapeutic outcomes. Furthermore, it aligns with European Union objectives to establish standardized, high-quality pharmaceutical care across Member States, thereby reinforcing the integrity of healthcare systems.

813. In addition to regulating prescription medications, the legislation provides explicit directives regarding OTC pharmaceuticals and the consequences of noncompliance. Article 3(8) of Law No. 105/2014 defines OTC drugs as medicinal products available for self-medication without the requirement of a physician's prescription.[203] Nonetheless, even these medications must adhere to strict requirements, including the need for proper formulation by a pharmacy when prepared for individual patients. Unauthorized distribution of prescription-only medications without the requisite authorization constitutes a violation subject to severe Criminalities. Pursuant to Article 63(1)(k) of Law No. 105/2014, such infractions attract

202. Law No. 105/2014, Art. 53, *"Classification of Medicines According to the Prescription Description": "1. For the purpose of granting a marketing authorization, medicines are classified into:*

a) medicines that are subject to a medical prescription;
b) medicines that are not subject to a medical prescription, such as OTC medicines.

2. Medicines are subject to a medical prescription only in cases where:
a) they pose a direct or indirect risk, even if used correctly, when used outside of medical supervision;
b) they are frequently and widely used incorrectly, and as a result, may pose a direct or indirect risk to human health;
c) they contain substances or their formulations, whose action and/or negative effects require further investigation;
ç) they are prescribed by a doctor to be administered parenterally." [author' translation]

203. Law No. 105/2014, Art. 3(g): *""Medicines sold without a medical prescription" are medicines that are used for self-medication and are sold and traded in pharmacies without a doctor's prescription (Over the Counter / OTC)."* [author' translation]

financial sanctions of 100,000 (one hundred thousand) lek for a first offense, escalating to 200,000 (two hundred thousand) lek for repeated violations, reflecting the legislator's intent to uphold the integrity of pharmaceutical distribution practices.[204]

814. The legal framework enforces strict limitations on the participation of medical practitioners in activities related to the commercial handling of pharmaceuticals. Article 60(1) of the Code of Medical Ethics[205] and Article 45 of Law No. 105/2014 categorically prohibit physicians from engaging in the commercial sale, storage, or preparation of medications, except in limited circumstances strictly confined to emergency scenarios or procedures directly linked to their professional responsibilities.[206] These restrictions are further reinforced through Criminalities, including fines, confiscation of unauthorized medicinal stock, and, in cases of recurrent violations, the revocation of professional licensure, as stipulated in Article 63(1)(i) of Law No. 105/2014.[207] These measures are integral to maintaining ethical boundaries and preventing conflicts of interest within the healthcare sector.

815. This extensive legal and regulatory framework emphasizes the paramount importance of safeguarding public health while advocating for a precisely organized pharmaceutical system. By defining the respective roles and obligations of healthcare professionals, establishing stringent oversight mechanisms, and imposing significant Criminalities for noncompliance, the legislation fosters a culture of accountability and professionalism. Moreover, by aligning with international standards, it ensures the delivery of equitable and high-quality healthcare, reflecting a commitment to the ethical stewardship of pharmaceutical resources and the well-being of patients.

816. The doctor is not allowed to enter and act in partnership with pharmacists, auxiliary staff or other persons for illegal profit purposes. The doctor is not allowed

---

204. Law No. 105/2014, Art. 63(1)(k), *"Administrative Offenses": "k) An action performed in violation of the provisions of Article 52, paragraph 1, of this law, involving the sale of medicines in pharmacies or pharmaceutical agencies without a doctor's prescription, except for OTC medicines, is punishable by a fine of 100,000 (one hundred thousand) lek. In case of repetition, the fine increases to 200,000 (two hundred thousand) lek."* [author' translation]

205. The Code of Medical Ethics, Art. 60(1), *"Medicine as a Business, Advertising, Partnerships": "1. A doctor is not allowed to enter into partnerships or act in partnership with pharmacists, auxiliary staff, or other individuals for illegal profit-making purposes."* [author' translation]

206. Law No. 105/2014, Art. 45, *"Restrictions for Doctors and Dentists": "1. The marketing, storage, and preparation of medicines for sale by doctors and dentists is not allowed. 2. Doctors and dentists may store and use medicines in their clinics in types and quantities sufficient only for emergency assistance or for necessary procedures related to the practice of their profession, according to the specifications set in the list approved by the minister responsible for health."* [author' translation]

207. Law No. 105/2014, Art. 63(1)(i), *"Administrative Offenses": "The following violations, when they do not constitute a criminal offense, are considered administrative offenses and are punished by pharmaceutical inspectors as follows: i) An action performed in violation of the provisions of Article 45 of this law, regarding the preparation and distribution of medicines by doctors and dentists, is punishable by confiscation of the medicines and a fine of 200,000 (two hundred thousand) lek. In case of repetition, the punishment includes confiscation and revocation of the license."* [author' translation]

to practice medicine as a business. He is categorically forbidden to make visits or consultations in premises and commercial environments where medicines are sold, other medical products, devices or equipment. It is forbidden for the doctor to engage in advertising or publicity of any kind, except for cases where these have a scientific or educational purpose. In this case, the doctor must make sure that the publicity is objective and in accordance with the rules of medical deontology. The doctor is not allowed to make any publicity in his favor, his personal activity or that of a certain institution (Article 60 The Code of Medical Ethics and Deontology).

§2. Nurses (Midwives)

817. According to Article 9 (3) of Law No. 10 107, dated 30.3.2009, on Health Care in the Republic of Albania, primary healthcare encompasses not only basic medical treatment, prevention, and rehabilitation when these do not require advanced techniques provided by other levels of healthcare, but also nursing care.[208] Nursing care is particularly fundamental in providing support for terminally ill patients. According to Article 15(1) of Law No. 10 107 (dated 30.3.2009), this care includes essential medical and nursing support during the final stage of a patient's life, particularly when the illness is deemed incurable by current medical advancements.[209] The primary aim is not to cure but to ensure comfort, manage symptoms effectively, and uphold the patient's dignity during this critical phase. This underscores the compassionate and supportive role of nursing in addressing both the physical and emotional challenges faced by terminally ill patients.

818. Healthcare professionals are guided by principles emphasizing collaboration, continuous improvement, and ethical practice. According to Article 10 of the Code of Medical Ethics, physicians are expected to maintain honest and respectful relationships with their colleagues and medical staff, including nurses.[210] This collaboration must uphold the professional independence of all parties while prioritizing the well-being of patients and preserving the integrity of the profession and the medical institution. To support these ethical commitments, healthcare professionals base their work on knowledge validated by the scientific community and consistently update their skills through ongoing study, research, and reflection on practical experiences. By engaging in critical thinking and lifelong learning, they ensure

---

208. Law No. 10 107, dated 30.3.2009, Art. 9(3), *"Primary Health Care": "Primary health care is provided without limitations related to disease, age, gender, economic status, or patient categories. Primary health care addresses the needs for basic medical treatment, nursing care, prevention, and rehabilitation, where these do not require treatments and examination techniques offered by other levels of health care."* [author' translation]

209. Law No. 10 107, dated 30.3.2009, Art. 15(1), *"Care for Terminally Ill Patients": "Care for terminally ill patients is medical and nursing care provided in the final stage of a patient's illness, which, with current possibilities, is incurable."* [author' translation]

210. The Code of Medical Ethics, Art. 10, *"Relations with Colleagues and Staff": "Doctors have the duty to maintain good and honest relations with each other and with other members of the medical staff, respecting the professional independence of each individual, in the interest of patients and the preservation of the good reputation of the profession and the medical institution."* [author' translation]

the quality and safety of their work. In addition, they consistently engage in planning, executing, and attending training sessions, meeting the demands of Continuing Education programs to remain leaders in their field.

819. A similar approach is emphasized in Article 12 of the Code of Medical Ethics for Nurses, which values collaboration within different professions in medical care. Professional collaboration in nursing is essential for addressing the healthcare needs of patients and the public.[211] Nurses play a pivotal role in fostering collaboration by working closely with other professionals, particularly physicians, to create an environment of mutual respect, trust, and shared responsibility.

820. Article 12 highlights that professional collaboration in nursing is vital for meeting the healthcare needs of both patients and the public. Effective patient care arises through interdisciplinary teamwork, where nurses in various roles contribute by developing skills, establishing care standards, managing healthcare environments, and expanding nursing knowledge. This teamwork requires recognizing and valuing the unique contributions of each healthcare provider, cultivating mutual trust, open dialog, and joint decision-making. Such collaboration ensures that all members of the care team, including nurses and physicians, work unitedly toward common goals.

821. Nurses are committed to supporting collaboration with all professionals involved in patient care, especially doctors, by adopting loyal and cooperative behaviors. This commitment reflects their acknowledgment of the specific contributions of other practitioners to the care process and their dedication to fostering a strong foundation for effective healthcare delivery. By supporting teamwork, nurses help establish a shared focus on achieving the best possible outcomes for patients while maintaining the integrity and quality of care.

822. Ultimately, this commitment to collaboration, as outlined in Article 12 of the Code of Medical Ethics for Nurses, represents the broader mission of healthcare professionals to provide compassionate, safe, and high-quality care. Through teamwork, critical thinking, and respect for one another's expertise, nurses and their colleagues address the complex challenges of modern healthcare, ensuring that the needs of patients and the public are met with excellence.

211. The Code of Medical Ethics of Nurses, Art. 12, *"Collaboration"*: *"Healthcare professionals are committed to supporting collaboration with other professionals involved in the care process, adopting loyal and cooperative behavior with colleagues and other operators. They recognize and value their specific contributions to the care process. When professionals and other members of the healthcare team collaborate to achieve a common goal in patient care, this is recognized as collaboration. Professional collaboration in nursing is essential for addressing the healthcare needs of patients and the public. Effective patient care occurs through interdisciplinary collaboration of nurses in various roles, who work together to: Learn skills, establish standards, Manage the healthcare environment, and Expand nursing knowledge. Collaboration requires mutual recognition, respect among healthcare team members, mutual trust, and open dialogue among all involved."* [author' translation]

823. In addition, Article 13 of the Code of Medical Ethics for Nurses states that healthcare professionals—meaning nurses—act based on their level of competence and, if necessary, use the advice and interventions of expert or specialist professionals, among others, doctors.[212] This means that nurses are expected to operate in alignment with their training, skills, and professional knowledge. When a situation exceeds their scope of competence, they are encouraged to seek the guidance and support of expert or specialist professionals, including physicians, to ensure the best outcomes for the patient.

824. This principle highlights the importance of collaboration and communication within the healthcare team. By recognizing the value of seeking advice and sharing knowledge, nurses contribute to a culture of safety and professionalism. The exchange of information and expertise between team members not only reinforces the quality of care but also ensures that complex patient needs are met through a collective effort. This approach aligns with the broader ethical duty of healthcare professionals to prioritize patient welfare and deliver care that reflects the highest standards of the profession.

825. Moreover, Article 16 of the Code of Medical Ethics for Nurses reinforces the principles outlined in Article 12 of the Code of Medical Ethics for Nurses, emphasizing the critical role of both intra-professional and inter-professional collaboration. It highlights that interaction and integration among healthcare professionals are essential elements in meeting the needs of individuals effectively.[213] This provision acknowledges that healthcare is inherently a team effort, requiring seamless coordination and communication across different roles and specialties. By working together seamlessly across different roles and areas of expertise, healthcare providers can offer care that is not only comprehensive but also tailored to the unique requirements of everyone. In practice, this means nurses and other healthcare providers must actively engage in teamwork, sharing knowledge, skills, and insights to create an integrated care experience. Article 16 reinforces the idea that collaboration is more than a professional responsibility—it is a vital element of high-quality, compassionate healthcare that prioritizes the dignity and well-being of every patient.

§3. Paramedical Professionals

826. Paramedical professionals in Albania, as defined by Article 1 of the Regulation on *"The Organization of Professional Practice for Health Professionals in the Republic of Albania"* are classified as healthcare workers who provide clinical services to patients under the supervision of a physician. A physician, as defined in

212. The Code of Medical Ethics of Nurses, Art. 13, *"Duty Bearer, Advice, and Information Exchange": "Healthcare professionals act based on their level of competence and, when necessary, seek advice and interventions from expert professionals or specialists."* [author' translation]

213. The Code of Medical Ethics of Nurses, Art. 16, *"Interaction and Integration": "Healthcare professionals recognize intra- and inter-professional interaction and integration as a fundamental element in responding to the needs of the individual."* [author' translation]

this regulation, is a professional with an official document of professional ability or qualification who has legally and independently practiced the profession for over three years. This framework establishes the foundational roles and responsibilities of paramedical professionals and their supervising physicians in the Albanian healthcare system.

827. Article 3 of the Regulation on "*The Organization of Professional Practice for Health Professionals in the Republic of Albania*" outlines the framework for developing professional practice among healthcare professionals in the country.[214] The aim of this process is to ensure the effective acquisition of practical, technical, and ethical knowledge, equipping practitioners with the necessary skills and a sense of public accountability for independent professional practice.

828. Professional practice must be conducted in healthcare institutions that meet the required standards to provide an environment conducive to the acquisition of essential competencies. This process is supervised by qualified professionals who have a minimum of three years of independent and lawful experience in their respective fields. In addition, the Ministry of Health plays a central role in approving and publishing a list of accredited institutions authorized to host trainees. This

214. Regulation on "The Organization of Professional Practice for Health Professionals in the Republic of Albania," Art. 3, *"Development of Professional Practice": "Professional practice ensures the effective acquisition of practical, technical, and ethical knowledge by the professional, guaranteeing them the necessary skills and public responsibility for independent practice of the profession. Professional practice is carried out in a healthcare institution that meets the required standards for fulfilling the demands and acquiring the practical, technical, and ethical knowledge of the trainee. Professional practice is guided and developed under the supervision and responsibility of a qualified professional with more than 3 (three) years of legal and independent practice of the profession. The Ministry of Health determines and approves the list of accredited institutions that are authorized to accept trainees. This list is published by the relevant authority. The relevant authority prepares, approves, and publishes the list of professionals who are authorized to lead and supervise trainees during professional practice. The trainee has the right to choose, from the published list, the institution and supervising professional for their practice. The Ministry of Health instructs the institutions and professionals supervising trainees to provide the necessary conditions and take on the necessary responsibilities for the proper development of the practice, in accordance with the program and the standard contract signed between the parties. The duration of professional practice is at least 9 (nine) months for medical and dental trainees, 6 (six) months (including any program training completed) for pharmacy trainees, and 3 (three) months for nursing and other professionals at this level. For a professional who has had more than five years of interruption in practicing the profession, the practice period (depending on the case) is at least 2 (two) months. The relevant authority, in cooperation with the academic staff of the Faculty of Medicine at the State University, determines and prepares the practice program. The relevant authority drafts the standard professional practice contract, which outlines the rights and obligations of the parties, to be respected during the practice and signed between the practice supervisor and the trainee. A candidate is exempt from the obligation to undergo professional practice if they prove that, for a specified period and in accordance with the specific criteria of the profession they belong to, they have been engaged in professional activity, within or outside the country, which has allowed them to gain sufficient professional experience in this field. To assess and verify whether the candidate's experience is sufficient to exempt them from the obligation to complete professional practice, the relevant authority relies on an official document issued by the institution where the candidate performed their professional activity."* [author' translation]

list is made publicly available to ensure accessibility and transparency. Furthermore, a governing body compiles and announces a list of qualified professionals who are authorized to supervise and guide trainees during their practice.

829. Furthermore, trainees are granted the freedom to choose their institution and supervising professionals from the approved lists. Institutions and mentors are obligated to create appropriate conditions for the practice, taking full responsibility for its proper implementation. The terms and expectations of this process are formalized in a standard contract signed by the involved parties. The required duration of professional practice varies depending on the field. For medical and dental trainees, the minimum period is nine months, while pharmacy trainees must complete six months, including prior program-related practice. Nursing and other equivalent professions require a minimum of three months. In cases where professionals are returning to their field after a break of over five years, the duration is no less than two months.

830. The governing body works in collaboration with the academic staff of the Faculty of Medicine to design a comprehensive practice program. It is also responsible for drafting a standard contract that delineates the rights and obligations of the parties involved, which must be signed by both the supervising professional and the trainee.

831. Exemptions from the professional practice requirement are possible for candidates who can demonstrate sufficient prior professional experience in alignment with the criteria of their specific profession. Such experience, whether acquired domestically or internationally, must be substantiated with official documentation from the institution where the professional activity was undertaken. This documentation serves as the basis for the governing body to assess and validate the sufficiency of the candidate's prior experience.

832. Paramedical professionals, as outlined in Article 6 and Article 7 of the Regulation on *"The Organization of Professional Practice for Health Professionals in the Republic of Albania,"* operate within a framework that delineates their rights and responsibilities during professional practice. These provisions ensure a structured, ethical, and developmental process, preparing them for independent and competent professional roles in healthcare.

833. Under Article 6 of the Regulation on *"The Organization of Professional Practice for Health Professionals in the Republic of Albania,"* paramedical professionals are entitled to have their professional practice agreements respected and fully enforced. This agreement establishes the foundation for their training and ensures institutional accountability.[215] They have the right to actively participate in

215. Regulation on "The Organization of Professional Practice for Health Professionals in the Republic of Albania," Art. 6, *"Rights of the Trainee": "Request the respect of the signed professional practice contract. Participate and be actively involved in all activities of scientific, professional, theoretical, and practical interest that are carried out. Follow and be engaged in the formats and*

all scientific, professional, theoretical, and practical activities that enhance their knowledge and skills. Furthermore, access to continuing professional education is guaranteed, enabling them to refine their technical abilities and broaden their professional expertise. In cases where their rights are violated, or face obstacles that disrupt the effective progression of their practice, paramedical professionals can escalate their concerns to the institutional leadership or the designated supervisory bodies.

834. The responsibilities of paramedical professionals, as specified in Article 7 of the Regulation on *"The Organization of Professional Practice for Health Professionals in the Republic of Albania,"* require adherence to professional and ethical standards. They must consistently attend their practice sessions and fully comply with the structured program, demonstrating a commitment to their professional development. Establishing and maintaining respectful and professional relationships with mentors, colleagues, institutional staff, and leadership is a fundamental obligation.[216] Their conduct must align with the principles set forth in the Code of Ethics and Deontology, reflecting high standards of professionalism, integrity, and ethical responsibility.

835. Paramedical professionals are further required to treat patients and the public with competence, dignity, empathy, and accountability. They must actively engage in acquiring practical and technical skills by participating in scientific activities, consultations, and other educational events that enhance their expertise. Compliance with the rules and regulations of the hosting institution is mandatory, reflecting their commitment to maintaining institutional order and discipline. Before beginning their practice, paramedical professionals are required to formalize their engagement through a standard agreement, and they must also register with the National Center for Continuing Education to facilitate their ongoing professional development.

---

programs of Continuing Professional Education that are relevant to their professional development. In case of actions that contradict these rights or any other action that creates obstacles or makes it difficult or impossible to effectively carry out professional practice, the trainee may file a complaint with the institution's supervisor, as well as with the relevant structures of the responsible authority." [author' translation]

216. Regulation on "The Organization of Professional Practice for Health Professionals in the Republic of Albania," Art. 7, *"Responsibilities of the Trainee": "The trainee has the responsibility to: Regularly participate in the practice and follow its program. Establish and maintain correct relationships based on courtesy and mutual respect with the professional leading the practice, colleagues, other staff members, and the institution's supervisor. Familiarize themselves with the Code of Ethics and Deontology and base their professional activities and behavior on the principles and provisions of this Code. Treat patients and the public with maturity, humanity, competence, and high professional responsibility in their interactions. Strive to acquire the maximum amount of practical and technical knowledge that contributes to their professional development. Follow and participate in scientific activities, consultations, etc... Adhere to and comply with the rules and statutes of the institution where the practice is carried out. Upon starting the professional practice, sign the standard trainee contract. Register with the National Center for Continuing Education."* [author' translation]

836. The provisions set forth in Articles 6 and 7 of the Regulation on *"The Organization of Professional Practice for Health Professionals in the Republic of Albania,"* establish a balanced framework that protects the rights of paramedical professionals while ensuring their accountability to the ethical and professional standards required in healthcare. This dual focus on rights and responsibilities fosters both individual development and the broader integrity of the healthcare system, ensuring paramedical professionals are well equipped to contribute effectively to their field.

837. Thus, the supervising professionals, as outlined in Article 9 and Article 10 of the Regulation on *"The Organization of Professional Practice for Health Professionals in the Republic of Albania,"* bear significant responsibilities and hold specific rights to ensure the effective and ethical implementation of the professional practice program for paramedical professionals. According to Article 9 of the Regulation on *"The Organization of Professional Practice for Health Professionals in the Republic of Albania,"* the supervising professional is required to fully understand the professional practice program and ensure that the trainee adheres to its structure and objectives.[217] This involves not only overseeing the trainee's practical activities but also embedding the ethical principles outlined in the Code of Ethics and Deontology into the daily conduct of the practice. Supervisors must ensure that these principles are upheld throughout the training period, fostering a professional environment that emphasizes ethical responsibility and accountability.

838. Additionally, the supervising professional is tasked with monitoring the trainee's attendance and documenting it meticulously in the official Practice Logbook. Beyond administration, the supervisor has a crucial educational role, contributing actively to the trainee's professional growth while maintaining an approachable and supportive demeanor. This ensures a collaborative environment where trainees feel encouraged to develop their skills. Supervisors are also responsible for upholding the terms of the signed agreement with the trainee, ensuring that both parties meet their obligations under the professional practice framework. Lastly, they must evaluate the trainee's progress by completing the official Trainee Evaluation Form with accuracy and professionalism, providing a clear assessment of the trainee's achievements and areas for improvement.

839. In addition to the supervisor's duties, Article 10 of the Regulation on *"The Organization of Professional Practice for Health Professionals in the Republic of*

---

217. Regulation on "The Organization of Professional Practice for Health Professionals in the Republic of Albania," Art. 9, *"Responsibilities of the Professional Leading the Trainee": "The professional leading the trainee must: Be familiar with the professional practice program and ensure its implementation by the trainee. Be aware of the principles of the Code of Ethics and Deontology and ensure their application and adherence throughout the practice. Ensure and be accountable for the proper execution of professional practice. Monitor the trainee's regular attendance and document it in the Practice Booklet. Contribute to the education and professional training of the trainee and maintain a supportive relationship with them. Ensure the respect and implementation of the contract signed with the trainee. Accurately and responsibly complete the Trainee Evaluation Form."* [author' translation]

Albania," highlights the responsibilities of the governing body (Professional Order) in overseeing the entire professional practice process. Through its designated structures, Professional Order ensures that the training environment operates smoothly and meets established standards. It acts as a regulatory body, gathering and evaluating formal complaints from all stakeholders, including the supervisor, the trainee, the institution's leadership, patients, the public, or even the media.[218] Where necessary, Professional Order initiates disciplinary procedures to address violations, thereby safeguarding the integrity of the professional practice program.

840. This comprehensive framework ensures that supervisors not only guide trainees toward professional competence but also uphold the ethical and operational standards of the healthcare system. By balancing educational mentorship with administrative oversight, the supervising professional plays a pivotal role in fostering the trainee's growth and maintaining the integrity of the professional practice program.

841. It shall be stated that according to Article 67 of the Code of Medical Ethics, this Code is legally binding not only for physicians but also for medical students assisting or replacing physicians on duty. It is the duty of all physicians, medical students, and medical trainees to be familiar with and adhere to the provisions of this Code throughout their professional careers.[219] The Code explicitly states that ignorance of its provisions does not exempt anyone from responsibility or disciplinary measures for any violations committed. This ensures that ethical standards are consistently upheld across all levels of medical practice.

842. To sum up, the interplay between Articles 6, 7, 9, and 10 of the Regulation on *"The Organization of Professional Practice for Health Professionals in the Republic of Albania"* establishes a structured and collaborative relationship between physicians, supervising professionals, and paramedical professionals. These articles collectively define the rights and responsibilities of trainees, the duties of their supervisors, and the oversight role of the governing body, creating a framework for professional development rooted in accountability, respect, and mutual growth.

843. Articles 6 and 7 of the Regulation on *"The Organization of Professional Practice for Health Professionals in the Republic of Albania,"* focus on the rights and responsibilities of paramedical professionals, ensuring access to educational

---

218. Regulation on "The Organization of Professional Practice for Health Professionals in the Republic of Albania," Art. 10, *"Rights and Responsibilities of the Relevant Authority": "In addition to the rights and responsibilities specified in the relevant articles of this regulation, the relevant authority performs the following: Through its structures, supervises and ensures the proper development of professional practice. Collects and evaluates written complaints submitted by the practice supervisor, the trainee, the institution's director, the relevant authority, patients, the public, or the media, and, as appropriate, subjects them to professional disciplinary review."* [author' translation]

219. The Code of Medical Ethics, Art. 67, *"Obligation to Respect the Code": "It is the duty of all doctors, medical students who assist or substitute for doctors on duty, as well as medical trainees, to know and adhere to the provisions of this Code throughout their professional careers. Ignorance does not exempt any individual from responsibility or disciplinary measures for any violation committed."* [author' translation]

opportunities and ethical accountability during training. Articles 9 and 10 of the Regulation on *"The Organization of Professional Practice for Health Professionals in the Republic of Albania,"* outline the roles of supervisors and governing bodies in guiding trainees, fostering their development, and maintaining a conducive training environment. This regulated relationship ensures paramedical professionals are adequately trained, integrated into the healthcare system, and respected as competent contributors. It emphasizes collaboration and mutual respect, promoting high-quality care and fostering a cohesive healthcare system where all providers work together effectively.

Chapter 3. Relationship with Healthcare Institutions

§1. Hospitals

844. In 2022, Albania adopted Law No. 55/2022 for the Hospital Service in the Republic of Albania (repealing Law No. 9106, dated 17.3.2003, "On hospital service in the Republic of Albania"). The object of this law is to determine the activity of the hospital service in the Republic of Albania, the way of organization, administration, management, and financing of this service, as well as defining the rules for the opening, the way of exercising the activity and the closing of public and private hospitals. This law aims to ensure and guarantee the provision of hospital services in the Republic of Albania, based on quality and safety standards of hospital care provision, in respecting the basic right of citizens to accessible qualitative health services. Hospital care is offered to citizens in need of diagnosis, examination, and/or hospital-centered treatment, which cannot be provided by primary healthcare, in accordance with referral system. Organization and operation of hospital healthcare services, public or private activities, are determined by a separate law (Article 10 Law No. 10 107, dated 30.3.2009).

845. The law has given hospitals autonomy in the form of decentralization, which addresses its gradual delegation in financial and administrative decision-making rights from government structures in general hospitals, as public healthcare institutions. The Charter of Hospital Autonomy is the legal instrument, which guarantees the granting of autonomy to public hospitals, which is given by the minister responsible for the hospital service according to the criteria as defined in this law and the bylaws issued in its implementation.

846. The hospital service is guided by the principles of universality and solidarity, equality and non-discrimination, guaranteeing respect for the right to care and quality health service, as well as equal access to services for all, through: (a) prevention, diagnosis, treatment, rehabilitation and palliative care; (b) providing urgent, general and specialized medical assistance; (c) improvement of public health indicators; (d) guaranteeing the safety and health protection at work of the medical personnel and non-medical; (e) maintaining confidentiality and the right of the patient both to be informed and for him approved the service offered to him; (f) maintaining professional ethics and medical deontological standards (Article 4 Law No. 55/2022).

847. The Ministry of Health is the institution that proposes policies and implements the governing program in the field of health and has the following powers: (a) designs policies and strategic plan in the field of hospital service; (b) designs and proposes the legal basis for the organization and operation of the hospital service; (c) proposes to the Council of Ministers the financing model of public hospitals according to the provisions of this law and the legal framework in force; (d) determines the criteria for opening and closing hospitals or/and hospital services according to approved hospital plan; (e) organizes, monitors and audits the activity of public hospitals according to the legislation in power; (f) inspects the activity of public and non-public hospitals in accordance with the provisions of legislation in the field of inspection; (g) determines the types of services provided by public hospitals based on location, needs of population, demographics, disease burden, human resources and equipment; (h) continuously ensures investments for the activity of public hospital institutions; (i) guarantees the establishment of quality standards for the accreditation of hospitals or hospital services (Article 5 Law No. 55/2022).

848. The Committee for National Hospital Planning is created as an advisory body of the Minister for hospital system development policies. The Committee for National Hospital Planning meets at the request of the responsible minister for health and performs the following functions:

a. submits the National Hospital Plan to the Minister for review.
b. gives opinions on: (i) drafting national strategies and programs in the field of hospital development; (ii) defining priority hospital policies; (iii) legislative improvements, which affect the development of hospital policies and the alignment of theirs with European ones; (iv) other hospital policy issues.

849. The Committee for National Hospital Planning has in its composition specialists in the field of health, as well as experts from other fields, who are indispensable in the decision-making for the drafting of the National Hospital Plan. The members of the Committee for National Hospital Planning are elected for a period of three years, with the right to re-election only once. Composition and mode of operation of the Committee for National Hospital Planning are determined by the decision of the Council of Ministers, with the proposal of the minister (Article 6 Law No. 55/2022).

850. The National Hospital Plan is the document that defines the national hospital capacities, based on territorial, demographic, socioeconomic criteria, the burden of morbidity, as well as meets the didactic and scientific requirements of medical education. The National Hospital Plan is approved by decision of the Council of Ministers, with the proposal of the minister. The National Hospital Plan defines: (a) the coefficients that will be applied at the national and regional level, based on the health situation, geomorphological and social-economic-cultural components, to extract the ratio between the number and distribution of beds, the distribution of human resources and the population; (b) planning for new beds, their distribution, including existing beds, between different sectors of hospital activity and at different functional organizational levels of the national hospital network; (c) the distribution of hospitals in the territory, as well as the needs for scientific research; (d) the organizational and functional criteria through which an active coordination is achieved between different structures that contribute to the creation of the national hospital system; (d) means and methods of financing by the state for the construction of new public hospitals, expansion, transformation and modernization of hospital structures (Article 7 Law No. 55/2022).

851. Regional hospital plans are drawn up by the Health Care Service Operator and are approved by ministerial order, based on the National Hospital Plan. Hospital plans at the regional level foresee meeting the needs of the of region population based on the demographic, epidemiological, morbidity and socioeconomic development of the region, orienting the development of the network of hospital services in the territory according to hospital level (Article 8 Law No. 55/2022).

I. Public and Non-public Hospitals

852. Hospitals are public and non-public. The division into public and non-public hospitals is based on the criteria of ownership, the method of financing and the purpose of the activity. A public hospital is a dependent institution of the minister, which is opened, administered and financed by the public structures defined by law, depending on the manner of its creation. Autonomous hospitals, depending on the type of autonomy, are opened according to the provisions Law No. 55/2022. The public hospital provides health services for hospitalized patients, as well as healthcare services for outpatients according to the provisions made in Law No. 55/2022 and acts bylaws issued in its implementation. A non-public hospital is a hospital licensed according to the legislation in force for the exercise of activity in the field of hospital care. The criteria and manner of licensing are determined by decision of the Council of Ministers. Non-public hospitals provide health services according to the criteria reflected in the object their activity and in the license obtained for the exercise of hospital activity according to legislation in force. Cooperation between public hospitals and non-public hospitals is based on agreements or joint memoranda, based on the legislation in force (Article 9 Law No. 55/2022).

853. Public and non-public hospitals are general and specialized hospitals based on the nature of the services they offer. General hospitals offer specialized consultations and hospitalization services for patients, such as: emergency, services in internal medicine, obstetrics-gynecology, pediatrics, laboratories, radiology, general surgery, as well as other necessary services. Specialized hospitals offer services mainly focused on a specific field, such as oncology, neurology, cardiology, internal medicine, dermatology, orthopedics, ophthalmology, pediatrics, obstetrics-gynecology and other specialized fields (Article 10 Law No. 55/2022).

854. Public and non-public hospitals are obliged to provide medical assistance to foreign citizens, insured or not, who need emergency hospital service. All non-resident foreign citizens, who perform a health treatment in public hospitals in the Republic of Albania, benefit from health treatment in these hospitals according to the rates determined by the governing bodies of the hospital itself. In the case of non-resident foreign citizens of the countries with which the Albanian state has reciprocity agreement, the payment of health expenses incurred is made according to the provisions of the agreement. In the case of non-resident foreign nationals, who are insured by a local insurance company to cover health expenses, payment of treatment fees will be carried out by the insurance company. Method of registration and completion of documentation for foreign citizens who receive health service in public and non-public hospitals will be carried out according to the provisions of the order of the minister. Public hospitals can offer health tourism services in accordance with instructions approved by the minister (Article 11 Law No. 55/2022).

II. Categories of Public Hospitals

855. Public hospitals by category are divided into (a) day hospitals; (b) hospitals at the municipality level; (c) hospitals at the district level; (d) regional hospital center; (e) tertiary hospitals; (f) hospitals/university hospital centers (Article 13 Law No. 55/2022). Regional hospital center is the organization of one or more general hospitals specialized and/or daily hospitals, for the effect of concentrated management of financial, human and capital resources in each territory. A hospital is a public or non-public healthcare institution with beds, which provides short-term or long-term emergency, preventive, diagnostic health services, therapeutic, rehabilitative and palliative. The day hospital is the institution that offers the service of consultation, diagnosis, treatment or surgical intervention or invasive procedure of patients under general, local anesthesia or sedation, within twenty-four hours, according to a preliminary hospitalization plan. The general hospital is the institution that provides hospital healthcare for citizens of all ages, who suffer from various diseases or physical injuries. The general hospital can serve the population of one or more districts/districts.

856. The specialized hospital is the institution that offers consultations and specific hospital treatment for a set of diagnoses and pathologies of a certain age group. Specialized hospitals may also provide general medicine or surgical consultation services, and any other services offered to the relevant categories of general hospitals, if they are necessary for the special nature of the specialized hospital.

857. Health tourism is the provision of health services for treatments and diagnostics for all foreign citizens according to procedure and fees health package. Day hospitals provide first aid for treatment and cure within twenty-four hours and carry out diagnosis, treatment and surgical interventions or invasive procedures, diagnostic or therapeutic of patients under general, local or sedation anesthesia.

858. Hospitals at the municipality level provide health services hospital for the population of one or more municipalities, based on demographic distribution. Hospitals at the municipality level provide internal medicine and pediatric services, as well as depending on the burden of morbidity, other specialized services. Hospitals at the municipality level can also be day hospitals with twenty-four-hour service. The organization of hospitals at the municipality level is defined in the regional hospital plan, based on demographic developments and morbidity.

859. Regional hospitals serve a certain district; they can be general or specialized, as defined in the act of their creation. General hospitals at the district level are those healthcare institutions that provide general medical services, internal diseases, general surgery, obstetrics and gynecology, pediatrics, radiology, laboratory, as well as other specified specialties from the ministry. The organization according to this point is defined in the regional hospital plan, based on demographic developments and morbidity, including other medical services estimated necessary.

860. The regional hospital center provides integrated hospital service, managing in one unique administration of human, financial and infrastructure resources of one or more general hospitals, specialized and/or day hospitals at the municipality or district level, with the purpose of the territorial organization of secondary and tertiary hospital care in function of the growth of access to hospital services in a certain area/region. The organization, according to this point, determined in the National Hospital Plan, based on demographic developments and morbidity, including other medical services deemed necessary.

861. Tertiary hospitals offer care and treatment with more specialized health personnel, with equipment and structures for scientific research and special treatment. Tertiary hospitals provide services based on the latest scientific knowledge, techniques and sophisticated equipment of use in medical facilities, as well as carry out research-scientific work.

862. Hospitals/university hospital centers perform diagnostic and treatment functions, in fulfilling the provision of tertiary healthcare, as well as teaching, scientific and research functions, to realize the university training of health specialists, as well as for students/trainees, who study at higher education institutions carried out teaching and research-scientific practices.

863. The governing body of the day hospital and municipal hospital is the hospital directorate. The way of creation, organization and operation of the day hospital and the municipal hospital is determined by order of the minister. The governing bodies of the regional hospital, the regional hospital center, the university hospital and the tertiary hospital are the general director, the management board and the medical commission. The method of creation, organization and operation of the regional hospital, regional hospital center, tertiary hospitals and university hospitals is determined by the decision of the Council Ministers (Article 14 Law No. 55/2022).

864. The referral mechanism in hospitals is the system that guarantees the patient's journey to healthcare and specifically the hospital one, as continuity of diagnosis, treatment, care and rehabilitation provided in primary care institutions when the complexity and degree of severity of diseases require specialized knowledge, drugs, medical equipment and special spaces treatment. The hospital is obliged to cooperate with primary healthcare institutions and to offer professional support during the provision of health services. Hospitalization and specialized consultations are provided within the hospital premises, but the hospital may have other units, part of its organization, that are offered outside its premises of the hospital.

865. The hospital organizes its work in such a way that the patient receives hospital services within the day without being hospitalized, except in cases where hospitalization is justified and imperative medical need. Cases in hospitals are managed either as medical emergencies or through the referral system from the lowest level to the highest level. The Minister determines by order the way of operation of the referral mechanism patients within the hospital system, using digital health systems (Article 15 Law No. 55/2022).

866. The public hospital is financed by: (a) the state budget; (b) health insurance institutions; (c) local government; (d) local and foreign donors; (e) income generated by services with third parties; (f) other legal income. Income from contracts, fees or payments from patients for clinical services and nonclinical, which are not covered by hospital financing institutions, are transferred to the hospital's account as secondary income. Secondary income, which has not been spent in a fiscal year, can be carried over to the next hospital fiscal year (Article 16 Law No. 55/2022).

867. Autonomy, as an integral part of the management of the public hospital system, guarantees equality, accessibility, quality, safety and timely delivery of health services to the patient. Hospital autonomous entities are organized in the form of a public legal entity, with rights, obligations and responsibilities defined in Law No. 55/2022 and the bylaws issued pursuant to it. Hospital autonomy aims to ensure: (a) effectiveness and transparency in the administrative management of financial resources and human resources; (b) increased transparency and accountability to citizens; (c) improvement of human and financial mobilization resources; (d) increasing the role of the community in decision-making.

868. The models of hospital autonomy are as follows: (a) the model of managerial autonomy guarantees the granting of administrative autonomy, organizational and regulatory of public hospitals, based on the definitions of the charter of hospital autonomy; (b) the model of financial autonomy guarantees the transformation of public hospitals into institutions that are self-financed, are financed from the state budget for certain services by the Council of Ministers and from other legal sources, based on the provisions of the charter hospital autonomy. The autonomy charter will be applied in an escalating and differentiated manner for each hospital, based on meeting the criteria for the benefit of hospital autonomy, according to a punctuation system, which will be determined by order of the minister. Autonomous hospitals apply the performance-based payment model for staff health, based on the rules defined by order of the minister.

869. Public hospitals benefit from hospital autonomy after fulfilling the defined criteria in the regulation of hospital autonomy, which is approved by decision of the Council of Ministers. The regulation of hospital autonomy defines: (a) the specific criteria that must be met by a public hospital to benefit from the autonomy for each of the models provided for Law No. 55/2022; (b) the procedure for evaluating the fulfillment of the criteria to benefit from autonomy; (c) scope and areas of autonomy that are granted; (d) the period of granting autonomy according to the model.

Autonomous public hospitals reorganize hospital services to improve utilization of infrastructure and human resources to provide an improved service in time and quality (Article 18 Law No. 55/2022).

870. The application for hospital autonomy is made by public hospitals to the Ministry of Health through a special form, approved by ministerial order, in which the formal elements of the request are reflected. The request must also contain data on the hospital services provided, the non-hospital services: diagnostic, therapeutic, rehabilitative, etc., the capacities of human resources and hospital management, to identify areas in which hospital autonomy can be exercised and to argue the reasons why hospital autonomy is requested or proposed. Granting hospital autonomy is done in an escalating way and based on the request of the hospital itself. The rules for the assessment of the request, the procedures and deadlines for its review are defined in the regulation of hospital autonomy. The Minister is the body responsible for accepting the request for hospital autonomy (Article 19 Law No. 55/2022).

871. The autonomy charter of the public hospital is the legal instrument, which indicates the areas in which autonomy can be exercised by the public hospital, including management, financing, resources human resources, procurement of funds and other areas, as appropriate, depending on the type of public hospital. Every public hospital has the right to apply for managerial and financial hospital autonomy in the ministry, which after evaluating the hospital and after fulfilling the criteria equips it with autonomy card (Article 20 Law No. 55/2022).

872. The governing bodies of the autonomous hospital are: (a) management board; (b) management team; (c) general administrator. The management board is the highest governing collegial body of the autonomous public hospital and is independent in its activity. The composition and functions of the board are defined in the regulation hospital autonomy. The composition and mode of operation of the governing board for university hospitals will be in accordance with the legislation in force for higher education. The management team of the autonomous hospital consists of the general administrator and technical and economic managers. The duties of the management team are defined in the internal regulations' operation of the hospital.

873. The general administrator of the hospital is the highest executive authority of the hospital autonomously and is appointed by the management board according to the procedures defined in the regulation hospital autonomy. The duties of the general administrator are defined in the regulation of the internal functioning of the hospital (Article 21 Law No. 55/2022).

874. Autonomous public hospitals have the right to conclude contracts with third parties, with companies' private insurance companies, as well as non-public hospitals for specific medical services. Autonomous public hospitals have the right to conclude agreements with the diplomatic services of foreign, international organizations and foreign corporations operating in Albania to provide services for their local and foreign personnel. Autonomous public hospitals can conclude contracts for scientific research with national and foreign institutions also for clinical tests with domestic and foreign pharmaceutical companies, based on the legislation in force. Autonomous public hospitals can contract non-health services with the private sector according to the legislation in force. The autonomous hospital uses the income from medical and non-medical activity, or even other revenues for goods and services as needed, as well as for infrastructure development, technology and human resources (Article 22 Law No. 55/2022).

875. The activity of the autonomous public hospital is supervised by the ministry according to the legislation in force. Autonomous public hospitals report annually to the responsible ministry for hospital service, for the activity of the autonomous hospital. The Ministry audits the autonomous hospital to evaluate and improve the operation of the hospital, according to a program previously approved by the minister. All financial resources, which provide and use autonomous public hospitals, are considered public funds and as such are subject to the rules of financial public funds management, public accounting and financial reporting rules and are controllable by the responsible minister for the hospital service. The financial resources of the autonomous public hospital are collected and recorded in the banking accounts of second level banks (Article 24 Law No. 55/2022).

876. The minister revokes the autonomy card when irregularities and violations are found that violate the criteria defined in the regulation of hospital autonomy or when legal acts or bylaws have been violated in force. The procedure for revoking the autonomy card is defined in the regulation of hospital autonomy (Article 25 Law No. 55/2022).

III. Opening of Non-public Hospitals

877. Non-public hospitals are licensed in accordance with the legislation in force on licensing. Non-public hospitals provide hospital services according to the rules and standards defined in this law and in the bylaws in its implementation. Non-public hospitals are categorized into general, specialized and daily hospitals. The supervision and inspection of the non-public hospital is done by the ministry and the responsible structure for inspection in the field of health. The criteria for opening and closing non-public hospitals are determined by the decision of the Council of Ministers (Article 28 Law No. 55/2022).

878. Non-public hospitals follow clinical standards and protocols approved by the ministry responsible for the hospital service. Non-public hospitals collect, process and report health data determined by the ministry and in application of the law on the protection of personal data. Public hospitals cooperate according to the legislation in force with non-public hospitals for the provision of mutual hospital services (Article 29 Law No. 55/2022).

879. The Minister revokes the hospital's activity license when he finds: (a) violation of laws and bylaws in force; (b) failure to meet the necessary conditions for the exercise of hospital activity according to the criteria defined in the license; (c) non-implementation within the conditions and deadlines of the tasks left by the ministry; (d) not exercising the activity for one year from the date of approval of the license; (e) non-fulfillment of the basic standards for accreditation according to the relevant legislation. The minister's decision to revoke the license can be appealed to the competent court for administrative matters, according to the legislation in force (Article 30 Law No. 55/2022).

§2. Preventive Healthcare

880. The Albanian healthcare system is regulated by Law No. 10 107, dated 30.3.2009 For Health Care in the Republic of Albania. This law defines the main principles and legal framework for regulation, organization and the functioning of the healthcare system in the Republic of Albania. This law is applied by all natural or legal persons, Albanian or foreign, who operate in the healthcare system. Healthcare in the Republic of Albania is guided by the following principles: (a) the right to healthcare is a fundamental right of the individual; (b) guaranteeing equal rights in healthcare, based on non-discrimination; (c) the healthcare system works based on the efficiency and quality of the service, ensuring patient safety and impartiality; (d) participation of different actors, patients, consumers and citizens; (e) accountability to citizens. Healthcare system is the organization, financing and distribution of healthcare services including: health promotion and prevention; the service diagnostic, therapeutic and rehabilitative; healthcare policies, laws, regulations and standards for the implementation of policies and cooperation of central, local government and public or private health services providers. Health promotion is the process of giving citizens the opportunity to improve their health. Health authorities are the Ministry of Health and its depending regional structures. Healthcare providers are public or private, natural or legal persons, such as non-profit organizations, which are registered by the Ministry of Health, to provide healthcare in accordance with this law. A patient is a person who is undergoing medical treatment in an institution of healthcare.

881. Healthcare encompasses all measures and activities undertaken by healthcare institutions, professionals, and citizens to enhance the overall physical, mental, and social well-being of the population. According to the World Health Organization's Constitution, health is defined as a state of complete physical, mental, and social well-being, not merely the absence of disease or infirmity. Healthcare services involve medical interventions aimed at protecting and improving health through prevention, diagnosis, treatment, and rehabilitation. These services are delivered by registered healthcare providers and can be offered in designated healthcare institutions, such as hospitals, clinics, and health centers, or in locations approved by the Ministry of Health (Article 29 Law No. 10 107, dated 30.3.2009).

882. Primary healthcare is the totality of measures and activities undertaken by a network of health professionals and institutions that provide basic medical services for the population. Health professionals are people equipped with the necessary scientific knowledge and professionals, practicing their profession in different fields and profiles of the health system. Registration of professionals is a mandatory process, which is carried out by the Ministry of Health. The Minister of Health approves, by order, Law No. 10 171, dated 22.10.2009 procedures and reregistration of health professionals (Article 31 Law No. 10 107, dated 30.3.2009).

883. The state exercises its activity related to healthcare in support of this law and undertakes to regulate the provision, supervision and administration of healthcare services. The state protects the principle of solidarity in the financing and provision of healthcare. The Minister of Health directs the policy, organization and supervision of the healthcare system. The Ministry of Health prepares the strategy of the healthcare system, which includes relevant health policies, programs and national treatment protocols. The Minister of Health drafts policies for the continuous professional education of human resources in healthcare. The Minister of Health is responsible for the identification and coordination of issues cross-cutting issues related to public health. The Minister of Health sets up special commissions or working groups to assist on certain issues. The organization, operation and activity of the public health service are regulated by special law (Article 12 Law No. 10 107, dated 30.3.2009). Public health programs and activities are financed by the State Budget and other sources determined by special law (Article 4 Law No. 10 107, dated 30.3.2009).

884. Pursuant to the legislation in force for local government, the units of local governments are responsible for the following: (a) creating and maintaining a healthy environment within the jurisdiction of their territory; (b) administration of healthcare service facilities owned by them; (c) involvement in policies and governing bodies of health institutions within their jurisdiction; (d) providing financial contributions to health institutions within their jurisdiction. Municipalities and communes exercise administrative control for health activity in the territory they administer, in accordance with the legislation in force, in coordination with the Ministry of Health. Municipalities, in coordination with the Ministry of Health, takes measures to provide primary healthcare services for the population within the jurisdiction of the municipality (Article 5 Law No. 10 107, dated 30.3.2009).

I. Responsibilities and Rights of Citizens

885. Every citizen is responsible for: (a) maintaining and improving personal and community health; (b) respecting the right of the other, which has to do with preserving and improving health, prevention of diseases, as well as their rehabilitation; (c) avoiding, in public spaces, the ways of behavior and activities, which, is based on studies done for this purpose, are known to be dangerous, in terms of the health of others; (d) providing assistance in financing healthcare services, through compulsory health insurance contributions and direct payments. According to this law, citizens enjoy the following rights: (a) to use healthcare services, which are part of the mandatory or basic benefits package, which are provided by public health institutions and providers in implementation of legislation in force; (b) to be informed about the preservation and improvement of health, in order to obtain decisions related to personal health and that of their families; (c) to be informed by health service providers about the features of the services healthcare, how to use them, for their rights, as citizens and patients, for the patient card and medical errors, as well as their implementation; (d) give consent for the healthcare that will be offered to them; (e) to participate actively, in accordance with the legislation in force, in programming and implementation of healthcare activities, especially, in terms of respecting the rights of the patient (Article 6 Law No. 10 107, dated 30.3.2009).

II. Integrated Health System

886. Healthcare is provided by an integrated system of health services and a network of public or private institutions and implements the referral system. The Ministry of Health prepares and updates, at least every three years, a network plan integrating public healthcare institution, to rationalize and increase to the maximum use of the capacity and performance of each hospital and to avoid overlapping services. The plan of the integrated network of public healthcare institutions contains the type and the number of services they offer, based on the needs of the population (Article 7 Law No. 10 107, dated 30.3.2009).

III. Primary Healthcare

887. Primary healthcare is provided through a network of professionals and health institutions, based on the principles of family healthcare. Primary healthcare is organized in such a way that every person living in the territory of the Republic of Albania has the opportunity to use primary healthcare providers, the right to choose a primary healthcare contact and register with selected primary healthcare provider (Article 9 Law No. 10 107, dated 30.3.2009). Health Institution is defined as a hospital, polyclinic, health center. A clinic is considered dental, pharmacy, where the intern carries out professional practice or part of it, in compliance with the program and its profile.

888. Primary healthcare is provided without limitations arising from illness, age, gender, economic status or categories of patients. Primary healthcare meets the needs for basic medical treatment, nursing care, prevention and rehabilitation, when these do not require treatment and examination techniques, from other levels of healthcare providers. The Minister of Health approves, by order, the regulations for the organization and operation of primary healthcare (Article 9 Law No. 10 107, dated 30.3.2009).

889. A medical emergency is defined as an acute injury or illness that poses an immediate risk to a person's life or their future health. A health emergency refers to a sudden disaster situation, such as an epidemic, or a natural or human-induced disaster, that endangers the life, physical integrity, and health of citizens or disrupts the functioning of health institutions. Such situations are declared by the Council of Ministers upon the proposal of the Ministry of Health for a specified period. Emergency medical services encompass clinical and pre-hospital care provided in life-threatening situations where a citizen is at risk. The need for emergency medical services ceases upon the stabilization of the patient's health condition or their admission to a hospital. The Minister of Health, by order, approves the regulations for the organization, operation, and financing of emergency medical services (Article 11, Law No. 10 107, dated 30.3.2009).

IV. Measures for Coping with Health Emergencies

890. The Minister of Health is responsible for preparing and maintaining an updated national health emergency plan, which outlines the measures to be implemented during a health emergency, following the guidelines of the World Health Organization. During such emergencies, citizens' rights as defined by law and regulations are upheld if they do not compromise the effectiveness of the measures taken or the overall well-being of the population. The Council of Ministers ensures the funding of extraordinary expenses incurred during health emergencies, utilizing the Council's reserve fund in accordance with the provisions of the National Health Emergency Plan. All healthcare institutions, both public and private, are required to cooperate in accordance with the National Health Emergency Plan and implement their respective emergency plans, which are developed in collaboration with the Ministry of Health (Article 35 Law No. 10 107, dated 30.3.2009).

V. Dental Health

891. Dental service is provided only by licensed professionals in the field of dental care. The rules of organization and operation of the dental service are regulated by law special (Article 14 Law No. 10 107, dated 30.3.2009).

VI. Care for the Terminally Ill

892. Terminally ill care is medical and nursing care at the last stage of a patient, a disease which, with current possibilities, is incurable. When a person has passed away, the provision of the service must be made based on the norms of medical deontology (Article 15 Law No. 10 107, dated 30.3.2009).

VII. Pharmaceutical Service

893. The pharmaceutical service is provided only by licensed professionals in this field. The rules of organization and operation of the pharmaceutical service are determined by special law (Article 16 Law No. 10 107, dated 30.3.2009).

VIII. Occupational Health Service

894. Professional healthcare includes preventive and protective measures, along with counseling for employers, employees, and their representatives to ensure the creation and maintenance of a safe and healthy working environment. This involves tailoring work conditions to match employees' abilities while considering their physical and mental health. It also encompasses the identification and evaluation of workplace risks, as well as monitoring environmental factors and work practices that could impact employee health. The Ministry of Health and the Ministry of Labor, Social Affairs, and Equal Opportunities collaborate to minimize workplace accidents and occupational diseases. The Minister of Health establishes detailed regulations for the organization and operation of professional health services in both hospital settings and workplaces through bylaws (Article 17, Law No. 10 107, dated 30.3.2009).

IX. Optical Service

895. The optical service consists of all the services provided by the optician and the optical laboratory technician, for the correction and rehabilitation of sight, by applying external methods correction, excluding, in this way, surgical intervention, which belongs to the specialty of medical ophthalmology. The rules for the organization and operation of the optical service are determined by the Minister of Health (Article 18, Law No. 10 107, dated 30.3.2009).

X. Rehabilitation and Sports Medicine

896. Rehabilitation medicine is a field of science focused on restoring lost or undeveloped skills resulting from an illness or other circumstances. This care is provided by a physiotherapist with a university degree. The physiotherapist collaborates with a multidisciplinary team of professionals with various competencies to restore autonomy in cognitive and psychological areas. This is achieved through the application of manual techniques, the use of electromedical devices, and efforts aimed at reducing disability, restoring health, enhancing remaining skills, and improving participation. Sports medicine, as part of healthcare services, provides specialized medical care to active athletes. The organization and operation of sports medicine services are regulated by bylaws issued by the Minister of Health (Article 19, Law No. 10 107, dated 30.3.2009).

XI. Alternative Medicine

897. Alternative medicine is the totality of preventive and curative health practices such as homeopathy, naturopathy, chiropractic and herbal medicine, which do not follow accepted general medical methods, and may not have a scientific explanation for their efficacy. The field of treatments, conditions and way of using unconventional therapeutics methods are determined by order of the Minister of Health (Article 20 Law No. 10 107, dated 30.3.2009).

XII. General Standards for Healthcare Institutions

898. Health service providers must, during the provision of care services health, act in accordance with the professional and ethical standards, determined by the Minister of Health and the orders of professionals. The Minister of Health, by order, approves the norms and standards of care services health. The Minister of Health approves, by order, the regulations related to the types and level of services of healthcare institutions (Article 21 Law No. 10 107, dated 30.3.2009).

XIII. Quality of Service

899. Quality and safety of healthcare in accordance with standards is a professional and ethical healthcare obligation. All healthcare institutions create programs and necessary mechanisms for the implementation of the national quality strategy, drawn up by the Ministry of Health. The purpose of quality management is to measure, evaluate and improve the delivery of patient care, as well as to develop and implement efficient management programs for disease, clinical protocols and medical guidelines (Article 22 Law No. 10 107, dated 30.3.2009).

XIV. Supervision of Healthcare Institutions

900. The Ministry of Health supervises the implementation of rules and standards in institutions of healthcare. Health institutions are obliged to accept supervision from the Ministry of Health. Supervision of health institutions includes internal supervision and inspection. Article 23 Law No. 10 107, dated 30.3.2009 (Amended point 3 by Law No. 51/2013, dated 14.2.2013).

XV. Internal Supervision

901. Internal professional supervision is organized and directed by the directors of healthcare institutions, in application of the internal operating rules, based on standards set by the Minister of Health. The supervision of the institution has as object the: (a) implementation of the law and bylaws; (b) implementation of professional and quality standards. All books, registers and other data, in electronic form or on paper, are made available to the authorized inspector, upon his request. Obstruction or prohibition of activities of the authorized inspector, by any official or employee of the healthcare institution, constitutes a violation (Article 24 Law No. 10 107, dated 30.3.2009).

XVI. Inspection

902. Inspection of compliance with the legal requirements, provided for Law No. 10 107, of the institution's healthcare is carried out by the inspectorate that covers the field of health in accordance with Law No. 10 107 and Law No. 10 433, dated 16.6.2011 "On inspection in the Republic of Albania" (Article 25 Law No. 10 107, dated 30.3.2009) (Amended by Law No. 51/2013, dated 14.2.2013). The appeal against the decision of the inspectorate is made in accordance with the law on inspection. The execution of the decisions is done according to the legislation in force for administrative offenses (Article 39 Law No. 10 107, dated 30.3.2009).

XVII. Accreditation

903. Health institutions are subject to the periodical accreditation process through the National Center of Quality, Safety and Accreditation, to assess the degree of compliance by their side of the standards predetermined and published by the Ministry of Health. The rules and the way of carrying out the process of accreditation of healthcare institutions are determined by the Council of Ministers. Article 26 Law No. 10 107, dated 30.3.2009. Accreditation of hospitals is a mechanism for continuous improvement of the healthcare service. Accreditation of hospitals is done according to the legislation in force for the accreditation of healthcare institutions. The purpose of accreditation is to determine the level of compliance with standards and protocols, overall performance and ongoing progress of the hospital service, to improve quality and patient safety. The structure responsible for the accreditation of healthcare institutions is the structure that follows the accreditation process of hospitals and/or hospital services. Every hospital has its own unit responsible for accreditation. The structure responsible for the accreditation of healthcare institutions publishes the program for accreditation and reaccreditation of hospitals and the time frame for the completion of accreditation of all hospitals (Article 12 Law No. 55/2022).

XVIII. Referral System

904. Contact of the citizen with the primary healthcare service provider or doctor of the family constitutes the starting point of the process of providing healthcare services and developed based on the system of referral/forwarding to other levels of healthcare. The Minister of Health determines the mode of operation of the referral/forwarding system of patients (Article 28 Law No. 10 107, dated 30.3.2009).

XIX. Health Information System

905. The Ministry of Health establishes and maintains a unique health information system, based on European health information standards. All institutions that collect health data are obliged to provide the Ministry of Health with access to this information, maintaining confidentiality. Providers of healthcare services, public or private, are obliged to periodically collect and report data according to the format and manner of reporting, which are determined by the decision of the Council of Ministers. The data of the health system is created through the collection and recording of data in the health documentation, which may be documentation that remains in the institution or owned by the patient. Health professionals are responsible for the accuracy of the data recorded in documentation and medical evidence, while healthcare institutions are responsible for maintaining confidentiality (Article 30 Law No. 10 107, dated 30.3.2009).

XX. Continuing Professional Education

906. The Ministry of Health administers a mandatory program for continuing professional education, known as the "Certification Program for Health Professionals." This program operates on a system of periodic cycles, during which healthcare professionals must earn a specified number of continuing education credits. These credits are awarded based on procedures, criteria, and standards established by the Council of Ministers. Certification is the process by which a healthcare professional completes the requirements of each cycle within the program, linking their participation to their career development and progression. Healthcare professionals are required to engage in continuous professional education to enhance their knowledge and skills, ensuring the delivery of high-quality healthcare services (Article 33 Law No. 10 107, dated 30.3.2009).

907. Employment or contracts in health institutions are suspended, if the health professional does not receive any continuing education credit. Regaining the right to employment or the contract with the health institutions is made after the professional has undergone the exam certification. If the health professional collects continuing education credits, but less than the required limit, he must undergo the certification exam within six months from the date of notification. If you fail the exam, employment or contracts in health institutions are suspended. Regaining the right to employment or contracts with health institutions is done after the professional successfully passed the certification exam. Public healthcare institutions are obliged to design and implement continuing education programs for their professionals. Healthcare institutions are subject to sanctions if they employ specialists who do not fulfill the requirements provided for in this article. Healthcare institutions facilitate continuing professional education of health professionals (Article 33 Law No. 10 107, dated 30.3.2009).

XXI. Healthcare Service for Foreign Nationals

908. Healthcare service, which is offered in healthcare institutions for foreign citizens residing in the Republic of Albania, based on relevant international agreements or based on the principle of reciprocity. In the absence of an international agreement or conditions where foreign citizens benefit from healthcare services based on the principle of reciprocity and the provisions of this law and the healthcare financing law. Foreign citizens, who need healthcare, in the conditions of a medical emergency, receive healthcare under equal conditions to those that apply to citizens of the Republic of Albania. In case of death of the foreign citizen in a health institution, the head of this institution immediately notifies the official representative of the country in question (Article 37 Law No. 10 107, dated 30.3.2009).

XXII. Administrative Offenses

909. Providing healthcare contrary to the provisions of this law constitutes an administrative misdemeanor and punished by the inspectorate that covers the field of health as follows: (a) non-fulfillment of the obligations provided for in Articles 21 and 22 Law No. 10 107, related to the general standards and quality of healthcare services, with a fine from 50,000 to 100,000 lek and, in repeated cases, with license revocation. (b) Refusal by the service provider of the process of state supervision, exercised by the responsible institutions, according to Articles 23, 24 and 25 Law No. 10 107, with a fine from 20,000 to 50,000 Lek. (c) Violation of Article 27 Law No. 10 107 by natural or legal persons, public or private, who provide healthcare in the Republic of Albania, is punished with a fine of ALL 500,000 and, in case of repetition, with five times the fine and denunciation to the competent bodies. (d) Non-registration of health professionals, according to the provisions made in Article 31 Law No. 10 107, with a fine from ALL 5,000 to ALL 10,000. The measure of fine is the main Criminality, while the measure of revocation of the license is a supplementary Criminality (Article 38 Law No. 10 107, dated 30.3.2009).

§3. Health Insurance

I. Law on Social Security

910. Law No. 7703, dated 11.05.1993 "On social security in the Republic of Albania" (as amended) regulates several aspects related to gender equality and some positive treatment of women's status in labor relations. The law on social security regulates the status of women, as employed for the purpose of social security due to pregnancy. It stipulates that in the maternity insurance branch, the following income are paid for pregnancy, income for compensation for pregnancy, as well as remuneration for the birth of a child. Maternity benefit is paid to the insured woman for pregnancy and childbirth, when she has twelve months of insurance period.

911. The benefit period provided by law is 365 calendar days, including a minimum of 35 days before and 63 days after the birth of the child. Maternity income for the insured woman is 80% of the daily average of the assessable base of the last calendar year for the period before childbirth and, for 150 calendar days after birth, and 50% of the daily average of the assessable base of the last calendar year for the next period in progress. This legislation equates adoptive mothers with natural mothers in terms of remuneration and leave.

912. Cases of pregnancy compensation when a woman changes her workplace due to pregnancy and is paid less in her new place are also regulated. Childbirth benefit is paid to an insured person who is the mother or father of a child being born, provided that one of them has contributed for a year before the birth of the child. The award will become payable only once and the mother will have priority in the benefit of the payment, in case she is insured. The reward for each born child will be an amount equal to 50% of the monthly minimum wage. Regarding pensions, the law on social security provides for gender differences in the treatment of men and women, in terms of retirement age and working seniority.

913. Regarding the full old-age pension, it is foreseen that:

- full old-age pensions for insured persons who enjoy them: men who reach the age of 65 and women who reach the age of 60 after completing thirty-five years of insurance. Mothers who have given birth to six or more children, which have grown up more than eight years, have the right to retire when they reach the age of 50 and have thirty years of insurance; and
- reduced old-age pensions, of which insured persons benefit must have completed at least thirty-five years of insurance and have reached the age of 62 for men and 57 for women, when the full old-age retirement age is higher older than these ages, when they do not perform economic activities as employees, employers or self-employed. Our law has a discriminatory attitude regarding the retirement age. These provisions are a rudiment of a time when the state tried to play a protective role toward women, seeing her as more fragile and vulnerable, more stunted than men by the burden of paid work and to "compensate" for her fatigue from the unpaid work at home that was not only performed de facto by women (rather than by men), but also that it was envisaged and expected by the whole society that this role be performed by her.

914. Partial old-age pension is granted to the insured person for a period of less than thirty-five years and more than fifteen years of insurance, when he reaches a certain age, which is 65 years for men and 60 years for women. The partial pension is set as part of the full pension. This pension is calculated by multiplying the full pension by the years of insurance and dividing by 35. The law also provides the conditions for its benefit. The law also deals with family pensions for dependents of the person who dies, who had conditions for benefiting from one of the types of pensions or was receiving a pension.

915. A widow has the right to receive a family pension, when it is proven that she is the supporter of a child who was dependent on the deceased, up to the age of 8, when she is unable to work or when she has reached the age of 50. For the most part, the law on social security is part of the legal basis of lawsuits filed in the courts related to requests for the payment of annual leave and amounts for the benefit of social security, in addition to requests for the payment of wages as compensation for the termination of the contract without reasonable cause.

916. Whereas, Law No. 9136, dated 11.9.2003 "On the Collection of Compulsory Social and Health Insurance Contributions in the Republic of Albania," in Article 6, point 2 thereof, provides that the employer is responsible for keeping the employee's contributions and for payment in tax authorities, along with employer contributions. Further, in Article 8 it is defined the method of calculating the contribution of the employer and the employee in favor of the Social Insurance Institute. The employer's contributions to the employee and the employee's own contributions are calculated according to the level determined on the gross salary of the employee and other allowances of a permanent nature arising from the employment relationship, within a minimum gross salary determined by the Council of Ministers and the maximum level that it is five times the minimum wage.

II. Assistance and Social Services

917. Law No. 9355, dated 10.3.2005 For Assistance and Social Services aims to: (1) Define social assistance and services for individuals and groups in need, who cannot ensure the fulfillment of basic vital needs, the development of personal skills and opportunities, and the preservation of integrity due to limited economic, physical, psychological and social skills and opportunities. (2) To alleviate poverty and social exclusion for individuals and families, as well as to create opportunities for their integration, through the provision of a system of interventions and services to improve their lives. This law regulates the financing and provision of assistance and social services in Albania (*see* 161, 164, 166, 170, 1195, 1200, 1201).

918. Social services are the set of services offered to individuals and groups in need, who are unable to meet, with the resources they have, their vital needs for the preservation, development and rehabilitation of individual opportunities, to overcome emergency or chronic needs. Social services, according to their nature, are divided into: (a) social care services; (b) social-medical care services. Social care services include the services offered to individuals, families, groups in need, communities, to meet their vital needs. Social-medical care services are provided by specialized personnel in residential reintegration and rehabilitation centers, in day care centers or in families, for individuals who are unable to live normally, due to temporary or permanent physical, psychic and mental deterioration. "Economic aid" as the support, in cash and in kind, of individuals with special status and families in need. Persons with disabilities receive a monthly payment, in Lek.

919. According to the way of organization and operation, social care services take the form of: (a) residential care services; (b) community care services. The service in residential institutions is offered to individuals, for whom care at home is not possible. Their placement in social care centers is done with the consent of the person, after assessing his social, economic and medical condition. Community care services are provided in day care centers, in individuals' homes or in foster families, according to the specific needs of the beneficiary groups.

920. A Person with disabilities is the individual whose ability is limited because of physical, sensory, intellectual, psychic-mental damage, born or acquired during life from accidents, temporary or permanent illnesses, which do not come from reasons related to employment. An individual becomes "Invalid for work" if he/she has been declared as such by the decision of the Medical Commission for Determining Ability to Work, which benefits from Law No. 7889, dated 14.12.1994 "On the status of the disabled," amended.

921. The basic principles on which the aid and social services scheme operates are: (a) respect and guarantee of the values and personality of the individual; (b) universality; (c) equality of opportunities; (d) the right to benefit; (e) partnership; (f) transparency and impartiality; (g) decentralization; (h) independence, social integration and participation in community life; (i) non-discrimination; (j) subsidizing character (Article 3, Law No. 9355, dated 10.3.2005 For Assistance and Social Services).

III. Beneficiaries of Assistance and Social Service

922. Beneficiaries of economic aid are: (1) Families in need. (2) Orphans over 25 years old, unemployed, who are not in institutions or under guardianship. (3) Parents with more than two children born at the same time, belong to needy families (Article 5, Law No. 9355, dated 10.3.2005 For Assistance and Social Services).

923. The beneficiaries of social services are children, young people up to the age of 25, the elderly, people with disabilities, women, girls in need (Article 6, Law No. 9355, dated 10.3.2005 For Assistance and Social Services).

924. Beneficiaries of the disability payment are: (1) The blind, with complete or partial lack of sight, born or acquired, who have been declared incapable of work by the decision of the Medical Commission for Determining Blindness. (2) Paraplegics and tetraplegics, who are declared by the decision of the Medical Commission for Determining Ability to Work to have become such, regardless of the cause and age. (3) Persons with disabilities who are declared unfit for work by the decision of the Medical Commission for Determining Ability to Work. (4) Persons, who have been declared disabled for work by the decision of the Medical Commission for Determining Ability to Work, who benefit from disability pension and a monthly supplement on top of it, according to the Status of Disabled for Work (Article 7, Law No. 9355, dated 10.3.2005 For Assistance and Social Services). Beneficiary persons defined in points 1, 2, 3 of Article 7 of this law, who by the decision of special medical commissions are determined to need care, also benefit from a paid guardian.

925. The following persons do not benefit from Law No. 9355, dated 10.3.2005 For Assistance and Social Services: (1) Albanian citizens living abroad as immigrants, except for persons and their families assigned to work near our diplomatic missions and international organizations. (2) Asylum seekers, who have not received asylum status. (3) Albanian citizens, foreign citizens or stateless persons who need emergency assistance because of natural disasters and wars (Article 9, Law No. 9355, dated 10.3.2005 For Assistance and Social Services).

926. Economic assistance is given in the form of a monthly installment, in Lek, or a monthly benefit, in kind. The monthly amount of economic assistance in value is determined by the decision of the Council of Ministers (Article 10, Law No. 9355, dated 10.3.2005 For Assistance and Social Services).

927. Payment for persons with disabilities is given in the form of a monthly installment, in Lek. The amount of payment for these individuals and their guardians is determined by the decision of the Council of Ministers. Beneficiaries defined in Article 7 of Law No. 9355, dated 10.3.2005 For Assistance and Social Services, classified by the decision of medical commissions of ability in the second disability groups, lose the right to disability payment at the time of their employment (Article 11, Law No. 9355, dated 10.3.2005 For Assistance and Social Services).

928. Economic assistance, which benefits families in need, is complete or partial. Families or individuals who have no income from: (a) economic activity; (b) assistance and social services programs or any other social protection system; (c) capital; (d) family members who are in emigration. Economic assistance is partial when the claimant family has insufficient income from: (a) land; (b) livestock, poultry, bees, viticulture and gardening; (c) pensions and other income (Article 19, Law No. 9355, dated 10.3.2005 For Assistance and Social Services).

929. Economic assistance and payment of disabled persons are distributed once a month by decision of the council of the local government unit. The request to benefit from economic assistance is made in writing by the head of the family and signed by all its adult members. Applicants submit the necessary documentation to the social administrator at the local government unit. The criteria and procedures for the benefit of economic aid are determined by the decision of the Council of Ministers. The request and documentation to receive payment for persons with disabilities are submitted to the social administrator in the local government units. The criteria for the benefits of payment for persons with disabilities are determined by the decision of the Council of Ministers. Requests and documentation to benefit from social care services are submitted to the social administrator in the local government units. The criteria for admission to social care institutions and community services are determined by the decision of the Council of Ministers.

930. The council of the municipality or commune has the right to approve specific criteria to provide economic assistance or provide care services, with local budget funds, for families with many members or families in need.

931. People who need social care services are admitted to public residential institutions free of charge, if their families have no income. Their expenses are covered by the State Budget (Article 22, Law No. 9355, dated 10.3.2005 For Assistance and Social Services). Persons who need social care services and have personal income are admitted to public care institutions against a payment in relation to their monthly income or the income of other responsible individuals. The amount of the contribution is determined by the decision of the Council of Ministers. Beneficiaries of social care services, who are placed in care institutions, are given an amount in Lek for personal expenses. This amount is determined by the decision of the Council of Ministers. The applicant whose request for the benefit of economic assistance, disability payment or social service is rejected by the decision of the council of the local government unit, has the right for appeal to the court.

IV. Management and Administration of the Assistance and Social Service Scheme

932. The State Social Service is a public institution, under the Ministry of Labor and Social Affairs. The Statute of the State Social Service is approved by decision of the Council of Ministers. The State Social Service is administered and directed by the Administrative Council, which is the highest decision-making body. The functions and membership of the Administrative Council are determined by the decision of the Council of Ministers. The State Social Service is responsible for implementing the policies of the Ministry of Labor and Social Affairs in the field of assistance and social care services for: (a) programming and control of the use of State Budget funds for economic assistance, payment of disabled persons and social care services; (b) the drafting of service standards and the proposal for approval of new services; (c) determining the unique documentation necessary for applicants and beneficiaries of social services, according to this law (Article 26, Law No. 9355, dated 10.3.2005 For Assistance and Social Services).

933. The Ministry of Labor and Social Affairs is the authority responsible for the drafting of policies, legislation, programming of economic assistance funds, payment for persons with disabilities and social services, norms and standards of services, as well as control and their implementation at all levels of central and local structures, in the public and private sector. The Minister of Labor and Social Affairs establishes the Inspectorate of Economic Assistance, Payment for Persons with Disabilities and Social Services, which controls the activity and the implementation of the legislation in the structures and institutions depending on it and the economic aid sections in municipalities.

934. The procedure for carrying out the control by this Inspectorate is determined by the decision of the Council of Ministers. The Ministry of Labor and Social

Affairs collects information, statistics and reports from local government units, to evaluate and monitor the implementation of policies, the achievement of standards for economic assistance, payment for persons with disabilities and social care services. Content, periodicity and statistical indicators are determined by decision of the Council of Ministers. The Ministry of Labor and Social Affairs drafts and submits to the Ministry of Finance the needs for funds from the budget for economic assistance, payment for persons with disabilities and for social care services.

935. The municipality or commune council has the following responsibilities: (1) Approves the fund and the number of families in the economic assistance scheme. (2) Approves the fund for the payment of disabled persons. (3) Approves the fund for social care services. (4) Drafts the plan for the development of social care services, based on local resources, needs and priorities. (5) Approves and supports the development of care services based on the assessment of local needs and priorities. (6) Makes decisions about persons, families, types of social services to be provided based on: (a) assessment of the needs of individuals and families, carried out by the social administrator; (b) financial possibilities for the provision of these services. (7) Establishes, in accordance with the legislation in force, the right and the measure of the benefit of economic assistance for the family, as well as the provision of special benefits, provided by law. (8) Authorizes the structures of the local government unit to contract with licensed private social service providers even in cases where these services are provided by public social services. (9) With its own funds, based on specific criteria, it supports families in need with economic assistance or other forms of immediate assistance. (10) Approves programs for conditioning economic assistance with work and services in the community. The criteria for conditionalizing assistance with work and services in the community are determined by the decision of the Council of Ministers. (11) Approves the structures of the institutions subordinate to it, which deal with the distribution of economic assistance, payment for persons with disabilities and the realization of care services under his jurisdiction. (12) Approves cooperation programs with NGOs, religious institutions and representatives of civil society, in accordance with the needs and national and regional plans of assistance and services of social care (Article 29, Law No. 9355, dated 10.3.2005 For Assistance and Social Services).

936. For the administration of the aid scheme and social services, the relevant structures are set up near the districts, municipalities or communes. Social administrators in municipalities are responsible: (a) to identify families in need of economic assistance, persons with disabilities and the needs of individuals for social care services; (b) verify the social and economic situation of families in need, when they enter the scheme for the first time, as well as twice a year all families that benefit from economic assistance; (c) to propose to the council of the municipality or commune the families in need, to benefit from economic assistance; (d) assist in the preparation of documentation for persons applying for the benefit of economic assistance, disability payment and social care services; (e) to participate in the drafting process of the draft decision for the families that will be treated with economic assistance, of the list of persons with disabilities and persons to be treated with social care services; (f) calculate and propose for approval in the aid and services section social care of the municipality the amount of economic assistance; (g) to draw up the request for the block aid and the payment fund of persons limited every two months for the local government unit; (h) to cooperate in the drafting of local and regional plans in support of persons in need; (i) assess the needs of individuals or families seeking to receive social services, in accordance with national and local priorities, the financial possibilities for covering these services, prepare documentation and proposals for approval in the council of the municipality or commune; (j) to collect and compile information, statistics and keep the register of beneficiaries, follow the expenses for economic assistance, payment of persons with disabilities and persons in need of social care services; (k) to gather information about the networks of public and private services operating in the territory of the municipality or commune (Article 31, Law No. 9355, dated 10.3.2005 For Assistance and Social Services).

V. Status of the Disabled Paraplegic and Tetraplegic

937. Law No. 8626, dated 22.6.2000 regulates the Status of the Disabled Paraplegic and Tetraplegic. The state creates conditions for paraplegic and tetraplegic patients, so that they can participate in social life in the same way as others, ensuring for them an economic level necessary to live in a normal way, dignified, suitable housing, living and working conditions, as well as creating normal opportunities for treatment, education, recreational, entertainment and sports activities. The Ministry of Health foresees every year in its expenditure budget the necessary funds for annual periodical checks by specialized doctors for paraplegic and tetraplegic patients (Article 3, Law No. 8626, dated 22.6.2000 the Status of the Disabled Paraplegic and Tetraplegic). The state protects paraplegic and tetraplegic patients from all types of exploitation, discrimination, abuse and insult.

938. Paraplegic and tetraplegic patients are provided with official identification. The criteria for providing the testimony and its form are determined by regulations of the Institute of Social Security and the General Administration of Aid and Social Services. Paraplegic and tetraplegic patients are exempt from direct taxes. In cases where they are self-employed as natural persons and are subject to small business tax, the fixed tax rate is half of that defined in Article 3 of Law No. 8313, dated 26.3.1998 "On Tax on Small Business" (Article 6, Law No. 8626, dated 22.6.2000 the Status of the Disabled Paraplegic and Tetraplegic).

939. Legal, state or private entities that employ paraplegic and tetraplegic patients, in addition to the criteria defined in Law No. 7955, dated 20.9.1995 "On promoting employment," benefit for every calendar year income tax reduction, equal to the percentage of the labor force of paraplegic and quadriplegic invalids. The Ministry of Finance issues the relevant bylaws based on this law (Article 7, Law No. 8626, dated 22.6.2000 the Status of the Disabled Paraplegic and Tetraplegic). The state favors the education of paraplegic patients in the higher schools of the state system. The Council of Ministers takes measures and determines funds for the establishment of schools and institutions for education, training and rehabilitation of paraplegic and tetraplegic invalids.

940. The state exempts paraplegic and tetraplegic patients from paying for health contributions and gives them the right to benefit from free medicines, covered by the health insurance scheme and healthcare. Paraplegics and tetraplegics, who have benefited from the status, benefit from an additional income to cover the costs of the necessary package with special hygiene-sanitary materials (Article 9, Law No. 8626, dated 22.6.2000 the Status of the Disabled Paraplegic and Tetraplegic). The measure, criteria and procedure of benefiting from this increase in income are determined by the decision of the Council of Ministers, changed by Law No. 9506, dated 3.4.2006 on the Status of Disabled Paraplegic and Tetraplegic.

941. Paraplegic and tetraplegic patients who are in a serious condition and unable to appear in state institutions, benefit from the service at home from the family doctor and the specialist doctor for those medical procedures that can be performed on an outpatient basis and in home conditions. The Ministry of Health issues the relevant bylaws for this purpose (Article 10, Law No. 8626, dated 22.6.2000 the Status of the Disabled Paraplegic and Tetraplegic). Urban travel of paraplegic and tetraplegic patients, together with their companions, is free on state and private means of transport, while interurban travel is reimbursed by the state 50% of the value (Article 11, Law No. 8626, dated 22.6.2000 the Status of the Disabled Paraplegic and Tetraplegic). Sick paraplegics and tetraplegics are exempt from customs duties for tools that help their integration into life, including vehicles adapted for their use (Article 16, Law No. 8626, dated 22.6.2000 the Status of the Disabled Paraplegic and Tetraplegic).

942. Paraplegic and tetraplegic patients are provided with telephones. They pay the first-level telephone rates, favored for the population defined at the time of entry into force of this law, and are exempt from other rates. The differences are paid by the state (Article 12, Law No. 8626, dated 22.6.2000 the Status of the Disabled Paraplegic and Tetraplegic). The state finances the activities organized by the paraplegic and tetraplegic disabled associations according to the financial resources planned for this purpose in the state budget. The state undertakes to make available and give free-of-charge facilities for the development of the activity of the association of paraplegic and tetraplegic invalids.

943. Paraplegic and quadriplegic invalids, regardless of the income they receive from the state, receive a cash supplement due to their paralysis, to the extent determined by the Council of Ministers. This allowance is not calculated in family income due to economic level effects. The disabled are entitled to a payment, to this extent, for their guardian, chosen according to legal procedures (Article 15, Law No. 8626, dated 22.6.2000 the Status of the Disabled Paraplegic and Tetraplegic).

944. The state undertakes priority treatment with housing, through loans given with favorable conditions for paraplegic and tetraplegic patients (Article 17, Law No. 8626, dated 22.6.2000 the Status of the Disabled Paraplegic and Tetraplegic).

The Ministry of Public Economy and Privatization determines reduced electricity consumption rates for paraplegic and quadriplegic patients (Article 18, Law No. 8626, dated 22.6.2000 the Status of the Disabled Paraplegic and Tetraplegic). The Ministry of Health takes measures to adapt and equip one to two rooms in hospitals of the second and third level for eventual hospitalization of paraplegic and tetraplegic patients (Article 19, Law No. 8626, dated 22.6.2000 the Status of the Disabled Paraplegic and Tetraplegic). In public places (airports, train stations, stadiums, hotels, etc.), environments are created for movement, stay and service for paraplegic patients according to Law No. 7889, dated 14.12.1994 "Status of the disabled."

945. According to the Council of Ministers Decision No. 31, 20.1.2001 regulating benefits from paraplegic disabled status and tretraplegia, the Medical Commission for the Determination of Ability to Work (KMCAP) in the district examines all requests submitted by persons who have become paraplegic or tetraplegic, for reasons related to employment, who benefit from Law No. 8626, dated 22.6.2000, regardless of age, of whether or not they are in employment, of the time or location of the absence or of the insurance cast. The Commission also decides the decree of invalidity, according to the following division:

1. The first group, which includes:
   a. tetraplegic patients, who have lost more than 55% of their ability to work, who do not have the physical ability to self-serve and who need a caregiver.
   b. paraplegic patients, who have lost more than 55% of their ability to work, who do not have the physical ability to serve themselves and who need a guardian.
2. The second group, which includes paraplegic patients, partially capable of selected work, who can serve themselves.

946. KMCAP issues the medical report to the interested party, determining the degree of disability and the need for a guardian. The disabled person, paraplegic or tetraplegic, must declare to the state administrator the name of the guardian who is recorded in a special register. The change of the guardian can be done whenever the disabled person, paraplegic or tetraplegic, sees fit, but is obliged to notify KMCAP immediately. Invalids, paraplegics or tetraplegics are provided with official proof of identification.

947. The amount of payment for invalids, paraplegics and quadriplegics, who have become such for reasons related to employment, is ALL 10,330 per month. Benefit measure for the caregiver of the paraplegic and tetraplegic invalid, becomes ALL 10,850 per month (Instruction No. 365 dated 21.09.2017 on the Implementation of Decision No. 31 dated 20.01.2001 of the Council of Ministers on "Benefits from the Status of Paraplegic Disabled and Tetraplegic").

948. This payment is granted irrespective of the recipient's age or income and is also extended to the caregiver of the disabled, including paraplegic and tetraplegic individuals. The specifics regarding the distribution and method of payment will be outlined in the instruction issued in accordance with this decision.

949. The period of service as a caregiver, for the paraplegic and tetraplegic invalid, who is not economically active, as well as does not receive income from the mandatory social insurance scheme, is an estimated insurance period, for the effect of pension benefits, maternity, accident at work and occupational disease, and health insurance. The contribution is paid based on the minimum wage, for the purpose of calculating the mandatory social insurance contribution and is borne by the State Budget. The State Social Service, based on the information sent by the local government units, draws up the lists of beneficiary guardians, every year and every time this list changes, based on which the funds needed for the payment of the contribution for this category are calculated of persons. The procedures for the implementation of this point are defined in the joint instruction of the Minister of Finance and the Minister of Labour, Social Affairs and Equal Opportunities. The disability payment is paid from the banking services or the Albanian Post, near the local government units where he resides the beneficiary. Decision No. 37 dated 19.01.2011, on Some additions to Decision No. 31 dated 20.01.2001 of the Council of Ministers on "Benefits from the Status of Paraplegic Disabled and Tetraplegic."

950. For each misappropriation, the responsible person will be given evidence for a period of up to three years and the provisions for administrative misdemeanors up to a report for criminal prosecution are also applied (Council of Ministers Decision No. 31, 20.1.2001 regulating benefits from paraplegic disabled status and tretraplegia).

VI. Disabled Status

951. Law No. 7889, dated 14.12.1994 regulates the status of the Disabled. The status of invalid (disabled) is enjoyed by a person who has an accident at work, is ill from an occupational disease or other diseases and receives a disability pension from the social insurance system according to Law No. 7703, dated 11.5.1993 "On social insurance in the Republic of Albania." Society and the state take protection of the disabled in order that they participate in social life on an equal basis with others, provide them with the economic level necessary to live in dignity, to have housing conditions, to use the external environment, to have a suitable job, as well as to create normal opportunities for treatment, education and leisure and entertainment activities. The state protects the disabled from all types of exploitation, discrimination, abuse, insult and ridicule. Disabled people are provided with official identification. The criteria for providing the testimony and its form are determined by the regulations of the Social Insurance Institute.

952. Nobody has the right to provide information about a person's state of disability without his consent (Article 5, Law No. 7889, dated 14.12.1994 on the status for the Disabled). The status of invalid continues even after reaching the age for old-age pension (Article 6, Law No. 7889, dated 14.12.1994 on the status for the Disabled).

953. Invalids who have been employed in state enterprises or institutions and former agricultural cooperatives and who are with occupational diseases or accidents at work are given by the state budget a monthly supplement on the disability pension as a disability benefit. Disability benefits are given on top of disability pension paraplegics who are paralyzed and all who need the service. Criteria for receiving the disability benefit and its measures are determined by the decision of the Council of Ministers (Article 7, Law No. 7889, dated 14.12.1994 on the status for the Disabled).

954. The Social Security Institute administers the device having problems with: (a) moving vehicles and various orthopedic equipment; (b) special auditory and visual aids; (c) with cardiac aids, etc. The criteria are determined by the regulations of the Social Insurance Institute. Disabled persons do not pay customs taxes for vehicles and aids (Article 8, Law No. 7889, dated 14.12.1994 on the status for the Disabled). The state designates certain areas for the disabled in coastal, mountain, and seaside holiday homes, where appropriate adaptations are made to remove architectural barriers for different categories of disabilities. They serve for the rest and rehabilitation of the disabled. The criteria for enjoying this right are determined by the Social Security Institute. For the paralyzed and severely disabled who do not move, medical service is organized at the residence free of charge. The Ministry of Health and Environmental Protection issues the relevant bylaws.

955. The travel of the disabled by means of public and private city transport is free. Traveling by means of state and private intercity transport is done with 50% of the ticket price. All city and intercity means of travel reserve special seats for the disabled. The ministry covers transport and communication issues with the relevant bylaws (Article 11, Law No. 7889, dated 14.12.1994 on the status for the Disabled). The entrance of the disabled to art shows, museums, matches and sports events is done with 50% of the ticket price. The ministry that covers culture, youth and sports issues the relevant bylaws (Article 12, Law No. 7889, dated 14.12.1994 on the status for the Disabled).

956. Environments of health, social care and public institutions are adapted for their use by the blind and paraplegic. The procedure and stages of adaptation are determined by the decision of the Council of Ministers. All new public constructions that are built after the entry into force of this law must provide opportunities for use by different categories of persons with disabilities. The ministry that covers construction, housing and territorial regulation issues the relevant bylaws.

957. Disabled people are employed and re-employed in state and private enterprises in appropriate work processes that are recommended by the Medical Commission for Determination of Ability to Work. The rules for the employment and re-employment of the disabled are determined by the decision of the Council of

Ministers. Disabled people are favored in attending professional qualification and retraining courses, as well as attending higher schools.

958. The disabled are exempt from direct taxes provided for in Law No. 7680, dated 3.3.1993 “On the tax system in the Republic of Albania.” When the disabled person exercises private activity, he is not exempt from taxes. The rights enjoyed by the disabled according to their status are displayed in visible places in public spaces. For violation of the rights sanctioned by this law, the disabled person has the right to go to court.

Selected Bibliography

Books

Academy of Sciences of Albania. *Albanian Encyclopedic Dictionary*. Tirana: Academy of Sciences of Albania, 1985.

Articles

Hoxha, Dorina, et al. "Albania, the Right-to-Not Be Treated, and COVID-19." *BioLaw Journal—Rivista di BioDiritto* 4 (2021): 417–425.

Koka, Enkelejda, Laert Sheme, and Denard Veshi. "The Enforcement of Human Rights by Albanian Constitutional Judges: A Focus on Individual Constitutional Complaints in Civil Matters." *Federalismi.it* 2 (2025): 186–209.

Lachman, Vicki D. "Voluntary Stopping of Eating and Drinking: An Ethical Alternative to Physician-Assisted Suicide." *Medsurg Nursing* 24(1) (2015): 56–60.

Veshi, Denard. "Albania's Judicial Approach to Consumer Protection and the Influence of EU Law." *Studi sull'Integrazione Europea* 1 (2025).

Veshi, Denard, Enida Bozheku, and Andrea Castaldo. "Reckless Medication (or Medical Negligence) in Albania: A Criminal Case Law Study." *Federalismi.it* 24 (2024): 279–297.

Veshi, Denard, Enkelejda Koka, and Laert Sheme. "The Application of Human Rights by Judges in Civil Cases: The Case of Albania." *Ordine Internazionale e Diritti Umani* 1 (2025): 87–103.

Veshi, Denard, et al. "End-of-Life Situations in Some Western European Countries: Towards a Common European Approach?" *BioLaw Journal—Rivista di BioDiritto* 1 (2024): 267–278.

www.ingramcontent.com/pod-product-compliance
Ingram Content Group UK Ltd.
Pitfield, Milton Keynes, MK11 3LW, UK
UKHW020135290926
15471UKWH00003B/500

9 789403 547091